Employment Relations in the Hospitality and Tourism Industries

Employment Relations in the Hospitality and Tourism Industries presents a detailed review of employment relations within a distinctive and significant part of the service economy. Uniquely combining employment relations and the hospitality and tourism fields, this book draws on recently published sources to give readers a comprehensive and internationally comparative perspective on the subject area.

The text boldly extends more traditional analysis of employment relations by integrating new topics into the discussion, such as the role of customers and the implications of gender at work. It also explores issues of continuity and change in a specific service sector, examining the industry by workplace size and sub-sector, and is illustrated with numerous case studies. Material is included from fifty countries, across all continents, ensuring a fully international view is presented.

Employment Relations in the Hospitality and Tourism Industries is an invaluable resource for anyone studying hospitality and tourism, industrial relations and human resource management.

Rosemary Lucas is Professor of Employment Relations and Director of the Centre for Hospitality and Employment Research (CHER) at Manchester Metropolitan University Business School.

Routledge studies in employment relations

Series editors: Rick Delbridge and Edmund Heery
Cardiff Business School

Aspects of the employment relationship are central to numerous courses at both undergraduate and postgraduate level. Drawing insights from industrial relations, human resource management and industrial sociology, this series provides an alternative source of research-based materials and texts, reviewing key developments in employment research.

Books published in this series are works of high academic merit, drawn from a wide range of academic studies in the social sciences.

Employment Relations in the Hospitality and Tourism Industries

Rosemary E. Lucas

Routledge
Taylor & Francis Group

LONDON AND NEW YORK

First published 2004
by Routledge
11 New Fetter Lane, London EC4P 4EE

Simultaneously published in the USA and Canada
by Routledge
29 West 35th Street, New York, NY 10001

Routledge is an imprint of the Taylor & Francis Group

Typeset in Baskerville by
Florence Production Ltd, Stoodleigh, Devon
Printed and bound in Great Britain by
TJ International, Padstow, Cornwall

British Library Cataloguing in Publication Data
A catalogue record for this book is available from the British Library

Library of Congress Cataloging in Publication Data
Lucas, Rosemary.
     Employment relations in the hospitality and tourism industries /
Rosemary Lucas.
     p. cm. – (Routledge studies in employment relations)
     1. Hospitality industry – Personnel management.   2. Tourism –
Personnel management.   I. Title.   II. Series.
TX911.3.P4L82 2003
647.94′068′3 – dc21   2003014694

ISBN 0–415–29711–7 (hbk)
ISBN 0–415–29712–5 (pbk)

For Patrick Hardy: a boy of considerable culinary refinement and an enthusiastic consumer of tourism

Contents

Illustrations

Tables

Boxes

Case studies

Acknowledgements

Writing this book was always going to be much more challenging second time around. Crucially, could anything new be said about employment relations in the hospitality industry within the relatively short time frame of less than a decade? Axiomatic to my task was the Workplace Employee Relations Survey 1998 (WERS98), which provided me with a rather more useful set of data than its predecessor survey the Workplace Industrial Relations Survey 1990 (WIRS3). There was also a good volume of post-1995 literature, not necessarily within the right areas, but encouraging nevertheless.

The reviewers all offered suggestions for further improvements, and have helped shape what I had hoped would become a very different book from *Managing Employee Relations in the Hotel and Catering Industry*. There is a much greater focus on employment relations internationally and tourism. I am grateful to the reviewers for their support and advice and to Routledge for commissioning the book. I would like to thank Francesca Poynter, Editor – Business and Management, and Rachel Crookes, Editorial Assistant, for helping me see things through to publication.

Finding the necessary time to assemble, read, analyse and evaluate the quantity of data to inform a book such as this is becoming increasingly difficult. A teaching quality assessment and a research assessment exercise intervened and thwarted publication at an earlier date. Fortunately it was possible to negotiate a period of reasonably free time during 2002. I would like to thank Professor Richard Murray, Dean of Hollings Faculty of Food, Clothing and Hospitality Management and Professor Richard Thorpe, now at Leeds University Business School, for encouraging and supporting my career and research efforts in the last few years.

I also wish to acknowledge the Department of Trade and Industry (DTI), the Economic and Social Research Council (ESRC), the Advisory Conciliation and Arbitration Service (ACAS) and the Policy Studies Institute (PSI) as the originators of the WERS98 data, as well as the UK Data archive at the University of Essex as the distributor of the data. I am indebted to John Forth, Neil Millward and Simon Kirby at the National Institute for Economic and Social Research (NIESR) for the provision of advice, assistance in constructing the data set and producing tabulations, and help in identifying and volunteering additional refinements. John has been inordinately patient in dealing with my endless queries and more than generous with his time. None of these organizations or individuals bears any responsibility for the author's analysis and interpretation of the data.

I have been supported by a hard-working and loyal team of researchers, notably Norma Lammont and Michele Langlois. Research students Hazem Halim, Jeremy Head, Shobana Nair Keegan, Nick Radiven and Bill Rowson have each made their own contribution to knowledge in employment relations and human resource management within hospitality, as has Milena Marinova, a researcher funded by the International Centre for Research and Consultancy. Thanks are also extended to other friends and colleagues, too numerous to mention, both at Manchester Metropolitan University and elsewhere, for the support, encouragement and advice that helped make this book possible.

No task such as this can be achieved without the love, support and encouragement of one's family. My husband Chris Adams has had to endure my long periods of self-imposed isolation, often starting very early in the morning. However, while Jack has thoroughly appreciated his early morning walks chasing rabbits, he has been less enthusiastic about trashing the endless chapter drafts that littered the floor of my study compared to the legendary Wasdale, now scattered to the ether in Fishing Cove Field, Trebetherick. My mother Elsie Lucas, who has shown considerable fortitude since the untimely death of my brother Nick, is still wondering what to make of me, but I hope she is proud of my achievements.

Any mistakes or errors are entirely down to me, but I trust these are minimal.

Abbreviations

ABI	Annual Business Inquiry
ACAS	Advisory, Conciliation and Arbitration Service
AES	Annual Employment Survey
AIDS	acquired immune deficiency syndrome
AIS	all industries and services
AML	additional maternity leave
BA	British Airways
BBPA	British Beer and Pub Association
BdS	Bundesverband der Systemgastronomie
BHA	British Hospitality Association
BII	British Institute of Innkeeping
BS	British Standard
CA	Court of Appeal
CAB	Citizens' Advice Bureau
CAC	Central Arbitration Committee
CBI	Confederation of British Industry
CIPD	Chartered Institute of Personnel and Development
CRE	Commission for Racial Equality
D/ES	Department for Education and Skills
DRC	Disability Rights Commission
DTI	Department for Trade and Industry
DWP	Department for Work and Pensions
EAT	Employment Appeal Tribunal
EC	European Commission
ECF	European Committee of Food, Catering and Allied Workers' Union
ECJ	European Court of Justice
EEA	European Economic Area
EEC	European Economic Community
EEOC	Equal Employment Opportunity Commission
EOC	Equal Opportunities Commission
ER	employee relations
ESRC	Economic and Social Research Council
ETLC	European Trade Union Liaison Committee

ETUC	European Trade Union Confederation
EU	European Union
EWC	European Works Council
EWCh	expected week of childbirth
FERCO	European Federation of Contract Catering Organizations
GB	Great Britain
GCSE	General Certificate of Secondary Education
GMB	General, Municipal and Boilermakers' Union
GNVQ	General National Vocational Qualification
HCIMA	Hotel, Catering and International Management Association
HCTS	Hotel, Catering and Tourism Sector
HERE	Hotel Employees and Restaurant Employees International Union
HI	hospitality industry
HIV	human immunodeficiency virus
HL	House of Lords
HOTREC	Confederation of National Associations of Hotels, Restaurants, Cafés and Similar Establishments in the European Union and European Economic Area
HRM	human resource management
HSC	Health and Safety Commission
HSE	Health and Safety Executive
H*t*F	Hospitality Training Foundation
IDS	Incomes Data Services
IER	Institute of Employment Rights
IHRA	International Hotel and Restaurant Association
IiP	Investors in People
ILO	International Labour Organization
IOD	Institute of Directors
IPA	Information and Participation Association
IRLR	Industrial Relations Law Reports
ISIC	International Standard Industrial Classification
ISO	International Standards Organization
IUF	International Union of Food, Agricultural, Hotel, Restaurant, Catering, Tobacco and Allied Workers' Associations
JCC	joint consultative committee
JIT	Just in Time
KFC	Kentucky Fried Chicken
LFS	Labour Force Survey
LOG	largest occupational group
LPC	Low Pay Commission
MBA	Masters in Business Administration
MNC	multinational corporation
NALHM	National Association of Licensed House Managers
NES	New Earnings Survey
NGG	Gewerkschaft Nahrung Genuss Gaststätten
NICs	National Insurance Contributions

NIESR	National Institute of Economic and Social Research
NLRB	National Labor Relations Board
NMW	National Minimum Wage
NVQ	National Vocational Qualification
NS	National Statistics
NTETs	National Targets for Education and Training
NTO	National Training Organisation
OML	ordinary maternity leave
ONS	Office for National Statistics
PAL	Personal Action Letter
PBR	payment by results
PCA	protected concerted activity
PLC	public limited company
PRP	performance-related pay
PSI	Policy Studies Institute
PSS	private service sector
RA	Restaurant Association
SDA	Shop Distributive and Allied Employees' Union
SME	small and medium-sized enterprise
SPSS	Statistical Package for the Social Sciences
SQ	service quality
SSC	Sector Skills Councils
SVQ	Scottish Vocational Qualification
SWU	Service Workers Union
TGWU	Transport and General Workers Union
TI	tourist industry
TUC	Trades Union Congress
TUPE	Transfer of Undertakings (Protection of Employment) Regulations
UK	United Kingdom
UNICE	Union of Industrial and Employers' Confederations of Europe
US	United States of America
USDAW	Union of Shop, Distributive and Allied Workers
VET	vocational education and training
WERS	Workplace Employee Relations Survey
WIRS	Workplace Industrial Relations Survey
WTR	Working Time Regulations
WTTC	World Travel and Tourism Council

Introduction

What is this book about?

Employment Relations in the Hospitality and Tourism Industries presents a detailed review of employment relations within a distinctive and significant part of the service economy. This represents a unique combination of the industrial relations and hospitality and tourism fields.

This book is a revised and expanded version of *Managing Employee Relations in the Hotel and Catering Industry* (Lucas, 1995a), drawing mainly from sources published since then, but necessarily retracing some of the central themes established earlier. The deliberately broader perspective makes the new version more comparative, international and comprehensive.

There are four key aims:

1   To convey a view of employment relations beyond Britain from North America to Europe to Asia-Pacific, and draw out some comparative themes.
2   To provide a detailed evaluation of the state of employment relations in British hospitality workplaces in the context of national and private service sector patterns.
3   To extend the analysis of employment relations by integrating some aspects that have not traditionally featured in industrial relations discourse, such as the role of customers and gender implications.
4   To explore issues of continuity and change in employment relations in a specific service sector.

The book shows that:

•   Hospitality employment across the globe can be characterized as 'vulnerable' employment, and is subject to regulation in areas such as minimum wages. Different economic, social, legal and political factors create particular cultures and diverse employment systems. Trade union membership is low but in some countries collective agreements have been extended to cover all workers. Knowledge boundaries need extending to convey a view of employment relations that is not western-centric and drawn from 'Anglo' countries.

- Employment relations in the British hospitality workplaces are different on a national and private service sector comparison. Employment policies and practices continue to conform to the management-driven 'unbridled individualism' thesis, based on cost-control, but may also reflect a more affiliated and liberal managerial approach within a customer-service ethos. Employees are not necessarily alienated, and may trade off low pay for other compensations demonstrating 'enfranchised realism'. The employment relationship is both transactional and relational, and may also reflect 'resigned realism' and exploitation. Hospitality employees are different, providing more compelling evidence that trade unions face an even more daunting task in attempting to recruit members and organize workplaces. We need to develop our understanding of why managers and employees do not share commonly held assumptions of 'good' employment relations. We also need to determine how far the employment relationship, rather than the personal values of employees, affects the state of the psychological contract.
- Customers, often interrelating with gender issues, are an important influence on the employment relationship. They are drawn into managerial control strategies in a number of ways including pay and reward systems based on tips and customer appraisal. Customer-service work can be highly rewarding, but unpredictable customers can both thwart managerial objectives, and make working stressful for employees. Labour may be manufactured to appeal to customers by internalizing (male) prejudices with strong gender implications for women. Flexible cost-control employment systems may perpetuate women's and young people's disadvantage. More studies are needed that embed customers, gender and youth within the analysis of employment relations.
- Continuity is evident from managerial evidence, but employee evidence enables us to reassess the state of employment relations, and largely reject the 'bleak house' and 'black holes' scenarios. The locus of a socio-economic customer-service employment relationship is a function of dimensions related to managers, workers and customers within particular types of work mediated by the state. There is scope to reappraise the notion of legally enforceable state-sponsored collective bargaining on an industry basis, a more sophisticated version of wages councils with wider application. The extension of employment rights to workers would also provide greater protection for 'vulnerable' hospitality workers.

Who should read it?

The book will be of interest to:

- hospitality and tourism management students;
- business management students;
- social science students.

For hospitality and tourism students studying human resource management (HRM) as a core subject, this book will serve as a textbook at higher levels of undergraduate study and postgraduate/Masters study.

For business management students studying HRM as a core subject or an option, this text will serve as secondary/further reading. As a sectoral source it builds upon introductions in organizational behaviour, people management or employee relations, and will be useful at higher undergraduate and post-graduate/Masters/Masters in Business Administration (MBA) levels.

Social science students may also be interested in the book, as industrial relations and the employment relationship are very important dimensions of the sociology of work. For them this text will represent a rich source of information on contemporary characteristics of service sector work that can exemplify theoretical sociological perspectives, such as fragmentation and feminization of labour, and inform debates on labour process theory. Here the book will provide secondary/further reading on optional courses.

What are the hospitality and tourism industries?

For the purposes of this book, the term *hospitality industry* (HI) serves as an overarching label for *businesses* whose primary purpose is to offer food, beverage and accommodation for sale on a commercial basis. The main activities or sub-sectors in the International Standard Industrial Classification of all Economic Activities (ISIC) Division 55 (Hotels and restaurants) are hotels, restaurants, bars (including pubs and clubs) and (contract) catering (International Labour Organization (ILO), 2001: 5–6). Table I.1 shows the numbers employed in hospitality-specific occupations in the UK. These are the sub-sectors covered by WERS (see Appendix 1), by comparable Labour Force Surveys (LFSs) in the European Union (EU) and by much of the academic literature and research.

Hospitality services are other hospitality activities that take place within other parts of the economy. These are mainly concerned with the provision of food and beverage in areas such as in-flight catering, and meals in schools, colleges,

Table I.1 Number of employees by sector (UK)

Hospitality activity	1998	2001
Hotels	239,500	237,720
Restaurants	429,500	387,978
Pubs, clubs and bars	290,800	248,768
Contract catering	144,400	110,720
Hospitality businesses	1,104,200	985,186
Hospitality services	683,300	384,285
Main jobs	1,787,500	1,369,471
Second jobs	115,900	108,463
Total employees	1,903,400	1,477,934

Sources: LFS (1998 and 2001) adapted from Table 1.2; Hospitality Training Foundation (HtF) (2002: 14).

Notes: These figures relate to hospitality-specific occupations only and do not show total employment in the industry, which stood at 1.9 million people in 2001. Ancillary occupations, including cleaners and domestics, are not included.

universities, hospitals, care homes and prisons. These activities are not identified separately because workers in these sectors are included in the ISIC for the main business, e.g. public administration, education or health. Although many employees work in hospitality services jobs (Table I.1) they have not been very widely researched.

There will also be reference to the *tourist industry* (TI), although some activities, such as transport, are only very loosely hospitality-related. Tourism is not defined by the ISIC, although some activities more closely related to hospitality can be identified (for example travel agencies and tour operators, and tourist assistance activities are ISIC class 6304).

There are three main reasons for the inclusion of the TI. First, the HI is not always recognized as a distinct entity and is considered to belong to the 'tourism characteristic industries' and therefore subsumed under tourism (ILO, 2001: 6). As much of the international data do not distinguish hospitality from tourism, we shall necessarily refer to tourism data in these circumstances. Even so, international comparisons remain impeded by the fact that 'Hard data on the hotel, catering and tourism sector are not easy to come by as it is rarely singled out from the services sector in general' (ILO, 2001: 2). Second, many HI activities are an integral part of the TI, notably in a holiday or leisure context, including resort hotels and country pubs. Third, some work is difficult to differentiate as either hospitality or tourism work, for example that performed by tour reps, back packers and flight attendants. These jobs share common attributes and are associated with both hospitality and tourism activities. In fact tourism literature rarely deals with employment issues, and one has to look within the social sciences to find any analysis of tourism work (for example Urry, 1990; Sinclair, 1997). Hence there are circumstances when we refer to the Hotel, Catering and Tourism Sector (HCTS).

What sources are used?

A full data set from the Workplace Employee Relations Survey

WERS (1998) is a nationally representative sample survey of workplaces in Great Britain (GB) with ten or more employees. This provides core empirical data about employment relations in the HI in two contexts – all industries and services (AIS) and the private service sector (PSS):

- Over 60 per cent of the sample of hospitality workplaces in WERS are small and very small workplaces, so this new data set provides a more rounded impression of employment relations than Lucas (1995a).
- Survey data have been gathered from employees for the first time, thus enabling a more balanced perspective of the employment relationship to be presented.
- Verbatim responses from the employee questionnaires have also been obtained, allowing extensive commentary from employees to be included.

Explaining the Workplace Employee Relations Survey

Readers of this book must refer to Appendix 1 (Methodology) to familiarize themselves with the details of the WERS sample and some of the associated
terminology:

- Appendix 1 contains substantial general background information about workplaces (size, status, employment, performance and change) and employees'
  occupations and other characteristics from the management questionnaire. It
  also contains a small amount of factual information from the employee survey.
- Specific employment relations observations from WERS are incorporated
  within chapters throughout the main body of the text.
- Key WERS characteristics are drawn together by way of summary in
  Appendix 2 for tutors' and students' further use in analysing and evaluating
  the state of employment relations in the HI by size of workplace and sub-
  sector.

Literature on employment relations and the hospitality industry published since 1995

An inter- and multi-disciplinary literature base, including the author's recent
research, forms the basis for exploring contemporary employment relations in the
HI across the globe, in theory and in practice. Examples from around 50 countries in all continents are included, but the available literature is richest for North
America, Asia-Pacific and Europe. Most research remains focused on hotels, typically the large companies at the upper end of the market, and ignores the smaller,
independent hotel businesses. Yet in Britain hotels comprise only 10 per cent of
HI establishments. There is growing interest in restaurant chains, notably in fast
food. While these organizations may be the most visible and accessible, there
are still huge swathes of the HI about which we know relatively little, in spite of
attempts to extend the boundaries of research enquiry into these areas (Lucas and
Langlois, 2000b; Sehkaran and Lucas, 2002). There is also over-reliance on
the managerial voice, although a number of studies have attempted to redress the
lack of employee perspective, hence the importance of the WERS employee
survey.

What does the book contain?

The book follows three broad themes. The Introduction and opening two
chapters are scene-setting, as they present background details and key contextual
issues. The next three chapters concentrate on managerial approaches to employment relations and the employment policies and practices that managers pursue
in relation to resourcing, development, fair treatment, reward and performance.
The subsequent three chapters focus on workers' issues, including representation,
participation, dispute resolution and employees' views about their job and workplace. Finally, the concluding chapter proposes a way forward to understand the
state of the employment relationship, and makes suggestions for reform.

Each chapter contains:

- learning objectives;
- core subject matter drawn from the British WERS and international literature;
- tables and boxes to illustrate comparisons;
- case studies on practice taken from companies, research and legal proceedings;
- topics for discussion and review.

Chapter 1, 'Whither employment relations and hospitality?', presents an overview of the historical development of employment relations in Britain, highlighting how these developments may influence employment relations in the HI where a triadic employer–worker–customer relationship is identified. Managerial frames of reference on employment relations are explained. Rules of employment and power relationships are discussed in relation to managers, workers and customers. The wider national and international contexts of employment relations are reviewed.

Chapter 2, 'Employment and work', identifies the importance and structure of HI employment and the main characteristics of the labour force and employment flows across the world. The structure and patterns of working time are discussed, and different approaches to labour utilization compared and located. Issues of skill and the deskilling of work are outlined. The nature and meaning of work, particularly customer-service work, is explored.

Chapter 3, 'The role of management in employment relations', identifies the characteristics of management style in the HI, and discusses different approaches to the management of employment relations, including HRM and the psychological contract. The ways HRM can be operationalized and managed in a customer-service context are developed. How management is organized for employment relations, managers' work responsibilities and managers' views of employment relations in British workplaces are outlined.

Chapter 4, 'Resourcing, development and fair treatment', reviews approaches to three key aspects of employment practice. Approaches to recruitment and selection are presented and evaluated. The state of training and development is assessed, drawing out some international comparisons. Measures designed to lead to fair treatment at work including family-friendly measures, diversity and equality opportunity policies, health and safety measures and work–life balance are discussed and evaluated.

Chapter 5, 'Pay, reward and performance', explains the nature and purpose of pay and reward systems. Pay regulation and its consequences across the world, including the role of a minimum wage and equal pay, are discussed. Pay determination systems, particularly those in the EU, are reviewed, while the role of managers in pay determination within British workplaces is explored. Monetary and non-monetary components of remuneration in a low paying industry are identified and evaluated within the triadic employment relationship. The role of performance appraisal is discussed.

Chapter 6, 'Representation, participation and involvement', identifies the principles of collective dialogue based on collective bargaining and social partnership, and explains why trade unions are not able to provide effective workforce representation in the HI within a variety of institutional frameworks throughout the world. The specific characteristics of trade union membership within Britain are identified. Alternative forms of non-union representation and industrial conflict are addressed. The purpose and function of different forms of worker participation and consultation are considered, with particular reference to the EU. Methods of employee communication and involvement are assessed, with a focus on British workplaces.

Chapter 7, 'Employment law and dispute resolution', summarizes the basic features of individual and collective employment law, and outlines the concept of an organizational framework of justice. The legal and institutional framework for dispute resolution is identified and considered. Issues within the grievance and disciplinary process are discussed, and the role of the employment tribunal system is evaluated. Collective disputes procedures are reviewed. While international themes are explored, the main emphasis is on the British experience.

Chapter 8, 'What do the workers think?', considers employment relations from workers' perspective and analyses and evaluates employees' perceptions of the state of employment relations in Britain from WERS.

Chapter 9, 'Conclusions and future issues', draws together the themes established from earlier chapters, and assesses the state of employment relations in the HI nationally and internationally. It considers how far the state of employment relations in the HI may have changed within the last ten years, and identifies key issues for the future.

Appendix 1, 'Background characteristics of the WERS98 sample', contains summary details about WERS and focuses on the new approach taken in this book, including methodology, data analysis and presentation of data. Substantial details of key supporting background data including workplace profiles, employee and occupational characteristics, workplace status, employment, workplace performance and workplace change are presented.

Appendix 2, 'Employment relations practices and outcomes', contains a number of tables summarizing selected employment relations practices and associated outcomes that have been discussed within the chapters.

Finally, an extensive bibliography uniquely draws together employment relations and hospitality literature. This is designed to overcome some of the difficulties of identifying and locating appropriate literature across both fields of study using existing methods of literature searching.

1 Whither employment relations and hospitality?

Learning objectives

By the end of this chapter you should be able to:

- appreciate the historical development of employment relations and its relevance as a field of study;
- understand how employment relations in the HI are defined;
- explain how managerial frames of reference affect the way we see employment relations;
- understand the nature of the rules of employment, and how their regulation is underpinned by power relationships;
- appreciate the influence of the wider international and national contexts on the employment relationship.

Historical development of employment relations

Interest in employment, now the preserve of many individuals, but not all, in western economies, derives from the fact that 'Work dominates the lives of men and women . . . the management of employees both individually and collectively remains a central feature of organisational life' (Blyton and Turnbull, 1998: 3). Before beginning an examination of employment relations in the HI, it is useful to outline the historical development of employment relations[1] and their relevance as a field of study, thereby introducing the reader to some of the key terms used throughout the book.

Establishing the collective model

According to Hyman (1989) academic interest in employment relations was prompted when the potential stability of social order was put under threat by militant behaviour among a growing number of unionized industrial manual workers, who were no longer prepared to tolerate very bad terms and conditions of employment. This challenge to social order, which began in the late nineteenth century, was met by two responses. First, the social welfare reformers, in keeping with their predecessors who had successfully campaigned for health and safety legislation earlier in the nineteenth century, urged legal intervention to improve the conditions under which work was performed and the terms under which it was undertaken. They achieved limited success, notably the introduction of minimum wages in four manufacturing industries in 1906.[2]

The second and main response, which was to characterize public policy on employment relations until 1979, was that voluntary collective bargaining provided the best means to secure order within employer–employee relations. Collective bargaining is a process whereby employers and trade unions negotiate the substantive terms and conditions of employment, such as pay and hours of work, and procedural agreements that facilitate the resolution of disputes between the parties. Industrial relations, the term in usage at the time, focused on the institutions of collective bargaining in fixing these 'rules' of employment, largely within male-dominated manufacturing environments. Collective agreements were not legally enforceable.

While public services such as the health service, the railways and the coal mines came to assume importance in industrial relations following the mass nationalization programme after the Second World War, private services remained the 'Cinderella' of British industrial relations. Even though the growth of private services such as retailing and hospitality opened up more employment opportunities for women, whose main work opportunities had been in domestic service in the earlier part of the century, unregulated, female service work was deemed not to be part of industrial relations. Even so, the lack of collective bargaining arrangements prompted the Labour government to extend the scope of minimum wage legislation to embrace these sectors. Thus in 1945 the newly named wages councils, a form of 'state-sponsored' collective bargaining, were able to fix remuneration (any pay including basic pay, overtime and shift premiums) and paid holidays for many 'unprotected' workers in private services.

Collective consensus and a more active state

Greater state intervention in employment matters was a response by both Conservative and Labour governments to the mounting economic difficulties of the 1960s, e.g. statutory and voluntary incomes policies. State intervention also constituted a response to the perceived failure of voluntary collective bargaining to provide an effective regulatory mechanism for social order and social welfare, notably to protect the interests of the low-paid, many of whom were women. This perceived breakdown prompted the government to appoint a Royal Commission in 1965, the Donovan Commission (1968), to investigate the state of employer–worker relations, in order to recommend how the 'system' could be reformed. The Donovan prescription sought to maintain voluntarism, and placed the onus on employers to improve the rules of employment, and to introduce more formal procedures for the resolution of disputes.

Donovan's prescription was not universal, because it could not be applied to large parts of private services comprising small, informally managed, non-union workplaces, where female and part-time employment was concentrated (Lucas, 1986: 97–131). A different approach based on legal intervention in employment relations began to develop, based on employment protection for individual employees. Early employment protection rights of the 1960s included the right to a written statement of terms and conditions of employment, statutory redundancy pay and equal pay. Workers lacking the protection of a trade union and with no recourse to formal workplace procedures could resolve employment disputes, that is those in scope of the law, by going to an industrial (now employment) tribunal.

The 1970s represented a significant turning point for legal intervention in employment relations. Britain joined the European Economic Community (EEC) in 1972. This heralded the start of a wide-ranging programme designed to establish a floor of new rights relating to matters including unfair dismissal, maternity leave, sex and race discrimination and health and safety at work. The main beneficiaries were to be those working in private services.

A challenge to tradition: the Thatcher and Major years

Events of the 1980s and early 1990s effectively killed the model of voluntary collective bargaining. In pursuit of an overriding objective to deregulate the labour market and employment, successive Conservative governments systematically dismantled institutions deemed to interfere with the free working of the labour market, notably the trade unions and wages councils. Paradoxically, in spite of the government's antipathy to the EU's social action programme and subsequent opt-out of the social chapter, the EU continued to influence British employment relations in a significant way. Rulings from the European Court of Justice (ECJ) obliged Britain to introduce new legislation, e.g. the transfer of undertakings[3] or the amendment of existing legislation relating to equal pay and sex discrimination. The floor of employment rights was both strengthened and extended.

Managers reasserted the right to manage increasingly flexible and non-standard workers under the banner of 'managerialism', in workplaces that might be labelled 'bleak houses' (Sisson, 1993). An alternative version of management thinking stressed the benefits of 'commitment' over 'control' (Walton, 1985). Both approaches came to signify the two variants of HRM. 'Soft' HRM emphasized fostering commitment, improving quality and developing the *human* resource, whereas 'hard' HRM was contingent and calculating in its utilization of the human *resource* (Hendry and Pettigrew, 1986; Storey, 1989, 1992). If organizations were to survive the effects of adverse economic conditions, globalization and increasing competition, the imperative was to integrate HRM within business strategy (Huselid, 1995; Storey, 1995; Guest and Hoque, 1996).

The impact of HRM on industrial relations was widely debated (Guest, 1987, 1989; Purcell and Ahlstrand, 1989; Guest and Hoque, 1996). Other key issues in the wider academic debate included the extent of continuity and change in industrial relations, the sharp decline in trade union membership, the impact of deregulation and whether employment relations could be re-regulated.

New Labour: new hope?

By the mid-1990s individual relationships were catapulted firmly to the forefront of analysis of the employment relationship (Edwards, 1995; Beardwell, 1996).

Recognition of this change had been apparent from WIRS in 1990 (Millward *et al.*, 1992), perhaps most notably within the HI (Lucas, 1995a, 1996a). HI managers are free to exercise a high degree of managerial prerogative in the absence of unorganized labour, termed 'unbridled individualism' (Lucas, 1996a).

The election of a Labour government for the first time in nearly 20 years in 1997 raised expectations that there would be a new agenda for employment relations, although Heery's (1997: 107) assessment was that 'it is extremely doubtful whether New Labour will issue in a new industrial relations'. New Labour's stakeholder economy is based on fairness and partnership. Fairness at work is to be achieved in two ways. The government signed up to the EU social chapter and set about introducing a new floor of minimum employment standards, including a National Minimum Wage (NMW), and family-friendly measures. Social partnership between employers and workers is designed to foster a more consensual and cooperative relationship between employers and employees. The Low Pay Commission (LPC), whose first task was to recommend the initial rate of the NMW, provides an early manifestation of social partnership comprising employer, worker and independent representatives. Although many of the Conservatives' trade union reforms remain in place, the introduction of statutory trade union recognition procedures might help reverse the steep decline in trade union membership.

By the time of WERS in 1998 the system of collective representation had crumbled 'to such an extent that it no longer represented the dominant model' (Millward *et al.*, 2000: 234). In reality employment relations could conform to different and diverse patterns (Millward *et al.*, 2000). Private service establishments employing 25 or more employees were numerically more important than private sector manufacturing and the public sector put together. Their share of employment increased from 26 per cent in 1980 to 44 per cent in 1998, reinforcing the point that alternative ways to view and reform employment relations were long overdue, particularly in circumstances of 'bleak house' (Sisson, 1993) or 'black hole' employment (Guest and Conway, 1999). Although we find these terms wanting in respect of the HI, they highlight the relevance of the industry as a unit of analysis. Consequently we shall show how these types of workplaces throw up major problems for employment relations reform.

Agenda for the twenty-first century

In calling for a new industrial relations paradigm, Ackers (2002) now argues that the new problem of social order focuses on links between employment and society, and that such a link provides an explicit ethical framework for policies like social partnership. He rejects the traditional industrial relations notion of workers as unattached individuals in their out-of-work lives, and argues that industrial relations can no longer ignore issues of work–life balance and corporate social responsibility. Indeed social concerns underpin 'Fairness at Work' and the 'Welfare to Work' programme (DTI, 1998), and family-friendly issues are a new addition to WERS. Hence a new definition of industrial relations as neo-pluralism:

> Employment relations is the study of the social institutions involved in the normative regulation of the employment relationship and business's interaction with other stakeholders in society.
>
> (Ackers, 2002: 18)

Thus Ackers rejects as inappropriate Kelly's (1997) industrial relations paradigm for the twenty-first century, which derives from a redefinition of Marxism based on socialism, workers' mobilization, economic militancy and strikes, and organized labour.

Edwards (2003a) identifies three pressing issues in contemporary employment relations: 'high commitment' or 'high involvement' work systems, the international context and economic performance. The first, although interesting, is very rarely found anywhere in Britain. Its alternative of 'low skills' and 'low wages' strikes right at the heart of much hospitality employment. This links to economic performance, where the absence of collective bargaining is likely to have contributed to income inequality and the perpetuation of low pay in the HI, although pay may be subsidized by the state through social security and taxation. The further subsidy of low pay through tips as a defensible employment practice is a matter of conjecture. We shall also explore if particular employment relations practices can be linked to successful performance outcomes. The international context and its implications for employment relations in the HI are considered below and in subsequent chapters.

A fourth pressing issue can be added. Employment relations discourse needs to recognize that prejudice and bias have been built into much of the theoretical and practical analysis, thus distorting its perspective. Gender is not the only example, but may be the most obvious. In spite of an increasing interest in what may be described as 'women's issues', such as (un)equal pay and employment opportunities, family-friendly policies and sexual harassment, one major barrier to understanding employment relations is an assumption that they are gender neutral (Forrest, 1993; Wajcman, 2000). The argument is that adding women's issues to the agenda is simply not good enough. Management, trade unions and the state are not gender neutral (Dickens, 1997, 1998; Edwards, 2003a), and therefore we need to recognize the gendered characteristics of the employment relationship and work and integrate this into our understanding of the field of employment relations. Other 'omissions' include age, ethnicity and the role of customers. We shall explore these issues throughout the book where it is possible or relevant to do so.

All these issues were placed under review in The Future of Work Programme launched by the ESRC in 1998. The Programme has supported 27 projects designed to rectify gaps in our understanding and improve the quality of information available to the policy-makers in the UK. Topics under investigation have included the future of unskilled work, business re-engineering and performance, the changing position of ethnic minorities and women in the labour market, the future for trade unions and the changing nature of the employment relationship (Taylor, 2001a,b, 2002a,b,c).

What are employment relations in the hospitality industry?

Three terms denote the relations between *managers* and *workers* in the employment relationship – industrial relations, employee relations and employment relations (Hollinshead *et al.*, 1999: 7; Salamon, 2000: 4–5; Leat, 2001: 5–7; Rose, 2001: 5–7). These terms are often used interchangeably, but can also convey subtle differences of meaning. They may coincide with other fields of academic inquiry and practical activity concerned with 'people management', namely personnel management and HRM.

Edwards (2003a: 1–36) provides an insightful analysis of the employment relationship, taking as his starting point the distinction made by Fox (1966) and Flanders (1974) between market relations and managerial relations. At the root is an economic exchange between capital (the employer) and labour (the worker), in which the price of labour is set as a contract of employment. In this economic exchange between the buyer (employer) and seller (worker) of labour, the parties do not share equal power resources. In common law the employer has the right to command and the employee has a duty to obey. The commodity at the heart of the bargain is the worker's labour power. The employer will seek to maximize control over that 'labour process' in order to generate a surplus as profit (Braverman, 1974; Friedman, 1977).

The employment relationship, as an exchange and in recognition of its broader context, has also been termed the effort–reward bargain: 'an economic, social and political relationship, for which employees provide manual and mental labour in return for rewards allotted by employers' (Gospel and Palmer, 1993: 3).

Labour only becomes useful if it can be persuaded by management to work, but this is only the beginning. Workers must demonstrate commitment, continue working to the required standards, and not deviate from those standards. In other words workers must follow 'rules', otherwise management may need to deploy corrective or punitive measures via the disciplinary procedure.

Bonamy and May (1997) argue that a weakening of employment relationships since the 1970s has given rise to the emergence of employment as a service relationship. This relationship demands increased recognition of the professional qualities of the 'autonomous' worker, which poses problems of incompatibility with an employment contract built upon subordination. Pay is determined by time worked, whilst idle time due to poor organization and absenteeism is reduced. This is manifested in new forms of employment contract (fixed-term and part-time), externalization of employment to agencies and the sub-contracting of activities.

Edwards (2003a: 1) notes that, if we were starting from scratch, 'employment relations' might be the best label.[4]

Employment relations do not rule out all variants within the employment relationship including:

- trade unions and formal collective bargaining;
- individually based management/workforce relations conducted informally;
- managerialism;

- more democratic and highly participative non-union relations;
- men, women and disadvantaged groups;
- employees and workers, including atypical workers and the self-employed.

Further:

- employment relations is the main term used in the WERS sourcebook (Cully *et al.*, 1999);
- industrial tribunals have been renamed employment tribunals;
- the cornerstone of New Labour's industrial relations policy is the *Employment Relations Act 1999*.

A necessary departure for this book, as noted earlier (Lucas, 1995a; Lucas and Lammont, 2003), is to relocate the nexus of the employment relationship to include a relatively ignored third actor in the employment relationship – *the customer*.[5] The notion of the customer in the employment relationship has been increasingly incorporated into the sociology of work (Hochschild, 1983; Wharton, 1993; Morris and Feldman, 1996; Erickson and Wharton, 1997), but less so in employment relations. Front-line workers, such as receptionists and servers in bars and restaurants, have to serve two 'masters': their superior manager and the customer. Individual workers can have a simultaneous and coterminous employment relationship with the organization and the customer.

Organizations in services are best seen as inverted pyramids, with most workers in direct customer contact (Redman and Mathews, 1998). Direct service workers engage directly with customers in an exchange that carries both economic *and* social connotations. Their ability to deliver successfully hinges upon a social relationship with indirect service workers, whose actions are also instrumental to the provision of good customer service, e.g. an enjoyable meal or clean bedrooms. Indirect service workers are not in regular customer contact, so customer influence may be more economic than social. Hence, customers cannot be excluded from an analysis of the employment relationship. As shown below and explained later, an earlier definition has been revised:

> Employee relations in hotels and catering is about the management of employment and work relationships between managers and workers and, sometimes, customers; it also covers contemporary employment and work practices.
>
> (Lucas, 1995a: 81)

> the locus of the employment relationship should change from an economic employer-employee exchange to a socio-economic employer-worker-customer exchange.
>
> (Lucas and Lammont, 2003: 84)

Frames of reference

Before exploring the facets of the employment relationship, we need to outline *why our attitude towards things influences the way in which we see any given situation, and how it*

> ### Box 1.1 Frames of reference in practice
>
> Triplets watch a local football match from adjoining seats, getting an almost identical view of the game. The result is United 5 City 1. One triplet is deliriously happy, the second feels very low, while the third is able to provide a balanced analysis of events, conceding that the result was a fair one, although two of United's goals were the result of dubious refereeing and City deserved more than a single goal.
>
> Why did their particular attitude affect their view of the game?[6]

may affect the way we interpret those events (Box 1.1). Let us now consider how these observations link to the theory and practice of employment relations.[7]

Fox (1966: 2) proposed two frames of reference as a means by which 'the problems of industrial relations can be seen realistically and laid more open to solution'. The *unitary perspective* is a 'management ideology' built on the belief that everyone in the organization shares the same goals, and that 'conflict' is pathological and derives from deviance. Trade unions are seen as an intrusion, competing with management for worker loyalty. Fox's main argument was that the unitary perspective was a naive and unrealistic frame of reference that might 'distort reality and thereby prejudice solutions'. Yet in reality many managers do perceive their organizations in unitary terms, regarding themselves as the sole source of authority. Unitarism has underpinned the 'human relations school' of management, including Mayo, Likert, McGregor, Schein and Herzberg (Pugh and Hickson, 1996: 155–77), and reasserted itself in 'managerialism' and HRM.

Fox suggested that the more realistic approach to managing people was to recognize that organizations are *pluralistic*, comprising various groups, each with their own basis of authority and sets of interests. The 'rules' of employment are not just the preserve of management. A new pay rate set by management will not necessarily be seen as fair by workers, creating an issue of potential dispute. Therefore conflict or differences between individuals and groups are inevitable. Management should recognize this inevitability, and find the ways and means to regulate such differences. As noted above, an institutional approach – collective bargaining between employers and trade unions, and the development of formal procedures to deal with disputes about pay, grievances and discipline – was considered to be the most appropriate solution. However, this is flawed to the extent that it implies both parties to the bargain have equal power resources at their disposal.

Later Fox (1974) revised his thinking and added a third perspective of *radicalism*, prompted by a wave of 'shop floor' discontent and 'wildcat' strikes at workplace level. Such worker behaviour was perceived as a reaction against exploitative and oppressive employers whose sole aim was to maximize profit. Conflict was caused by the economic disparity of society as a whole, with the principal disparity between capital and labour – employers who own and manage the means of production and workers who have their (human) capital to sell. This view underpins the labour process approach (Braverman, 1974). This approach stresses the contradiction of managerial goals, with regulation and control having to be balanced by the need to gain workers' consent (Edwards, 1995).

Even today Edwards (2003a) argues that unitarism cannot be written off as naive and outdated any more than radicalism because of the apparent disappearance of discontent. Ackers' (2002) neo-pluralism refocuses the employment relationship beyond the workplace by connecting the old pluralist and voluntary frames of reference with new questions raised by contemporary society. The health of society is put first, encouraging industrial relations policy initiatives that are driven by social concerns, not just a business agenda. Further he argues that the employment relationship bears hidden ethical considerations of trust and responsibility in relation to human beings.

As we shall show, both managers and workers in a variety of work and employment situations in the HI do see their workplaces in unitary terms, but this does not necessarily infer the absence of conflict. Areas of potential dispute, conflict and difference do exist between managers and workers, between managers and other managers, and between workers and customers, demonstrating that workplaces are pluralistic. In cases where workers 'fiddle' or 'pilfer' from their employer (Mars *et al.*, 1979), the nature of their behaviour is more in keeping with a radical perspective. Thus it is possible to observe facets of unitarism, pluralism and radicalism in the same employment relationship in which management, for the most part, remains the more powerful.

Even so, areas of common interest self-evidently exist otherwise all these relationships would break down. Consent provides the basis for resolving conflict and achieving cooperation. Cooperation is built on trust between individuals engendered at workplace level rather than through elaborate organizational mechanisms. Yet securing workers' consent is neither a straightforward nor certain process. Therefore, a mix of overt and covert conflict and cooperation underpins all employment relationships and, as we shall argue, workplace harmony owes more to pragmatic acceptance and accommodation among the parties in the employment relationship than to ideological belief.

The rules of employment and power relations

We have already noted that the employment relationship is underpinned by rules, hence the continuing validity of Clegg's (1979: 1) definition of industrial relations as 'The study of the rules governing employment' which Edwards (1995: 5) explains in more detail:

> This does not limit the subject to the collective relations between managements and trade unions, for a rule can derive from other sources, and there are rules governing non-union groups; nor does it restrict analysis to one sector, for it covers all paid forms of employment. A rule is a social institution involving two or more parties which may have its basis in law, a written collective agreement, an unwritten agreement, a unilateral decree or merely an understanding that has the force of custom. In non-union settings, as much as union ones, rules determine rates of pay, hours of work, job descriptions

and many other aspects of employment. The subject is about the ways in which the employment relationship is regulated. To regulate means to control, to adapt or adjust continuously or to adjust by rule.

Managerial issues

While rules may be the substantive rules of employment, e.g. pay and conditions of employment, implicit in the notion of *rules* affecting people is the concept of *behaviour*. Management's job is to control and direct workers' behaviour to perform work to the desired standards, and thereby ensure that the rules of employment are adhered to.

Four key issues arise:

* Rules are not always absolute and may be gendered.
* Managerial control of workers' behaviour is underpinned by a power relationship.
* This power relationship is unequal and may be gendered.[8]
* Managers have a choice of means to maximize control.

The first point is that one should *caution against perceiving rules in too absolute a sense*. At one end of the spectrum rules embodied in the law of the land provide a good example of formal rules. Any breach may incur very severe penalties, e.g. health and safety. In a workplace setting rules in practice may derive from informal understandings that can in one set of circumstances be interpreted by the worker as a permissive concession or in a different set of circumstances as something to be observed at all costs (Edwards, 2003a). Strawberries as a worker's perquisite during the Wimbledon lawn tennis championship are a good example. Experienced workers know that taking home unwanted strawberries is 'permitted' during busy periods. When fewer staff are needed, increased managerial surveillance will be deployed to dismiss staff caught in possession of company property (Lucas, 1995a: 119–20).

Rule-learning is part of what Polanyi (1967) refers to as 'tacit skills'. As argued elsewhere:

> Tacit skills, such as learning to deal with customers, are learnt in and through the very act of doing, often involving trial and error and not from following a body of procedurally-designed rules. They are seen as an interpretive achievement of the user as to how the 'rules' fit the task in hand. By mastery of the rules comes the power to extend them.
>
> (Lucas and Lammont, 2003: 61)

This example embracing the customer provides a developmental point to Edwards' (1995, 2003a) observation that rule-making is difficult, and that rules have to be interpreted in action for them to have any real meaning. Specifically in the labour contract this is because the worker's ability to work is only realized as useful labour in the course of carrying out that work, hence 'a rule is a complex social institution'.

In service work physical appearance and 'personality', or 'aesthetic labour', are an implicit part of the employment contract (Tyler and Abbott, 1998; Warhurst *et al.*, 2000). Only female flight attendants, not their male colleagues, are subjected to regular weigh-ins to ensure they comply to specified weight:height ratios. This demonstrates clearly how a *rule may be gendered* (Tyler and Abbott, 1998).

The second point to note is that the *very essence of management seeking to control workers' behaviour is underpinned by a power relationship.* Power is the capacity to pursue one's own interests individually and collectively, involving the capacity to oppose the actions of others and to pursue one's own objectives, and is embedded in continuing relationships (Edwards, 2003a). This does not mean power has to be exercised by either party in an overt sense. The threat of power may be sufficient to maintain broadly consensual employment relationships, such that any disputes or differences (conflicts) are resolved amicably without recourse to either party seeking to deploy sanctions against the other.

The third point assumes a *power inequality in the employment relationship.* Self-evidently an employer is more powerful than an individual worker. The employer's ability to terminate a worker's services is likely to be more detrimental to the worker than to the employer, in spite of employment protection legislation. Yet the individual behaviours of workers, such as high labour turnover, may be detrimental to an employer, even though they are not concerted. When workers combine collectively, with or without the backing of a trade union, there is some tilt in the balance of power, because collective sanctions may be imposed against the employer.[9] Ultimately the outcome of the process by which each side seeks to gain concessions will depend on the relative power of the parties. For example, a plentiful supply of suitable workers in the labour market makes existing workers more readily dispensable and replaceable on the employer's terms. The opposite would be true for workers with scarce skills who can command high wages.

As Wajcman (2000) argues, gender relations are power-based and women's subordination in the workforce and workplace owes as much to trade unions as it does to managers. Spradley and Mann (1975) provide a graphic account of how the subordination of one group of female workers was brought about by another group of male workers who were the custodians of the male proprietor's trust. The male bartenders controlled the orders, and sought to make the cocktail waitresses' job difficult by giving orders in an inconsistent and confusing way. Any mistakes became the waitresses' responsibility, even if they had been caused by the bartenders. Such was the power of the bartenders that pleasing them became more important than pleasing the customers.

The fourth point is that *managers have a choice of means to maximize control* over workers. Friedman's (1977) 'direct control' is a variant of Taylorism (the separation of mental and manual labour or scientific management). Management is responsible for planning, designing and organizing the labour process, while cheap, unskilled workers perform standardized, simple repetitive tasks. Fast food is a good case in point, and also epitomizes McDonaldization, a social critique of how contemporary society and culture are being shaped by rationalist scientific management (from Weber's theory of rationalization and Taylorism) (Ritzer, 1996). While Taylorism sought to control the organization of work,

McDonaldization is based on rationalization, replication, standardization of products and service, and quantification. In this low trust strategy (Fox, 1974) worker behaviour is controlled through the use of standardized scripts in the service encounter (see Chapter 2).

In Friedman's alternative of 'responsible autonomy', a high trust approach, managers delegate control to relatively privileged skilled workers who may already have elements of job control and discretion. The objective is to get workers to identify with the competitive aims of the organization so they will behave responsibly with minimum supervision. An obvious example of where such an approach might be used is in a luxury hotel, but it is also associated with empowerment and much customer-service work.

As we shall argue in Chapter 3, and implied in the example of cocktail waitresses above, these and other similar approaches including 'hard' and 'soft' HRM provide a useful framework for analysis, but are not necessarily alternatives. The history of hotel internationalization has been characterized by American chains that secure control and integration through highly standardized procedures and manuals of operational procedures (Nickson, 1997). Yet a 'soft' focus on the service encounter as the driver of competitive advantage necessitates developing a culture of customized service (Jones *et al.*, 1998). Mass customization illustrated by Burger King's 'have it your way' slogan as a challenge to McDonald's hold on the market is proposed as an alternative paradigm to McDonaldization (Taylor and Lyon, 1995).

Workers and customers

Other tensions within the employment relationship impinge upon the rules of employment and power relationships. If management is about the achievement of organizational goals through people it can be argued that managers will be successful to the extent that these goals coincide with the aims and aspirations of those people, be they workers or customers. This 'matching' of broadly reciprocal needs between employers and workers may be referred to as a 'psychological contract' (Schein, 1978; McLean Parks *et al.*, 1998; Guest and Conway, 1998, 2002), or set of contracts (Mumford, 1995). It suggests managers and workers can share goals, but this is not at all straightforward. There is not a necessarily clear-cut distinction between boss and worker, or a 'them and us' scenario. Further we must also account for a psychological contract with customers.

Two key points are noteworthy:

* Organizations comprise people and are, therefore, social organizations.
* People, as social animals, may behave in unpredictable ways.

Workers

Human beings do not necessarily behave consistently or predictably, even in the same sets of circumstances. People are citizens and customers as well as employees, and these multiple identities bring different and sometimes conflicting expectations of the organization (Heery, 1993). This makes the management of the employment relationship an uncertain process within which there is a blend of contradictory principles around the need to control and to gain the consent of workers. Workers may seek to regain control individually or collectively when they perceive that management has operated outside the rules. At that point workers' consent has been withdrawn and management will need to find ways to restore order and regain consent.

In Lucas (1995a: 93–5) workers' individual response to organizational rules is seen in three main ways – to conform or be deviant in employment, or to terminate their employment. These responses are similar to Marchington's (1992) 'getting on', 'getting by' and 'getting back'. These are behaviours deployed in circumstances where customer care and service quality are dependent on workers' use of their tacit skills, which contain both technical and attitudinal elements. Limiting the definition of tacit skills to employer–employee relations is too narrow. Marchington overlooked how workers exhibit their tacit skills in ways other than in respect of their relationship with the employer (Lammont and Lucas, 1999; Lucas and Lammont, 2003), notably the customer. The point that 'getting back', 'getting by' and 'getting on' are as much resistance strategies in the labour process as coping mechanisms is developed in Chapters 2 and 6. These behaviours can also be deployed collectively. How workers' interests may be served collectively through trade union and non-union representation will be discussed in Chapter 6.

At workplace level personal relationships are likely to be closely connected to morale and success. Managers often 'muck in' when required. In small workplaces the existence of a single leader, often the owner, may serve to inspire loyalty from the workforce, but it is not a one-way process, as workers' respect has to be earned. Is it realistic to suggest that Mina, Jo and Sadie, who wait on table in the restaurant, share all the same goals as their boss? The hotel may not be doing very well, so there may be mutual concern for the survival of the business. Yet these ladies' main goal may be to serve their customers cheerfully and effectively, while at the same time enjoying some social banter among themselves and with their customers in the process of earning a reasonable wage.

Customers

Within the triadic employment relationship a simultaneous and coterminous relationship with the organization and the customer directly impinges on how workers carry out their work, and such interactions may be rewarding or stressful. The consequent effect on workers' performance may have positive or negative implications for the rules of employment: what they can earn (from good tips to no tips), their prospects of promotion (satisfactory manager and customer appraisal) or actually keeping their job (customer complaint leading to disciplinary sanctions or closure). Unequivocally the worker–customer relationship affects the rules governing employment[10] and workplace behaviour. But so do employer–customer relationships, hence the employment relationship embodies a triadic set of power relations.

This relationship embodies a socio-economic exchange, and is not simply an economic exchange around the price of labour. Fox (1966) provides a useful starting point, since he noted that organizations are social organizations and how people behave is a crucial issue in the employment relationship. Even Edwards' (2003a: 14) point that 'a rule is a complex social institution' does not adequately encapsulate our position. The main justification for widening the scope of this relationship derives from the fact that the service encounter is the interaction of the producer and consumer of services, and is a more complex phenomenon where financial considerations are interwoven with social ones (Offe, 1985; Urry, 1990). In hospitality the social function of service work derives from the provision of a 'home away from home' (Offe, 1985). The service encounter entails 'emotion work' (Hochschild, 1983) – the assumption of a social-self, which effectively masks the individual's own personal dispositions to act, including the need to smile and be pleasant in an uninvolved way. We have already noted that 'aesthetic' and sexual labour may also be inherent in service work. It is the 'normalizing' social role of service labour that distinguishes it from other wage labour (Hochschild, 1983). Service work cannot be understood in terms of economic rationality alone. Examination must be based on the supposition that service work is the intended outcome of a necessarily social process in which some social interaction occurs between one or more producers and one or more consumers.

The relations between three groups of people – managers, workers and customers – embody the potential for contradiction between, on the one hand, uncertainty, unpredictability, conflict and difference and, on the other hand, consent, team effort and concerted performance. The practical benefit this book seeks to convey accrues from an understanding of the nature and scope of the rules of employment in this triadic employment relationship, and how it is regulated, primarily at workplace level.

The employment relationship in a wider context

This chapter concludes by considering some key external contextual influences on workplace employment relationships at two levels – internationally and, in more detail, nationally in Britain.

The international context

The national context of British employment relations increasingly needs to be understood within a much wider international context. Three international dimensions have particular resonance for this book:

- International competition has created more open economies that have attracted investment from foreign-owned businesses. For example the French-owned groups Accor and Envergure have respectively opened hotels within their Novotel and Campanile brands in the United Kingdom (UK).
- On a larger scale American multinational corporations (MNCs) have created world brands. McDonald's, Burger King, KFC (formerly Kentucky Fried

Chicken) and Marriott are among those that are now household names in many countries across the world.[11]

- Spin-offs from European integration, especially on employment law in Britain, have provided an important underpinning to the employment relationship in the HI.[12]

Foreign investment and MNCs are clearly important factors underpinning the expansion of hospitality and tourism not only in Britain but also in developing countries. Examples of 'better' employment practices, in so far as they may exist in the British HI, have been associated with foreign-owned businesses (Lucas and Laycock, 1991; Price, 1994; Hoque, 1999a, 1999b).

Aspects of the American model of employment relations, that is non-union and market-driven, may seem to reflect some aspects of observed employment relations practice in the British HI (Lucas, 2002a,b), but the similarity has been overstated (Taylor, 2001a). The United States (US) has substantially more legal regulation than Britain, which has benefited American HI workers, while the trade unions are not entirely powerless – issues we highlight in later chapters. The European model based on social partnership designed to forge a common agenda between capital and labour is considerably more diverse and different across the member states than is often acknowledged (Taylor, 2000b). While we cannot expect it to reflect current developments in HI employment relations in most British workplaces, it has not necessarily produced wholesale benefits for HI workers across the EU either.

The British experience is not necessarily mirrored in other countries across the world. Differences in other countries' institutional arrangements and cultural considerations are among the factors that will affect their employment relations systems. Detailed comparison with other countries is beyond the scope of this book, but key instances of international employment relations within hospitality and tourism are cited throughout the remaining chapters.[13]

The British context

Workplace employment relationships cannot be immune from wider economic, social, legal and political contextual influences. Contemporary examples, which may be influential in Britain today, are shown in Table 1.1. The distinctions between these sets of influences are not always clear-cut as they can be interrelated (for a detailed account, see Salamon, 2000: 40–73).

The state

Although we have already touched upon some aspects of the state's interest in employment relations, we need to examine its role in a little more detail. The state is not a single or cohesive body, and comprises a number of institutions that have an interest in the employment relationship, whose objectives do not necessarily coincide. Parliament is the legislature, government ministers form the executive, the judiciary enforces the law, and civil servants are the administrators.[14] The state

Table 1.1 Contextual influences on the employment relationship in contemporary Britain

Economic	Social	Legal	Political
Economic prosperity	47% of the labour force is female; 25% of all employment is part-time	No restoration of collective representation and joint regulation that existed prior to the 1980s	New Labour government in second term of office with large majority
Low unemployment, but high youth unemployment	25% of young people are from ethnic minority groups	Statutory trade union recognition procedures	Public policy: the Third Way embracing a 'partnership' and a 'stakeholder' economy
Low inflation	An ageing population with increased life expectancy for men and women	NMW	Private finance initiative to fund public sector expenditure
Three-quarters of employment is in the service sector	The working population contains a high proportion of workers over 50	Family-friendly measures including improved maternity and paternity rights	Fewer people voting in General Elections and in local elections
Increasing gap in wage inequality	Society is class based, with widening gap between the 'rich' in work and the 'poor' not in work	Threefold rise in number of employment tribunal cases between 1991 and 2001	
Internationalization, globalization and liberalization of trade	Making work pay policy effected through social security, e.g. New Deal for the unemployed, and taxation, e.g. Child and Work Tax Credits to top up low earnings	EU Directives and decisions reached by the European Court of Justice influence employment law	
Deregulated and flexible labour markets	More highly educated population		
Technology, especially information technology	Trade union density is 29%, but is much lower among workers under 30		
The power and influence of MNCs	The power and influence of the mass media		
Rise in self-employment			

sponsors specialist agencies in the field of employment, and has done so since the end of the nineteenth century.[15]

Three government departments impinge on employment relations within a much wider brief. The most important is the DTI, which has overall responsibility for employment relations, small firms and competitiveness (www.dti.gov.uk/er). The Employment Relations directorate is responsible for developing policy and legislation affecting individual workers and trade unions, EU legislation, promoting partnership and best practice, regulation of employment tribunals and the dates of public holidays. The DTI publishes consultation documents, research papers, practical guidance on how to implement employment legislation and regulations, and codes of practice on matters such as picketing.[16]

The Department for Education and Skills (D*f*ES) is responsible for developing the skills of young people and adults (www.dfes.gov.uk). The Department for Work and Pensions (DWP) delivers support and advice in areas of work and work-related benefits, including New Deal, sickness and accidents at work, and retirement (www.dwp.gov.uk).

Although publicly funded, other state agencies and bodies are independent of government because they are controlled and managed by their own executive. The main institutions discussed later in the book are ACAS, the Central Arbitration Committee (CAC) and employment tribunals (Chapter 7).

The Equal Opportunities Commission (EOC), Commission for Racial Equality (CRE) and Disability Rights Commission (DRC) each have overall responsibility for specific types of anti-discrimination or equal opportunities legislation. The Health and Safety Commission (HSC) and Health and Safety Executive (HSE) have responsibility for health, safety and welfare legislation. Their roles include the publication of codes of practice.

Other bodies assist with the enforcement of minimum employment standards. The Inland Revenue's powers include obtaining information from employers, issuing enforcement notices requiring employers to pay the NMW and imposing penalties on employers not observing the NMW. Environmental Health Officers are responsible for the enforcement of health and safety standards.

Other institutions

Many other institutions, some of which may have a political bias, offer a mixture of fact and opinion on employment relations. National bodies, which take either an employer or management view, include the Confederation of British Industry (CBI), the Institute of Directors (IOD), and the Chartered Institute of Personnel and Development (CIPD). The British Hospitality Association (BHA), Restaurant Association (RA), the British Beer and Pub Association (BBPA), the Hotel, Catering and International Management Association (HCIMA) and the British Institute of Innkeeping (BII) are specific to the HI.

The H*t*F, formerly the HI's National Training Organisation (NTO), is recognized by government as the employer-led voice on all issues relating to hospitality training, education and qualifications.[17] The H*t*F also carries out research, and produces useful statistical information about the labour market (H*t*F, 2000, 2002).

The Trades Union Congress (TUC), Institute of Employment Rights (IER) and the Low Pay Network serve to defend workers' interests. The HCIMA can also be regarded as having a worker perspective since, as the professional body of hospitality managers, it serves to defend their interests as well as disseminating good management practice. Three large unions have special sections for hospitality workers: the General, Municipal and Boilermakers' Union (GMB), the Transport and General Workers Union (TGWU) and the Union of Shop, Distributive and Allied Workers (USDAW). The National Association of Licensed House Managers (NALHM) was self-standing for many years, but has recently become part of the TGWU.

Discussion and review topics

Viewing employment relations in the HI

Industrial relations are associated with trade unions and the formal institution of collective bargaining. Employee relations place emphasis on strong management often denoted by the term 'managerialist', but not all workers are afforded employee status.

- Specifically in relation to the HI, suggest why these labels may be problematic.

Frames of reference

Take examples of different managers for whom you have worked:

- Which frame of reference guided their approach to employment relations?
- What specific instances of their behaviour or actions have led you to reach this conclusion?

Employment rules

Drawing from your work experience:

- What were the main rules of employment?
- Which of these were formal written rules?
- Which of these rules were learnt in practice?
- Can you identify any rules that were ignored in particular circumstances and enforced in others, and explain why this occurred?

Power and control

Drawing from your work experience, discuss examples of where:

- managers sought to oppose the actions of others;
- managers sought to pursue their own objectives;
- workers sought to oppose the actions of others;
- workers sought to pursue their own objectives;
- managers sought to control workers through 'direct control';
- managers sought to control workers through 'responsible autonomy'.

Workforce behaviour

Based on your work experience:

- What were the circumstances when managers and customers operated outside the rules of employment?
- What was the workers' response, either as individuals or as groups?

The context of employment relations

Using data about the HI from elsewhere and from this book (e.g. trade union density is 2 per cent):

- produce a new Table 1.1 that more specifically outlines the national context of hospitality employment relations;
- see if you can add any new contextual influences;
- analyse and evaluate the potential effects of these influences on workplace relations.

2 Employment and work

Learning objectives

By the end of this chapter you should be able to:

- recognize the importance of hospitality and tourism employment;
- identify the main characteristics of the labour force, including occupations, skills and the nature of employment flows;
- identify the structure and patterns of working time;
- compare different approaches to flexible labour utilization, and understand the circumstances in which they are used;
- explain the nature and meaning of work, and identify how customer-service work impinges upon the employment relationship.

The importance and structure of employment

Worldwide employment in tourism, including the HI, stands at 192.2 million, and by 2010 is expected to have grown to 256.1 million jobs, accounting for one in 11 jobs in the formal economy (World Travel and Tourism Council (WTTC), 2000). The importance of tourism employment varies among countries, with some showing rapid employment growth, e.g. in Spain tourism employment increased by 24 per cent in the 1990s (Incomes Data Services (IDS), 1998c; Appendix 1 for WERS). In some developing countries international tourism is high status and provides secure employment, while in others it may be low status and exploitative (Baum *et al.*, 1997). Exceptionally employment may be between 10 and 30 per cent in small island economies such as Cyprus, Malta and Anguilla. In Europe tourism employment is of greater importance to southern countries such as Spain (8.3 per cent) and Italy (5.9 per cent). In other 'westernized' economies the figure is nearer 5 per cent (Australia, US, UK), while in 'emerging' tourism economies such as Bulgaria and Slovakia it represents 2 per cent of employment. Tourism is essentially a small and medium-sized enterprise (SME) industry. In Europe 94 per cent of the 2.7 million SMEs are micro-enterprises employing fewer than ten people (ILO, 2001: 48).

In some countries, including industrialized ones, there is a high proportion of unpaid labour, reflecting a large number of small entrepreneurs and their

Table 2.1 Number and percentage of establishments by size (GB)

Size of establishment	Hospitality businesses (% in brackets)		AIS (% in brackets)	
1–10 employees	226,610	(85)	1,074,922	(76)
11–24 employees	29,326	(11)	190,895	(14)
25+ employees	10,664	(4)	150,778	(11)
Total	266,600	(100)	1,416,595	(100)

Source: Calculated from H/F (1999: 9, 10) and Office for National Statistics (ONS) (1996: 97).

Notes: Column percentages do not sum to 100 due to rounding. Based on Annual Employment Survey (AES) (1996) and LFS (1998), excluding hospitality services.

Table 2.2 Number and percentage of employees in employment by size of establishment (GB)

Size of establishment	Hospitality businesses (% in brackets)		AIS (% in brackets)	
1–10 employees	410,400	(36)	3,907,000	(18)
11–24 employees	262,200	(23)	2,982,200	(14)
25+ employees	467,400	(41)	14,856,300	(68)
Total	1,140,000	(100)*	21,745,500	(100)

Source: Calculated from H/F (1999: 15, 20) and ONS (1996: 97).

Notes: *Excluding the self-employed. Based on AES (1996) and LFS (1998), excluding hospitality services.

non-remunerated family members. Peru has the highest proportion of unpaid employment (70 per cent), followed by Korea (55 per cent). Greece (48 per cent), Italy[1] and Belgium (45 per cent) have the highest proportion of unpaid employment in Europe, while in Spain and Portugal it stands at one-third. Unpaid employment is much lower in Northern, Central and Eastern Europe. Figures are not available for the US or the UK. In the EU 1,412,987 hotel and catering enterprises employ 6,544,710 people, an average of 4.6 per enterprise (ILO, 2001: 70). Table 2.1 shows that the HI accounts for almost 19 per cent of all establishments in Britain, making it a highly visible part of economic activity, and employs an average of 5.3 employees per establishment. Although larger establishments employing 25 or more employees employ a sizeable share of employment (Table 2.2), most HI employment is in small and micro-establishments (59 per cent), although this is not the case for firms in the British economy as a whole.[2] Workplace profiles from WERS differ because they do not include workplaces with fewer than ten employees (Tables A.3 and A.4).

Expansion of branded chains since the 1970s has created large multi-site organizations in fast food, themed bars, roadside catering and budget hotels (Goss-Turner, 1999; Tables A.16 and A.17 for WERS). Many characterize Levitt's (1972) industrialization of services, as they offer less labour-intensive products and use new technology. One-third of HI businesses, and over half of all restaurants are owned or managed by self-employed proprietors (H/F, 2000; Tables A.16 and A.17 for WERS).

Labour force characteristics

Both the TI and the HI rely heavily on young and/or female labour. In terms of the former, for both females and males it may be their first entry into the world of work as students working part-time during the term and vacations (ILO, 2001; Lucas and Langlois, 2001). The ready availability of jobs and working hours that can be fitted around study time suggests there is a coincidence of needs between employers and students (Lucas and Ralston, 1996; Lucas, 1997b; Curtis and Lucas, 2001). The flexible nature of working hours may also be convenient to people with family or care obligations later in their lives, which tend to be women. The proportion of women in the global TI is estimated at 46 per cent. Most occupy the lower levels of the occupational structure[3] and, consequently, many are low paid (see Chapter 5):

- In 1996 in US restaurants 52 per cent of employees were women and 34 per cent of employees were aged between 16 and 24 years (Soeder, 1998).
- In 1995 in Austria women accounted for 60 to 70 per cent of HCT employment (Weiermair, 1996).
- In Italy there is a 50:50 split between men and women, while in Spain 57.5 per cent of HI employment is male (ILO, 2001: 49).

In the vast majority of European countries women account for 60 per cent or more of those in paid employment (ILO, 2001: 11–12). In the UK over 60 per cent of HI employment is female (Table 2.3) while young people aged 16 to 24 make up almost one-third of the workforce (Table 2.4) (for WERS see Tables A.7 to A.13).

Students are clearly an important and growing segment of the global youth labour force.[4] Nearly three-quarters of Australian fast food workers are aged 18 and under (Allan *et al.*, 2000). One-quarter of all tourism employees in Denmark are full-time students (Hjalager and Andersen, 2000). Nearly half of all teenagers in Britain in employment are full-time students, but this rises above 70 per cent

Table 2.3 Employment by gender, 2001 (UK) (%)

	Male	*Female*
All hospitality	38	62
AIS	55	45

Source: H*t*F (2002: 19) and NS (2001: 20).

Notes: Based on occupations from LFS (2001). Figures include hospitality services, where 96% of occupations are held by females, and second jobs.

Table 2.4 Employment by age, 2000 (UK) (%)

	<20	*20–24*	*25+*
All hospitality	17	13	70
AIS	5	8	87

Source: H*t*F (2000: 23–4).

Table 2.5 Employment by ethnicity, 2000 (GB) (%)

	White	Non-white
All hospitality	90	10
AIS	95	5

Source: H*t*F (2000: 21).

Note: Based on occupations, inclusive of hospitality services.

in the HI (Curtis and Lucas, 2001). The presence of large proportions of young, mobile people induces high labour turnover and is also an important contributory factor to low trade union density.

Between 13 and 19 million children and young people under the age of 18 (10–15 per cent of all TI employment) are engaged in a wide variety of jobs (ILO, 2001: 75), both in developing and developed countries, where they may be subjected to harsh conditions. Of particular concern is child sex tourism, particularly in Asia, which led to the Worst Forms of Child Labour Convention (No. 182) and recommendation No. 190 in 1999 (ILO, 2001: 76–8).

Multiple job holding has been observed (Lucas and Lammont, 1998; Lucas and Langlois, 2001), and it is estimated that around 7 per cent of jobs are second jobs, well over half of which are in bars (H*t*F, 2002: 14). However it is much less easy to estimate the size or importance of the 'informal economy'. Although it is widely reported that many workers are paid in cash (Lucas, 1995a: 114; Lucas and Langlois, 2001), it is impossible to know which of these are not recorded officially 'on the books'. There is a suggestion that illegal immigrants may constitute such 'undeclared labour' (ILO, 2001: 79).

Some countries rely significantly on migrant labour, such as Spain (51 per cent) and Germany (31 per cent) (ILO, 2001: 78–9).[5] The dismantling of national and labour market boundaries within the EU has created increasingly elastic labour market migration into the UK and Finland. Three-quarters of Pret à Manger's retail staff, who work mainly in London, are from elsewhere in the EU and come to the UK to improve their English (IDS, 2003). Immigrants and ethnic minority groups are frequently segmented into secondary labour market jobs. As Table 2.5 shows, ethnic minority groups are more likely to be working in the HI in Britain (Tables A.12 and A.13 for WERS).

Skill and occupation

Hospitality work is generally regarded as semi-skilled and unskilled (Wood, 1992; Tables A.14 and A.15 for WERS), but in practice presents a more complex picture than its common descriptor of low skills would suggest (Nickson *et al.*, 2002).[6] On the other hand expansion of the industry across the world has created an acute shortage of qualified and highly skilled staff (ILO, 2001: 43), a problem that continues to feature prominently in Britain (Lucas, 1995a: 58–9; H*t*F, 1999, 2001, 2002). The skill deficit is a sign of the failure of the British vocational education and training system (VET) to prepare individuals for more highly skilled work, compared to Germany and the US (Finegold *et al.*, 2000) (see Chapter 4).

Conversely embedded knowledge and organizational routines suggest that many skills are not unique to the HI and are transferable to other industries (Hjalager and Andersen, 2000). Hence, skill shortages may increasingly be seen as generic, e.g. communication, people management and problem solving (Nickson *et al.*, 2002: 34–8). The industry is reluctant to give formal recognition to acquired skills (ILO, 2001). This may stem from a fear of claims for higher wages, and because companies fear that trained staff will be poached by competitors.

A western-centric view of low skills may be inappropriate to the Solomon Islands, Sri Lanka and the Cook Islands (Burns, 1997). Baum (1996) argues that the stereotypical skills model is woefully inadequate in analysing work in many developing countries, particularly in services offered to international standards. The technical nature of work, e.g. the equipment used in food services in a modern international hotel, is far more alien to an Indian or Tanzanian recruit than to their 'western' counterparts. Similarly soft and social attributes, including the need to understand guests' expectations and the ability to communicate verbally and non-verbally, may be absent.

Feminist analysts see skill as a social construction, a classification imposed on certain types of work by virtue of the sex and power of the workers who perform it (Phillips and Taylor, 1980). Hence skilled work derives from an association with male apprenticeships entailing a period of several years' training and on-job experience, whereas unskilled work is a job that a typically female worker would naturally know how to do, such as cooking and cleaning. By defining many hospitality and tourism jobs as unskilled 'women's work' employers have been able to keep their costs low.

Burns (1997) argues that the application of the terms skilled and unskilled to a post-industrialized workforce is anachronistic and, in the case of front-line service workers, creates a myth that undermines their contribution to organizational success. Rather, the terms 'hard' and 'soft' skills would more usefully encapsulate the difference inherent in the traditional manufacturing/service dichotomy. We shall develop these issues further below in relation to customer-service work.[7]

Growing standardization and routinization of hospitality work has led to deskilling in the HI (Nickson *et al.*, 2002). One problematic is that one's definition of skill therefore influences perceptions about the extent to which hospitality work has become deskilled, and its attendant consequences, notably in fast food (Leidner, 1993; Reiter, 1996; Ritzer, 1996, 1998). Both Levitt (1972) and Braverman (1974) foresaw that technology would give rise to work organization entailing practices and experiences more in keeping with factory work than service work. The introduction of automatic dishwashing machines caused a substantial drop in the proportion of kitchen hands from 21 per cent to 4.2 per cent between 1951 and 1971 (Bagguley, 1987).

The reorganization of work, or McDonaldization (Ritzer, 1996), is built upon the principles of efficiency, calculability, predictability and control which restructure the labour process according to cost-minimization.[8] Allan *et al.* (2000) add that linking standardized production systems to numerical flexibility creates low cost 'Just in Time' (JIT). McJobs are low trust labour practices. Yet even fast food workers interact with customers, although the degree of engagement may be

Table 2.6 Numbers employed by occupation, 2001 (UK)

Occupation	Number
Managers	129,538
Chefs/cooks	216,717
Waiting staff	181,926
Bar staff	192,245
Front line staff	31,290
Receptionists	19,866
Housekeepers	34,027
Hotel porters	8,697
Kitchen porters and catering assistants	354,855
Total	1,169,161

Source: Adapted from H*t*F (2002: 17).

Notes: Main hospitality-specific occupations only. 247,600 cleaners/domestics worked in all hospitality in 1999 (H*t*F, 2000: 19), but are excluded from the figures in H*t*F (2002).

relatively superficial at the level of 'impression management' or 'surface acting' (Seymour, 2000).

The automation of service jobs may serve to diminish the degree to which workers can deploy their tacit skills involving judgement, intelligence, sensitivity and subjectivity. Yet Gabriel (1988) observed how fast food workers did break the rules to meet intense demand and break the drudgery of work, and that managers turned a blind eye to the ways in which these workers were able to maintain a measure of autonomy.

The main hospitality-specific occupations in the UK are shown in Table 2.6. We can roughly estimate that around half of these groups are most likely to engage in direct customer-service work, by excluding the main occupations involved in food preparation. However, kitchen work is still geared to serving customers, if in a less direct way than work with a direct customer interface, and still embodies customer-related consequences. More generic occupational groups from WERS are shown in Tables A.14 and A.15.

Employment flows

Labour turnover

High labour turnover is by no means a British problem,[9] since we have already noted that the HCTS across the globe employs a large proportion of young, mobile people (ILO, 2001: 49). Hence the HI internationally is considered to have the highest occupational mobility in hourly and managerial levels (Paraskevas, 2000). In fast food turnover rates as high as 300 per cent have been reported (ILO, 2001: 54–5). Figures in excess of 50 per cent have been reported for the US and Hong Kong, with Australia (45 per cent) and Singapore (42 per cent) not far behind (Cheng and Brown, 1998).

Table 2.7 Turnover in last 12 months in context and by size of workplace (%)

	AIS	PSS	HI	<25	25–49	50–99	100+
No turnover	8	7	2**	0	9	0	0
<=20%	59	51	33**	33	36	23	40
<=50%	29	36	46	52	27	42	36
<=100%	4	5	9	0	23	28	17
>100%	1	1	12	14	5	7	7
Mean	19	23	42**	43	37	49	31

Source: WERS98.

Notes: All weighted cases where leaver/new employee data matched well (AIS, N = 1,565, PSS, N = 903 and HI, N = 73). Column percentages do not sum accurately due to rounding. Means are rounded. **Significantly different at the 5% level from AIS.

Table 2.8 Turnover in last 12 months by sub-sector (%)

	Hotel	Campsites	Restaurants	Bars	Canteens
No turnover	0	0	5	0	0
<=20%	43	25	33	32	16
<=50%	28	75	27	63	84
<=100%	23	0	9	0	0
>100%	5	0	25	6	0
Mean	39	20	61	33	23

Source: WERS98.

Notes: All weighted cases where leaver/new employee data matched well. Column percentages do not sum accurately due to rounding. Means are rounded.

The HI is frequently cited as the industry with the highest levels of turnover (48 per cent) in Britain (H*t*F, 2002). Pub and restaurant staff have turnover levels of between 54 and 170 per cent, averaging 93 per cent (IDS, 2003). In pubs part-timers have higher rates (140 per cent) than full-timers (105 per cent), influenced by the high incidence of casual and temporary employees. Turnover figures do not separate out non-standard part-time jobs from full-time posts, so it is difficult to ascertain how problematic high rates of labour turnover may be. High turnover may reflect a rapid churn in particular jobs, and not across all jobs in an establishment. It is also most likely to occur in the first three months of employment (Lashley and Best, 2002). Labour turnover figures for Britain from WERS have been computed in cases where leaver and new employee data approximately match the associated data on the growth/decline of the workplace (Tables 2.7 and 2.8).

Many employers perceive high turnover as inevitable with so many 'transient' workers, and find it difficult to retain staff. Others believe it arises from poor management and, therefore, is self-inflicted (Iverson and Deery, 1997;[10] Rowley and Purcell, 2001). High turnover is a key cost issue affecting the bottom line incurring both direct costs (e.g. recruitment, training) and indirect costs (e.g. low morale, poor customer service, decreased productivity) that may undermine business strategy, business efficiency and reputation (Rowley and Purcell, 2001). Woods (1999) estimates the average cost of losing an hourly worker at \$2,500–3,000, but indirect costs could add another \$1,600 (Cheng and Brown, 1998). Replacement costs for managers could be five times greater than for operatives (Lashley and Best, 2002).

Much turnover research has been directed at work-related attitudes, particularly job satisfaction and job involvement, organizational commitment and work performance (Paraskevas, 2000). High turnover does not necessarily mean work dissatisfaction in circumstances where workers construct informal work groups and form strong group affiliation (Lee-Ross, 1999). Employees frequently cite low pay as a cause for leaving, although this may owe something to the unreasonable level effort being demanded of them in return for modest levels of reward. This is indicative of a negative turnover culture, where employees leave because they are dissatisfied (Deery and Shaw, 1997, 1999).

As many HI firms are small, there are limited career opportunities so that many employees' only chance of 'getting on' or developing new skills may necessitate moving to another workplace within or outside the organization (Nickson *et al.*, 2002). This represents a positive turnover culture, as employees' perceive advantages in obtaining another job (Deery and Shaw, 1997, 1999). Labour turnover can benefit the business where a regular influx of workers brings new skills, enthusiasm and experience (Rowley and Purcell, 2001). Most individuals make a trade-off between these 'push' and 'pull' factors.

Although Huselid (1995) maintains there has been relatively little concern about how effective recruitment and selection will improve turnover and image, some organizations do believe high turnover can be managed (Rowley and Purcell, 2001). Strategic HRM policies to minimize turnover primarily through the recruitment, selection and induction processes are in place in large hotels in Australia and Singapore (Cheng and Brown, 1998). Conversely poor management practices, including weak HR strategies, contribute to high turnover (Rowley and Purcell, 2001).

Leavers

WERS shows that leaver rates in the HI are significantly higher than in AIS and PSS (Table 2.9). Leaver rates of 50 per cent or more are four and three times greater than in AIS and PSS respectively. Smaller workplaces and restaurants and bars (Table 2.10) sustain the highest overall leaver rates. The main reason why employees leave is resignations, with significantly more HI workplaces having 300 or more resignations per 1,000 employees. Large workplaces are least affected and bars most affected. Dismissals are also significantly more commonplace, and HI workplaces are significantly less likely to have had no dismissals. The mean number of dismissals per 1,000 employees is nearly three times the national average, and may indicate a more extreme case of numerical flexibility in these workplaces. Small workplaces and bars have the highest dismissal rates. By contrast redundancies are relatively rare, with well over eight in ten workplaces in AIS, PSS and

Table 2.9 Leavers in last 12 months in context and by size of workplace

	AIS	PSS	HI	>25	25–49	50–99	100+
Total leavers							
Mean number	12	12	19	10	26	36	60
As % of total employees							
1 year ago	27	33	78	70	115	68	45
Reasons							
Resignations							
Mean number	9	10	16	8	19	33	55
Mean per 1,000 employees	175	220	515*	527	542	491	341
Dismissals							
Mean number	1	1	2	1	4	2	4
Mean per 1,000 employees	23	26	66*	61	112	34	24
Redundancies							
Mean number	1	1	b	b	2	b	b
Mean per 1,000 employees	26	35	13*	4	47	5	2
Retirement							
Mean number	2	1	b	b	1	b	1
Mean per 1,000 employees	26	26	10*	7	25	3	7

Source: WERS98.

Notes: All weighted cases where there have been leavers (AIS, N = 2,094, PSS, N = 1,297 and HI, N = 137). Means are rounded. b Fewer than 0.5%. *Significantly different at the 5% level from AIS and PSS.

Table 2.10 Leavers in last 12 months by sub-sector

	Hotels	Campsites	Restaurants	Bars	Canteens
Total leavers					
Mean number	32	6	19	16	12
As % of total employees					
1 year ago	72	19	93	85	24
Reasons					
Resignations					
Mean number	28	4	16	13	10
Mean per 1,000 employees	401	142	524	636	170
Dismissals					
Mean number	3	b	1	2	2
Mean per 1,000 employees	59	1	33	94	51
Redundancies					
Mean number	b	1	b	1	0
Mean per 1,000 employees	5	46	b	27	0
Retirement					
Mean number	1	1	b	1	b
Mean per 1,000 employees	9	8	b	17	11

Source: WERS98.

Notes: All weighted cases where there have been leavers. Means are rounded. b Fewer than 0.5%.

Table 2.11 Working days lost through absence or sickness in last 12 months in context and by size of workplace and sub-sector (%)

	AIS	PSS	HI	<25	25–49	50–99	100+
None	5	7	24*	35	13	0	0
Mean	5	4	5	6	3	6	5

	Hotels	Campsites	Restaurants	Bars	Canteens
None	5	0	34	30	0
Mean	4	1	10	4	4

Source: WERS98.

Notes: All weighted cases where there have been days lost (AIS, N = 1,831, PSS, N = 1,115 and HI, N = 135). Means are rounded. *Significantly different at 5% level from AIS and PSS.

the HI having made no workers redundant[11] (see Appendix 1 for other data on job losses from WERS). Retirements are significantly less common in the HI.

Absence

Work-related factors similar to those fuelling high turnover may also affect absenteeism (Pizam and Thornburg, 2000). In Britain significantly more HI workplaces (Table 2.11) did not lose any working days through employee absence or sickness compared to AIS and PSS. However, this is confined to HI workplaces employing fewer than 50 employees, while above average numbers of restaurants and bars lost no working days. This may be linked to the highly flexible work practices found in these sub-sectors.

Structure and patterns of working time

Issues in working time

In full-time work the employment contract presupposes the marriage contract freeing men from domestic responsibility (Wajcman, 2000), and EU working time regimes bear the 'imprint' of a male breadwinner arrangement (Fagan, 2001). The HI has a reputation for long hours and arduous workloads. The appearance of being at work for long hours, or 'resigned behavioural compliance', has long been a feature of hotel management (Nickson, 1997).

There has been growing concern among governments, employers and trade unions of the importance of developing policies that accommodate employees' working time preferences and their ability to coordinate the time demands of their jobs with other areas of life (Fagan, 2001; Ackers, 2002; Taylor, 2001b, 2002c). This is often referred to as the work–life balance, which has family-friendly implications (see Chapter 4), but it is also a health and safety issue related to a link between excessive hours and ill health. In the EU the Working Time Directive prohibits a working week in excess of 48 hours, which may be averaged over a specified reference period. Selected examples of how EU countries deal with

Case study 2.1 Hospitality and tourism employment and working time in Europe

Spain

780,400 workers are employed of which 213,122 are agency temps. Provincial and company level collective agreements lay down maximum annual and weekly hours of work, minimum daily and weekly rest breaks, and nightwork premiums.

Italy

An estimated 1.8 million employees work in 260,000 companies. The black economy accounts for half of tourism employment, and many companies exist off the record. Only Rome, Venice and Florence have an all-year-round trade. Seasonal workers comprise 45 per cent of the total, and around 30 per cent are employed on either temporary or daily (*lavora extra*) contracts. Under the collective agreements a single establishment cannot recruit more than 22 per cent agency workers or staff on fixed term contracts. Working time is specified as annual hours because of seasonality, typically 38 hours per week over six months. Hours beyond count as overtime with a 35 per cent premium. Part-timers must be employed for a minimum of 15 hours. Any hours in excess of normal contracted hours are subject to a premium of 30 per cent.

Sweden

100,000 employees (3 per cent of all employment) work in 1,600 hotels and 9,000 restaurants. About 70 per cent are aged below 35 years and 55 per cent are female. Many work on permanent contracts, but agency contracts account for one-third of all contracts.

Netherlands

227,500 workers work in 22,494 restaurants, 19,321 bars and 2,886 hotels. There is an equal gender distribution, and 42 per cent are aged between 20 and 29. Half are employed on part-time contracts. About 38 per cent work on on-call contracts and are entitled to a minimum of three hours' pay per call up after six months' service. Fixed term contracts may be renewed twice only, becoming permanent thereafter.

Source: IDS (1998a,b,c, 1999).

working time are shown in Case study 2.1. A 35-hour week is now in force for all French employees, and has been beneficial to employers and employees (Taylor, 2001b).

In Britain the Working Time Regulations (WTR)1998 enable workers to opt out of the maximum 48-hour period if they sign waivers. Employers do not have to keep records of hours worked by each opted-out worker, only a list of their names. The opt-out provisions seem unlikely to be renewed after expiry in November 2003. All workers are also entitled to four weeks' paid holiday, but there are special rules about how entitlement accrues during the first year of employment. The entitlement is limited during the first year to the amount that has accrued on a month-by-month basis. Calculation is particularly difficult for casual workers whose working patterns fluctuate significantly. Employers commonly enhance the basic hourly rate to cover holiday pay, in effect a prepayment. Workers may then take the appropriate period of time off as unpaid at a later stage.[12]

Work has become more concentrated and intensified in late twentieth-century Britain (Green, 2001; Taylor, 2001b, 2002c). Yet Goss and Adam-Smith (2001) conclude that, as currently implemented, the Directive will do little to change established working time practices. Coincidence with current practice, easy 'escape' options and non-compliance help explain the lack of employer post-implementation protest. Individual opt-outs may be forced on employees who are prepared to pay the price of long hours for lack of job security (Nickson *et al.*, 2002).

The working time of young workers has been regulated in many countries across the world for a long time, particularly in respect of school children (Clay and Stephens, 1996). In the EU the Young Workers Directive regulates the hours of young persons aged 16 and 17. In the UK these provisions have been implemented by the WTR, and by a subsequent amendment in 2002. The main restrictions on work are a daily limit of eight hours, a weekly limit of 40 hours and working at night. This is normally 10 p.m. to 6 a.m. but a lesser restriction applies in catering, hotels and restaurants, prohibiting work only between midnight and 4 a.m. A young person is entitled to compensatory rest for working during what would normally be the restricted period. The *Children and Young Persons Act 1933* also remains in force.[13]

Part-time employment

Part-time employment varies in importance within EU countries, and is increasing (Clifford *et al.*, 1997; Raghuram *et al.*, 2001).[14] Within the HI the share of part-time employment averages 26 per cent, but it is more important in Northern Europe, where the Netherlands and Denmark (ILO, 2001: 60) have the highest rates. Southern European counties sustain much lower rates of part-time employment.

British part-time figures for the period 1997 and 2001 indicate some puzzling major fluctuations. The ILO (2001) figures show a rate of 49 per cent in 1997, while H*t*F (1999, 2002) data indicate that part-time employment dropped from 59 per cent to 27 per cent between 1998 and 2001 (see Table 2.12) (Tables A.7

Table 2.12 Distribution of employment, 2001 (UK) (%)

	Full-time	Part-time
Hospitality businesses	74	26
Hospitality services	43	57
All hospitality	73	27
AIS	75	25

Sources: H*t*F (2002: 18); NS (2001: 20).

Note: AIS excludes second jobs.

to A.13 for WERS data). There are two possible explanations. First, part-time hours are increasing, based on individual part-time employees' perceptions that they now work full-time, as the LFS allows respondents to classify themselves. This does not necessarily take more employees above the 30-hour weekly threshold used in some statistical surveys to differentiate full- and part-time employment. Second, they arise because the ways in which national statistics been collected and reported have changed in the last few years (see Chapter 2, note 2).

A Joint Declaration of the European Committee of Food, Catering and Allied Workers' Union (ECF) within the International Union of Food, Agricultural, Hotel, Restaurant, Catering, Tobacco and Allied Workers Associations (IUF) on Flexibility of Labour and Organization of Working Time, Part-time Work and the Creation of Jobs (1995) recognizes that part-time working presents advantages to employers and workers. The main problem is that it can create a secondary labour market, where workers are treated less favourably as regards training and pay, and cannot participate in the collective bargaining process. Government employment creation policies that reduce the charges payable on part-time labour can encourage over-reliance on 'cheaper' labour, to the detriment of full-time jobs (Case study 5.6).

The Part-time Workers Directive was implemented into UK law in 2000. All part-timers must not be treated less favourably, pro rata, than full-timers, but comparability requires that the comparator is in the same category. Workers who are not employees cannot compare with employees or vice versa. Comparators must be employed by the same employer at the same establishment and perform the same or broadly similar work. If there is no full-timer at the establishment a comparator at another establishment can be relied upon, provided the other conditions are satisfied. There is no provision for full-time workers to make a comparison in reverse.

Part-time employment is important to the HI in Britain (Table 2.12). The reasons why employers seek part-time workers and why workers seek part-time jobs are complex. The stereotypical view is that the nature of labour supply serves to allocate men and women to different jobs; notably women are attracted to part-time jobs because of domestic responsibilities (Hunter *et al.*, 1993). Walsh and Deery (1999) note employees' expectations and responses are 'assumed' from employers' policies and practices. Hakim's (1995) assertion that part-time work is typically chosen voluntarily by the great majority of women has been subject to challenge. Others argue that women's choice is constrained by the lack of alternatives and weak bargaining position because they have to accommodate domestic responsibility (Ginn *et al.*, 1996). Balchin (1994) maintains that increased legal employment protection for part-time workers (removal of the requirement to work for a minimum of 16 hours) has not affected their employment prospects because employers necessarily have to match labour supply to trading patterns and the need to cover peak hours.

Part-time employment is not homogeneous, and may be segmented (Walsh, 1999). First, there are variations in the quality and content of part-time jobs. Tilly (1992) differentiates between retention part-time jobs, designed to attract valued workers who prefer working part-time, and secondary part-time jobs, which allow employers to secure competitive advantage through low remuneration costs and temporal flexibility. Hakim (1997) identifies three common modes of part-time work: reduced hours (30 or more per week), half-time (15–29 hours) and marginal (below 15). Second, there are differences in the motivations of part-time employees seeking and accepting part-time employment. Financial imperatives might be the primary reasons for students working part-time. People with dependent children or relatives and retired males might choose to work part-time voluntarily. Equally it is also the case that some workers work part-time involuntarily because suitable full-time work is not available. Third, part-time orientations and commitment to work may be variable and subject to change over the family life cycle and part-time work is not, as Hakim (1995) asserts, chosen voluntarily by the great majority of married women. Commitment among part-timers in professional jobs exceeds that of full-timers in lower occupational levels (Fagan, 2001).

Atypical jobs

Atypical jobs denote a wide variety of working arrangements that are temporary and contractually non-permanent, often referred to as contingent jobs (Purcell and Purcell, 1998). Examples include a full-time fixed-term contract for one year, a part-time seasonal contract and casual work where an employer can offer occasional work at any time, but where there is no obligation on the worker to accept work each time it is offered. Many countries find it difficult to sustain year-round employment within the HCTS. Spain and Italy have around a 50 per cent seasonal variation in employment. In France, Finland, Italy, the Netherlands and Austria, 30 per cent or more of tourism employees are on fixed-term contracts. Casual workers account for over 50 per cent of HI employment in Australia (Whitehouse *et al.*, 1997). In France and Switzerland casual workers enjoy the same legal rights as full- and part-time workers. The European Trade Union Confederation (ETUC) has reported that temporary agency work is increasing all over the EU (Smith, 2000).

In temporary work the risks associated with the employment contract are displaced from employer to employee. These working arrangements generally apply to less than 10 per cent of the workforce. In the UK some two million workers are temporary agency workers (Ward *et al.*, 2001). Spain and the Netherlands are notable exceptions, largely attributable to legislation specifically promoting the

---

Case study 2.2 **Leading cases of atypical workers' contract status**

In the UK in *O'Kelly and others v Trusthouse Forte plc* [1983] IRLR 369 the Court of Appeal (CA) ruled that while mutuality appeared to exist between employer and worker, employee status was denied. In *Carmichael v National Power plc* [1999] IRLR 43 the House of Lords decided that a casual/zero hours worker was self-employed because the minimum mutuality obligations necessary to create an employment relationship were not present. More recently in *Montgomery v Johnson Underwood* [2001] IRLR 269 the CA ruled that 'mutuality of obligation' and 'control' are irreducible minimum legal requirements for the existence of a contract of employment.

---

promotion of atypical work (Tregaskis, 1997). In the Netherlands 38 per cent of the HI workforce are on on-call contracts.

'Peripheral' workers, especially temporary employees, in a five-star Australian hotel were most dissatisfied and least committed to the organization in spite of a strong orientation to work and high levels of motivation (Walsh and Deery, 1999). A majority wanted regular, more permanent jobs, which would lead to increased job satisfaction and higher customer satisfaction.

In the UK zero hours contracts are a variation of on-call contracts. These entail no specific guarantee of hours, as employers can offer work when available and will pay when work is accepted and undertaken. Leighton and Painter (2001) argue that only the employer benefits, because workers are excluded from most of the basic statutory employment rights (Case study 2.2). It is hard to assess the extent of the use of zero hours contracts in the HI. Head (1998) found that 45 per cent of hotels used zero hours contracts, while WERS showed that they are used in only 7 per cent of HI workplaces, mainly in hotels and bars.

More effective regulation of atypical work has been brought about by the implementation of the Fixed-term Work Directive in 2002. Fixed-term is extended from time-fixed contracts to include contracts for a specific task or future event. All employees except apprentices and agency workers (unless employees of the agency) have the right to be treated no less favourably than comparable permanent employees, unless objective justification can be shown. For example a fixed-term contract worker could be paid a higher rate of pay to compensate for the lack of other benefits. After four years (from July 2002 only) of successive fixed-term contracts the employee automatically becomes permanent. The right to waive redundancy rights has been abolished, but only if the contract started or was renewed or extended after 1 October 2002 or the waiver applied on or after that date.[15]

A draft Agency Workers Directive proposes agency workers should be entitled to the same pay and conditions as normal employees unless the assignment is less than six weeks or staff are employed by the agency. The proposals are still subject to debate and implementation is not expected before 2006/7.

Flexible labour utilization

What is flexibility?

The flexibility debate was sparked by Atkinson's (1984) core–periphery model of functionally and numerically flexible labour. Functional flexibility enables multi-skilled workers to perform various jobs, while numerical flexibility enables the ready engagement and dispensation of various forms of atypical labour. The main benefit of functional flexibility is that a multi-skilled worker can be deployed across tasks according to demand, thus maximizing labour productivity. Multi-skilling differs from multi-tasking, because the worker is trained in different skills. Numerical flexibility enables the firm to adjust labour costs to changes in the market. Hence, in circumstances of uneven and unpredictable demand the HI has long functioned on the basis of high proportions of contingent labour. Restaurants have been described as 'the ultimate "JIT" deliverer of goods and services' (ILO, 2001: 48).

Most commentators still broadly conceive of labour utilization in core–periphery terms, the core being more regular workers who may be given relatively favourable terms and conditions of employment and the periphery having a more casual employment relationship. Core employees in hotels are skilled and enjoy good conditions of employment, while the periphery which has less job security and less favourable terms of employment acts as a buffer to protect core employees from shifts in demand (Guerrier and Lockwood, 1989). Core employees are not necessarily full-time or skilled employees, especially in small HI workplaces, where core practices centre on more fine-tuned flexibility involving the use of non-standard labour (Case study 2.3). Similarly peripheral workers can be highly skilled, such as an employee of the local accountancy firm who does the accounts for a few days a month in a small hotel. In the HI it is common to find core and peripheral workers working together in the same jobs, including waiting at table or serving behind the bar.

The nature and scope of these core–periphery constructs is recognized as highly variable and contingent. Functional flexibility may not necessarily represent a 'high road' quality-enhancing approach any more than numerical flexibility is always a 'low road' cost-minimization option, since both approaches may be used within the same workplace. Within hotels some departments are more prone to cost-minimization measures than others, and may have different job tenure and working time arrangements from others. However defined, employers' use of core–periphery is not necessarily a straight choice of one or the other or even a strategy. The boundaries of different groups of workers are being continuously redrawn (Grimshaw *et al.*, 2001). Rather, the managerial issues are what is an appropriate mix and how can both groups be managed effectively.

Why employers pursue labour flexibility

Strategic use of contingent segments of the labour force developed strongly in the 1990s, and is expected to continue although the picture is not uniform (Purcell

Case study 2.3 **Fine-tuned flexibility in hotels**

Hotel A employs 70 staff (41 full-time, 13 regular part-time and 16 casual part-time).

Departmental delineation between types of staff and age groups is highly demand influenced. Young part-time student labour is employed mainly in the restaurant and bar in the evening. Students start work with food service and can move to bar work at 18. Older part-time females do the breakfast shift. Older full-time workers work in housekeeping and general kitchen jobs. Reception work, because it is technology- and systems-based, is the most skilled after chefs' work.

Hotel B employs 47 staff (16 full-time and 31 part-time, 23 of whom are casuals). Twenty-one staff are aged 21 and under (six under the age of 16, ten aged 16–17, five aged 18–21).

Under 16s are used for washing up at weekends under adult supervision. They are highly flexible and keen to work at any opportunity. This might be once a fortnight, which would not be unacceptable to an adult. Casual students of 16 and 17 are used to manage fluctuating demand as both parties can pick and choose when to work, while 18–21-year-olds have the right personality and confidence to do bar work, and are more personable to customers than younger workers. The sizable core of casuals, including students, could work 40 hours one week and none the next.

Source: Lucas and Langlois (2000b).

and Purcell, 1998). Others have challenged the notion that striving for flexibility is a strategy at all (Rubery, 1989; Pollert, 1991; Hunter *et al.*, 1993), suggesting that opportunism might be a more accurate description. Walsh and Deery (1999) argue that emphasis on employers' pursuit of flexibility provides an overly managerialist account of workforce restructuring. Walby (1987) and Bagguley (1990) have argued that particular kinds of labour flexibility presuppose gendering of the labour force, such that males are functionally flexible, and females are numerically flexible. This presumption has been challenged (Bird *et al.*, 2002). Female functionally flexible workers in four- and five-star hotels are more core than male workers, and usually better qualified with greater opportunities. Flexibility is geared to employers rather than to employees and family needs with adverse gender consequences (Dickens, 1997). Hence flexibility is a function of cost control in conditions of fluctuating demand, and not about retaining key workers such a women returners (Bird *et al.*, 2002). Recent legal measures addressing employees' requirements to work more flexibly, which reflect good practice in the work–life balance, are considered in Chapter 4.

Kalleberg (2001: 479) proposes 'two distinct strategies of flexible labour utilisation: enhancing employees' ability to perform a variety of jobs and participate in decision-making and reducing costs by limiting workers' involvement in the organisation'. The former focuses on high performance work systems, while the latter emphasizes externalization. Osterman (1999) concludes that it is difficult for organizations to implement high performance work practices if they employ contingent workers who will only be around for a short time. The use of contingent workers depends on management's ability to minimize the risk of low quality performance (Timo, 2001). In hotels where there is a strong traditional departmental culture, departmental managers have considerable influence to engender loyalty or to squeeze out misfits. This regulates performance levels and also serves to diffuse conflict and reinforce the managerial prerogative.

In terms of functional flexibility based on multi-skilling, even though competency may be lower in the worker's secondary skills, there is still a net gain in productivity and job satisfaction, although stress may be caused where there is high work intensification (Kelliher *et al.*, 2000). More widespread use of functional flexibility in the HI may be hindered by two factors. First, because firms may not have skilled jobs and provide training, and, second, because workers are status conscious and have strong job identity. Institutional and cultural considerations apart, the main policy issues for managers who do seek to introduce functional flexibility embrace breadth (which departments, which staff) and depth (all skills, selected skills).

Flexibility in practice

In spite of the growth of contingent labour generally (Purcell and Purcell, 1998), it is argued that, as the use of part-time, seasonal and casual labour has always been high in the HI, the potential scope for significant further growth must be limited (Lucas, 1995a). It has always been easier for the HI to do something other than invest in functional flexibility (Riley, 1992; Krakover, 2000). Achievement of a 'flexible factory' depends on sophisticated information systems that can generate appropriate data to inform the planning and forecasting process (Riley and Lockwood, 1997). Small firms get by on a simple form of cost-control management, relying heavily on the external labour market to provide them with a readily available supply of appropriately skilled labour. Even within the regulated Australian economy, trade unions' attempts to negotiate a transition from casual to permanent part-time employment (see Timo, 2001) have proved difficult, with permanent part-time employment failing to confer significant improvements (Whitehouse *et al.*, 1997). In hotels mobility across traditional organization structures and occupational identity serve to hinder more functionally flexible jobs (Kelliher *et al.*, 2000). Here flexibility becomes a social process that needs to be embodied in the wider social life of the organization.

It is therefore of interest to highlight three recent contrasting cases from the UK, Australia and the US. The first is concerned with the introduction and implementation of functional flexibility (Kelliher *et al.*, 2000; Gore *et al.*, 2002). Gore *et al.* (2002) propose different typologies depicted on a matrix that compares the level of intensification of work with the necessary requirement of management to control and effect through behavioural-cognitive change. Four main benefits

Case study 2.4 Functional flexibility in a hotel and a pub

Resort hotel

In order to maintain service standards in a resort hotel during the low season, staff in various departments were trained in selected secondary skills (highly cognitively demanding/low work intensification). For example, non-reception staff were trained in telephone work and guest-receiving procedures, but not in computerized techniques involving reservations and accounts. Perceived benefits included greater staff stability.

Pub

All staff were trained to do everything, enabling fewer staff to be employed and worker value maximized because of the relatively high wages prevailing in the labour market (some increase in cognition/high work intensification). Perceived drawbacks were increased levels of worker stress.

Source: Gore *et al.* (2002).

---

accrue: cost reduction, improved staff motivation, greater teamwork and improved quality. Conversely employees may experience some stress and loss of identity where they are moved to a department with lower status. Two contrasting examples are given in Case study 2.4.

The second attempts to provide a theoretical framework that accounts for changes in the pattern of labour utilization in Australia (Case study 2.5), where over half of hotel workers are casual or contingent workers (Timo, 2001). Employers' labour use choices are theoretically constrained by industry or occupational awards and by workplace agreements (see Chapters 5 and 6). Awards define regular employment categories on the basis of the number of hours worked per day or per week, and connect working time with the pay system. However HI employers have coined their own terms of core and periphery by differentiating between regular and irregular casuals and part-time workers. The crucial difference is the *variability* of irregular workers' hours, which places them outside the scope of the awards. New working time systems have cut labour costs by reducing idle and non-productive time. Their low-road response has created different employment systems built around regular and irregular job tenure (see Case study 2.5). By circumventing the award system hotels have been able to introduce workplace change without the need for cooperation, consultation and negotiation with employees under workplace bargaining.

Case study 2.5 Core–periphery in luxury Australian hotels

Regular job tenure, i.e. regular and continuing employment relationship with career intentions:

- Core tenure (permanent and regular hours part-time subject to award constraints), e.g. administration, accounts, front office, sales and marketing.
- Retentive job tenure (regular part-time and on-going casuals with variable hours drawn from list of regular 'just-in-time' workers), e.g. chefs, cooks, bar, waiting, accommodation.

Irregular job tenure, i.e. subject to gaps in employment relationship and availability of work and no career intentions:

- Peripheral tenure (numerically flexible irregular casuals and part-time as needed), e.g. semi-skilled waiting, portering, cleaning.
- Contingent job tenure (very highly numerically flexible), e.g. lower skills and wages.
- Seasonal tenure (short fixed-term during holiday periods although subject to awards and not strictly numerically flexible), e.g. students, backpackers.

Source: Timo (2001).

Case study 2.6 Flexibility in US hotels post-11 September 2001

Some hourly paid workers were forced or agreed to give up work hours to preserve their jobs. Employees in other hotels suffered no hours reduction but were assigned additional duties. At a unionized hotel agreement was reached in New York City and Chicago allowing employees to decide whether to give up hours to preserve other workers' jobs.

Source: Sherwyn and Sturman (2002).

The third illustrates how unexpected events can also trigger responses in flexible working that are rather more pragmatic and opportunistic (see Case study 2.6). A drop in business after 11 September 2001 forced many American hotels to lower labour costs and lay off staff.

The meaning of work

Perceptions and the status of hospitality work are considerably diverse across the globe. For those who work, it provides income and a sense of identity and self (see Case study 2.7). Yet this experience may not necessarily be a positive or fulfilling one. Employers' competitive position depends not only on the knowledge and skills of their workers, but also on their ability to persuade workers to realize those attributes in useful and productive work.

There is no unambiguous rule that all workers place a high value on work and employment, or even want the same things from their jobs (Simons and Enz, 1995).[16] A distinct segment of workers, e.g. students, may have different orientations to their part-time work. Financial considerations may be important to students who have to 'pay their way' at university in 'western' economies such as the US, Canada, Australia and the UK. Career opportunities may be more important to students in economies in Central and Eastern Europe where education remains state-funded and part-time jobs are relatively scarce (Lucas and Langlois, 2001; Johnson and Lucas, 2002; Lucas *et al.*, 2003).

Ross (1997) found that travel agency work was of most interest to females because it provided the opportunity for achievement, teamwork, initiative and writing skills.

Case study 2.7 **Work and occupational community**

Resort hotels

Six hotels in Great Yarmouth employ four groups – year-round live-in and live-out staff and seasonal live-in and live-out staff. Seasonal workers, particularly live-in staff, tend to form a distinct occupational community, focusing on a work situation characterized by hedonism and close social bonding rather than on the job they do. Live-in staff are often 'problem' children with difficult family backgrounds, for whom the workplace provides a home. Live-out staff were more family-orientated and rarely shared social occasions with work colleagues. Year-round live-out staff aspired to career progression, while seasonal live-out workers took the work for convenience.

Pubs

Employees have high job satisfaction, particularly those who see themselves as future landlords. The close relationship between job satisfaction and commitment to the pub industry is a strong indicator of occupational community.

Fast food

The needs of McDonald's are for part-time, low-skilled, low-paid jobs. In Britain the workforce comprises mainly young students with limited work experience. Some 65 per cent of the British workforce are under 20, for whom work is fun and provides a social experience. In Germany the workforce is mainly older foreign guest workers and economic migrants for whom McDonald's provides a 'family'. Labour turnover is relatively low.

Sources: Lee-Ross (1999); Riley *et al.* (1998); Royle (1999c).

Working tourists in a Kibbutz orientated towards social rather than economic exchange type of relations with their hosts are more likely to develop a positive attitude towards them (Pizam *et al.*, 2000). Similarly tour reps describe their job as a novel and intensive experience, where group cohesion is heightened because a small group of them are living and working together (Guerrier and Adib, 2002).

There is a sizeable body of literature arguing that hospitality and tourism work is gendered (e.g. Purcell, 1996; Sinclair, 1997), an issue we develop below. Purcell (1996) identifies three main categories of female occupation:

- contingently gendered (employers seek cheap labour that happens to be female);
- sex-typed (sexual attractiveness is a desired attribute);
- patriarchally prescribed (based on the tradition of women's work and role as carer and cook).

Customer-service work

The growth of service work,[17] accounting for around three-quarters of employment in Britain, Europe, North America, Japan and Australia, represents a transformation in work and employment. Warhurst *et al.* (2000) argue that the occupational classification focus on form of jobs, rather than on the content of labour, has led to insufficient sensitivity to the heterogeneity of work and employment within services (also Warhurst and Thompson, 1998). The job of waiter may vary from highly customized personal silver service in a traditional restaurant to routine standardized speedy service in fast food (Seymour, 2000). This draws attention to a matrix of skills – technical, social and aesthetic. New organizational practices are based on using aesthetic skills to commercial advantage (Warhurst *et al.*, 2000).

In direct service work the social composition of the producers is part of the product. Employers seek workers with personal characteristics likely to make them interact spontaneously and perform effectively. Thus sociability, friendliness, drive, honesty/integrity, conscientiousness and adaptability are more important selection criteria than technical skills (Warhurst *et al.*, 2000). Control of emotions, behaviour and appearance are legitimate managerial strategies in the name of customer care. The aesthetic content of labour, in the form of language and dress codes, shape and size of body, manner and style, is deliberately manufactured to appeal to customers' visual and aural senses.

Such labour may also be sexualized (Adkins, 1995). Sexy uniforms and 'job flirt' (Hall, 1993; Seymour, 2000) produce a style of service encounter that is more or less a routine part of the job. Different behaviour is demanded of men and women. Gilbert *et al.* (1998) note that, although TGI Fridays teach both men and women to flirt, its consequence is that male status is reduced, which may also be reinforced by reference to sexual identity and assumptions of being gay. Today's conception of a waiter has moved a long way from Mars and Nicod's (1984) ideal waiter as an invisible and de-sexed 'non-person'.

When staff meet customers there is a complex intertwining of labour and leisure. Within a culture that increasingly emphasizes the self as a consumer rather than a producer, Guerrier and Adib (2002) argue that customer-service work has become construed as a consumer product. Jobs in restaurants (Marshall, 1986), night clubs (Sosteric, 1996), pubs (Lammont and Lucas, 1999) or with a tour operator (Adib and Guerrier, 2001; Guerrier and Adib, 2002) afford the potential for workers to enjoy some of the pleasures of consumption at work. Interaction with the customer is one the main pleasures of direct service work, while dealing with abusive customers is of critical importance to these workers and managers. Ultimately dissatisfied customers will have job consequences for all workers and the business, so no amount of good direct customer service can ever compensate for food or rooms that do not reach an acceptable standard.

Managing the service encounter

Labour as part of the service product poses particular difficulties for management, an issue we shall pursue in greater depth in Chapter 3. Scripts may be adequate where the encounter is brief and organizational control is extended to structure customer expectations, e.g. mass advertising (Jones *et al.*, 1997). The longer the delivery takes, the more important for the consumer is the intimacy and quality of the service (Urry, 1990). Therefore a worker's interpersonal attributes and public relations skills, such as speech, appearance and personality, may be treated as legitimate areas for intervention and control by management in order to retain a positive attitude to guests (Sosteric, 1996). 'Work includes more and more relational dimensions of co-production' (Bonamy and May, 1997: 557). Interdependencies have grown considerably and the efficiency of production organization and quality depend on these dimensions.

Age and intelligence can be used as means to control labour (Lucas, 1997a; Curtis and Lucas, 2001). It cannot be coincidence that in the UK students account for 15.3 per cent of the total labour force, and over 70 per cent of teenagers working in the HI are students (Johnson and Lucas, 2002). Being slim, youthful and intelligent are not necessarily aesthetic attributes, since older females may embody the aesthetic capacities and attributes required by hotels to serve breakfast to their guests or by fashion retailers of clothes for larger ladies (Lucas and Langlois, 2000b).

Hochschild (1983) notes how monitoring and controlling 'emotion work' becomes increasingly difficult in circumstances of work intensification. Flight attendants working under increasing pressures tended to 'smile less broadly ... thus dimming the company's message to the people' (Hochschild, 1983: 127). The problem for management is how to manufacture these 'moments of truth' to ensure that what is consumed at the point of delivery meets the appropriate level of service quality.

Kivelä and Chu (2001) argue that effective management of the service encounter in restaurants is an internal issue requiring a thorough understanding of the behaviour of front-line staff that can result in favourable or unfavourable service encounters. Favourable service encounters greatly encourage repeat customers who bring revenue to the business, and provide enjoyment and security for the employees.

The service encounter also affects internal customers where one department in a hotel services another. Gummesson (1991) uses the term 'tribal warfare' to signify that these encounters represent a compromise between partially conflicting parties which have a loyalty to their department, rather than to the organization as a whole. Paraskevas (2001) illustrates the gendered nature of a three-way conflict involving front office, which requisitions rooms serviced and checked by housekeeping, who identify any possible maintenance problems and report them to maintenance. Housekeeping's performance and efficiency depends on maintenance's response, and conflicts frequently arise because of different perspectives on the main priorities between male maintenance workers and female housekeeping staff. If female front office staff want something really urgent from housekeeping, they ask a male colleague to make the call. Similarly Mars and Nicod (1984) observed rivalry between waiting and kitchen staff, aggressive tendencies in waiters, and instances of verbal abuse by senior to junior waiters. Yet these workers dealt with customers in a calm and reassured manner, indicating a split personality

Experiencing the service encounter

'The process by which the employee attempts to manage the guest in a subtle way whilst giving the impression that the guest is in control is a normal part of hotels' guest-employee encounters' (Guerrier and Adib, 2000: 703). Seymour (2000) rejects Braverman's (1974) thesis that service work has necessarily been standardized and job tasks have little complexity or scope for discretion. Fast food and traditional restaurant workers both consider that wearing a uniform signifies that customers can treat them as servants they can be rude or abusive to. Although fast food uniforms are unisex, short skirted black and white uniforms necessitate females in the traditional restaurant to endure 'groping with a smile' in order to generate high tips. The scripted work routine and the fact that customers can be 'stooges' sent by head office to check on their performance force fast food workers to contain their emotions. Without a script traditional service workers put more of their real self into their job performance, thereby engaging in 'deep acting' (Hochschild, 1983). In terms of using their social skills to control and personalize the worker–customer interface, speed of service in fast food affords minimal interaction, even though some workers are able to personalize service to defend self. Traditional workers developed their own formulaic approach of greeting and conversation that enabled them to estrange themselves.

Much emphasis has been placed on the negative consequences of emotion work, such as feeling phony (Hochschild, 1983), emotional exhaustion and burnout (Wharton, 1993; Zapf, 2002) and boredom (Sandiford and Seymour, 2002), but this experience may more routinely embrace both positive and negative outcomes (Lammont and Lucas, 1999; Zapf, 2002). This may depend on whether customers are regulars or strangers. Smith (1985b) notes how emotion work is not necessarily gendered, as male publicans depend on the social and relational network of regulars. Publicans' social lives may be dominated by work contacts, as Smith (1985a) noted in the case of a publican who spent more time in front of the bar than behind it, highlighting a social and community role addition to his managerial responsibilities.

Case study 2.8 Containing resistance among tour reps

Bout of gastric illness

The tour reps' actions were directed towards influencing the way the holi-daymakers saw the situation by attributing the cause to an airborne bug, not food poisoning because that could have been attributable to the hotel. The reps could not back the guests because the company would become liable, yet they had to give sympathy to customers while also protecting the company. The space of the hotel was organized by the tour operator and the hotel's management, enabling them to manage the rules of behaviour. Senior managers intervened and spoke to families individually, enabling resistance to be controlled and contained.

Airport delay

An airport delay was nothing to do with the company and beyond the reps' call of duty, although the holidaymakers vented their frustrations on them. The reps experienced a loss of power and control. If they had been able to pass on knowledge and information this might have formed a significant part of the process of empowerment.

Source: Adib and Guerrier (2001).

Employees in their work also have to maintain control over their customers, and may lose it in circumstances beyond their control (Adib and Guerrier, 2001). Tour reps provide emotional labour and act as agents of power (Foucault, 1979). When something goes wrong they are most likely to see resistance from the targets of power – the tourist. Case study 2.8 illustrates how the space in which they have to work, the knowledge and information at their disposal, and their status are key determining factors of the extent to which resistance can be contained.

Not only do workers have to handle personal abuse, but also they must ensure that customers' misbehaviour does not affect the service received by other guests. Workers' emotions are not wholly commodified as they seek to reconcile customer and managerial demands through a simultaneous and contradictory process of compliance (Guerrier and Adib, 2002) and resistance (Lammont and Lucas, 1999). Surprisingly tour reps are cooperative and compliant, generally behaving for the benefit of the company even when they are being exploited.

Front-line service workers bearing the brunt of any abusive customer behaviour such as 'air rage' (Guerrier and Adib, 2000) or drunkenness (Smith, 1985b) may need to be protected. Harassment and bullying are an abuse and misuse of power (see Chapter 4). Indeed in the 'Bernard Manning' case two black females won compensation because of their employer's failure to 'protect' them from his racist and sexist jokes. While workers have to subordinate themselves to guests' power because management tells them to, they can also adopt complex sets of strategies to make sense of such harassment, entailing outright objection, compliance or more subtle ways to resist control (Lammont and Lucas, 1999; Guerrier and Adib, 2000).

Workers may experience particular difficulties when faced with ambiguous sexual innuendo. Female receptionists may be asked if there is 'anything extra in the room rate?'. Guerrier and Adib (2000) report the example of a male guest who asked a male employee if the hotel provided any entertainment and could he send one of his female colleagues up to his room? When the employee pointed out that she would be unlikely to agree, the guest then suggested he 'would do', to which the employee replied that the hotel did not provide that kind of service. Here the power of the guest is such that if the employee complained about the guest he could deny asking for a sexual favour, yet the worker could be admonished if the guest complained that no one would come to his room.

Workers may have to manage their emotions for financial reward (Sandiford and Seymour, 2002). The lack of resentment among workers about their poor working conditions may be explained by a perception that they are not really working for pay (Marshall, 1986), since work may provide a 'social life in the workplace' (Lucas, 1997a: 609).

The issue of customer-service work is developed within approaches to HRM in Chapter 3, and in relation to involvement schemes based on empowerment and teamworking in Chapter 6.

Discussion and review topics

Skill

Devise a gender-neutral method that enables you to compare and objectively justify the skill levels of the following jobs:

- Chef
- Receptionist
- Waiting staff
- Bar staff
- Kitchen assistant

Working time

- How can managers organize working time more effectively to meet unstable demand and maintain service quality?
- Do current working time arrangements in the HI serve to reinforce and institutionalize women's disadvantaged position in the labour market and in society?
- Should the working time of full-time students be regulated?

Core and periphery

Take examples of workplaces with which you are familiar:

- Which workers were core or peripheral?
- What were the main differences between core and peripheral workers' jobs, and other conditions and employment including pay, hours and training?
- Can you discern any patterns among similar types of workplace?

The role of work

Here is a description of the work of a famous chef and that of a humble kitchen porter. The former owns a gastronomic restaurant. He appears regularly in a television show, and is transported to the studio in a chauffeur-driven car. He almost always works in a designer kitchen. Much of his work is his own creation. He exerts a powerful influence on a large contingent of the UK population that has purchased his cookery books. All of these activities are highly lucrative. Our kitchen porter works in a hot and badly organized part of the kitchen in cramped conditions. He is constantly bombarded by rudely expressed requests for clean pots and pans, often being sworn at by kitchen and waiting staff alike in racist overtones, for he is Bangladeshi. He frequently finishes work well past midnight, and has to walk home. He is paid the NMW in cash and doesn't get a pay slip. He hasn't been given any paid holidays since he started work six months earlier, but doesn't know what he can do about this.

Compare and contrast what work means to these two individuals?

3 The role of management in employment relations

Learning objectives

By the end of this chapter you should be able to:

- appreciate how choices and constraints influence management style in the HI;
- differentiate approaches to the management of employment relations, including HRM;
- understand how the service encounter influences managers' approach to employment relations management;
- understand how management is organized for employment relations at organizational and workplace level;
- describe the main areas of managers' work responsibilities;
- identify managers' views of the state of workplace employment relations.

Understanding management style in the hospitality industry

It is widely accepted that managers' approach to employment relations, often referred to as management style,[1] is the result of choices that are influenced by certain constraints (Salamon, 2000; Hollinshead, 1999). The nature of the product and labour markets, organizational status and structure, including size of workplace, and culture are chief among the factors thought to place constraints on managers. Managers, as much as workers and customers, are never truly free agents. We have already noted in Chapter 1 how economic, technical, social, legal and political factors external to the workplace provide boundaries that may constrain managers' behaviour and actions. We also discussed how managers' personal frame of reference will inform the choices they make about the strategies, policies and practices they pursue, and why power relationships are integral to this process. Of particular note here is the virtual absence of trade unions to act as a countervailing force to counteract managerial power. The HI sustains a mere 2 per cent trade union density (DTI, 1999).

Managers must be able to exercise choice otherwise we would not be able to account for variations in management style among similar types of firm. In seeking to control events managers may be constrained by their own rational thinking of what is good and bad, failing to recognize that opposites are often very closely related and may even coexist simultaneously. The right to manage is so deeply ingrained into behaviour and thinking that it may dominate over their tacit acceptance of a more pluralist ethos. Hence 'a constant underlying pressure within management both to resist any extension of joint regulation and to restore unilateral regulation wherever and whenever circumstances allow' (Salamon, 2000: 235). HRM is often seen as unitarist (Guest, 1989) and a reassertion of managerial prerogative, especially the 'hard' version, even though the 'soft' variant contains some positive attributes.

While we can debate the extent to which particular constraints affect the choices that particular managers make in particular circumstances, this approach still implies a rationality that does not account for pragmatism, opportunism and reacting to events. This approach is beginning to emerge as an alternative (Edwards and Gilman, 1999; Grimshaw *et al.*, 2001; Gilman *et al.*, 2002). That said, we take as a universal truth that all HI employers place high priority on seeking to control labour costs (Appendix 1 for WERS).[2] As we shall argue this is achieved predominantly through 'low road' practices that may be both intentional and/or the result of pragmatism or opportunism. This approach is so successful that managers have no incentive to take the 'high road'. Organizations that focus on quality in the service encounter exceptionally approach the management of employment by the 'high road' using more sophisticated and developmental HRM practices, but not necessarily in respect of the workforce as a whole.

Constraints and choices

To cope with *market uncertainties* managers can opt for the external regulation of employment matters, choose to develop their own internal responses, or use a combination of both (Gospel, 1992). Grimshaw *et al.* (2001) argue that internal and external market pressures mutually interact to shape employment strategy, generating a wide range of possibilities for different workforce groups. The weakening of national regulatory and collective bodies in the UK, and the accompanying widening of scope for managerial prerogative, have made managing an even more uncertain process (also Beynon *et al.*, 2002).

Marchington and Parker (1990) suggest that stable product markets will encourage the development of 'high road' practices based on partnership, job security, systematic recruitment, selection, training and development, two-way communications and formal procedures. Turbulent market conditions, which affect large parts of the HI (Appendix 1 for WERS), militate against long-term policies, even in larger companies (Guerrier and Lockwood, 1989). They will drive 'low road' practices based on hire and fire, ad hoc recruitment, selection, training and development, low pay, one-way communication, if any, from management, and lack of procedures, reinforcing a culture of macho management.

If the economic climate deteriorates firms may be forced to change route towards 'low road' practices, graphically illustrated by the case of British Airways (BA) (Blyton and Turnbull, 1998). Keenoy (1997) identifies a wide-ranging programme of 'soft' measures, including improvements to communications and leadership, while maintaining a 'hard' approach to headcount. In respect of cabin crew, Boyd (2001) argues that 'soft' HRM in the form of a sanctimonious mission and policy statement may have provided a smoke screen for short-term, cost-rational HRM leading to work intensification.

Case study research has identified a more complex pattern of highly firm-specific policy solutions in response to a variety of different internal and external pressures (Lucas and Langlois, 2000a,b; Gilman *et al.*, 2002). Contradictory outcomes emerge as new policies capitalize on changing external conditions at the expense of organizational demands. New policies may be unsustainable where on aggregate they fail to develop workforce skills or fulfil career expectations (Grimshaw *et al.*, 2001). Considerable emphasis on recruitment and training in hotels, which is symptomatic of labour flux, militates against uptake of new HRM initiatives of a longer-term nature (Kelliher and Johnson, 1997).

Organization status and structure, including *size of workplace* will also serve to constrain the extent to which managers can exercise choice. Not all managers own and control their own business, and in larger hotel companies, restaurant and public house chains, and contract catering firms, managers are themselves also workers reporting to a more senior manager. Managers' choices are constrained by organizational policies, as well as by the actions of other managers and subordinates. Management is necessarily a messy business. Achieving organizational goals through people is a complex and political process, political in the sense that it involves choosing how to reconcile differences among colleagues of different status and power who may be senior managers, peers or subordinate workers (Case study 3.1). Some large HI organizations comprise many small workplaces (Appendix 1 for WERS), so we cannot necessarily generalize their management style to single-site workplaces.

Owner managers of *small firms* have more freedom to make rules on the 'hoof', as there are no precedents or constraints from any higher authority (Scase, 1995). Surplus labour supply of amply skilled labour, and the simple division of labour are conducive to an ad hoc management style within the economic determinism approach of externalization (Lucas, 1995a; Riley *et al.*, 2000). As Riley *et al.* (2000) note, productivity is largely a matter of matching supply to demand in the short term, because of the almost instantaneous impact of customer trends on labour supply. This dynamic instability based on stochastic demand creates and continually reinforces a short-term perspective where small unit structure creates a style of management that is good at improvising. Reliance on a plentiful supply of unskilled labour from the labour market and hire and fire serve to enhance managerial power. The manager may be aware of the constraint of unfair dismissal legislation. By making a simple risk assessment, the manager will calculate that a fired worker will probably not bother to make a claim, if eligible, because alternative work is easily secured (and a replacement easily obtained). If the worker does proceed to employment tribunal, at worst there will be a cheap out-of-court settlement, because of the worker's low pay and short service (Head, 1998).

Culture can be considered on three levels – *organizational, national and occupational* – with some crossover between the first two in the case of MNCs. Two American

---

Case study 3.1 **Workplace structure in the Australian hotel industry**

Hotels may appear to be structured bureaucracies under the control of a general manager, but are essentially organic structures within which departmental managers have considerable autonomy and responsibility. Each department is a unique entity controlled by a manager skilled in that work who hires and fires, and determines the categories of labour to be used, the tasks to be performed and the timing of work.

The autonomy and responsibility invested in departmental managers encourages an informal management style and a system of rule-making that shapes the pattern of labour use (initial engagements tend to be casual), and encourages the growth of informal work practices between manager and worker designed to engender loyalty and commitment. Departmentalization and labour flexibility forms part of the hierarchy of control, shifting transaction costs (of uncertainty) to the worker, protecting the hotel from unfair dismissal litigation, and using behaviour and discipline to determine permanent employment status.

Weak and low-status HRM within hotels militates against participation in new HRM practices, such as multi-skilling, because managers fear other departments may poach good staff. This acts as a barrier to strong internal labour markets, so the external market becomes a significant mechanism for the allocation of skill.

Source: Timo (2001).

MNCs, McDonald's and Disney, have been hailed as 'influential models of excellence in the development of particular organisational cultures or systems of production and job design with their respective implications for management and the conduct of employee relations' (Hollinshead, 1999: 108). International chains display more sophisticated HRM, e.g. in Greece (Paraskevas, 2000). Larger units and those owned by foreign chains appear to veer towards the 'best practice' models of HRM (Lucas and Laycock, 1991; Price, 1994; Kelliher and Johnson, 1997).

Organizational culture encapsulates 'the way we do things around here'.[3] Culture and values underpin the organization's identity and core purpose and new initiatives in employment relations and HRM may entail programmes of culture change, especially where there is a conscious shift towards a service quality (SQ) culture. Redman and Mathews (1998) argue that the traditional dichotomy between the 'high road' and the 'low road' has been increasingly challenged by effective quality management systems resulting in both improved quality and reduced costs. This reflects a new approach to corporate management. 'Organisational culture is rooted in the future and change' whereas work-based culture is rooted in the here and now (Cameron *et al.*, 1999: 233). Occupational culture may be more readily identifiable within skilled occupations such as chefs,

---

Case study 3.2 **Effects of institutional change on large hotels in New Zealand**

A major change in the law in 1991 was designed to shift employment relations from a highly regulated environment to a minimalist and market-led regime. In spite of the opportunity presented for firms to innovate on the basis of high commitment work practices, there was neither any evidence of a complete displacement of the traditional pattern of collective relations nor any indication of HRM practices designed to secure workforce commitment. Rather, any changes made to improve communications did not diminish the level of managerial control typical of the industry.

Source: Haynes and Fryer (1999).

---

and may create adversity in the employment relationship where professional values conflict with commercial values.

Employment relations systems reflect the *society* in which they operate.[4] Hofstede (1980, 1991) has shown that people in different countries approach work in different ways. Interestingly many of the countries discussed in this book (Australia, Canada, Britain, New Zealand and the US) display 'Anglo' characteristics – a belief in equality, acceptance of uncertainty, emphasis on personal initiative and achievement, and the right to a private life. Money and material standards are important. By contrast European countries, largely in relation to geographical location, fall into four groups and are more diverse (see Pugh and Hickson, 1996: 91). Approaches that may work well in one country do not necessarily transplant well to other countries. Local managers may resist the incursion of expatriate managers who are socialized in a different culture (Jones *et al.*, 1998). The application of western practices to transitional economies such as Bulgaria (Anastassova and Purcell, 1995), and Russia (D'Annunzio-Green, 2002) may be difficult to achieve, particularly in Slovakia where there are few MNCs (Lucas *et al.*, forthcoming). Differences in national institutional arrangements and the extent to which employment systems rely on detailed regulation and labour codes contribute to national cultural differences. Changes to national institutions have not necessarily impacted upon employment relations practices (Case study 3.2).

Models and maps

Models and maps of employment relations have developed from the constraints and choices approach in an attempt to depict variations in the management style of employment relations. A useful start point is Purcell and Sisson's (1983) five ideal types of industrial relations management:[5]

- *Traditionalists* are hostile to trade unions, exploit their workforce and believe in management's right to manage.

- *Sophisticated paternalist/human relations* embodies strong management, but with concern for employees' welfare. Unions are kept at bay by giving employees good pay and terms of employment.
- *Sophisticated moderns* accept trade unions as a positive force, and there is strong emphasis on developing and maintaining informal and formal procedures for resolving disputes. There are two types of sophisticated moderns. 'Consulters' accept unions but also deploy techniques designed to enhance individual commitment. 'Constitutionalists' place more emphasis on collective agreements.
- *Standard moderns* take a pragmatic approach to industrial relations with recognized trade unions, with line managers taking the lead.

In reviewing management styles we have discounted any model that embraces trade unions and a collective approach because, to all intents and purposes, these are not relevant to the HI in Britain.[6] Indeed Streeck's (1987) system of industrial governance without trade unions bears a remarkable resemblance to the way in which many HI managers have traditionally 'done business'. The managerial line of command and authority is the only institution necessary to maintain control in highly uncertain market conditions, hence the perceived legitimacy of a unitarist form of employment relations. While we do not include the McDonaldization model here, we can note that managers often display a management style derived from an individualist and unitarist approach (Allan *et al.*, 2000). HRM is dealt with separately (see pp. 60–72).

Of course models and maps are not absolute constructs, as Kessler and Purcell (1995: 347) note:

- Style is a preferred way of managing employees that may be amended in practice.
- Firms may have no real style, being essentially opportunistic in reaction to events, and cannot be depicted.
- Styles may differ in relation to different groups, notably managers, highly skilled workers and peripheral workers.

We can add a fourth point – management styles may be gendered. Rutherford's (2001) study of male and female managers in an airline confirms differences in their approach to management. Men tend to follow a more command and control style with a distancing of personal self, while women are more communicative and caring, with more emphasis on people skills such as listening rather than mere performance of the task. That said the business function is the most important determinant of management style.

The locus of management style for employment relations in the HI is best identified as falling somewhere within the models and maps of non-union relations shown in Box 3.1. All authors, with the exception of Scase (1995), attribute directly or implicitly their particular approach as applicable to the HI. We should note that Lucas's (1996a) and Sisson's (1993) approaches were based on WIRS3. In the light of new evidence discussed in subsequent chapters, notably WERS, we shall review the efficacy of this depiction in the concluding chapter.

Box 3.1 Approaches to non-union employment relations

'Traditional' cost-minimization/no collectivism (Kessler and Purcell, 1995)
- Labour is a cost and factor of production
- Employee subordination part of the natural order
- Fear of union interference → opposition or kept at arm's length
- Low pay and no job security
- Little or no training

'Fraternal autocracy' (derived from Scase, 1995*)
- High financial rewards to obtain short-term commitment from skilled workers
- Owner-managers work alongside employees
- Managerial prerogative conditioned by weak market position of most employees who are unskilled
- Low pay, poor working conditions
- Non-union

'Bleak house' (Sisson, 1993)
- Unorganized conflict (high labour turnover and accidents)
- No grievance and health and safety procedures
- No communications and employee involvement
- No consultative committees
- Lack of employment security, including temporary contracts
- High rate of dismissals

'Black hole' (Guest and Conway, 1999)
- No HRM or industrial relations
- Small privately owned organizations
- Pragmatic and authoritarian cost-cutting approaches
- Low-skill, short-service marginal workers
- Low pay and insecure conditions of employment
- Little employee involvement

'Unbridled individualism' (Lucas, 1996a)
- High degree of managerial prerogative in the absence of organized labour
- Employers regard workers as a commodity to be controlled and constrained
- Low pay
- High employee quit rates, sickness, absence, injury, and use of grievance procedure
- High use of disciplinary sanctions and dismissal

- More limited opportunity for employees to challenge management
- Little consultation, especially on health and safety, or employee involvement

'Determined opportunism' (Head and Lucas, 2004b)
- High degree of managerial prerogative in the absence of organized labour
- Workforce structuring includes high reliance on so-called casuals with no contract
- Majority of workforce ('peripheral' unskilled) are subject to more 'hard' form of HRM
- Not constrained in dismissing workers, failing to comply with many minimum legal requirements, or observing the law in spirit
- Extreme instance of 'retaining control/cost-control' management

Note: *A combination of fraternalism and autocratic, because both styles reflect features that could be applied within the HI where demand is unpredictable.

HRM: an appropriate benchmark for the hospitality industry?

Doherty (2002) argues that the way in which the state of employment management in the HI is perceived depends on how it is benchmarked, either as industrial relations/personnel management or HRM (Storey, 1992: 35). She argues that the unfavourable picture drawn from the non-union approaches depicted in Box 3.1 is still rooted in the trade union/collective industrial relations paradigm. She suggests that the measure of HRM may invite more positive conclusions, especially in larger organizations and workplaces.

There may be some truth in this where the issue of service quality has been embraced, predicated on a redefinition of organizational purpose and a programme of culture change that embraces a clear strategy for long-term success and competitive advantage. Here there is some considerable interest in HRM within hotel and restaurant chains (Lashley, 1995b; Watson and D'Annunzio-Green, 1996; Gilbert and Guerrier, 1997; Hoque, 1999a,b,c; Lashley and Watson, 1999; Kelliher and Perrett, 2001). Hyams and Fryer (2000) cite the case of a luxury hotel in New Zealand where a distinct set of HRM practices introduced in support of the strategic decision towards quality enhancement demonstrated very positive outcomes against key performance indicators, especially overall guest satisfaction and financial performance. Indeed Hoque (1999a) asserts that hotels are more interested in HRM than manufacturing firms. Conversely Kelliher and Perrett (2001) do not find a clear relationship between business strategy and the approach to HRM in designer restaurants.

However, there are two problems with Doherty's argument. First, the approaches to employment relations in Box 3.1 have all been developed explicitly as an alternative to the trade union/collective industrial relations paradigm. Second, her conclusion that HRM is about managerial control gained through indirect and direct methods is not necessarily a good deal for the workers. Indeed one major piece of evidence she cites in support of this comes from research about management development, which suggests that managers may be the beneficiaries of 'soft' HRM, but not the workers, reaffirming that this variation of HRM is directed only at managers (Legge, 1995a; Storey, 1995, 2001). Rather it infers a cost-minimization route for the majority (Worsfold, 1999), and is symptomatic of McDonaldization where labour flexibility and work standardization militate against the development of strategic HRM systems and internal labour markets (Allan *et al.*, 2000).

In discussing the role of HRM in the management of employment, we begin with an overview of key issues that encapsulate the way in which HRM has emerged and become established in mainstream thinking. Not everybody subscribes to a new HRM model and orthodoxy of 'people management', notably those maintaining the broadly personnel management tradition. Even then among both camps there is a considerable divergence of view as to what HRM (or personnel management) is and means, how it can be operationalized and its effects measured, and its relationship with corporate performance. As Woods (1999) suggests HR(M) is a paradox that has never really been mastered. We then turn in more detail to issues that have most relevance to the management of hospitality employment, notably to account for a psychological contract and service work.[7]

Key issues in HRM discourse

HRM is a phenomenon of the 1980s when, according to Streeck (1987), the key issue for management was to find ways of managing in an unprecedented degree of economic uncertainty, which derived from a need for continuous rapid adjustment to an increasingly turbulent market. Hence the imperatives that HRM issues should be integrated with business strategy, and that HRM should be able to demonstrate its contribution to business performance (from the expectancy model, see high performance practices below). Issues such as commitment, quality, flexibility and adaptability became important (Guest, 1987). And so HRM was born (Fombrun *et al.*, 1984; Hendry and Pettigrew, 1986; Guest, 1987; Storey, 1989, 1992). HRM also stresses the importance of the devolving the ownership and delivery of HR initiatives from specialist HR managers to line managers.

Others deny that HRM represents anything different or new. Armstrong (2000: 586) claims HRM is a 'construct largely invented by academics and popularised by consultants', yet Grant and Oswick (1998) found a majority of practitioners agreed that HRM was different from personnel management. Gennard and Kelly (1995) and Torrington *et al.* (2002) are among those who regard HRM as the next stage in the evolution of personnel management. Equally there has been a growth in the proportion of specialists using HR in their title. These specialists are better qualified, more involved in strategic planning, more likely to use HRM practices than their counterparts using the title 'personnel', and most likely to be found in foreign-owned firms (Hoque and Noon, 2001).

One outcome has been a realignment of the personnel/line manager relationship, with more personnel work being devolved down the line (Hall and Torrington, 1998).[8] Yet in the more cost-conscious and value-added environment line managers are making more, not less, use of their specialist personnel advisers. The personnel function does contribute to corporate objectives by being delivered in many different but flexible forms (Gennard and Kelly, 1997). It is not necessarily the case that an organization not acting strategically will mean that the workforce is not managed in a strategic way. Hence strategic management of people is not purely within the domain of the HR department, and can be diffused throughout the organization and owned and directed by the line (Truss *et al.*, 2002).

The emphasis within HRM discourse has remained largely managerialist because of the emphasis on management's cost and performance concerns (Gibb, 2001), hence a management practice research agenda. The management of employment also tends to be discussed in terms of bipolar opposites in and around the metaphors of 'hard' and 'soft'. Key instances include high and low trust work practices (Fox, 1974), direct control vs. responsible autonomy (Friedman, 1977), control vs. commitment (Walton, 1985) and 'high road' vs. 'low road' (Cooke, 2001). Here managers may exercise strategic contingency choice in terms of which approach best fits their organization. In some respects these divergences are symptomatic of some of the differences between personnel management and HRM. Within personnel management people are more likely to be recognized and treated as human beings, whereas in HRM they are treated as people in the 'soft' variant and resources in the 'hard' variant.

A further criticism of HRM is that it is not gender neutral (Dickens, 1998), with Townley (1994) being an exception in making gender more visible within her analysis. Dickens (1998) argues HRM policies and practices perpetuate rather than challenge gender inequality. In terms of securing employee commitment assumptions about women being less committed than men will affect the shape of the core–periphery, and determine which jobs are full-time or part-time. Cost-cutting 'hard' HRM has underpinned existing sex segregation. Wajcman (2000) echoes these observations, pointing out that men are most likely to be found in occupations where management is convinced of a high quality strategy, whereas women are most likely to be found in low-skill jobs where management feels competition on costs is the most viable option.

'High road' or 'low road' HRM?

There are two broad approaches to HRM, both of which have been found wanting. The first, a 'high road' version, is generally agreed to comprise a list of tangible practices, with 'best practice' HRM or 'bundles' of practices having the greatest impact on performance (Pfeffer, 1994, 1998; Huselid, 1995; Wood, 1995; Patterson *et al.*, 1998; Guest, 2001). Two groups of practices can be identified:

- High performance practices support the components of the expectancy model in that careful selection and training will produce high quality workers who will translate into high work performance.

- High commitment practices are antecedents of high commitment and job satisfaction in that good family-friendly policies will aid retention and regulate the work–life balance of employees.

Some practices may be core requirements, e.g. selection, training, communications and reward. Others are more marginal because they do not necessarily have general application, e.g. family-friendly policies, profit-related pay and share ownership (Guest, 2001).

An alternative approach stresses that HRM may be contingent, with 'best fit' HRM differing according to the stage in the business life cycle (Kochan and Barocci, 1985; Goss-Turner, 1999), the strategy–structure configuration (Fombrun *et al.*, 1984) and the business strategy being pursued (Legge, 1995a). Schuler and Jackson (1987) identify three alternative 'best fit' strategies – innovation, quality enhancement and cost-reduction – but acknowledge that organizations may pursue two or more competitive strategies simultaneously. Hence 'best fit' may embrace both 'high road' and 'low road' approaches.

Espousal of the 'best practice' approach suggests that the 'sophisticated paternalist' and 'consultative' models of industrial relations management (Purcell and Sisson, 1983) triumph over 'bleak houses' (Sisson, 1993) and 'black holes' (Guest and Conway, 1999), in effect denying them legitimacy when they undoubtedly exist (Cully *et al.*, 1999). Legge (1995b) proceeds from the basis that HRM has never been anything but 'hard'. 'Some managements have always preferred a unitarist approach and have exploited their workers – HRM may have provided a language to justify that approach but was not responsible for it' (Armstrong, 2000: 586). Marchington and Grugulis (2000) point out that the rhetoric of HRM disguises the way in which it reinforces managerial control, sometimes against workers' interests or wishes. Indeed the rhetoric of 'best practice' HRM can be turned on its head to depict 'low road' HRM as the following examples show:

- The practice of teamworking can be regarded as a means to replace over the shoulder managerial control by peer surveillance.
- Empowerment is about getting workers to take more responsibility with no commensurate increase in reward.
- Using the management chain to cascade information simply denies employees any voice in what is going on around them.

In support of the contingency approach Cappelli and Crocker-Hefter (1996) caution against 'best practice' and benchmarking, suggesting each organization should develop its own set of core competencies to reflect its own distinctiveness. Conversely others have observed that international pressures have driven countries and companies to adopt similar HRM concepts, regulations and practices (Clark *et al.*, 1999; Walsh, 2001).

Purcell (1999) considers that a 'best practice' prescription is a cul-de-sac, while contingency and 'best fit' HRM are a chimera. Both are predicated upon the logic of rational choice and neglect other organizational processes at work.

Importantly they fail to identify circumstances in which particular HRM practices are successful. Others share Purcell's scepticism, denying that HRM can exist in the diametrically opposite forms of 'soft' and 'hard' (Legge, 1995a,b; Keenoy, 1997; Truss *et al.*, 1997). Policies are always both 'hard' and 'soft', e.g. McDonald's provides all the support that employees need to perform to the required level, yet it deploys a 'no excuses' policy if they do not conform. Legge (1995b) sees the implementation of Walton's soft model of mutuality being restricted to knowledge-based industries seeking value added. Even though the majority of employees may fall within this larger than normal privileged core, there may still be a minority for whom harder conditions exist.

Keenoy's (1999) metaphor of HRM as a hologram, or virtual image, usefully encapsulates why the HRM debate has become somewhat sterile. As a hologram HRM changes its appearance as we move around its image, and appears different each time we look at it. It is akin to quality, something that is always in the process of becoming (a continuous and never-ending process).

The paradox remains why so few American (Milkman, 1998) and British workplaces (Cully *et al.*, 1999) take the 'high road' to employment management. While the UK historical tradition does not favour this approach (Cooke, 2001), it is also likely to have been undermined by the devolution of HR activities and associated budgets, which are necessary to measure the contribution of HRM. Thus line managers' HR actions will be driven by adherence to short-term financial targets, and working to budgets will drive a short-term employment relations agenda (Marginson *et al.*, 1993), encouraging a deterioration towards 'low road' practices.

Ultimately people are always expendable. Labour costs may be a significant proportion of operating costs, and are always far easier to trim than other fixed costs. BA cannot cut the cost of fuel or new aircraft, so it is cheaper to sack and re-employ sizeable numbers of workers because re-employment costs are lower than exit costs (Boyd, 2001). It is hardly surprising, then, that the overall conclusion from WERS was that the broad approach to employment relations management in Britain was 'one of retaining control and doing what they could to control costs' (Cully *et al.*, 1999: 295).

As the HI product is highly diverse and ever-changing, there is no reason why 'high road' HRM should be effective, and there will be circumstances in which other HRM strategies, including cost-control will be effective. Indeed support for this comes from contingency models of HRM, as we show later in the chapter. In new businesses the personal influence of the founder and an entrepreneurial spirit will predominate over a clearly defined organization or HRM structure (Goss-Turner, 1999; Kelliher and Perrett, 2001). As organizations mature and become more complex quality assurance, standardization, systems, structures controlling costs and increasing efficiency begin to emerge. These are heightened where there are plans to expand a chain under franchises (Goss-Turner, 1999). Concurrently more attention is given towards systematic 'people management', including motivating managers, spreading values and developing a service culture, in order to sustain the business. In short there is a mix of 'hard' and 'soft' measures that conforms to Lashley's 'promise of control and commitment' (Box 3.3, p. 70).

A psychological contract

A further problem with the 'best practice' approach is that it does not take account of employees' view of HRM within the psychological contract (Gibb, 2001; also Mabey *et al.*, 1998; Guest, 1999). Renewed interest in the psychological contract and taking account of employees' expectations has become an increasingly important dimension of HRM (Guest *et al.*, 1996; Mabey *et al.*, 1998; Grant, 1999; Guest, 1999; Gibb, 2001).

The concept of the psychological contract, where employees' needs are necessarily satisfied to ensure commitment to organizational objectives that will translate into business success, has remained the keystone of Torrington's philosophy of HRM as an emergent version of personnel management (Torrington *et al.*, 2002). Grant (1999) identifies two approaches. The first derives from Argyris (1960) and Schein (1978) who focus on employer–employee perceptions to the exchange implied by the employment relationship within the broader context of social processes. Alternatively perceptions are shaped in the mind of the employee. All approaches draw from expectancy theory, where the state of the psychological contract is influenced by our desired goals and outcomes, while the experience we have of these goals and outcomes determines our motivation to work and our behaviour at work. Two types of contract can be identified (Rousseau, 1990, 1995; Guest *et al.*, 1996):

- Transactional – characterized by short-term security with most emphasis on financial reward.
- Relational – where long-term employment security is based on a mixture of loyalty, commitment and financial reward.

The nature of the contract following recruitment appears to be linked with new recruits' career motivations and intentions to stay (Rousseau, 1990). In transactional contracts workers may perceive regular job change as a prerequisite to career development, a point frequently noted in respect of hospitality workers (Riley *et al.*, 2000). Consequently they may expect less from their employer in terms of consultation, appraisal and job security in the knowledge that they will be moving on. While in one sense 'soft' HRM is implied in a relational contract, and 'hard' HRM is implied in a transactional contract, Grant (1999) questions the extent to which HRM policies and practices viewed across these dichotomies have led to a change in the nature of the psychological contract. Indeed employees may experience both types of psychological contract simultaneously, as noted in the case of part-time students, but it is important to emphasize that their financial reward is relatively poor (Curtis, 2002; Lammont and Lucas, 1999).

Employees draw on past and current employment experience in order to rationalize and create their own sense of reality in relation to work. A satisfied employee will adopt and believe the prevailing HRM rhetoric (Grant, 1999). Gibb (2001) also argues that bringing employees into the equation will help to shed light on whether HRM leads to real benefits or exploitation and injustice. Fears that employees are more likely to display a preponderance of negative work attitudes have not been borne out by the WERS findings of general employee satisfaction at work (Cully *et al.*, 1999; also Chapter 8). Employees are generally appreciative and positive about HRM systems, while unhappy employees may still experience effective HRM (Gibb, 1999).

HRM and service work

The growth in importance of service work has pointed to the need to develop new theories of alternative forms of work organization and HRM (Frenkel, 2000; Korczynski, 2002). This is particularly challenging in transitional countries in Central and Eastern Europe in the post-Communist era (Anastassova and Purcell, 1995; D'Annunzio-Green, 2002; Lucas *et al.*, forthcoming). Clearly, front-line service work is heterogeneous. Some forms of service work, e.g. call-centres, have been transformed by advances in digital technology. Technology cannot necessarily substitute for the personalized nature of service work that is integral to many hospitality and tourism activities. However, intensified international competition, with its attendant concentration on marketing and operational strategy, has prompted businesses to focus greater attention on managing the service encounter (Mattson and den Haring, 1998; Lashley, 1998; Lashley and Taylor, 1998; Haynes and Fryer, 2000). The behaviour and performance of indirect service workers are also important, as poor quality food or rooms cannot be compensated by a high standard of direct service delivery. The character of service work and the HRM practices deemed necessary to support a 'best practice' SQ approach are contained in Box 3.2.

We have already noted that the extent to which management is able to achieve its organizational goals through people will depend on the extent to which workers' or customers' aims and aspirations are met. The need to draw the employee–customer relationship into the analysis of HRM derives from the critical role of employee in determining SQ, as Redman and Mathews (1998: 59) note:

> to a very real extent the employee is the service, given the absence of any tangible artefact. They carry the responsibility of projecting the image of the organisation and it is in their hands that the ultimate satisfaction of the consumer rests.

'Delighting the customer' may be marketing objective to ensure repeat business, but it is also highly dependent upon management's ability to 'manage' employees so that they display the right attitude and behaviour, an issue discussed in the previous chapter. The simple point is, if managers are not meeting employees' or customers' expectations, this has negative implications for organizational performance, reinforcing need to consider a three-way psychological contract.

Branded hotels in particular are inevitably very concerned about customer service and quality standards. Hoque's (1999a,b) work indicates that larger hotels do attach a large degree of importance to strategic HRM issues (Case study 3.3), although the findings should not be extrapolated to smaller hotels where 'poor' practice may be commonplace[9] (Price, 1994). McGunnigle and Jameson's (2000) study of high commitment in the top 50 hotel groups challenges Hoque's

---

Box 3.2 Service quality and Human Resource Management

The character of service
- Intangibility of services – cannot be evaluated until consumed.
- Inseparability of service producer from consumer – immediacy and importance of encounter.
- Heterogeneity and variability – every service encounter is different.
- Perishability – the service disappears if not consumed.

Eight key HRM practices
- Recruitment and selection – based on identification of personality and skills needs, and uses a range of methods.
- Retention – effective programme.
- Teamworking – semi-autonomous, cross-process and multi-functional teams.
- Training and development – quality-related including teamworking process and interpersonal skills.
- Performance appraisal – goals focus on quality goals and effective behaviour, utilizing customer-driven data.
- Reward – payment systems linked to achievement of quality goals.
- Job security – high security, including support where redundancies necessary.
- Employee involvement – fosters open, supportive and participatory employment relations climate.

Source: Derived from Redman and Mathews (1998).

Case study 3.3 HRM and performance in hotels

The relationship between HRM and performance is dependent upon:

- a hotel's business strategy;
- hotels having a quality focus within that strategy;
- HRM being introduced as an integrated and coherent 'bundle' of packages.

While it is not claimed or shown that a quality-enhancing approach leads to high performance, this study is claimed as unique in demonstrating strong contingency effects, possibly because it is a single industry study. In short high commitment HRM is practised only when there is a 'fit' with product and service strategy.

Source: Hoque (1999a,b).

The role of management 69

conclusion that the hotel industry has undergone change, including finding new ways of managing staff. They take Peccei and Rosenthal's (1997) lead that recruitment and selection, and training and development, including performance appraisal, are all important in developing individual commitment to customer service and culture change. A clear desire for commitment, recruitment and selection is not found to be commensurate with this aim, where there is little development for line managers or strategic integration of training. In designer restaurants:

> the lack of coherency both in terms of internal consistency across policy areas and the ways in which different staff groups were managed, suggest that the relationship between approaches to HRM and business strategy is a more complicated one than that suggested by the models based on notions of fit.
>
> (Kelliher and Perrett, 2001: 435)

Lashley (1998) argues that the amount of employee discretion required to fulfil a particular customer-service need is crucial to understanding 'best fit' between the service offer and the management of employees. His model of four ideal types of HRM relates to the amount of employee involvement and participation in shaping the service encounter, hence the kind of empowerment employees are afforded (Box 3.3) (see also Chapter 6). The variations on the vertical plane reflect the fact that service work is a mix of tangibles and intangibles, with the latter being regarded as the defining feature of services. Their relationship is an influential factor in determining employment strategy and the form that HRM takes. Although within food and beverage service vending machines are wholly tangible, fast food is high in tangibles (high technology, standard products), and the intangibles of the service encounter are standardized by use of scripts. Highly personalized service in a gentleman's club might incorporate a high element of intangibles where 'delighting the customer' and considerable discretion are exercised in the conduct of work. The extent to which work needs to be standardized or customized is the most important influence on HRM strategy.

Horizontally the parameters of 'external control' and 'internal control' are broadly in keeping with the 'hard' and 'soft' approaches to the management of employment noted earlier, including direct control vs. responsible autonomy (Friedman, 1977) and control vs. commitment (Walton, 1985). Lashley argues these approaches are misleading in service work because employment strategy is concerned with both control and commitment, and because they fail to recognize the importance of employee discretion as an element of job design, which is crucial to an understanding of the service delivery. While Lashley's model is a helpful start point to understanding employee management in hospitality and tourism, in practice there are likely to be many variations that reflect the fact that professional, participative, command and control and involvement are not four discrete alternatives. Further he overlooks how employee attitudes to customer service and individual and group behaviour may affect HRM practices and organizational performance in services (Peccei and Rosenthal, 1997; Haynes and Fryer, 2000). As many firms continually seek to reposition themselves the market place to achieve competitive advantage, these approaches are not static (Case study 3.4).

Box 3.3 Approaches to the management of human resources in service organizations

Customized offer

Involvement style
Service shop, e.g. TGI Fridays
Product: standardized menus, decor, uniforms.
Service: some standardization, e.g. time targets, but more customized direct service and individualization of uniforms. Low labour intensity.
Employees: limited discretion.
Performance management: good benefits, tips, bonuses on sales, training, team briefing.

Professional style
Professional service, e.g. gentlemen's club
Product: highly customized.
Service: highly personal and individual, involving complex tasks.
Employees: high discretion and responsible autonomy.
Performance management: power to shape objectives, moral involvement – psychological needs, trust culture.

External control   ⟶ Internal control

Service factory, e.g. McDonald's
Product: highly standardized, efficient, predictable, calculable, controllable.
Service: short, simple, low labour intensity.
Employees: little, limited discretion.
Performance management: extensive training, observation checklists.

Mass service, e.g. Harvester Restaurants
Product: standardized around English pub theme.
Service: quite labour intensive and leisurely.
Employees: high discretion in customer complaints, ambience creation.
Performance management: training emphasizing intrinsic controls, teamworking, team briefing, participation at task level, strong social dynamic.

Command and control style   *Participative style*

Standardized offer

Source: Derived from Lashley (1998: 28).

Case study 3.4 Quality enhancement in a luxury New Zealand hotel

A luxury hotel pursued a strategy of quality enhancement over a six-year period to be at the top of the market. Bundles of HRM practices, including changes to work design and organization structure, achieved measurable positive effects on the key indicators of service used. The approach changed from traditional hotel management incorporating elements of command and control to an involvement style.

Source: Haynes and Fryer (2000).

Mayer (2002) claims that strong HR practices in hiring, development, providing appropriate support systems and retention have led to the delivery of superior guest services in a Florida Theme Park. Nankervis and Debrah (1995) observe differences in the way HRM practices are implemented within SQ in hotels in Singapore and Australia, attributing these to national, cultural, social and labour market phenomena, a finding also applicable in the US (Partlow, 1996).

Halim's (2001) comparative case study research of six SQ hotels and six non-SQ hotels evaluated the degree of effectiveness of the SQ philosophy in achieving better HR practices in the Room Service Division of five-star hotels in Egypt. Differences in the implementation of approaches to the philosophy within SQ hotels were revealed, as well as some significant differences between SQ and non-SQ hotels. Factors were also identified that affect the implementation of the SQ philosophy to achieve better HR practices (Case study 3.5). A model modifying the HR aspects of the Malcolm Baldrige National Quality Award has also been developed to provide simplified guidelines on effective implementation.

Largely in support of Lashley (1998), Nickson *et al.* (2002) conclude that HRM in hospitality is more 'best fit' than 'best practice'. A 'best fit' approach to designing HRM contingent upon the particular notion of 'good service' seems apposite. Hence practices will differ across market segments, and between tangible and intangible aspects of service production. Although good practice has been identified by Hoque (1999a) and Kelliher and Perrett (2001) in upmarket organizations, it may also be found in small firms (Jameson, 2000). For many firms high pay, extensive training and job security are unlikely to be cost effective (also Riley *et al.*, 2000). Poor practice may reflect a number of reasons but is not immutable, and the 'high road' is not the only route to competitive advantage (Keep and Mayhew, 1999). Case study 3.6 illustrates an example of Lashley's (1998) command and control style at Pret à Manger.

While moving towards greater customer responsiveness and an SQ philosophy may be a longer-term objective in post-Communist countries such as Slovakia, hotels have found it difficult to move away from the traditional rigid 'socialist' type of personnel management. They have yet to reach a point in terms of current practice that is fully adequate to the new economic environment, and remain a

Case study 3.5 Service quality and effective HR practices in five-star hotels in Cairo

The SQ philosophy gives management the opportunity to create a better quality culture, select the most qualified staff, set an efficient job design, design effective job training plans, and establish an appropriate base that can sustain the achievement of quality objectives, provided that hotels use the proper approaches to implement the philosophy.

Factors that affect the effective implementation of SQ to achieve better HR practices are lack of sufficient knowledge about the philosophy, lack of expertise among some senior managers, bureaucratic management, central- ized management and the heavy involvement of hotel owners in operations. Insufficient allocation of financial resources, too much emphasis on achiev- ing profit rather than on improving quality and absence of detailed guidance to aid implementation militate against effectiveness. Behavioural norms of employees embedded in their ways of performing duties and high turnover also contributed. Quality approaches need to be integrated into all elements of a hotel's operations. The unstable political climate in the Middle East and some Egyptian labour laws are perceived as inhibitors to reaching the desired quality standards.

Total involvement and employee empowerment, and employee evalua- tion of their own performance, are difficult to implement due to the low level of education in some departments.

Source: Halim (2001).

long way from achieving a 'western' model of HRM (Lucas *et al.*, forthcoming). Residues of the Communist ideology and practices are still apparent and hand- icap the wish to compete for increasingly demanding global tourism clients in Bulgaria. Deeply entrenched custom and practice present formidable obstacles to change (Anastassova and Purcell, 1995). While a growing number of foreign hospi- tality companies are willing to invest in Russia (Upchurch *et al.*, 2000), a production-oriented viewpoint is challenging in terms of developing an SQ- focused ethos (D'Annunzio-Green, 2002).

Management organization for employment relations

While we have noted how HI managers approach employment relations and HRM, there is a dearth of literature since Lucas and Laycock (1991) about the way in which managers are actually organized and their role and responsibilities, with the exception of Goss-Turner's (1999) study of regional multi-unit managers. Here we rely largely on WERS to tell us something about these issues for work- place managers, their supervisors, and their superiors, who may have board-level responsibility. In so doing it is important to remember that over three-quarters of workplaces are part of a larger organization, and do not portray an owner-

Case study 3.6 Pret à Manger: 'best fit' and 'best practice'

Rated as one of the top ten places to work in Europe, Pret à Manger employs 2,400 staff in 120 shops producing high quality hand-made sandwiches and coffees, appealing to the urban professional.

Empowered employees

Staff are scripted only to greet and thank customers. They have discretion over speech during the service encounter, can detect and remedy product faults, and can upsell using their own approach.

Resourcing, diversity and development

Although the shops are based mainly in London, three-quarters of staff are from elsewhere in Europe. There are clear job descriptions and people are invited to work for a day, allowing the manager and shop staff to determine suitability. There is a three-hour introduction to the company within an initial ten-day training plan. Training covers health and safety, food hygiene, customer service and food preparation procedures. Each employee has two weeks' training per annum. An in-store career structure allows staff to progress from team member to manager, while the opportunity to move to another store has reduced overall company labour turnover.

Pay and performance

Performance is reviewed after three months' service and then every four months. In mid-2002 average front-line pay was £6.25 (with bonus), some £2.00 above the NMW. Bonus is based on mystery shoppers, with 80 per cent of stores achieving it weekly. Staff can exchange up to 15 per cent of salary for additional holidays and medical care. There are paid breaks and the company spends £250,000 on staff parties twice a year.

Involvement and communications

Team meetings occur twice a day, supplemented by a longer monthly staff meeting, which sets goals and targets for the next quarter.

Source: Nickson *et al.* (2002).

manager perspective. We also identify where workplace managers may seek external advice on employment matters.

Workplace management

The HI has significantly fewer personnel specialists than AIS, and employment relations are most likely to be managed by a general manager. HR/personnel specialists are concentrated in large workplaces (Table 3.1), although variations in the HI sub-sectors are less clear-cut (Table 3.2). Regardless of job title managers in AIS, PSS and the HI spend around one-third of their time on employment relations, with just over 30 per cent spending half or more of their time on employment relations matters. On average all these managers had been in their current job for six years.

Responsibility for employee relations matters is most likely to be combined equally with HI managers' other job responsibilities, such as financial management

Table 3.1 Workplace managers' role in context and by size of workplace (%)

Job title	AIS	PSS	HI	<25	25–49	50–99	100+
HRM/personnel, etc.	20	17	10**	2	24	8	59
Owner/partner	18	21	6*	2	20	0	0
Finance	9	11	4***	6	0	6	0
General manager	53	50	79*	89	56	86	41
Other	1	1	1	1	0	0	0
Mean time spent on employment relations	32	31	35	31	42	38	47
ER is major job responsibility ff	22	19	13	8	24	12	31
ER is of equal responsibility ff	39	42	48	50	37	60	43
Formal HR qualification ff	35	30	39	40	51	21	39

Source: WERS98.

Notes: All weighted cases unless otherwise stated. Column percentages for job title do not sum to 100 due to rounding. *Significantly different at the 5% level from AIS and PSS. **Significantly different at the 5% level from AIS. ***Significantly different at the 5% level from PSS. ff Excludes cases where managers are more concerned with other responsibilities.

Table 3.2 Workplace managers' role in context and by sub-sector (%)

Job title	Hotel	Campsites	Restaurants	Bars	Canteens
HRM/personnel etc.	14	10	4	9	26
Owner/partner	10	0	7	2	10
Finance	0	0	3	9	0
General manager	77	90	83	81	65
Other	0	0	3	0	0
Mean time spent on employment relations	31	36	29	40	36
ER is major job responsibility ff	10	0	6	17	22
ER is of equal responsibility ff	53	94	63	31	68
Formal HR qualification ff	41	100	30	24	88

Source: WERS98.

Notes: All weighted cases unless otherwise stated. Column percentages for job title do not sum to 100 due to rounding. ff Excludes cases where managers are more concerned with other responsibilities.

(48 per cent), and is a major responsibility in only a minority of cases (Table 3.1). These two groups taken together can be regarded as more 'specialized' managers involved in employment relations and are found in six in ten HI workplaces. These managers have around 15 years' experience in employment relations in all groupings, but HI managers are more likely to have a formal HR qualification.

HI managers' work responsibilities span the full range of employment relations activities, with payment systems most likely to be someone else's responsibility. This suggests a much more diverse picture of sustained involvement across most activities than is portrayed in the more selectively focused literature discussed above. Although recruitment, selection and training are important, it is hard to argue that grievance handling and health and safety are not integral to HRM, however defined, although the literature rarely deals with them explicitly (see Box 3.2). Indeed HI managers are significantly more likely to deal with training,

Table 3.3 Workplace managers' work responsibilities in context and by size of workplace (%)

HR aspects	AIS	PSS	HI	<25	25–49	50–99	100+
Pay or conditions of employment	78	82	86	85	91	86	85
Recruitment or selection	93	92	96	100	93	85	95
Employee training	87	86	95*	99	94	85	88
Payment systems	55	59	58	58	65	52	46
Handling grievances	92	92	98*	100	100	92	87
Staff planning	87	85	89	89	96	84	78
Equal opportunities	88	85	85	82	96	82	85
Health and safety	83	82	92*	94	94	80	78
Performance appraisals	82	81	85	84	95	85	68
None of these	0	1	1	0	0	6	0

Source: WERS98.

Notes: All weighted cases. *Significantly different at the 5% level from AIS and PSS.

Table 3.4 Workplace managers' work responsibilities by sub-sector (%)

HR aspects	Hotel	Campsites	Restaurants	Bars	Canteens
Pay or conditions of employment	95	10	75	88	98
Recruitment or selection	92	100	94	100	95
Employee training	92	100	92	100	95
Payment systems	62	72	67	51	50
Handling grievances	97	100	97	100	98
Staff planning	96	96	77	91	93
Equal opportunities	93	96	89	74	98
Health and safety	92	96	81	98	90
Performance appraisals	88	96	77	88	90

Source: WERS98.

Note: All weighted cases.

grievance handling and health and safety than their counterparts in AIS and PSS (Table 3.3). This is more marked in small and large workplaces, but does not show much variation by sub-sector (Table 3.4). Most HI managers have a personnel 'team' of only one or two staff.

Workplace supervisors

In terms of non-managerial supervision (Tables 3.5 and 3.6) three-quarters of HI workplaces have few or no non-managerial employees who have job duties that involve supervising other employees. This is related to workplace size, such that non-managerial staff supervision is most evident in large workplaces. However, in workplaces where non-managerial employees supervise others, HI supervisors have an active role in most employee relations matters noted in Tables 3.3 and 3.4, which is similar to their counterparts in AIS and PSS. All these supervisors have very limited authority, especially in deciding pay increases for their sub-ordinates or dismissing workers for unsatisfactory performance. HI supervisors (one in four) are significantly more likely to make the final decision in recruitment than managers in AIS. HI workplaces are significantly more likely to have most supervisors trained in HR skills than in PSS.

Strategic organization

As Tables 3.5 and 3.6 illustrate a good majority of multi-site workplaces (Tables A.15 and A.16) have the support of an HR Director who spends most of his/her time on employment relations. There is also evidence of strategic planning and integration. Workplace strategic plans that set out objectives and how they will be achieved are fairly widespread, and the significantly higher proportion of HI work-places accredited as Investors in People (IiP) suggests a strong level of strategic integration in half the HI workplaces. Almost 40 per cent of HI workplaces without IiP had applied for IiP recognition in the previous five years. The ways in which higher-level management becomes involved in workplace employment relations will be considered later on.

Goss-Turner's (1999) study of multi-unit managers in branded hotel, pub and restaurant chains sheds light on managers whose role has been enhanced as a result of management delayering. Harvester Restaurants' new service strategy around culture, organization, people and systems led to the removal of two layers of management (Lashley, 1997). With increased accountability multi-unit managers become the company's ambassador in the key interface between the strategic plan and unit managers and their front-line staff, becoming policy implementers and policers of standards. Fulford and Enz's (1995) study of restaurants found that the HR function was not perceived as a strategic partner, was not sufficiently involved in decision making, and line managers did not feel HRM made a substantial contribution to business success. Weak HRM that does not articulate at workplace level may lead to local cultures that detract from company image (Barron and Maxwell, 1998).

Table 3.5 Strategic and supervisory organization for employment relations in context and by size of workplace (%)

	AIS	PSS	HI	<25	25–49	50–99	100+
Organization g							
HR Director l	60	63	71	78	64	53	86
Higher-level manager spending most time on ER k	76	76	71	69	75	66	85
Workplace							
Formal strategic plan	74	69	75	75	67	78	93
Few non-management staff supervising others d	63	65	74	78	71	67	53
Most supervisors trained in HR skills f	25	23	38***	34	48	39	44
Member of organization cc	55	62	63**	57	70	65	74
No external help with ER	52	51	75*	90	54	57	25
Investors in People	34	31	50*	62	30	31	50
BS5750/ISO9000	24	21	11*	16	0	9	15

Source: WERS98.

Notes: All weighted cases unless otherwise stated. d Below 20%. l Excludes Head Offices. k Private sector including Head Offices. g Where part of larger organization. f 60% and above where non-managerial employees supervise other workers. cc Trade or employer. *Significantly different at the 5% level from AIS and PSS. **Significantly different at the 5% level from AIS. ***Significantly different at the 5% level from PSS.

Table 3.6 Strategic and supervisory organization for employment relations by sub-sector (%)

	Hotels	Campsites	Restaurants	Bars	Canteens
Organization g					
HR Director l	57	100	61	82	100
Higher-level manager spending most time on ER k	37	93	55	94	82
Workplace					
Formal strategic plan	69	100	83	70	86
Few non-management staff supervising others d	72	90	82	79	28
Most supervisors trained in HR skills f	38	100	45	29	63
Member of organization cc	75	100	70	47	78
No external help with ER	63	90	84	77	67
Investors in People	32	10	68	48	66
BS5750/ISO9000	5	0	2	11	60

Source: WERS98.

Notes: All weighted cases unless otherwise stated. d Below 20%. l Excludes Head Offices. k Private sector including Head Offices. g Where part of larger organization. f 60% and above where non-managerial employees supervise other workers. cc Trade or employer.

Table 3.7 Where managers agree about employment relations issues in context and by size of workplace (%)

	AIS (agree)	PSS (agree)	HI (agree)	<25 (agree)	25–49 (agree)	50–99 (agree)	100+ (agree)
Employees frequently asked to work beyond job requirements	52	50	55	52	59	62	57
Employees sometimes take unfair advantage of management	25	27	34	32	30	44	49
Employees led to expect long-term employment	77	79	74	80	63	80	58
Up to individual to balance work and family	84	85	90	93	96	68	74
Top managers best placed to make workplace decisions	54	57	49	42	53	73	48
Unions help find ways to improve workplace performance	26	21	23	27	26	12	4
Rather consult directly with employees than with unions	75	82	88**	84	100	92	72
Change not introduced without implications being discussed with employees	72	66	57**	59	51	55	52
Employees fully committed to values of organization	72	73	69	74	52	76	69
Most decisions made without employee consultation	16	20	23	21	22	33	30

Source: WERS98.

Notes: All weighted cases. Row percentages do not sum to 100 due to rounding. Agree includes strongly agree responses. **Significantly different at the 5% level from AIS.

Sources of external advice

Where HI workplaces belong to another organization, this is most likely to be connected with trade, such as trade association and Chamber of Commerce. Over a quarter belong to an employers' association.[10]

Significantly fewer HI workplaces than in AIS and PSS sought external advice on employee relations in the preceding 12 months, especially in very small workplaces, and restaurants. However most large workplaces had sought external advice, mainly from ACAS or external lawyers. In general the main HI source is external lawyers (15 per cent) with even less use of ACAS, management

Table 3.8 Where managers agree about employment relations issues by sub-sector (%)

	Hotels (agree)	Campsites (agree)	Restaurants (agree)	Bars (agree)	Canteens (agree)
Employees frequently asked to work beyond job requirements	55	28	45	58	80
Employees sometimes take unfair advantage of management	25	10	36	33	64
Employees led to expect long-term employment	89	90	86	57	79
Up to individual to balance work and family	85	28	90	100	52
Top managers best placed to make workplace decisions	67	18	43	48	18
Unions help find ways to improve workplace performance	8	82	44	28	0
Rather consult directly with employees than with unions	96	22	95	87	52
Change not introduced without implications being discussed with employees	67	90	50	52	67
Employees fully committed to values of organization	79	96	58	67	85
Most decisions made without employee consultation	11	6	36	24	16

Source: WERS98.

Notes: All weighted cases. Row percentages do not sum to 100 due to rounding. Agree includes strongly agree responses.

consultants, accountants, employers' associations, other professional bodies and government agencies. External accountants and other professional bodies are used in a sizeable minority of small and large workplaces.

In those HI workplaces that have sought ACAS advice, it has been mainly for advice on industrial tribunal case/conciliation (46 per cent) and dismissals (23 per cent). These reasons account for all ACAS contact in very small and small workplaces. In large workplaces ACAS is used mostly for these reasons and for advice on other aspects of employment law. ACAS is also used for the more proactive reason of improving employee relations in one-third of large workplaces, all of which are hotels and restaurants.

Table 3.9 Managers' views about employment relations issues by size of workplace (%)

	HI			<25			25–49			50–99			100+		
	A	N	D	A	N	D	A	N	D	A	N	D	A	N	D
Employees frequently asked to work beyond job requirements	55	9	36	52	9	39	59	13	27	62	3	35	57	5	38
Employees sometimes take unfair advantage of management	34	14	52	32	14	54	30	13	57	44	21	36	49	9	42
Employees led to expect long-term employment	74	17	9	80	13	7	63	38	10	80	6	15	58	22	20
Up to individual to balance work and family	90	9	2	93	7	0	96	4	0	68	19	13	74	19	7
Top managers best placed to make workplace decisions	49	15	36	42	17	41	53	18	28	73	5	22	48	11	40
Unions help find ways to improve workplace performance	23	31	46	27	26	48	26	29	45	12	52	37	4	50	36
Rather consult directly with employees than with unions	88	10	2	84	14	2	100	0	0	92	4	3	72	23	5
Change not introduced without implications being discussed with employees	57	19	24	59	18	23	51	15	34	55	28	17	52	34	14
Employees fully committed to values of organization	69	19	12	74	18	8	52	20	28	76	18	6	69	20	11
Most decisions made without employee consultation	23	20	57	21	25	55	22	7	70	33	18	49	30	20	50

Source: WERS98.

Notes: All weighted cases. Row percentages do not sum to 100 due to rounding. Agree and disagree columns include strongly agree/disagree responses.

Table 3.10 Managers' views about employment relations issues by sub-sector (%)

	Hotels			Campsites			Restaurants			Bars			Canteens		
	A	N	D	A	N	D	A	N	D	A	N	D	A	N	D
Employees frequently asked to work beyond job requirements	55	2	42	28	72	0	45	18	37	58	4	39	80	15	5
Employees sometimes take unfair advantage of management	25	14	61	10	72	18	36	23	41	33	10	56	64	0	36
Employees led to expect long-term employment	89	8	5	90	10	0	86	7	7	57	31	12	79	10	11
Up to individual to balance work and family	85	13	2	28	72	0	90	3	7	100	0	0	52	48	0
Top managers best placed to make workplace decisions	67	9	23	18	4	78	43	18	39	48	6	46	18	74	8
Unions help find ways to improve workplace performance	8	43	48	82	18	0	44	17	48	28	24	48	0	81	19
Rather consult directly with employees than with unions	96	3	1	22	0	78	95	4	1	87	11	2	52	48	0
Change not introduced without implications being discussed with employees	67	21	12	90	4	6	50	25	25	52	14	34	67	24	10
Employees fully committed to values of organization	79	20	2	96	4	0	58	20	22	67	19	14	85	13	2
Most decisions made without employee consultation	11	14	76	6	0	94	36	20	44	24	24	51	16	15	69

Source: WERS98.

Notes: All weighted cases. Row percentages do not sum to 100 due to rounding. Agree and disagree columns include strongly agree/disagree responses.

Managers' views about employment relations

Tables 3.7 and 3.8 summarize managers' views about employment relations issues, using the 'agree' responses only (the neither agree nor disagree, disagree and strongly disagree are not shown). There are two aspects of significance with AIS only. First, HI managers would rather consult directly with employees than with unions. Second, HI managers are more likely to introduce change without discussing its implications with employees. Elsewhere HI managers' views are broadly in keeping with those in AIS and PSS, but there are some variations by size of workplace and sub-sector. A more complete HI breakdown is shown in Tables 3.9 and 3.10 as the basis for discussion.

Discussion and review topics

Models and maps of employment relations

Taking a workplace with which you are familiar, map or model the management style of:

- the organization;
- your line manager.

Can you identify any differences that may be gender-based?

A service quality approach

Using Lashley's model in Box 3.3 design an approach to employee management for the following organizations:

- A regional restaurant chain that incorporates a Michelin starred restaurant and four city centre restaurants trading under the chef's name.
- An independent three-star hotel operating along traditional lines employing 80 staff.
- A national public house chain operating three brands: family-friendly, young professional and high entertainment.

Employment relations from WERS

What are the main distinguishing features of the management of employment relations within HI workplaces in terms of:

- the way management is organized;
- how managers routinely deal with employment relations issues;

- the support managers get from within the organization and workplace and from elsewhere?

What do these features suggest about organizations' approach to the management of employment relations?

Managers' views on employment relations

Using the data presented in Tables 3.9 and 3.10, analyse and evaluate managers' views about:

- their role as managers;
- trade unions and workforce participation;
- their employees.

What does this tell us about managers' overall approach to employment relations by size of workplace or by sub-sector?

4 Resourcing, development and fair treatment

Learning objectives

By the end of this chapter you should be able to:

- understand the nature of recruitment activity, and explain approaches to recruitment and selection;
- compare approaches to induction and training within national training frameworks;
- identify the legal framework for preventing discrimination and promoting fair treatment at work;
- appreciate how policies for equal opportunities, managing diversity, and health, safety and welfare contribute to the achievement of fairness, equity and work–life balance.

Recruitment and selection

Recruitment activity

High levels of recruitment activity can be attributed to specific conflicting pressures. On the one hand the HI worldwide reports skill shortages and fails to fill current vacancies (IDS, 1998b; ILO, 2001; H*t*F, 2000, 2002), inferring a quality problem. Employers may not be targeting appropriate groups of people or national training frameworks may be inadequately geared to the industry's needs. Considering only locals as a source of labour may be outdated in a global economy (Choi *et al.*, 2000). Technological advances facilitate the finding of required labour by targeting recruitment in developing countries, where there are high rates of unemployment among skilled workers, e.g. in Bangladesh 40 per cent of people with a Master's degree are unemployed or under-employed. The increasing presence of MNCs in tourism, in countries such as India, may not necessarily be met by an adequate supply of skilled workers (Singh, 1997). Skills shortages in Florida are overcome by recruiting from Puerto Rico (Mayer, 2002).

On the other hand the consequences of employment flows, which management may seek to perpetuate, and cost-minimization policies encourage recruitment systems that are highly responsive, flexible and ad hoc. Given high leaver rates

Table 4.1 Recruitment in last 12 months in context and by size of workplace

	AIS	PSS	HI	<25	25–49	50–99	100+
Total recruits							
Mean number	13	14	20	10	25	42	53
As % of total employees							
1 year ago	27	34	63*	62	72	64	33
New permanent							
Yes (%)	91	93	93	93	89	100	100

Source: WERS98.

Notes: All weighted cases where there have been recruits (AIS, N = 2,142, PSS, N = 1,331 and HI, N = 154). Means are rounded. *Significantly different at the 5% level from AIS and PSS.

Table 4.2 Recruitment in last 12 months by sub-sector

	Hotels	Campsites	Restaurants	Bars	Canteens
Total recruits					
Mean number	29	2	21	15	10
As % of total employees					
1 year ago	59	5	66	71	24
New permanent					
Yes (%)	97	100	97	88	100

Source: WERS98.

Notes: All weighted cases where there have been recruits. Means are rounded.

noted in Chapter 2, it is not surprising to find a high rate of recruitment in Britain (Table 4.1). HI workplaces are significantly more likely to have workforces with 50 per cent or more new employees, and this is three times greater than in AIS. Large workplaces have the lowest rates of recruitment activity (Tables 4.1 and 4.2).

In the twelve months prior to WERS HI workplaces were most likely to have vacancies for unskilled and sales staff. HI workplaces were significantly more likely to have vacancies for personal service, sales staff and routine unskilled manual workers, and significantly less likely to have vacancies for professional, technical and scientific, clerical and secretarial and operative and assembly workers. Half the workplaces in AIS, PSS and the HI had no difficulty filling vacancies, while skilled and unskilled job were most problematic in a small minority of HI workplaces. Considerable variations within sub-sectors reflect the different skill bases within them.

A different set of pressures is observed in post-Communist Russia, where bringing in new staff to respond to new demands is difficult to achieve. Overstaffing is rife because of low pay, problems making people redundant and the social responsibility to keep staff in jobs. Consequently staff become bored and lazy (D'Annunzio-Green, 2002).

Approaches to recruitment

Recruitment and selection are an important part of managerial work and work-place life. To proponents of the quality-enhancing employment approach 'employee selection is an important issue. Investing in techniques and skills which improve the selection decision is essential for organisational success' (Barclay, 2001: 96). Good recruitment and selection is based on an assessment of work values, personality, interpersonal skills and problem-solving ability (Redman and Mathews, 1998). Testing potential employees can be used to control 'type' and help mould organizational culture (Storey, 1992).

On the other hand those pursuing a cost-minimization approach may have little incentive or will to deploy other than the most basic of methods, and may respond in an ad hoc way. Using casual staff as ports of entry not only maintains control over staffing levels but also over behaviour and discipline, as casuals can be more easily dismissed (Allan *et al.*, 2000). Ease of dismissal may act as a barrier to the adoption of more systematic recruitment and selection, especially where there is a plentiful supply of labour (McGunnigle and Jameson, 2000). Lack of job security is likely to undermine the achievement of SQ (Redman and Mathews, 1998), and may also reflect the low status of the personnel function or its absence (Allan *et al.*, 2000).

The 'employment decision', when the vacancy is filled by an appropriate candidate, is a mutual and voluntary decision, based on employers' and candidates' freedom to withdraw from the process at any time. The process involves chance and risk. Managers have considerable discretion but are never in complete control (Torrington *et al.*, 2002: 189–90). Managers' own ways of maximizing cost-effectiveness have different meanings within firms' own employment standards and different labour market conditions.

Studies consistently report high levels of informality, including 'word of mouth' recruitment (Ryan, 1996; Kelliher and Johnson, 1997; IDS, 1998b; Cheng and Brown, 1998). Most British students gain employment by initiating contact themselves or through friends and family (Lucas and Ralston, 1997; Lucas and Lammont, 1998; Lucas and Langlois, 2001), which is even more common in Bulgaria, Hungary and Slovakia (Johnson and Lucas, 2002). Greater formality may be found in larger hotel firms (McGunnigle and Jameson, 2000), but is by no means comprehensive (Hoque, 1999a). Larger hotel companies looking overseas for staff are providing more accommodation as a first temporary step in the first two months of employment (IDS, 2001).

A large majority of British HI workplaces in WERS are significantly more likely to treat internal and external candidates equally than in AIS and PSS. Consequently they are also less likely to give preference to internal candidates over external candidates except in medium and large workplaces (one-third favour internal candidates). This is mirrored in slightly lower levels of internal recruit-ment in the HI. Goss-Turner (1999) notes that multi-unit managers are normally recruited internally on the basis of perceived task and people orientation, without any systematic selection procedures.

Recruitment criteria

We noted in Chapter 2 how in customer-service work recruitment is more likely to be based on people's personal and aesthetic skills than technical skills (Warhurst *et al.*, 2000), while the preceding discussion suggests availability is also important. Dickens (1998) argues that attitudes, behaviour and personality tend to interact with gender and racial stereotypes, which may lead to discrimination in recruitment. Managers' preference for recruitment is made on the basis of personality (ILO, 2001: 90). Aesthetically employers can signal the type of labour required by using terms such as 'smart young person' in an advertisement, or requiring the enclosure of a photograph with applications. By presenting themselves in person young people enable employers to screen for aesthetic skills (Lucas and Lammont, 1998; Lammont and Lucas, 1999; Lucas and Langlois, 2001). Hence recruitment (and training) is on the basis of customer focus, interpersonal skills, emotional control and empathy. Training in grooming and deportment may follow.

The 'personality' criterion is to an extent confirmed by WERS, which shows that the four most important recruitment criteria in the HI are motivation, references,[1] skills and availability; each is used in three-quarters or more workplaces. The three most important criteria in AIS of experience, skills and motivation apply in 86 per cent or more workplaces. Availability, experience and personal recommendation are significantly more important in the HI than in AIS and PSS. Qualifications are more important in AIS and PSS. Availability is of major importance to restaurants, while age is more important in bars than in any other sub-sector.

We know from Chapter 2 that a combination of volatile demand, age-related factors, and worker attributes makes young workers, particularly students, a valuable commodity within the HI. Yet firms have not fallen to the temptation of employing more young workers on officially sanctioned lower rates of pay under the NMW (Lucas and Langlois, 2000a,b). This fits with their pay structures, policies on employing particular age groups for particular jobs or periods of time, or legal restrictions on the serving of alcohol and the operation of dangerous machinery.

Selection methods and tests

The interview remains popular with managers and candidates alike, as it is simple, quick and cheap, in spite of reliability and validity concerns. It fulfils a social function, enabling social and aesthetic aspects that are so integral to customer-service work to be addressed, however inadequately. Behavioural interviewing, where standard questions address how the candidate dealt with past situations that are likely to arise in their new job, provides better quality information and encourages a more reciprocal approach to employment decision-making (Simons, 1995; Barclay, 2001). Like other simulated group exercises its limitations are assumptions that actual behaviour will be in line with intentions, and that a snapshot view is representative of general behaviour. Competency-based interviewing has produced exceptional performers and reduced turnover levels at the Buckhead Beef Company (Warech, 2002).

Paraskevas (2000) suggests that HI managerial selection techniques should be aimed at the application of skills, rather than their possession. Personality is an important consideration, and HI selectors are as likely to accept the validity and usefulness of sophisticated selection techniques as their counterparts in other sectors. Hotels do not use them because of cost and reliability concerns.

According to WERS personality and attitude tests have limited use in general, more so in the HI than in AIS and PSS. They are more likely to be used in HI firms employing 25 or more employees. While performance or competency tests are used by half of AIS firms significantly fewer HI workplaces (one-quarter) use them. They are most likely to be used in the largest HI workplaces but are rarely used in bars. One view is that tests are best suited to jobs involving special know-ledge and abilities. Hence such tests have limited application among a largely unskilled workforce (Berger and Ghei, 1995).

Appointment

Terms and conditions of employment (pay, hours, sick leave, grievance proce-dures, training opportunities and holiday) are made available in writing in most HI workplaces. However 13 per cent do not convey any of these details in writing, over twice the proportion in AIS and PSS. Restaurants are the worst offenders (one-quarter). Three-quarters of AIS, PSS and HI workplaces have standard employment contracts for their largest occupational group (LOG),[2] although one-fifth of bars do not give their LOG contracts.

Retention

The recruitment and retention of managers and skilled workers is a global HCT sector problem (Barron, 1997; MacHatton et al., 1997; Barber and Pittaway, 2000; ILO, 2001). While Redman and Mathews (1998) contend that effective retention programmes will achieve higher levels of SQ, there is a view that the most talented people leave the sector, while the less competent stay for fear of becoming unem-ployed (ILO, 2001). In spite of the increase in hospitality management programmes and more hospitality graduates (Ineson and Kempa, 1997), there are poor graduate transfer rates (Barron, 1997) and demand outstrips supply (Purcell and Quinn, 1996). Part of the problem may lie in unsystematic graduate recruit-ment and selection that relies upon impressions and subjective judgements of character, and pays little regard to academic achievement and performance and supporting evidence from tutors (Ineson, 1996). Poor impressions created by work placements may prompt hospitality graduates to seek careers elsewhere.

A number of the larger hotel companies have adopted training initiatives to improve retention in a tight UK labour market. The Thistle Tower Hotel introduced Modern Apprenticeships in-house, while employees at Harrington Hall were given the chance to study National Vocational Qualifications (NVQs) (IDS, 2001). The London Heathrow Marriott offers a wide range of courses including Modern Apprenticeships, graduate training schemes, NVQ programmes and English lessons for non-English speaking staff, while Accor also offers

NVQs and Modern Apprenticeships (IDS, 2002). Rowley and Purcell (2001) note how leading edge employers' retention policies include anything, short of raising pay.

Training and development

Training frameworks

The state has a vested interest in VET in seeking to develop a more highly skilled labour force to improve economic performance and competitiveness. National systems vary considerably in general and in their specificity towards hospitality and tourism, with many developing countries not yet providing sufficient state support (Esichaikul and Baum, 1998). In India the framework of tourism education is inadequate to a growing tourism sector where increasing professionalism, particularly at managerial levels, is required (Singh, 1997). Russia may have a highly literate and well-educated workforce, but this presents challenges to bringing managerial staff to the requisite level of skills and competencies where cultural attitudes are non-western (D'Annunzio-Green, 2002).

The training culture of the US can be described as voluntarist and largely uncoordinated, and places emphasis on individual effort and individual payment – a 'protean' career (Finegold *et al.*, 2000). Germany, France and Sweden have directed and more centralized systems. In Spain many employees (43 per cent) have no school-leaving certificate. A state-funded scheme entitles employers to financial aid on presentation of an annual training plan. Employees are eligible to up to 150 hours training on full pay (IDS, 1998c). In Australia McDonald's offers employees access to an approved fast food accredited traineeship of 12 months' duration in return for a government subsidy (Allan *et al.*, 2000). These arrangements have been incorporated into sectoral agreements. The British system is voluntarist, and not particularly industry-oriented since the demise of the industry training boards in the 1980s. Examples of national VET systems are shown in Case study 4.1.[3]

Hospitality and tourism management education is provided in many countries, but not in Denmark, Sweden or Japan. The corpus of knowledge for hospitality management is the preserve of the HCIMA, which represents 24,000 managers in 106 countries (Powell and Wood, 1999). Baum and Nickson (1998) press the case for a stronger pedagogical base in the learning experience of HRM in higher education, arguing that responding to industry demands may perpetuate existing (poor) HRM practice and make little or no contribution to change. Even major chains do not have any involvement with leading UK and US Business Schools (Goss-Turner, 1999).

In response to the 1997 National Targets for Education and Training (NTETs) for the UK, the HI's target for 2000 for the proportion of employers offering NVQs and SVQs (Scottish VQs) was 50 per cent from a base of less than 1 per cent in the mid-1990s (H*t*F, 1997). The target for employees to have job-related qualifications increased to 60 per cent from 30 per cent. Such highly ambitious targets, even if met, would still leave major gaps in training provision (Lucas

Case study 4.1 National vocational, educational and training frameworks for hospitality and tourism

France

A highly centralized system of public provision is based on nationally recognized qualifications at staged levels from the craft *Certificat de l'Aptitude Professionelle* to the management-orientated *Brevet de Technicien Supérieur*. Higher education tends to be private, often with the cooperation of the local Chamber of Commerce.

Italy

Training is highly fragmented, with no industry-level training body. Secondary education is available in Hotel and Catering Schools and Schools of Tourism. Placements in hotels last only one or two weeks and are ineffective. Tourism is a recent innovation in higher education, but there is no provision for hospitality.

Spain

Escuelas de Hosteleria provide craft training, while *Escuelas de Turismo* provide more general training leading to hotel reception, travel agency or tourist guide work. A degree has recently been developed for both industries but is criticized by employers for its lack of practical skill development.

Netherlands

Training is well regulated and well developed. All adults are entitled to three days' training per annum. Apprenticeships involve four days' working and one day's study a week. Three higher-level state-run hotel schools offer degrees and 11 middle-level schools offer diplomas. In both cases there is a one-year industrial placement and qualifications are recognized internationally. Diploma courses are rigorous, including international law, languages and personnel management.

Germany

There is a highly regulated system based on apprenticeships, including two languages, which are subject to national practical and theoretical examinations. Two-year post-apprenticeship training is undertaken at a *Fachschule*. Most hotel general managers have taken this route. Most college graduates have a related degree.

UK

NVQs are a workplace competency-based assessment of tasks a worker can perform. There is no training requirement, and many workers do not complete enough modules to gain a qualification. There is no external examination. Over 300 colleges and universities provide courses ranging from craft-level NVQs to Masters degrees. Registrations for NVQs/SVQs have risen and the most popular is food preparation and cooking. Work-based training Modern Apprenticeships have high uptakes but also high drop-out rates. Enrolment on General (G)NVQ, further and higher education courses has been falling. A new network of SSCs replaced NTOs in 2002. Most college graduates have industry-related qualifications.

US

Vocational preparation is rare, and apprenticeships are very rare. Alternatively hotels have formal relationships with colleges for students, which are more formal where hospitality programmes are taught. Twenty per cent of food and beverage operatives are full-time students. There are no national hotel skill standards. A few high-profile universities provide qualifications recognized by the leading international and national hotel companies.

Sources: Burrell *et al.* (1997); IDS (1998b); Finegold *et al.* (2000); H*t*F (2002).

and Langlois, 2000b). Fifteen per cent of people working in the HI do not have qualifications of any kind, while 17 per cent have a qualification below General Certificate of Education (GCSE) grades A–C or equivalent, which could be an NVQ/SVQ. The majority has a qualification at or above this level (H*t*F, 2002).[4]

Baum *et al.* (1997) suggest that the NVQ/GNVQ framework developed in the UK in the early 1990s was done without specific sectoral consideration or recognition of the hospitality and tourism industries' policy priorities, leading to a skills gap. Hales *et al.* (1996) contend that NVQs have considerable potential in small hospitality firms, as they give a sharper focus to training activities and improve candidates' perceived job satisfaction, morale and career prospects. However the system is seen as weak in the absence of external examination (Finegold *et al.*, 2000). Other government initiatives such as Modern Apprenticeships and New Deal may be viewed negatively by HI employers, and those that have experience of them may be unwilling to use them again (Lucas and Langlois, 2000a,b).

Recent employer-led initiatives in Britain include the BHA's Excellence Through People, which identifies and disseminates 'best practice' in recruitment and selection, development, recognition and reward, and communications.

However, only 0.6 per cent of all HI establishments had been certified (H*t*F, 2002). Hospitality Assured, developed by the HCIMA and promoted by the BHA, deals with 'best practice' from a customer perspective, enabling those holding an award to benchmark their customer service against the best in the industry.

Approaches to training

Training can be formal or informal, applied selectively to particular workers, on- or off-job, accredited or non-accredited, occur over variable periods of time, and be provided by the firm or an outside body. Firms' ability and willingness to train depends on the available resources of time, money and staff. An unstable work-force base built upon volatile demand also constrains firms' ability to provide training. Where organizations appear to support external training, they are not prepared to pay high fees, even for managers (Shaw and Patterson, 1995). Where demand is more volatile, and jobs involve more numerous tasks, training becomes more difficult. Full-time students with career aspirations elsewhere cannot or are unwilling to participate in formal training even if available. Where demand is steady, employers can subdivide jobs and closely monitor defined tasks. Hence formalized training is likely to be found where there is a clearly defined skills base, usually in food preparation (Lucas and Langlois, 2000b).

Storey (1992) regards training and development as the 'litmus test' of HRM (see Case study 4.2). Redman and Mathews (1998) suggest the extent of quality-related training in 'soft' areas such as teamworking processes and interpersonal skills are positively related to increased SQ. IiP brings benefits in terms of workforce development and improved business efficiency (Claytor, 2002), and can reduce turnover and absenteeism where it is part of an SQ philosophy. However failure will result where training budgets are low and needs assessments are poorly executed (Breiter and Woods, 1997). In Singapore the use of guests' comments and employee consultation to inform training needs is regarded as a strength

---

Case study 4.2 Training and development in UK designer restaurants

A training manager coordinates, supports and executes training throughout the group. All new recruits attend induction training in the first two weeks. Staff use training manuals to conduct on-job training for kitchen and restaurant staff. Chefs learn through job rotation. Waiting staff are provided with lists of menu ingredients, and are expected to attend periodic tastings, especially when the menu changes. Chefs are encouraged to experiment with new dishes, and an exchange scheme was being piloted with a restaurant in California. Day release is available for achieving NVQs, with several managers working towards NVQ assessor awards to carry out in-house accredited training.

Source: Kelliher and Perrett (2001).

Case study 4.3 The San Francisco Hotels Partnership Project

A consortium of 12 hotels and the four largest union locals found a collective solution to skill development and career progression. The collective agreement included joint problem-solving groups and a state-subsidized training programme. All workers were offered 100 hours of training in team building, technical skills and English as a foreign language. This released the potential capability of room attendants with degrees to advance to higher positions. Cross-training enabled them to gain experience as food servers during periods of holiday cover.

Source: Finegold *et al.* (2000).

(Cheng and Brown, 1998). Training and development supported by performance appraisal is a primary tool of culture change and communication strategy (Watson and D'Annunzio-Green, 1996; Guest and Conway, 2002). People-focused organizations like BA, Singapore Airlines, Marriott and Ritz Carlton do engage in systematic training and development programmes (Baum *et al.*, 1997). Case study 4.3 illustrates how trade unions have made a positive contribution to training in the US.

Limitations to managerial training and development feature widely in the literature (McGunnigle and Jameson, 2000; Taylor and Berger, 2000). The bringing together of all hotel managers at the company's training centre in pairs is lauded as enabling international managers to network and thereby develop a better understanding of global aspects and company philosophy (Jones *et al.*, 1998). Perceptions of limited promotion opportunities are not justified in major airlines, international hotel groups and theme parks (Baum *et al.*, 1997).

In McDonald's management training is replaced by an operation and training manual, which contains all facets of owning and operating a store (Allan *et al.*, 2000). There is an interesting slant to management development. Most line managers start as casual or part-time crew members, and may internalize the leadership or managerial style of the owner or franchisee. This is important in terms of how careers are defined and how future franchises are created.

In Chapter 2 we noted Baum's (1996) reservation about the application of a traditional skills model to developing countries. India, Indonesia and Thailand may have plentiful labour pools, but major investment in training and development is necessary to overcome the lack of cultural and communications skills of front-line employees. Hence training needs in developing countries and other countries with an international market centre on the 'soft' competencies of generic service skills, including the ability to anticipate guests' verbal and non-verbal communication styles (Mallinson and Weiler, 2000).

Small HI firms with informal HRM relying on casual, part-time and seasonal labour are likely to make a poor investment in training (Casey *et al.*, 1997; Lucas and Langlois, 2000b). Rather they rely on buying in skills from the external labour market or, if they train, a regular churn of statutory and skills training is needed to service staff turnover (McGunnigle and Jameson, 2000). Because career progression is dependent upon moving to another employer, there is a reluctance to invest in training that will benefit a competitor (Lucas and Langlois, 2000a). Recession in post-Communist Bulgaria has curtailed investment in training and development in hotels (Anatassova and Purcell, 1995).

Induction and training in Britain

The first day at work is critical in shaping an employee's attitude to the company, influencing performance, satisfaction, commitment or intention to leave (Young and Lundberg, 1996; Lashley and Best, 2002). Within Britain standard induction[5] for the LOG is widespread in the HI, the PSS and AIS (three-quarters of workplaces), but is most likely to be used in workplaces employing 25 or more employees. However, over one-quarter of hotels have no such programme, which may be linked to high turnover (Table 2.7). Short induction programmes of one day or less are more common in HI workplaces (four in ten) than in the PSS and AIS (one-third), and these are more likely to be found in medium and large workplaces (over half).

Supervision, job descriptions, induction/initial training and ongoing training are the main methods used to make employees aware of their job responsibilities in all groupings, and these apply in three-quarters or more of HI workplaces. Individual objectives and targets are least used in the HI (30 per cent), with team targets and competency standards (both 31 per cent) also featuring relatively less often. There are variations by size and sector, with most continual reinforcement of job responsibilities occurring in large workplaces.[6]

Many studies find that worker training is basic, and that the unskilled nature of the work enables workers to reach experienced worker standard within a few weeks (Ryan, 1996). There is normally a statutory requirement to provide general training in respect of food hygiene, health and safety and fire regulations (McGunnigle and Jameson, 2000). More specific skills training is related to sub-sectors with a defined skills base, e.g. silver service and wine waiting in restaurants. While some firms may pay a lower training or starter rate to reflect the trainee's lower contribution, there appears to be little uptake among HI firms for two reasons. The duration of training is short and training occurs while the worker is actually working, so lower pay cannot be justified (Lucas and Langlois, 2001). There has been little use of the development rate of the NMW for adult trainees (LPC, 2000).

New starters in the LOG in the HI are able to do their job as well as experienced employees significantly more quickly than is the case in the PSS and AIS, which is symptomatic of the low skills base (Ryan, 1996). Within one month new starters would be up to experienced worker standard in over half of HI workplaces compared to only one-third of the PSS and AIS workplaces. Very few HI workplaces have any employees who take more than six months to become experienced, which is significantly different from AIS and the PSS. One-third of HI workplaces offered no off-the-job training compared to one-quarter in AIS and the PSS, and overall HI employees are less likely to have received off-job training. Limited training (below 20 per cent of the LOG) is most often found in very small workplaces (two-thirds) and restaurants (eight in ten). Even so, those HI employees who do benefit from off-job training received similar amounts of time in training as their counterparts in the PSS and AIS. One-quarter of HI employees benefiting from off-the-job training received less than one day. Off-the-job training of five days or more affects almost one-third of HI workplaces and is more likely to be found in restaurants and small workplaces.

HI workplaces are significantly more likely to give off-the-job training in health and safety (89 per cent), customer service/liaison (85 per cent) and quality control procedures (67 per cent) and significantly less likely to provide training in computing skills (19 per cent) than in the PSS and AIS. Quality control is particularly important in small workplaces and restaurants (over eight in ten). Reliability and working to deadlines is significantly more important in the HI than in AIS. Teamworking, operation of new equipment, and improving communications affect 50 per cent or more HI workplaces. The different needs of firms in AIS and the PSS make for a more diverse pattern of matters covered by off-the-job training. Although these workplaces provide off-the-job training in the matters noted above, these tend to happen in a sizeable minority of workplaces, and it may be the case that they are covered in on-the-job training.

In one-third of AIS, PSS and HI workplaces around half or more of the workforce in the LOG has been formally trained to do jobs other than their own. High levels of workers who are functionally flexible are most likely to be found in HI workplaces employing between 25 and 49 employees, and are least likely to be found in the very small workplaces and restaurants.

Fair treatment at work

Equal opportunities and anti-discrimination law

The origins of equal opportunities lie in the social and political agenda of the 1960s and 1970s, in which the US civil rights movement was a powerful driving force for social justice. Perhaps surprisingly, given the free enterprise culture and

---

Case study 4.4 **Peculiar discrimination at Joe's Stone Crabs**

The EEOC brought a case of sex discrimination against this Miami restaurant, although no individual had claimed discrimination. The EEOC decided that Joe's had a reputation for hiring men only, and therefore women would have been discouraged from applying. The employers were required to review their HR practices, analyse their workforce, and re-examine their recruitment and selection criteria.

Source: Sherwyn *et al.* (1999).

deregulated American approach to employment relations noted in Chapter 1, the US is at the forefront of legal compliance in the form of anti-discrimination legislation in relation to gender, race, age and disability. The Equal Employment Opportunity Commission (EEOC) deals with all complaints of discrimination on grounds of sex (see Case study 4.4), race, national origin, religion, retaliation and disability, aids complainants, undertakes research and produces publications with a view to removing barriers (Sargeant, 1999). Historically Europe's agenda has been more restricted, focusing largely on gender equality (sex discrimination and equal pay), but is now changing. There is no monitoring body independent of government in France (Burrell *et al.*, 1997).

Sex and race

Within Europe only Britain deals with race discrimination[7] in a similar way to sex discrimination for persons seeking employment and those in employment. The *Sex Discrimination Act 1975* (sex and marital status) and the *Race Relations Act 1976* (race, colour, nationality, ethnic and national origin) are designed to prevent three types of discrimination – direct, indirect and victimization, which can include harassment.[8] Customers are within the scope of sex discrimination law because it is unlawful for an employer to discriminate on sex grounds in the provision of goods, facilities or services as part of a business, such as service in a restaurant or the letting of rooms. If race (or sex) is a genuine occupational qualification, then an employer can lawfully discriminate in favour of a person from a particular racial group. If an employer refuses to train a woman simply because she is a married, that is directly discriminatory. The imposition of an age requirement for a post might be indirectly discriminatory where the effect is that a significantly smaller proportion of men, women or married persons are able to comply with it compared to persons of the opposite sex or single persons. Both Acts cover selection, promotion, transfer, training and other benefits, but pay and pensions are within scope of equal pay legislation (see Chapter 5). Two separate bodies, the EOC and the CRE, exercise specific responsibilities for this legislation.

There is no maximum limit on the amount of compensation that employment tribunals may award to a successful claimant. Although only a very small proportion of total cases reach tribunal (most are settled or disposed of by other means or withdrawn), in 2000/1 compensation of £3.75 million was awarded in sex discrimination cases. The highest award was £1,414,620 and the median award £5,000. However the number of claims dropped sharply from 17,200 to 10,092, and those that are made are becoming increasingly complex. Victims of race discrimination fare less well, with total compensation standing at £0.75 million, the highest award £66,086 and the median award £5,263 (Employment Tribunals Service, 2002).

In critique of the effectiveness of extant British anti-discrimination law, Dickens (1997) notes that the emphasis is to desist from doing negative things. There is no legal requirement to do anything positive to promote equality such as workforce monitoring or attempting to increase the proportion of under-represented groups in the workplace.[9] Positive discrimination such as preferential hiring quotas is unlawful. Equal opportunities policies are voluntary, and depend on a business case argument rather than being based on a social case. Business arguments are contingent (Dickens, 1994), resulting in selective and partial action in which employers prioritize gender over race. Putting equal opportunities policies into practice is impeded by men's resistance to sex equality (Weber, 1998; Wajcman, 2000). There are circumstances when women can break through the 'glass ceiling' and achieve senior management positions (Maxwell, 1997; Knutson and Schmidgall, 1999). An organization-based approach is no use to women in highly feminized employment who remain stuck to a 'sticky floor' because it does not lead to 'a transformation in access to power and the nature of it' (Dickens, 1994: 15). Hence the economic benefits of equal opportunities need to be articulated at a level beyond the organization, but may not produce desirable outcomes (Case study 4.5).

Dickens (1998) also argues that HRM concepts and policies perpetuate rather than challenge gender inequality (also Cassell, 1996). The reality of work intensification, increased surveillance and managerial control, and the shifting of risk to employees revealed in more critical empirical reviews of HRM have a disproportionate effect on women and other disadvantaged groups. In pursuit of flexibility, cost-cutting 'hard' HRM has utilized and underpinned existing sex segregation, with the core being defined partly by reference to masculine attributes. Perceptions of women's (lower) commitment also shape the core–periphery, determining who is hired, trained and developed. Assessment in selection, appraisal and reward needs to be understood in terms of power-based relations. Increasing reliance on attitudinal characteristics exacerbates the problem because attitude, behaviour and personality tend to interact with gender and racial stereotypes and lead to discrimination in selection. Working as cabin crew is defined as women's work by employers, customers and employees. Emotional labour is not gender neutral as work containing significant amounts is dominated by women (Taylor and Tyler, 2000).

Sexual harassment

Harassment is unwanted behaviour of a sexual nature including physical, verbal and non-verbal behaviour.[10] In the US the company is responsible for a manager's persistent harassment (Sherry, 1995). The issue of what constitutes a hostile environment has proved difficult to define and sexual harassment need not be so severe as to cause psychological damage. Employers cannot seek a judgement to dismiss charges unless they have a properly implemented policy (Aalberts and Seidman, 1996). Where there is no policy, employers will be liable for the hostile environment created by supervisors (Sherwyn and Tracey, 1998).

Harassment is a pervasive and frequent occurrence (Woods and Kavanaugh, 1994). Managers and customers can be the perpetrators of sexual harassment (Gilbert *et al.*, 1998; Worsfold and McCann, 2000). It mainly affects women, reflecting the gendered division of work and existing power differentials (Purcell, 1996; McMahon, 2000). Customer harassment is one of the least rewarding aspects of the interpersonal relationship, and is exacerbated where service staff are

---

Case study 4.5 **Women in hotels in Italy and the UK**

Italy has a stronger legal framework supporting women, but job opportun-ities are limited and favourable maternity rights appear to be damaging women's employment prospects. Women returners are considered out of touch, and they are offered chambermaids' jobs. Family-friendly policies are unknown, even to large hotel groups. The pay gap is smaller because all sectors are regulated by legally binding collective agreements. Some employers pay above the minimum in cash to avoid higher tax and social insurance costs.

In the UK increased opportunities are in numerically flexible jobs which are vulnerable to economic fluctuations. As in Italy, restaurant and bar jobs are contingently gendered, as employers seek cheap labour of either sex. Women are largely excluded from kitchen work, but not from nightwork, the reverse of what is observed in Italy. Company economic performance is the most important factor in setting pay. There is greater awareness of gender issues.

Source: Doherty and Manfredi (2001).

---

encouraged to sell sexuality or to flirt (Adkins, 1995; Gilbert *et al.*, 1998). The more authentic the performance, the more difficult it is for the customer to recognize there is no promise of associated consequences, which may be exacerbated by alcohol (Worsfold and McCann, 2000). Individual employee re/action may make things worse, as most managerial harassment comes from an immediate superior or more senior manager. The extent of harassment is likely to be under-reported, unless there is a strong policy and effective channels for challenging such behaviour that by-pass superiors. Consequently individuals sustain stress and poor working relationships, and may quit.

Disability

The European approach to disability has generally been based on compulsory employment quota systems, e.g. France, Germany and Spain, and extensive state intervention in contrast to the US model of civil rights and strong anti-discrimi-nation measures (Goss *et al.*, 2000). The US model is based on the premise that discrimination owes more to society's attitude and structural barriers than personal limitations caused by impairment or disability. The *Rehabilitation Act 1973* provides for affirmative action, which could include the achievement of preferential quotas, while the *Americans with Disabilities Act 1992* recognizes disabled people as a group whose relative lack of power has prevented them from achieving fair or equal treat-ment in the face of societal prejudice. Case study 4.6 illustrates some early court decisions on disability and acquired immune deficiency syndrome (AIDS), which have become more difficult to document due to HI organizations settling out of

***Case study 4.6* Disability and AIDS**

A New York City hotel was ordered to pay its former accountant, who was sacked less than two weeks after confiding to colleagues that he had AIDS, $13,546 for disability, plus medical bills and $1,000 compensation for pain and suffering. Sheraton stated that termination was for excessive absences. The accountant had been voted Employee of the Year two months earlier.

A waiter in a Texas lodge with AIDS was awarded $60,000 by a jury for disability discrimination, rejecting the company's claim that he was dismissed for excessive tardiness.

Source: Barrows *et al.* (1996).

court to avoid expensive litigation and adverse publicity. Such cases may arise from the misconception that AIDS can be transmitted by casual contact, e.g. food handling, with the implication that companies need to maintain ongoing employee educational programmes in the context of strong policies (Barrows *et al.*, 1996).

Britain diverged from the general European model with the *Disability Discrimination Act 1995*, which defines disability, covers direct discrimination and victimization, but not indirect discrimination, and places a duty on employers to make positive adjustments to the workplace to accommodate disabled people[11] (Doyle, 1995; Stacey and Short, 2000). The DRC exercises responsibility for the legislation. Even so, almost all British workplaces, including those in the HI, do not employ disabled workers (Tables A.11 and A.12). In 2000/1 employment tribunals awarded £1.5 million compensation to successful claimants, with a maximum figure of £215,000 and a median of £6,019 in the small proportion of cases that proceeded to tribunal.

Age

The US has the longest experience of age discrimination legislation with the *Age Discrimination in Employment Act 1967*. Canada, France, Ireland and Australia are examples of other countries with legislation, with New Zealand having recently followed suit. In the US the law only protects those aged 40 and over (no upper age limit), and employers cannot make employment decisions on hiring, firing, training or grading on the basis of age. In 1997 age complaints accounted for 20 per cent of all complaints received by the EEOC (Sargeant, 1999). Australia and New Zealand's legislation was a response to the 'demographic timebomb' – a shortage of young people entering a labour market increasingly dominated by older age groups. New Zealand legislation embodies an assertion that age per se does not determine a person's ability or productivity, and should not be used as a criterion in any part of the employment cycle. Reliance should be placed on the person's ability to perform the task required. Hence Qu and Yee Cheng (1996) report how the hotel industry in Hong Kong targeted workers aged 55 and over to alleviate labour shortages. Their favourable attributes, including being hard-working, responsible and cooperative, are perceived to outweigh their weaknesses, including lower productivity and higher employment cost. Conversely in Britain high reliance on young labour, coupled with a given set of managerial attitudes and prejudices, serves to disadvantage 'mature' workers who may be as young as 30 (Lucas, 1995b).

Britain introduced a Code of Practice on Age Diversity in Employment in 1999, which seeks to introduce good practice into employers' policies on recruitment, selection, promotion, redundancy and retention. Loretto *et al.* (2000) suggest the Code's impact is likely to be small because its non-statutory basis has more draw-backs than merits. As Sargeant (1999) notes, the Code will not outlaw a provision contained within an advertisement for stewards/stewardesses to work on Eurostar that states 'we want to hear from you if you are aged 20–35'.

Current and future developments

The legal framework within Europe is changing following the adoption in 2000 of the EU Directive on equal treatment in areas other than sex or race legislation, and anti-discrimination legislation will be extended to other areas including age and disability after extensive consultation.[12] Many aspects of the race and disability proposals are already covered by extant UK legislation, but changes are already taking place:

- New regulations in 2003 change the definition of indirect discrimination in race cases, introduce a definition of racial harassment, and shift the burden of proof in direct discrimination to the employer, in keeping with sex discrimination.
- New regulations in 2003 outlaw discrimination on grounds of sexual orientation[13] and religion. Both are based closely on the principles of the *Race Relations Act 1976*. The regulations cover orientation towards the same sex, opposite sex or both. Religion covers grounds of religion or belief (religious belief or similar philosophical belief). Religion is not defined, and there is a genuine occupational qualification exemption.
- New anti-discrimination regulations in 2004 widen the definition of disability discrimination, outlaw harassment as a form of discrimination, and remove the small employer exemption (below 15 employees). Further legislation arising from an internal review is expected to widen the scope of the definition of disability, possibly to include human immunodeficiency virus (HIV) and cancer.
- Age legislation must be in place by 2006, and is unlikely to be earlier, so the continued survival of compulsory retirement age will remain unresolved until then.[14] However some relaxation is necessary to allow future generations to defer their pensions and work longer to enhance their 'pension' provision in a longer living population.

Managing diversity

In the last 40 years there has been a shift in emphasis from providing equal opportunities in employment to managing diversity of employment. Managing diversity has emerged as an alternative approach to managing the individual, and positively values differences (Liff and Wajcman, 1996). It takes account not only of race, sex and disability but also other factors, including culture, work experience, personality and workstyle (Kandola and Fullerton, 1994; Iles, 1995). Maxwell *et al.* (2001: 469) identify two factors that differentiate managing diversity from equal opportunities. First, there is emphasis on the positive perspective of difference among staff in contrast to a negative perspective of disadvantage and discrimination against staff. Second, diversity factors beyond those covered by law are embraced.

A motivating force for addressing diversity polices arises from widespread demographic changes in the US and Europe producing a gradually ageing workforce. Changes in the ethnic mix of the labour force are occurring. In the US most growth in the non-white workforce will come from Asians and Hispanics who together will comprise 20 per cent in 2020, while the black population will only account for 11 per cent (Woods, 1999). These groups are generally clustered in lower-level occupations in the HI. Sixty per cent of line-level personnel in US restaurants are from an ethnic minority, where diversity needs to be acknowledged through cross-cultural training (Lee and Chon, 2000). Conversely there were only 35 black general managers in 45,000 US hotels (Charles and McCleary, 1997). Companies are advised to use mentors and to take more affirmative action.

The extent to which diversity policies complement or supplement equal opportunities approaches is debatable. Maxwell *et al.* (2001) argue that equal opportunities is outdated in a changed social and political climate where employers need to embrace diversity as a strategic issue for economic and competitive success. As noted above Dickens (1994, 1997, 1998) finds the business case unconvincing, and argues that only regulatory changes at the macro level will lead the greater equality. Studies of diversity programmes in practice have noted ill-defined

---

Case study 4.7 Managing diversity in San Francisco hotels

The labour mix in an international hotel chain reflects a diverse labour market. The chain demonstrates a reactive diversification approach. Discrimination and bias are discouraged but affirmative action is not taken. High quit and fire rates may have reflected managers' inability to manage diversity. Employees are expected to assimilate to the organization rather than the organization adapt to them. Trade unions have a positive impact on the hotels and in helping them move towards diversity management, but managers need to move forward and value diversity to become more multicultural.

Source: Groeschl and Doherty (1999).

goals. For example in American chain restaurants the programmes rarely do more than improve employees' awareness, and do not seek to work towards organizational change (Woods and Sciarini, 1995). Case study 4.7 also illustrates the limited nature of diversity programmes. Alternatively Iverson (2000b) identifies a model based on the concerns of a diverse group of employees, but acknowledges that strong and committed leadership from the top is needed to make this work effectively.

Putting equal opportunities and diversity into practice

From WERS, while most workplaces have written policies on equal opportunities and managing diversity, and these are slightly more widespread in the HI, there is less likelihood that the effects of these policies will be measured (Table 4.3). While a majority of medium workplaces and hotels do not have policies, those that do are more likely to measure their effects. The forms of equality of treatment and discrimination that these policies address are similar in AIS, the PSS and the HI. Ethnic minority or racial groups are most likely to be included, with sex/gender and disability following. Although this suggests that legislation in these areas may have promoted most workplaces to include them, the same does not apply in the case of union membership, which is least likely to be included. Religion, sexual orientation and age, where anti-discrimination legislation does not yet apply, have more widespread application than trade union membership, which is included in only a large minority of workplaces.

Most workplaces in AIS, the PSS and the HI use the staff handbook to inform their employees about these policies. The letter of appointment is rarely used in the HI and, as with grievance and discipline procedures, is significantly different

Table 4.3 Equal opportunities policy in context, by size of workplace and sub-sector (%)

	AIS	PSS	HI	<25	25–49	50–99	100+
Equal opportunities or diversity policy	67	62	70	75	67	48	78
Any attempt to measure effects++	16	9	9	8	6	23	7

	Hotels	Camp-sites	Restaur-ants	Bars	Canteens
Equal opportunities or diversity policy	45	100	69	78	86
Any attempt to measure effects++	10	0	3	2	56

Source: WERS98.

Notes: All weighted cases. ++Where policy exists.

from AIS and the PSS. Where there is no formal written policy, the main reason in all groupings is because it is deemed unnecessary, a reason that is especially marked in restaurants and very small workplaces. The second and third reasons are that there is a policy, but it is not written down or the firm aims to be an equal opportunities employer. Given that most workplaces do not measure the effects of equal opportunities policies either, there is a clear indication that the management of equality and diversity is not taken very seriously. By contrast the management of sales, costs, profits and labour costs where there is extensive monitoring is afforded very high priority (see Appendix 1).

Slightly more HI workplaces (six of ten) do not apply practical proactive equal opportunities measures. Hence recording, measuring, monitoring and reviewing specific practices or making adjustments for disabled employees are not at all common.

Family-friendly measures

In the US the *Family and Medical Leave Act 1993*, applicable only to companies employing 50 or more people, gives employees the right to take 12 weeks' leave per 12-month period without pay for specific family and medical purposes. These include the birth or adoption of a child, a personal medical condition, and caring for ill close relatives (Wyld, 1995). However the lodging industry lags behind other industries in the provision of parental leave (Paxson, 1995). Here practices are more open to managerial discretion, but have not affected business effectiveness as being too onerous or costly.

Although WERS took place prior to some important legal changes being implemented (see pp. 105–6), UK workplaces are also not very family-friendly. HI workplaces demonstrate a significantly different approach to employees needing a day off at short notice. Employees are more likely to be required to take unpaid leave than to benefit from paid arrangements (Table 4.4), and there is quite a bit of sub-sectoral variation (Table 4.5).

Although a minority of AIS, PSS and HI workplaces make no arrangements for males to take time off when a child is born, significantly fewer HI workplaces have a written policy giving entitlement to special leave for male employees.

Table 4.4 Time off at short notice in context and by size of workplace (%) hh

	AIS	PSS	HI	<25	25–49	50–99	100+
Make up time later	19	23	20	18	31	13	31
As leave without pay	18	20	48*	51	52	42	18
As sick leave	5	5	5	6	2	4	7
As special paid leave	24	18	6*	8	0	6	8
As annual leave	24	24	12*	7	7	32	32

Source: WERS98.

Notes: All weighted cases. hh Five most frequently mentioned responses. *Significantly different at the 5% level from AIS and the PSS.

Table 4.5 Time off at short notice by sub-sector (%) hh

	Hotels	Campsites	Restaurants	Bars	Canteens
Make up time later	41	4	23	6	29
As leave without pay	22	18	44	74	17
As sick leave	2	0	13	2	2
As special paid leave	9	6	14	0	1
As annual leave	22	72	3	2	50

Source: WERS98.

Notes: All weighted cases. hh Five most frequently mentioned responses.

Table 4.6 Family-friendly work practices in context and by size of workplace (%) hh

	AIS	PSS	HI	<25	25–49	50–99	100+
Parental leave	34	27	20**	24	11	15	18
Working at/from home	13	10	5**	6	1	5	5
Term-only contracts	16	10	19	13	38	25	14
Switch from full-time to part-time	46	43	54	47	62	76	55
Job sharing	26	19	20	18	30	11	30
None of these	38	42	36	41	33	20	33

Source: WERS98.

Notes: All weighted cases. hh Five most frequently mentioned responses to multi-response question. **Significantly different at the 5% level from AIS.

Table 4.7 Family-friendly work practices by sub-sector (%) hh

	Hotels	Campsites	Restaurants	Bars	Canteens
Parental leave	9	6	33	21	9
Working at/from home	2	0	14	0	7
Term-only contracts	17	0	32	17	2
Switch from full-time to part-time	43	18	62	53	71
Job sharing	15	0	21	17	53
None of these	54	72	34	28	23

Source: WERS98.

Notes: All weighted cases. hh Five most frequently mentioned responses.

One or more family-friendly practices can be found in the majority of workplaces, but a comprehensive range of measures is still quite a long way from being widespread in AIS, the PSS and the HI (Table 4.6). The significant differences noted in Table 4.6 are likely to be related to the high proportion of employees without dependent children (see Chapter 8), and because most HI work cannot be carried out at or from home. There is some variation by size of workplace and sub-sector (Table 4.7). Workplace nurseries and financial help towards childcare are almost non-existent in AIS, the PSS and the HI.

Recent UK legal changes

The *Employment Relations Act 1999* simplified and extended maternity rights, and introduced unpaid parental and urgent family need leave, providing a more coherent, potentially fair and effective legal regime (Lewis, 2000):

- All employees are entitled to take *reasonable unpaid time off work* to attend to the needs of a dependant (i.e. spouse, parent, child or person relying on employee). This is limited to 'emergencies', including illness, death and disruption of care arrangements, and does not extend to personal needs, e.g. dentist.

The *Employment Act 2002* introduces an equal pay questionnaire in employment tribunal cases, and makes some important additional improvements to family-friendly policies. The actual periods of leave for the purpose of childcare are extended from April 2003. The period of leave, which is payable at the rate of Statutory Maternity Pay (£100 per week or 90 per cent of weekly earnings if this is less than £100), has also been increased.

The Maternity and Parental Leave Regulations 2002 and the Paternity and Adoption Leave Regulations 2002 contain the following main provisions:

- Women are entitled to take up to 26 weeks' paid ordinary maternity leave (OML) and 26 weeks' unpaid additional maternity leave (AML). There are increased notification periods for a woman's start and early return dates from maternity leave. Maternity leave is not transferable between partners, but this may be changed after the current review of anti-discrimination legislation.
- Men are entitled to 13 weeks' unpaid parental leave and two weeks' paid paternity leave. A father cannot take both paternity leave and adoption leave. Women who are same-sex partners or one of an adopting couple not taking adoption leave are entitled to paternity leave.
- One adoptive parent is entitled to the same periods of paid and unpaid leave that apply to mothers. The person must have 26 weeks' continuous service by the time they are matched with the child for adoptive purposes. The other parent will be entitled to take two weeks' paid leave (equivalent to paternity leave), if so eligible. Both adoptive parents will, in addition, also be entitled to take 13 weeks' unpaid parental leave.

There is no service requirement for OML. In cases of AML and paternity leave the person must be an employee with at least 26 weeks' continuous service by the fifteenth week before the expected week of childbirth (EWCh). Thus working mothers require only 40 weeks' service to benefit from the enhanced maternity arrangements in full. There is reimbursement of maternity, paternity and adoption payments, with a full 100 per cent recoverable by small employers and a further compensation payment on top.

The *Employment Act 2002* also places a duty on employers to give serious consideration to requests from parents of young children to work flexibly, which has been effected by two sets of Flexible Working Regulations 2002. Employees must have

26 weeks' service, not have made such a request in the previous 12 months, and be the parent responsible for child. The child must be under six (or 18 if disabled), and the request must be for the purposes of caring for that child. Flexibility is not just part-time, but could include variation in daily hours or place of work. The employer must convene a meeting within 28 days, at which the employee must address specific details, including how the employer may deal with any effects arising from the proposed change, and may be accompanied by a fellow employee or worker.[15] There are 14 days to reach agreement. Employers can refuse requests on one of eight grounds, including cost, the inability to reorganize or find suitable alternative staff and, where this would have a detrimental effect on customers, quality and performance. There is a right of appeal within 14 days, with a further 28 days for the procedure to be exhausted, after which the employee may complain to a tribunal. Tribunals can award only a statutory maximum of eight weeks' pay, and it is possible that complainants may also allege indirect sex discrimination.

These provisions, which apply to men and women, are likely to be used widely, particularly by returning mothers. Hospitality firms experiencing recruitment and retention difficulties are recommended to adopt a flexible approach towards all employees, as this also helps employees address work–life balance (DTI, 2001a). New mothers may opt for different modes of flexibility (subject to the 12-month rule), seeking different arrangements, such as term-time working, once the child is of school age.

Hardy and Adnett (2002) argue that the Parental Leave Directive (1996), which has driven recent changes, has not led to the creation of an adequate or consistent framework to enable parents to achieve a desirable work–life balance. Low take-up by fathers effectively reinforces gender inequalities in the labour market. Taylor (2001b) argues that the word balance is inappropriate, as it implies a settled equilibrium. Rather, the current issue is about a continual need to reconcile the conflicting pressures of home and workplace for everyone in work, not just working parents. There is also little indication that employers are going beyond the minimum legal requirements for family-friendly work (Taylor, 2002b) and adopting good practice (DTI, 2001b).

Health and safety

The issue of health and safety as a discrete topic rarely features in employment relations or HRM texts. Rather it emerges as an underlying theme in discussions about absence, working time, representation, consultation and involvement.[16] Its low-key status is all the more surprising, because nationally a larger proportion of working days are lost from relatively long spells of absence compared to industrial disputes (James *et al.*, 2002). LFS statistics show that 2.2 million days were lost through sickness in the autumn quarter alone (Barham and Leonard, 2002) compared to 525,000 working days lost through industrial disputes in the whole of 2001 (Davies, 2002).

There are also legal, commercial and ethical reasons why healthy and safe workplaces serve the interests of employers, workers and customers.[17] Such workplaces

---

Case study 4.8 Work intensification for airline cabin crew

The use of computer programming was used to manipulate shift patterns within legal limits. This resulted in extended working hours and combined day and night working in the same week. Short period turnarounds gave very little time for meal and rest breaks. Crew numbers were reduced to the absolute legal minimum. Untrained junior staff were required to stand in for more senior staff. Occupational health was afforded low priority, with only major illness and injury recorded. Crew members frequently complained about faulty equipment and poor air quality.

Source: Boyd (2001).

---

are considered more likely to make a positive contribution to company economic performance, while helping achieve fair treatment, well-being and job satisfaction among employees (Cully *et al.*, 1999). More efforts are being directed at raising awareness of health and safety issues in small firms (HSC, 2001).

Boyd (2001) challenges the assumption that people-centred management automatically leads to first-class health and safety management, using the case of airlines, where standard EU and UK health and safety legislation does not apply. Sanctimonious HRM mission statements belie cost-minimization and productivity maximizing strategies. These have a derogative effect on health and safety standards by creating a worse working environment, more stressful work and more intensive work patterns, as Case study 4.8 illustrates.

Taking a constructive approach to employee welfare is also integral to creating an effective work–life balance. Hence good employers are recommended to offer counselling for stress, work issues, domestic issues, health and disability, and drug and alcohol problems, in addition to assistance with childcare (DTI, 2001a).

Injury and illness

An estimated two million people believe they suffer ill health caused by work, resulting in 18 million days lost and costing society £10 billion per annum (HSC, 2001). Disabled workers tend to be those suffering long-term health problems. Echoing government and TUC calls for more measures on rehabilitation at work, they advocate better job retention and return-to-work measures based on a 'case management' approach.

WERS enables us to make a closer examination of injuries and work-related illness in the HI. Although the mean number of employees injured per workplace is small, HI employees are more likely to sustain injuries than their counterparts in AIS and the PSS, especially in very small workplaces, and in restaurants where food preparation is a major activity (Table 4.8). In terms of areas of significant difference, burns account for most of the HI workplace injuries (56 per cent), while fewer HI workplaces (37 per cent) reported no injuries in the last 12 months. Although the incidence is relatively small, there is an above-average level of injury from physical assault at work in bars. There were 100+ injuries per 1,000 employees in half of HI workplaces compared to one-quarter in AIS and under one-third in the PSS.

Work-related illness is less widespread in the HI, but is well above average in very small workplaces and restaurants (Table 4.9). A skin problem is the condition most likely to have been exacerbated by work in the previous 12 months in the HI (13 per cent of workplaces). Stress is the most frequently mentioned recent work-related condition in one-quarter of AIS workplaces but stress, like limb disorders, is significantly rarer in the HI. In the last 12 months, there was a rate

Table 4.8 Employees injured at work in last 12 months in context and by size of workplace and sub-sector

	AIS	*PSS*	*HI*	*<25*	*25–49*	*50–99*	*100+*
Mean number of injuries per 1,000 employees	98	127	198**	284	117	96	47
Mean number injured	4	4	5	5	4	6	7
			Hotels	*Camp-sites*	*Restaur-ants*	*Bars*	*Canteens*
Mean number of injuries per 1,000 employees			64	42	409	112	335
Mean number injured			4	6	11	2	7

Source: WERS98.

Notes: All weighted cases. **Significantly different at the 5% level from AIS.

Table 4.9 Work-related illness and absence in last 12 months in context and by size of workplace and sub-sector

	AIS	*PSS*	*HI*	*<25*	*25–49*	*50–99*	*100+*
Work-related illness per 1,000 employees	73	66	57	97	28	26	13
Mean number absent	3	2	1**	1	1	2	2
			Hotels	*Camp-sites*	*Restaur-ants*	*Bars*	*Canteens*
Work-related illness per 1,000 employees			22	71	96	78	27
Mean number absent			1	20	2	1	1

Source: WERS98.

Notes: All weighted cases of numbers absent where absence occurred. Figures have been rounded to nearest whole number. **Significantly different at the 5% level from AIS.

of work-related illness of 100+ per 1,000 employees in one-fifth of AIS, PSS and HI workplaces.

Stress

Stress can play a positive role in creating alertness at work, but becomes counter-productive once excessive levels of unresolved physical and psychological discomfort begin to affect the health, safety and well-being of the workforce. Stress has a negative effect on workers' motivation, commitment and performance, as well as being a major contributor to sickness and absence (Earnshaw and Morrison, 2001). Smith (2001) estimates that five million workers – 20 per cent of the British workforce – may experience very high stress levels, and that 91.5 million days are lost every year from stress-related illness.[18] There is little evidence of progressive health and safety policies, with organizations providing only a limited counselling service (Earnshaw and Morrison, 2001).

Within the HI Law *et al.* (1995) attribute the principal causes of stress to management (poor work organization) and managerial behaviour (lack of communications/involvement). Stress also arises from long hours and work intensification, financial insecurity, the lack of opportunity for advancement, pressure to perform well and outside work factors (Faulkner and Patiar, 1997).

Although undue stress is not occupation-specific, it is more likely to affect customer-service workers (see Chapter 2), because they are subject to competing, contradictory and conflicting demands from managers and customers (Hochschild, 1983; Law *et al.*, 1995; Faulkner and Patiar, 1997; Adib and Guerrier, 2001; Buick and Thomas, 2001). Poor service poses a serious threat to performance (Ross, 1995), especially where it leads to lost customers (Sosteric, 1996). There are circumstances when service workers may also find customer relationships rewarding (Marshall, 1986; Smith, 1985b; Lammont and Lucas, 1999). As we noted earlier, workers can develop coping mechanisms where stress is within their personal capacity to manage. Otherwise prolonged job stress can lead to burn-out or breakdown, which is more likely to affect women than men (Buick and Thomas, 2001).

Discussion and review topics

Recruitment and selection

- Why does the HI perpetuate an approach towards recruitment and selection that undermines the 'high road' that many managers claim they seek?
- Can this be excused?
- What implications does this have for workforce diversity and SQ?

Training

- Discuss the allegation that the 'any hands will do' approach has any foundation by way of a summary of the HI's approach to training.
- Can you suggest and justify circumstances where organizations might afford differential treatment to particular occupational groups?
- Assess the importance of VETs and suggest how they can be made more effective.

Facilitating workplace fairness

Advise the manager of a nightclub in Manchester's Gay Village aiming to pursue an integrated policy covering recruitment, selection, training and health and safety designed to overcome sexual harassment, stress and promote AIDS awareness.

Topical health and safety issues

Discuss the issue of managerial responsibility towards workers and customers in relation to:

- the serving and consumption of alcohol;
- smoking;
- violent customers;
- breast-feeding mothers.

5 Pay, reward and performance

Pay and reward systems

This chapter develops some of the issues introduced in Chapter 1 surrounding one of the most important sets of employment rules – pay and pay determination – but in the reverse order because pay is the outcome of the process of pay determination. As Rubery (1995: 640) observes, 'Payment systems are a mechanism or a medium through which the employment relationship is constituted and codified . . . development of a new payment system may be seen as part of a reconstitution of power relations'. In particular we show how pay and reward systems constitute one of the central facets of a managerial cost-control approach, with a strong gender effect.[1]

Pay defines a worker's status and standard of living, and can affect motivation and commitment to work, so low pay may be detrimental on a number of grounds. Pay may be used by employers to signal they are good employers, to attract the best workers, to maximize control, to motivate workers, to improve performance, and as part of a change management programme (Torrington *et al.*, 2002). While some of these objectives are allied to higher pay, we must not assume that employers will apply all, or any, of these principles to every occupational group within the same organization. We have already noted in Chapters 1, 2 and 3 that more beneficial conditions may be applied to a privileged core, while the rest of the workforce is subjected to less favourable and more controlling conditions, including low pay.

The term 'total reward system' has traditionally been used to describe remuneration in the HI (Mars and Mitchell, 1976; Mars *et al.*, 1979). Employees in hotels and restaurants, but not necessarily in other sub-sectors, are assumed to receive all or most of the following variable reward system:

> basic pay + subsidized lodging + subsidized food + tips or service charge + 'fiddles' and 'knock-offs'.

The wider application of this package may well have been overstated in an attempt by employers to justify that employees are not really low-paid. The stark reality is that the HCTS is low-paid, regardless of how pay is measured. Most of the elements of the total reward system can be applied to workers in other sectors, who may benefit from other more favourable monetary and non-monetary benefits. Hence shop workers can 'fiddle' by short-changing customers, while there are a host of occupations where workers can readily pilfer small items from their employer such as pens, sellotape and stationery. Tipping is common practice in hairdressing.

The unpredictable and variable nature of the total reward system says a great deal about the nature of the employment relationship in the HI. In spite of the legal and institutional framework, managers are able to exert strong control through individual contract making, and unilateral management determination of pay (Lucas, 1996a; Gilman *et al.*, 2002; Head and Lucas, 2004a). Informal practices are not the preserve of any particular type of workplace or activity. In fast food stores practices involve the distribution of rewards and favours according to informal systems of individual bargaining, including access to days off and favourable rosters (Allan *et al.*, 2000). An informal deal may bind a worker to a tacit understanding that may later be used as a sanction against her/him. The lack of transparency about reward systems reduces workers' bargaining power by isolating individuals (Rubery, 1995). It is not surprising that the HI sustains high quit rates in these circumstances. Reward is not seen as a component part of culture change (Watson and D'Annunzio-Green, 1996).

Apart from keeping pay low, there are other circumstances and conditions under which managerial control may be intensified. For example, control on wage costs and employee performance is achieved through high reliance on tips, particularly in pubs and bars. Work intensity is maximized by the provision of live-in facilities, enabling staff to be summoned to work at short notice. Tightening up on a 'blind eye' approach to 'fiddles' and pilfering when business slackens and dismissing the miscreants can be used to control employee numbers, e.g. strawberries at the Wimbledon lawn tennis championships (see Chapter 1). On the other hand managerial control has been weakened by the poor economic situation in Russia. The lack of funds to pay employees has led to demands for copious time off (D'Annunzio-Green, 2002).

Pay regulation and determination

Global commitment to a minimum wage and the equalization of pay between men and women provide the central foundation to the regulation of the pay of many HCTS workers. Both principles have been given legal effect in many countries throughout the world. While law-abiding employers will pay at least the minimum rate, and uprate it as required, the issue of narrowing the gender pay gap is far more problematic. We also consider how far collective bargaining has served the interests of employers and workers, although we shall show in Chapter 6 that its application and effects can be patchy and largely ineffectual. Hence the primary actor in pay determination is management.

Minimum wages

By 1980 the ILO's minimum wage Convention had been ratified by 194 countries[2] to the benefit of many hospitality and tourism workers. Large swathes of the British HI were within scope of wages councils system between the mid-1940s and mid-1990s (Lucas, 1986). Abolition of the system in 1993 led to the deterioration in pay in the HI (Radiven and Lucas, 1996, 1997a,b, 2001; Lucas and Radiven, 1998).

Although the objectives of a minimum wage can vary (Lucas, 1989), one purpose is to provide a pay floor (LPC, 1998). However, the level at which the wage is set affects its 'bite'; a wage set very low and sporadically uprated will be largely symbolic. Three-quarters of minimum wage workers in the US work in the HI, and industry leaders are renowned in their fight to hold down the wage (Woods, 1999). Lower-level jobs in the HI in the US are paid at the same level as other industries, ostensibly because of minimum wage laws (Sturman, 2001). In Australia and Singapore one-third and two-thirds of hotel workers respectively are paid above the minimum (Nankervis and Debrah, 1995).

Favourable differential rates may apply to casuals and young workers, reinforcing their importance as integral to cost-minimization. Under the award system in Australia casuals receive a loading (about 20 per cent) above standard rates and a minimum pay guarantee (2–3 hours) in lieu of annual and sick leave, but are not entitled to premium payments for weekends. It is alleged that McDonald's dismiss workers when they reach the age of 20 to avoid paying full adult rates (Allan *et al.*, 2000). Most other studies have found no evidence to support the employment of young workers as a means to evade the minimum wage (Ryan, 1996; Lucas and Langlois, 2000a,b).

The UK National Minimum Wage

The introduction of a NMW in the UK (Case study 5.1) has caused a pay spike at the minimum rate, showing that workers actually benefited from its introduction (LPC, 2000, 2001a,b, 2003).

The arrival of the NMW has not been a discrete event in a stable world. Individual firms do have scope for discretion, and to take random, opportunistic decisions (Lucas and Langlois, 2003). However, there has been a tendency for hospitality firms to take a 'low road' approach (Lucas and Rowson, 2002). Hotels have tended to adopt a cost-minimization strategy rather than pursue a quality enhancement route (Brown and Crossman, 2000).

***Case study 5.1* Introducing the UK National Minimum Wage in hospitality**

The NMW was introduced in April 1999. Two rates were set – a full adult rate of £3.60, and a lower development rate for young workers aged 18–21 and adult trainees in the first six months of a new job. By October 2003 the full rate was £4.50 and the development rate £3.80. Rates of £4.85 and £4.10 have been provisionally accepted to apply from October 2004, subject to the LPC's advice in light of economic circumstances.

The NMW has been introduced successfully, with employers given plenty of warning about forthcoming increases. The HI has been disproportionately affected because it has the highest proportion of low-paid jobs, particularly among females, and employs large proportions of young people, the group most likely to suffer (un)employment effects. Twenty-three per cent of hospitality jobs, 300,000 in total, benefited from a major hike in the NMW of 40p in 2001. Waiting and bar staff are among the occupational groups most affected. The impact on the wage bill of 0.7 per cent is less than at the time the NMW was introduced.

Employment has increased by 200,000 since 1999. Many firms have deployed a wide variety of coping strategies, including increased cost control, adjusting hours, employment restructuring, increasing prices and reducing profits. A pay spike at the level of the full adult rate has developed, with a mezzanine floor some 30–40p higher, reflecting tight labour market conditions in some parts of the country. Small firms have been more affected, because large companies' pay was already at or above the NMW rates.

The youth development rate is below the market rate and most employers pay the full rate at age 18. Most employers are likely to welcome the introduction of a lower rate for 16- and 17-year-olds in 2004, subject to the LPC's recommendations. There has been little take-up of the adult development rate, mainly because firms find it hard to recruit at this rate, recruits already have the skills and it is unfair/divisive.

Sources: LPC (1998, 2001a,b, 2003); Lucas and Radiven (1998); IDS (2001); Lucas and Langlois (2000a,b, 2001, 2003); Rowson (2002); Lucas and Rowson (2002).

In the UK three aspects of the NMW have particular resonance within the HI: tips and gratuities, an accommodation offset and the differential treatment of young workers. Employers may use tips or a service charge collected through the payroll to 'top up' hourly pay to the NMW, whereas cash tips paid to and kept by workers do not count (see p. 130). As there was a limited call to the LPC's suggestion that the rules for treatment of tips and gratuities be reconsidered, this remains unchanged (LPC, 2003).

An accommodation offset of £24.40 per week (£26.25 from October 2004) can be deducted from the NMW to pay for accommodation. Where accommodation is for less than a full week, the offset must be a corresponding reduction, which replaces specified hourly and daily rates (LPC, 2003). Employers can charge more provided the deduction does not bring the hourly rate to below the NMW. The BHA estimates that the average cost of accommodation is £42 per week, and that employers typically charge between £40 and £50 (IDS, 2001). Other sources suggest wider weekly variations of between £20 and £95 (IDS, 2002) and £35 and £65 (LPC, 2003).

While youth pay is generally lower than adult pay (LPC, 2003), many employers have been uneasy about the exclusion of 16- and 17-year-olds from any form of minimum wage protection (Lucas and Langlois, 2000a). Some believe that the absence of regulation will lead to a vulnerable group being exploited by ruthless employers, while others consider exclusion is discriminatory or not justified on grounds of equity. The government's decision to ask the LPC to consider the case for introducing a minimum wage rate for workers of these ages is likely to be uncontroversial. Some 25 per cent of students in employment aged 16 and 17 work in the HI, and a number of major fast food employers, including Burger King, already apply the full NMW rate from age 16 (IDS, 2003).

The government's continued rejection of the LPC's advice to apply the full NMW rate at age 21, rather than 22, remains an anomaly and irrelevance for most firms (Lucas and Langlois, 2000b). Yet there are still pockets in the economy where employers use the lower youth rate, including rural North Wales (Sehkaran and Lucas, 2001). The method of job evaluation, which can be used to determine equal value claims for equal pay (see p. 116), offers one way to establish the reasons for the differences in adult and youth pay and to assess whether differences can be objectively justified. This approach, based on job content and employee attribute analysis, has been used in North Wales (Sehkaran and Lucas, 2003), as Case study 5.2 illustrates.

Case study 5.2 Is lower youth pay objectively justified: small hospitality firms in North Wales?

Employers perceive a positive relationship between age and employee attributes, rating under 18s' attributes consistently lower than the rest of the workforce. Some attributes such as solving problems, making decisions, and interpersonal skills are developed through experience, hence lower pay. In most cases work also involves fewer tasks and responsibilities. The exception is fast food, where workers of all ages receive the same starter rate, as they are subject to the same tasks, responsibilities and working conditions.

Workers aged 18–21 are to an extent disadvantaged on lower pay, because they appear to be performing the same tasks as older workers. Employers appear to place more emphasis on the possession of higher personal attributes by older workers.

Source: Sehkaran and Lucas (2003).

The LPC was placed on a permanent footing in 2001, with a view to monitoring the impact of the NMW and making uprating recommendations. The pattern has been to recommend increases on a two-year basis from October, with the proviso that the second stage increases are reviewed nearer the time. Although the initial NMW rate was set 'prudently' because of the unknown effects, subsequent increases have been above average earnings. These have been of most benefit to workers on lowest decile earnings who are less likely to get incentive or overtime pay. Assuming the 2004 increase is implemented, estimates suggest that the NMW will have increased from 88.7 per cent to 94.5 per cent of half median male earnings in its first five years (LPC, 2003).

Equal pay

The principle of equal pay for equal work regardless of gender is more recent than a minimum wage, emerging from 1951 ILO Convention on Equal Pay. Equal pay was integral to the Treaty of Rome 1957 and has been addressed in subsequent EU Directives. In Britain the *Equal Pay Act 1970* enabled equal pay claims to be made between men and women on the basis of like work or work rated as equivalent under a job evaluation scheme. The Act was amended in 1983 to allow women to claim equal pay for work of equal value, even where no job evaluation scheme was in place. Hence a female canteen worker could claim her job was of equal value to a male painter and decorator. Same sex claims between part-time and full-time workers were not possible until the Part-time Employees (Prevention of Less Favourable Treatment) Regulations were introduced in 2000. However, minimum wage and equal pay legislation have had a limited effect on pay relativities.

In 2003 implementation of a provision of the *Employment Act 2002* introduced an equal pay questionnaire in equal pay cases at employment tribunal, to make it easier for applicants to request key information from the employer when deciding whether to bring a case. Completion is not compulsory but failure to reply may lead to inferences from the tribunal.[3]

Institutional constraints

Men earn more than women, because every labour market in the EU is gender segregated (Almond and Rubery, 1998). Full-timers earn more than part-timers, although the differential is smaller among women than among men. Strong collective bargaining and minimum wage regimes reduce the percentage of low-paid workers, but the benefits of regulation do not extend to women, especially part-timers, as much as to men (Almond and Rubery, 1998; Robson *et al.*, 1999). There is also a strong sectoral effect whether or not national arrangements are in place (Arrowsmith and Sisson, 1999).

'It is extremely unlikely that both differences in systems of wage determination between countries and changes to wage structures would not have consequences for the relative pay of women and men' (Almond and Rubery, 1998: 675). Hence in the US, Canada and UK where pay determination systems are decentralized and fragmented, between 19 and 25 per cent of the full-time female labour force is low-paid compared to 6 per cent in Scandinavia where solidaristic bargaining prevails. That said, women executives in the US have lower starting salaries than their male counterparts, and pay inequality persists where directors are believed to be able to 'get more for less' (Coffey and Anderson, 1998). Whitehouse *et al.* (2001) conclude that the prosecution of pay equity cases has been limited by progressive decentralization in Australia and Britain, although in different ways.

The failure of minimum wage systems to deliver gender equity in the EU arises from strong political pressure not to increase minimum wages as a symbol of wage restraint and to promote a more flexible labour market. Unusually, a stated objective of the UK's NMW was to promote gender equality; over 70 per cent of beneficiaries were women, and around two-thirds of jobs below minimum wage levels were part-time (LPC, 2001b). The gap between male and female hourly pay has narrowed, particularly among part-timers, but still remains at 82 per cent for full-timers and 89 per cent for part-timers.

In Western Europe collective agreements reached at multi-employer (sectoral and economy-wide) have coverage that is greater than union density. This is because even firms with few union members participate in sectoral bargaining and statutory procedures extend the terms of the agreement to all employers in the sector (Robson *et al.*, 1999). Selected examples from EU countries are shown in Case study 5.3. In the US the wages of highly unionized occupations in the hotel, gaming and restaurant industry in Las Vegas are significantly higher than the wages of identical non-union occupations in Reno (Waddoups, 1999).

In the US the *Fair Labor Standards Act 1938* created two classes of employees – those paid for the hire of their labour and those undertaking administrative, professional or executive duties who are paid a salary. The latter are exempted from minimum wage laws. Incorrect classification of employees can be costly (Case study 5.4).

The role of managers in pay determination

The nature of skills (readily available and transferable) and unpredictable demand tend to create a low market rate for jobs (Riley *et al.*, 2000). We identify how British managers are able to exercise considerable discretion over pay within the legal and institutional frameworks outlined above.

Which managers?

Which managers are involved in determining pay will depend on whether workplaces are multi- or single-site; in the WERS sample over three-quarters of HI workplaces are multi-site. In just under half the HI workplaces higher-level managers beyond the workplace and the Board of Directors are directly involved in determining the pay rise, although workplace management is involved in 37 per cent of cases. Where the decision about pay change was made at the establishment (one in eight HI cases), higher-level managers are not consulted in two-thirds of cases. While hotel managers are most likely to be involved, a majority consulted

Case study 5.3 Pay determination in the European hospitality industry

Spain

In 1996 a binding four-year sectoral agreement replaced a labour ordinance (*ordenanza laboral*) which contained a cumbersome pay structure. The new agreement lays down basic conditions regarding grading systems, disciplinary procedures and training, which is monitored by a joint committee (*comision paritaria*) of the signatory partners. Pay is determined by an extensive network of collective agreements. Some 555,083 workers (71 per cent of the total HI workforce) were covered by 104 company and 47 provincial agreements.

Italy

In 1999 four new collective agreements set minimum pay and conditions for three years, including increases to the number of atypical working arrangements, new options for managing working time and measures to improve training. Some 800,000 employees are covered by the agreements, but in some areas half of employment is in the black economy. The right to bargain locally has been recognized since 1993. In practice company bargaining has continued for organizations employing more than 15 employees. There is a new option for smaller companies and companies where it has not been customary to bargain regionally (*territorialmente*). To encourage firms to enter the formal economy special clauses (*clausole di ucscita*) may be negotiated at this level, allowing agreed pay increases to be implemented in an alternative way.

Sweden

Sectoral agreements are combined with local agreements. Employers who are not members of the main employers' organization may be bound by the terms of the sectoral agreement through signing an auxiliary agreement (*hangavtal*). This is common among small companies who are not members of an employers' organization, and for around half of those workplaces with union members who have no company agreement. Although collective agreements set minimum pay, most employees earn above these amounts.

Germany

Collective agreements have the force of law, acting as a minimum wage, and cover 80 to 90 per cent of the German workforce, although trade union membership is low. McDonald's and other fast food establishments broke away from the HI collective agreement by establishing a new employers' federation *Bundersverband der Systemgastronomie* (BdS) and negotiating separately with the *Gewerkschaft Nahrung Genuss Gaststatten* (NGG). The fast food collective agreement on pay and conditions includes pay in lieu, overtime, sick pay and the washing of uniforms. The lack of works councils in stores means there is no guarantee that the agreement will be adhered to.

Netherlands

Employees are covered by a three-part national collective agreement. Part A contains conditions that are binding on the whole sector. Parts B and C give individual establishments the option to negotiate at local level with a works council or other representative body provided the agreement is superior to the sectoral agreement. There is one pay scale covering eleven grades, and 120 job categories have their own job descriptions. A two-year agreement reached in 1998 provided for pay increases in 1998 and 1999, new early retirement provisions in 2000, greater scope for local level negotiations and changes to working time arrangements.

UK

There is no state-sponsored collective bargaining, so most employers are guided by the NMW introduced in 1999. Two of the largest hotel companies, Jarvis and Thistle Hotels, have entered into company collective agreements. The Jarvis agreement includes a probationary hourly rate (first three months) set at the same rate as the NMW, and a minimum rate that is 18p above the NMW, both applicable at age 18. Premiums apply for designated nightwork (63p per hour) and unsocial hours (59p per hour). Higher rates apply in London and within the M25 orbital.

Sources: IDS (1998a,b,c, 1999, 2001); Royle (1999a).

their higher-level colleagues. While pay is largely management-determined in AIS and the PSS, HI workplaces, unsurprisingly, are significantly less likely to involve union representatives in this process.

Pay setting arrangements for different occupational groups differ within AIS, the PSS and the HI, and by size of workplace and sub-sector. The most common method is shown in Tables 5.1 and 5.2. One must be careful about drawing too many inferences from these because the limited presence of some occupational groups means that numbers of cases can be very small (Tables A.14 and A.15). Even so, higher management clearly takes a leading role in setting pay in the HI, suggesting strong emphasis is placed on organizational cost control.

How often is pay reviewed?

Although two-thirds of HI workplaces in WERS have an annual pay review, workers in the LOG in these workplaces are significantly less likely to benefit from an annual pay review than their counterparts in AIS and the PSS where nine in

Table 5.1 Pay-setting arrangements for different occupational groups in context and by size of workplace (%)

	AIS	PSS	HI	<25	25–49	50–99	100+
Managers/administrative	HM (43)	HM (50)	HM (60)**	HM (57)	HM (71)	HM (60)	HM (50)
Professional	WM (27)	WM (39)	WM (30)	IN/SOW (45)	WM (46)	WM (55)	HM/WM (48)
Technical/scientific	WM (36)	WM (38)	HM (51)	OCB/HM (50)	HM (100)	HM/WM (50)	WM (58)
Clerical and secretarial	WM (34)	WM (42)	WM (36)	SOW (41)	HM (68)	WM (61)	WM (49)
Craft and skilled manual	WM (37)	WM (37)	HM (38)	IN (59)	HM (72)	WM (65)	WM (56)
Personal service	HM (32)	HM/WM (39)	HM (37)	HM (30)	HM (67)	WM (58)	WM (47)
Sales	HM (45)	HM (50)	HM (61)	HM (65)	HM (66)	HM (50)	WM (56)
Operative and assembly manuals	WM (41)	WM (42)	HM (83)*	HM (100)	HM (100)	HM (34)	HM/WM (50)
Routine unskilled manual	WM (33)	WM (42)	HM (38)	HM (33)	HM (55)	WM (60)	WM (50)

Source: WERS98.

Notes: All establishments where any employees in occupational category (Tables A.13 and A.14). The most common method used where any employees in particular occupational groups. HM = higher management, WM = workplace management, CB = collective bargaining with more than one employer, OCB = collective bargaining at organizational level, WCB = workplace collective bargaining, IN = negotiation with individual employees, SOW = some other way. In cases where two arrangements rank first equal, both are shown. *Significantly different at the 5% level from AIS and PSS. **Significantly different at the 5% level from AIS.

Table 5.2 Pay-setting arrangements for different occupational groups by sub-sector (%)

	Hotels	Campsites	Restaurants	Bars	Canteens
Managers/administrative	HM (55)	OCB (72)	HM (57)	HM (75)	CB (45)
Professional	WM (69)	HM (100)	SOW (93)	IN (70)	IN (75)
Technical/scientific	HM (51)	OCB (95)	WM (100)	HM (100)	–
Clerical and secretarial	WM (53)	OCB (72)	SOW (44)	SOW (61)	CB (55)
Craft and skilled manual	WM (52)	OCB (78)	HM (56)	HM (54)	WCB (40)
Personal service	IN (42)	HM (78)	SOW (39)	HM (85)	CB (78)
Sales	WM (63)	HM (100)	WM (51)	HM (80)	CB (71)
Operative and assembly manuals	HM (60)	HM (100)	HM (85)	HM (100)	WM (100)
Routine unskilled manual	WM (50)	WM (72)	HM (43)	HM (52)	CB (65)

Source: WERS98.

Notes: All establishments where any employees in occupational category (Tables A.13 and A.14). The most common method used where any employees in particular occupational groups. HM = higher management, WM = workplace management, OCB = collective bargaining with more than one employer, CB = collective bargaining at organizational level, WCB = workplace collective bargaining, IN = negotiation with individual employees, SOW = some other way. In cases where two arrangements rank first equal, both are shown.

Case study 5.4 The cost of misclassifying restaurant managers under the *Fair Labor Standards Act*

Employee misclassification cost Waffle House more than $3,000,000. Restaurant managers working an average of 89 hours per week were classified as exempt executives. Factors that counted against the company were:

- Unit managers served as grill cooks on the busiest shift.
- The primary training objective was to become a proficient grill operator, with exposure to management duties and responsibilities coming second.
- Managers often substituted for other employees.
- Other employees regularly stood in for absent managers.

Under the *Fair Labor Standards Act* the managers were entitled to be paid overtime for all hours worked in excess of 40 per week.

Source: Pollack (2001).

---

ten workplaces operate an annual review. However, workers in the LOG in one-fifth of HI workplaces are significantly more likely to benefit from more frequent pay reviews. Pay is reviewed less than once a year in 10 per cent of HI workplaces, especially in restaurants (over one-quarter). One in 12 HI workplaces had not actually changed pay at the last review. Workers were most likely to have received an increase of between 3 and 4 per cent, although settlements in hotels were more typically at 4 per cent and above. The HI had slightly more cases of the lowest and highest increases at the last pay review.

In the interim six-year period between the abolition of wages councils and the introduction of the NMW, the lack of a reference point for reviewing pay created pay inertia among small HI firms, widening the pay gap between them and larger companies (Lucas and Radiven, 1998). Some two years after abolition pay had stayed the same or decreased in nearly one-third of the companies surveyed. In the absence of the review date specified in the wages order, almost half the firms had no fixed review date. Personnel directors stressed that the single major change since abolition was a new flexibility in their company's approach to pay-setting, largely in relation to skills pay, thus widening pay differentials above the minimum rate (Radiven and Lucas, 1997a). As there was nothing to prevent the paying of higher rates under the wages councils, this may be a reflection of a relative decline in pay for those on minimum rates. The main determinants of pay reviews were the local labour market and competitors' pay rates, followed by company economic performance and cost of living/inflation. Wages councils clearly had a significant impact upon pay determination procedures, pay levels and pay structures in the HI.

Even in the two-year period leading up to the introduction of the NMW, many HI firms did not adjust pay in advance, waiting until 1 April 1999 when it became a legal necessity (Lucas and Langlois, 2000a). In the early stages of the NMW only 50 per cent of small HI firms increased pay annually. Pay increases were highly variable and unstructured (Gilman *et al.*, 2002). Nevertheless, the NMW, as noted above, has been an important influence on HI workers' pay in conjunction with tight labour market conditions. Many firms across the HI, particularly pubs and restaurants, have moved their anniversary dates to October and now review pay to coincide with increases in the NMW (IDS, 2001, 2002, 2003).

The major hotel companies have more highly variable review dates. Adverse business conditions in the hotel sector following the foot-and-mouth epidemic and the slump in international tourism and business travel post-11 September caused a number of the major companies to cancel or delay their pay review. Others froze recruitment, allowing turnover and natural wastage to reduce staff numbers. However, skill shortages in a tight labour market created recruitment and reten-tion problems in key jobs, with pay rises for those affected. However, in many of the large chains, including De Vere, Hilton International, Jarvis Hotels, Thistle Hotels and Whitbread (Marriott) starter rates were at or very close to the NMW rate of £4.10. The median pay of waiting and bar staff, room attendants and commis chefs was 30–40p an hour above the NMW (IDS, 2002).

How is pay structured?

Much of the HI is characterized by the absence of grading schemes, and a lack of well-defined differentials between jobs (Lucas and Radiven, 1998; Lucas and Langlois, 2000a,b). This, coupled with the lack of job evaluation, is likely to exacerbate pay discrimination (Dickens, 1998). Loosely defined and variable pay structures can be explained in terms of the interplay between labour and product markets, firms' own choices and shocks such as the NMW (Gilman *et al.*, 2002). Managers may structure pay to maximize cost savings by limiting hours and ensuring that employees earn below the threshold for National Insurance Contributions (NICs) (Case study 5.6). An overspend on wages can be compen-sated by reducing the hours of part-time workers on variable hours contracts and the numbers of casual workers on a daily or weekly basis (Lucas and Langlois, 2000b).

The majority of the major hotel companies have pay progression scales for different departments or employee groups, almost all of which are subject to performance (IDS, 2001). Individual performance reviews are also common in fast food, noted below (p. 133) (IDS, 2003). Up until 2001 employers were able to increase pay for the lowest paid without any repercussions for those further up the scale. The 40p hike in the NMW in 2001 led to a narrowing of differentials within hotels' pay structures, necessitating increases for junior supervisory staff (IDS, 2002). The 2001 increase also caused McDonald's to shift from paying adult rates at 16, and to reintroduce age-related pay, with different rates for restaurant crew below 18, aged 18–21 and 22 years and over (IDS, 2003). While national chains set national rates, a number also have differential location-based pay for the provinces, and London and the South-east, in addition to other tight labour markets such as out-of-town retail parks (IDS, 2002, 2003).

Case study 5.5 **Pay structures and the UK National Minimum Wage**

The new NMW wage structure did not match the practice of most firms. Firms' initial response was to 'pick and mix' or do the minimum required, which meant increasing some adult workers' pay while leaving others' pay at the same level. Even though young workers were already being paid more than the development rate, their pay was also increased at the same time adult workers' pay was adjusted to comply with the NMW.

Notional adult minima might apply at age 18 or age 21, but managers exercised considerable discretion to give accelerated progression, so there was no strict wage-for-age policy. There was informality and flexibility about how managers determined individuals' pay as they saw fit. Many could not adequately explain the basis of their pay structures and how employees progressed to higher pay.

Most young workers aged 18–21 and many exempt 16- and 17-year-olds were paid more than the development rate.

Differentials were generally maintained because there was still a sizeable gap of £2.00 per hour or more between most workers and the higher paid. In one case the hourly differential between three supervisors had reduced from 50p to 25p. The manager was prepared to restore the differential if asked to do so because it would not be costly.

Source: Lucas and Langlois (2000b, 2001).

In small independent firms largely informal pay determination provides considerable scope for discretion within a framework of either individual employer–employee bargaining or unilateral management determination (Gilman *et al.*, 2002), in spite of the NMW (Case study 5.5). In a low-paying region (North Wales) nearly one-third of small employers were making use of the development rate (Sehkaran and Lucas, 2001). As noted earlier, they justified lower pay for young workers who were less experienced, had lower skills and were less productive, but age in itself was not a determinant of pay.

The components of remuneration

Understanding low pay

Although relatively few countries provide comparable earnings data, as a general rule hotel and restaurant workers across the world earn less than workers in socially comparable positions, and the differential tends to be higher in developing countries and for occupations requiring more skills and responsibilities (ILO, 2001: 132–3).[4]

Working conditions in the EU (1996) include potentially problematic areas such as irregular working hours, frequent Sunday work, wages without a fixed element in 25 per cent of cases and widespread absence of overtime premiums; wage levels are generally 20 per cent below the EU average. Similar problems are observed in North America. Even where overtime premiums exist, they may rarely be paid (Royle, 1999a). We should note major problems with comparative statistics. Tips are not always declared for tax and will not be shown, and differences in the skill and training content of occupations in sub-sectors, such as waiting staff, mean that comparisons may not be made on a like-for-like basis. Weekly earnings show a bigger gap than hourly earnings because men work more overtime (Doherty and Stead, 1998).

Women's consistently low pay can be explained by three main sets of factors: occupational segregation by gender, methods of pay determination and the concentration of low pay in certain industries (Doherty and Stead, 1998), which makes it especially trenchant in the HI. Broadbridge (1997) provides support for arguments made in Chapters 2 and 6, showing that nature of skill and trade union activities have been constructed against women. Rubery (1995) warns that trends towards performance-related pay (PRP) pose a potential threat to pay equality as discretion in pay determination increases and there is no clear relationship between earnings and job grade. She also suggests that devolving HRM to line managers who are less aware of gender issues will also impact negatively on pay equality.

The size of the pay difference varies across countries, and there are exceptions. Tourism in North Korea is a low-wage sector but is more advantageous to women in terms of earnings inequality and level of earnings (Lee and Kang, 1998). While women have lower pay expectations at career entry and career peak than men, organizational issues such as a 'glass ceiling' blocking entry into higher paying positions are indicative of discrimination (Sparrowe and Iverson, 1999; Iverson, 2000a). By placing more emphasis on relationships in the workplace than on status women rule out jobs which might bring higher rewards.

The position in Britain may be even more polarized. A survey of the major hotel companies (2000), which might be expected to be 'market leaders', did find that pay was well ahead of the NMW (IDS, 2001). Only a minority pay premium rates for night or weekend work, and only two-fifths pay overtime at premium rates (IDS, 2002). New Earnings Survey (NES) data for the hotel sub-sector consistently show adult full-time earnings at two-thirds of average earnings for the whole economy, with overtime pay, shift pay and bonus payments comprising a very small part of total earnings compared to the rest of the economy (IDS, 2001, 2002). The same is also true for the HI as a whole (Tables 5.3, 5.4[5] and 5.5).

The lowest-paid HI workers (lowest decile) rarely receive overtime or incentives (LPC, 2001a). Low pay is linked to a wide range of factors, many of which are specific to the establishment and its competitive strategy (see Case study 5.6). The incidence of low pay is high in single establishments and low in small establishments that are part of a larger organization (McNabb and Whitfield, 2000). Basic pay is 100 per cent of total earnings in two-thirds of small HI firms (Gilman *et al.*, 2002).

In 2002 the median pay of waiting and bar staff, luggage porters, room and leisure centre attendants and commis chefs was between £4.41 and £4.50. By contrast head chefs and sous chefs enjoyed relatively good pay, with median rates in South-east England exceeding £11 per hour (IDS, 2002).

Table 5.3 Patterns of pay for all employees on adult rates (2002)

	Average gross annual pay (£)	Average gross weekly pay (£)	Increase April 2001/2 (%)	Average hourly pay (excl. O/T) (£)	Average total weekly (hours)	Average weekly overtime (hours)
Full-time						
AIS	24,603	465	4.6	11.73	39.6	1.8
HI	15,762	299	3.7	7.28	40.9	1.2
Part-time						
AIS	7,903	148	6.0	8.09	19.6	1.0
HI	5,080	93	13.3	6.11	17.9	0.6

Source: NES (2002); ONS (2002).

Table 5.4 Patterns of pay for male employees on adult rates (2002)

	Average gross annual pay (£)	Average gross weekly pay (£)	Increase April 2001/2 (%)	Average hourly pay (excl. O/T) (£)	Average total weekly (hours)	Average weekly overtime (hours)
Full-time						
AIS	27,437	514	4.8	12.59	40.9	2.4
HI	18,051	331	2.2	7.87	41.9	1.3
Part-time						
AIS	9,485	165	7.7	10.08	19.2	1.5
HI	–*	100	17.1	7.56	17.8	0.5

Source: NES (2002); ONS (2002).
Note: *See note 5, this chapter.

Table 5.5 Patterns of pay for female employees on adult rates (2002)

	Average gross annual pay (£)	Average gross weekly pay (£)	Increase April 2001/2 (%)	Average hourly pay (excl. O/T) (£)	Average total weekly (hours)	Average weekly overtime (hours)
Full-time						
AIS	19,811	383	4.5	10.22	37.5	0.7
HI	12,984	257	4.7	6.48	39.6	1.0
Part-time						
AIS	7,593	144	5.8	7.72	19.7	1.0
HI	4,822	89	10.5	5.57	17.9	0.7

Source: NES (2002); ONS (2002).

Table 5.6 Full-time annual male earnings in context and by size of workplace (%)

	AIS	PSS	HI	<25	25–49	50–99	100+
<£9,000	7	11	47*	34	42	56	47
£9,000 to <£12,000	15	18	23	26	31	17	23
£12,000 to <£16,000	24	24	12*	9	16	12	13
£16,000 to <£22,000	28	19	9*	12	5	8	9
£22,000 to <£29,000	15	12	5*	12	4	4	4
>£29,000	12	16	4*	7	3	3	5

Source: WERS98.

Notes: Aggregate percentage of all weighted cases. *Significantly different at the 5% level from AIS and PSS.

Table 5.7 Full-time annual female earnings in context and by size of workplace (%)

	AIS	PSS	HI	<25	25–49	50–99	100+
<£9,000	18	24	57*	57	58	62	50
£9,000 to <£12,000	25	25	19	14	18	19	24
£12,000 to <£16,000	23	21	13**	13	12	12	14
£16,000 to <£22,000	20	16	8**	14	6	5	7
£22,000 to <£29,000	10	8	2*	3	2	1	2
>£29,000	4	5	1*	1	2	0	2

Source: WERS98.

Notes: Aggregate percentage of all weighted cases. *Significantly different at the 5% level from AIS and PSS. **Significantly different at the 5% level from AIS.

Table 5.8 Full-time annual male earnings by sub-sector (%)

	Hotels	Campsites	Restaurants	Bars	Canteens
<£9,000	48	69	50	37	34
£9,000 to <£12,000	20	10	28	32	26
£12,000 to <£16,000	14	6	7	17	4
£16,000 to <£22,000	9	7	10	10	3
£22,000 to <£29,000	6	1	1	4	15
>£29,000	4	1	4	1	18

Source: WERS98.

Notes: Aggregate percentage of all weighted cases.

Table 5.9 Full-time annual female earnings by sub-sector (%)

	Hotels	Campsites	Restaurants	Bars	Canteens
<£9,000	54	76	54	51	64
£9,000 to <£12,000	21	7	20	27	12
£12,000 to <£16,000	14	6	10	17	10
£16,000 to <£22,000	8	11	12	0	10
£22,000 to <£29,000	1	0	2	2	4
>£29,000	1	0	2	2	2

Source: WERS98.

Notes: Aggregate percentage of all weighted cases.

Table 5.10 Employees earning less than £3.50 per hour in context, by size of workplace and sub-sector (%)

	AIS	PSS	HI	<25	25–49	50–99	100+
None	67	57	40*	47	19	34	40
50%+	8	12	33*	34	49	15	8
			Hotels	Camp-sites	Restaur-ants	Bars	Canteens
None			41	4	35	35	80
50%+			18	0	31	48	12

Source: WERS98.

Notes: All weighted cases. *Significantly different at the 5% level from AIS and PSS.

WERS data indicate a similar disparity across all sub-sectors (Tables 5.6, 5.7 and 5.8). Differences in the actual pay levels of full-time employees differ between the AIS, the PSS and the HI, between men and women. The main reason (from a multi-response question) for significant differences in pay levels is hours worked in over two-thirds of HI workplaces. Job grade/classification (59 per cent) and skills/core competences (47 per cent) are of second- and third-order importance. In AIS and the PSS the two most important factors are job grade/classification and hours worked, with overtime and skills/core competences being the second and third most important factors respectively. Tables 5.6, 5.7, 5.8 and 5.9 also indicate that earnings patterns by size of workplace and sub-sector are not clear-cut. The reasons given for these differences are also similarly diverse. In terms of low pay HI workplaces are significantly more likely to have workers earning less than £3.50 per hour and to have half or more workers that are low-paid (Table 5.10).

Tips

Tipping is culturally specific (Casey, 2001) and more prevalent in countries characterized by strong needs for achievement and power, where intolerance of uncertainty, anxiety and neuroticism are greater, and where citizens place greater value on status and prestige (Lynn, 1997, 2000). In Egypt, the US and Argentina, where people are extroverted and status-seeking, it is customary to tip many service workers. Very few service workers receive tips in Japan, Iceland and Scandinavia, where there is greater emphasis on social than on economic relations (see Case study 5.7).

While one view of tipping is that it is the most efficient way of monitoring and rewarding the efforts of service workers, and may motivate workers to perform well (McCarty et al., 1990), workers set a price for service that is personalized and difficult for managers to monitor (Shamir, 1984). The relationship between tipping and service quality is weak, even though managers and employees perceive such a relationship (McCarty et al., 1990; Lynn, 2001; Bodvarsson and Gibson, 2002). A range of behavioural variables are thought to affect tips, including good appear-

Case study 5.6 Pay, income tax and National Insurance Contributions

Low pay serves the immediate mutual interests of employer and employee as an avoidance strategy for employment taxes, but this may have other longer-term and more damaging consequences. Avoidance maximizes employees' net pay and minimizes employers' labour costs, but employees are not eligible for a range of benefits, including pensions.

In Britain the threshold at which NICs became payable increased to the same level as the income tax threshold in 2000, a year after the NMW was introduced. This combined threshold was £84 per week when the NMW stood at £3.60 per hour. Thus a worker paid the NMW would only become liable for both deductions after working 23 hours, with the employer being subject to NICs only.

Two contrasting effects have been observed.

In 1999 when the NMW and the NIC threshold was still below the income tax threshold, some low-paying employers realigned the hours of their part-timers to keep their pay below the NIC threshold. One small firm had to increase the number of employees to cover the same workload over the same hours at mutual cost benefit. This was not 'real' job creation.

In 2000 the changes increased the wage:hour ratio of 'exempt' employees thus providing employers with an incentive to increase their part-time work-force on longer hours.

Sources: Purcell *et al.* (1999); Lucas and Langlois (2000b).

---

ance, being on first name terms, particular dress codes and touching and smiling. Uncertainty of pay may be detrimental to job satisfaction and commitment, and even lead to dysfunctional behaviour, e.g. cheating and pilfering (Casey, 2001). For customers tipping functions in part as a status display (Shamir, 1984; Lynn, 1997), to gain social approval or to compensate poorly paid workers (Holloway, 1985).

The extent to which tips increase gross pay or total reward is highly variable (see Case study 5.7), and appears to be higher where the employee has more control, i.e. takes tips individually. Purcell *et al.* (1999) found that workers in pubs and bars could enhance their hourly pay by up to £2.00 per hour in larger establishments and by up to £1.00 per hour in smaller establishments. Restaurant workers could only achieve up to £1.00 per hour, but only for evening work in busy city centre establishments, and also received very few fringe benefits. In hotels where an employee sharing system or employer distribution of tips is the norm, tips amount to less, but other terms and conditions are generally better. Case study 5.8 illustrates how tips distributed from a tronc relate to status, and may give greatest benefit to those staff with no direct customer interface who are already paid higher rates.

Case study 5.7 **Tips in practice across the world**

US

Tipping is almost universal. Waiting staff depend on tips for a living wage, where a set percentage of the bill is automatically expected. Tips can exceed basic pay, and credit card tips often get pooled among staff. Hotel bellmen could double the amount of tips by providing a full service, rather than a limited service.

Spain

Tipping is very common but amounts to no more than a few coins, and credit card tips are almost unheard of.

UK

Staff keep cash tips, either individually or on a pooled basis, and do not pay tax on them, unless they are declared. Staff working in pubs, bars and restaurants are more likely to benefit from tips than hotel staff. Staff are not entitled to receive tips or a service charge that are added to a credit card in addition to the NMW, although employers can use these payments to top up pay to the level of the NMW. This situation was finally confirmed by a ruling of the European Court of Human Rights in 2002. Where tips are paid into a tronc, the tronc master shares them among employees who are taxed on them.

Italy

Restaurants may add 10–15 per cent to meals but customers are normally expected to add 10 per cent. Credit card tips are passed on to waiting staff.

New Zealand

Tipping is not widespread in restaurants. Managers consider that tips are a private transaction between server and customer and are not taken into account when setting pay.

Australia

Tipping usually applies only in high-class restaurants. Credit card tips are usually divided among staff.

Sources: Purcell *et al.*, (1999); Lynn (1997, 2000); Casey (2001); Lynn and Gregor (2001); Wilson (2002); LPC (2003).

Case study 5.8 The tronc and hierarchical pay in designer restaurants

Each employee is awarded a number of points according to their position. Departments are allocated a set percentage of the tronc, which is divided by the total number of points based on total employees per shift. Chefs view the tronc as a bonus to their salary, whereas it is a supplement to low basic wages for waiting staff.

Source: Kelliher and Perrett (2001).

In City Centre Restaurants, which operates chains such as Caffe Uno and Garfunkels, it is claimed that waiting staff in London make so much in tips they could work without being paid a basic wage. Basic rates, set low, are topped up to the NMW with centrally collected tips. Pizza Express introduced a similar system when the NMW was introduced, but soon abandoned it amid adverse publicity. The company now encourages individual staff to keep their own tips, believing it is morally wrong to use tips or a service charge to subsidize wages (IDS, 2003).

Incentive- and performance-related pay

On a global basis variable pay linked to performance is not yet common, but is emerging in countries such as the US, the UK and Australia, particularly among large hotel groups (ILO, 2001: Millett, 2002). Incentive pay falls broadly into two categories: PRP and payment by results (PBR). The former normally measures performance against previously determined criteria expressed as targets or objectives and has particular resonance with both a customer service-focused ethos and an HR philosophy designed to generate motivated and committed employees. A payment system that rewards employees for attaining quality goals is more likely to result in improved SQ (Redman and Mathews, 1998). By comparison PBR schemes, which measure fixed outputs, may be more appropriate to the factory production line. However, it is also important not to lose sight of fact that employee control also underpins both PRP and PBR, with PRP reflecting a tightening of the way in which individual performance is regulated (Rubery, 1995; Beynon *et al.*, 2002). Hence increased performance may be required for the same or less pay where schemes replace non-performance based systems or provide for a derisory performance-related element.

Another set of circumstances driving incentive pay centres upon improving recruitment and retention, and reducing high turnover (IDS, 2002, 2003). Dermody (2002) reports how US restaurants use incentive programmes to retain employees. Schemes are most often tied to business volume and generally offer servers incentives to sell more items. Independent restaurants use creative incentive practices, such as unique gifts and team incentives more frequently than chain restaurants, which apply daily contests with a cash increase tied to individual performance. Few front office or back-of-house staff benefit from such schemes.

Other schemes as part of performance management may be more selective, targeting managers, e.g. Wolverhampton and Dudley, which runs family-friendly pubs, or key workers, e.g. TGI Fridays, Pret à Manger, KFC, Select Service Partner and Welcome Break, which have all succeeded in reducing turnover markedly (IDS, 2003). Competency-based pay linked to the completion of training modules is also widely used (see Case study 5.9). McDonald's employees can gain an extra 15p increase per hour every four months if they achieve 93.5 per cent performance. In practice only a small minority benefit because performance review sheets are not completed on time or even at all (Royle 1999a).

Profit-related and sales-related schemes are the most common basis for incentive pay among major hotel companies, 70 per cent of which operate some form of bonus scheme (IDS, 2002). The criterion of good customer service is less common, with a few instances of chefs being rewarded according to gross profit on food or by minimizing food costs. Profit sharing and share ownership may be segregated by gender as more benefits accrue to full-time workers who are more likely to be male (Dickens, 1998). The criteria for PRP for Flightpath Telephone Sales staff were based on hard skills (e.g. individual sales targets) and soft skills (e.g. handling calls). Supervisors could listen to and tape employees' performance, hence employees' ability to 'deep act' directly shaped their pay (Taylor and Tyler, 2000).

From WERS variable pay schemes, including dividend-based schemes, are slightly more common in the HI and the PSS (just over 60 per cent) than in AIS (53 per cent). Above average proportions of large workplaces and bars have such schemes. In all groupings profit-related payments or bonuses are the most common type of variable pay. While just over half of HI workplaces have profit-related payments or bonuses and deferred profit-sharing schemes, the proportion rises to over three-quarters in large workplaces and bars. Conversely most restaurant workers do not benefit from these schemes. Employee share ownership schemes are also more common in the HI than in AIS and the PSS. Individual or group performance-related schemes are less likely to be found in the HI than in AIS and the PSS.

PRP on its own is not widespread, as it applies in only one in nine HI workplaces, affecting managers and administrative staff in three-quarters of these workplaces. The pattern of usage among other occupational groups is different from in AIS and the PSS. In the HI professional staff and manual workers (craft, skilled and unskilled) are more likely to benefit from such schemes than their equivalents in AIS and the PSS. Conversely clerical and secretarial and sales staff in AIS and the PSS are more likely to have PRP than their counterparts in the HI. Some of these variations are likely to arise because of the different occupational characteristics of each group. The application of PRP to occupational groups also varies by size of workplace and sub-sector because of their different occupational make-up (Tables A.14 and A.15).

Where PRP applies to non-managerial employees in the HI (N = 15) a greater proportion of them are included in the scheme than in AIS and the PSS. Where PRP has been paid to non-managerial employees in the last 12 months, all have been included in the scheme in just over half of these HI workplaces. Individual

***Case study 5.9* Contemporary incentive, performance and competency-based pay in Britain**

The Marriott Hanbury Hall Hotel has profit share for managers and team leaders. Waiting staff can earn extra pay for selling additional coffees and desserts. A variety of non-cash recognition awards are available to reward very good performance.

Accor Hotels provides in-house skill-based programmes that link pay increases to the achievement of new skills.

McDonald's moved to a single performance review for merit-based pay in 2002. Staff are assessed between July and September, with the corresponding increase awarded at the end of September. Individual performance pay ranged from 0 per cent (needs improvement) to 6 per cent (excellent). Most received 3 per cent (satisfactory), and others 4.5 per cent (good).

Select Service Partner (UK Rail Division) introduced a new pay structure in 2002 based on completion of relevant training modules. Each stage takes around three months, and the company has applied for recognition under the NVQ scheme.

Pub retailers commonly link pay progression to training. The BII estimates one in four pub workers is studying for an NVQ/SVQ.

Pizza Express pays a discretionary bonus to back-of-house staff who are not in a position to earn tips, linked to the profitability of the restaurant.

Pret à Manger pays a weekly bonus worth 75p per hour on top of basic rates for every hour worked. Mystery shoppers visit all shops and award points for efficiency, quality and speed of service. The shop has to score 90 per cent or over to qualify. A card for outstanding service worth £50 in cash can also be awarded.

A contract catering company paid £100 to a supervisor whose idea of filling confectionery machines with home-made or branded cookies increased gross profit from 18 per cent to 40 per cent. Staff could also earn £100 for leads to new business, plus a further £250 if the contract was successful. One-quarter of new business came from such suggestions.

Sources: Rowley and Purcell (2001); IDS (2001, 2003).

performance/output is significantly less likely to be used as the basis for PRP in the HI, where schemes are most likely to be group- or team-based. Individual performance/output is usually measured or assessed by a supervisor, whereas other measures of output are more likely to be used in AIS and the PSS.

Other terms and conditions of employment

Although details of global practices are rarely reported, workers within the EU are entitled to four weeks' paid holiday, while pensions are highly variable among

Table 5.11 Non-pay terms and conditions in context and by size of workplace (%)

	AIS	PSS	HI	<25	25–49	50–99	100+
Employer pension scheme	65	55	36*	43	20	30	34
Company car/allowance	15	15	0*	0	0	1	5
Private health insurance	15	20	9***	3	19	17	18
4 weeks+ paid leave (excl. public holidays)	83	78	67**	71	53	69	72
Sick pay in excess of statutory requirements	64	61	43*	43	36	51	48
None of these	11	14	30*	29	43	18	26

Source: WERS98.

Notes: All weighted cases. *Significantly different at the 5% level from AIS and the PSS. **Significantly different at the 5% level from AIS. ***Significantly different at the 5% level from PSS.

Table 5.12 Non-pay terms and conditions by sub-sector (%)

	Hotels	Campsites	Restaurants	Bars	Canteens
Employer pension scheme	35	78	37	27	81
Company car/allowance	2	0	0	0	0
Private health insurance	19	0	10	0	19
4 weeks+ paid leave (excl. public holidays)	84	78	70	50	93
Sick pay in excess of statutory requirements	49	78	40	32	89
None of these	12	22	27	48	7

Source: WERS98.

Note: All weighted cases.

member states. In Spain employees retiring at 65 usually receive three months' salary (subject to a minimum of 15 years' service). Provincial and company agreements also provide incentives to retire early for longer-serving employees, e.g. an extra eight months' pay at 60. Evidence suggests that some hospitality businesses, mainly small firms, had to increase workers' basic holiday entitlement and introduce holiday pay to meet the requirements of the WTR (Lucas and Langlois, 2000a). Some of the larger hotel companies now give between 21 and 30 days per annum related to service (IDS, 2002). Meals, drinks and uniforms, which may be free or subject to a small charge, and discounts are among the most commonly provided fringe benefits (Lucas and Langlois, 2000a, 2001; IDS, 2002).

The most frequently given non-pay terms and conditions from WERS are shown in Tables 5.11 and 5.12. These indicate just how badly HI employers fare compared to counterparts in AIS and the PSS, especially in bars.

Performance appraisal

Performance appraisal, one facet of performance management (Millett, 2002), has a number of different purposes beyond providing the basis for reviewing pay.

Case study 5.10 **Performance appraisal in US hotels**

Performance appraisal is conducted annually for all staff. Most managers use more than one type of appraisal, and appraisals have more than one purpose. Half the managers use a management-by-objectives approach. However not all managers use follow-up sessions to feedback the results. The most frequent application of performance appraisals is for compensation decisions, followed by assessing whether objectives have been met, establishing training needs and determining promotions. A majority considered that appraisals were important to their business.

Source: Woods *et al.* (1998).

Annual or six-monthly appraisal in Australia and Singapore forms part of employee development, with management by objectives being almost universal (Cheng and Brown, 1998). While systems distinguish between managerial and operative staff in both countries, appraisal is more commonly used to determine pay in Singapore than in Australia where award rates of payment, rather than individual contracts, govern pay rates. Managers have more scope to vary pay in Singapore because of workplace collective agreements. US experience is shown in Case study 5.10.

Within Britain appraisals are regarded as an essential business tool by HR managers to improve company and individual performance (Anon., 2003b). Performance appraisal goals focusing on quality goals, behaviour critical to achieving those goals and use of customer-driven data are more compatible with improving SQ (Redman and Mathews, 1998).

The identification of training and development needs and evaluating individual performance are the main reasons performance appraisals are used in the private sector in Britain, with most large organizations appraising all employees (Anon., 2003b). From WERS the four main purposes of appraisal in the HI, which also apply in AIS and the PSS, are to give feedback on an employee's performance, to set/evaluate training and development needs, to give employees a chance to discuss future career moves, and to review and set objectives. Performance appraisal is more likely to be used to determine a pay increase in the HI (half the sub-sample) than in AIS and the PSS. However, performance appraisal is not directly linked to reviews or changes in individual employees' pay in almost all of those cases, the exceptions being found only in large workplaces.

WERS shows that in Britain managers and administrative staff in the HI are significantly more likely to be appraised formally than their counterparts in AIS and the PSS. Conversely professional, technical and scientific, and clerical and secretarial staff are significantly less likely to be have formal appraisals. A minority of workplaces in AIS and the PSS (one-quarter) and 18 per cent of HI workplaces do not formally appraise any of the specified occupational groups. Further details about appraisals from WERS are given for non-managerial employees only.

Formal performance appraisal schemes covering all or almost all staff have been observed in a large hotels (Kelliher and Johnson, 1997; Hoque, 1999a; McGunnigle and Jameson, 2000) and designer restaurants (Kelliher and Perrett, 2001). WERS shows that performance appraisal of non-managerial employees is less likely to occur in the HI (56 per cent of all cases), and where it applies coverage is slightly less comprehensive.

Most private sector schemes operate a formalized process with an annual interview between manager and subordinate, typically of between one and two hours' duration. Within hospitality and leisure Sodexho and David Lloyd Leisure carry out regular reviews outside the appraisal process, in the latter case informally as a precursor that could lead to formal disciplinary action (Anon., 2003b). WERS shows that where appraisal is used, all employees are included in the scheme in half of HI workplaces compared to 65 per cent in AIS and 73 per cent in PSS. The HI is significantly less likely to operate annual appraisals and significantly more likely to have appraisals that do not conform to a fixed pattern. In all groupings appraisal is most likely to be conducted by the employee's immediate superior, with the wider involvement of another manager occurring in a large minority of cases, especially in restaurants.

Employees are often suspicious of appraisals which, when conducted badly, can side-step crucial issues and lead to one party unleashing pent-up frustrations, leading ultimately to a deterioration in the employment relationship (Anon., 2003b). Dickens (1998) argues that impression management rather than good performance may count for more in obtaining a good rating. Appraisers are usually men who may use proxy measures for measuring commitment, such as visible hours at work and working beyond contract which penalize women (also Rubery, 1995).

Discussion and review topics

Perspectives on pay

- How can you reconcile the conflicting objectives of using pay for managerial cost control and to ensure a fair wage?
- Consider this dilemma in the context of different sizes of firm and by industry sub-sector.

Pay regulation

How can the UK's NMW be reformed to provide better wage protection for hospitality workers?

Tips

Is the use of tips by employers to subsidize low pay an ethically and morally defensible practice?

Designing a pay structure

Sue Smallridge and Paul Tait are opening a new restaurant in an affluent suburb of Birmingham. The restaurant, seating 120 customers, has a French café-style theme. It will be open from 7.30 a.m. to 11.00 p.m. Monday to Friday, and from 8.30 a.m. to 12.00 p.m. on Saturday and Sunday. The restaurant will serve breakfast, morning coffee, lunch, afternoon tea and dinner.

Your brief as a consultant is to:

- design the organization structure and to specify the number and type of staff in each section;
- design a pay structure including other benefits and a payments system for all the staff, including the manager;
- justify and explain the basis upon which you have designed the pay structure;
- estimate the cost of the wage bill in the first year.

6 Representation, participation and involvement

Learning objectives

By the end of this chapter you should be able to:

- understand the principles of collective dialogue based on collective bargaining and social partnership;
- explain why trade unions are not able to provide effective workforce representation in the HI within a variety of institutional frameworks throughout the world;
- recognize the specific characteristics of trade union membership within Britain;
- identify alternative forms of non-union representation and the circumstances in which they may operate;
- explain the purpose and function of different methods of employee communication and involvement, and worker participation.

Collective dialogue

Collective bargaining

Collective bargaining is a rule-making process for contract-making and contract-changing (Welch and Leighton, 1996). Terms and conditions of employment are determined and regulated through the formal process of negotiation[1] between representatives of management and employees. The outcome is a binding agreement for those employees within the bargaining unit, e.g. at national, enterprise or workplace level. It is based on management's legitimization of employee involvement and influence over aspects of decision-making, and involves a power relationship in which employee representatives may regulate managerial authority. Acknowledgement of the right to strike is embodied within this process. Variations in the scope and coverage of collective bargaining are a reflection of different regulatory regimes across the world.

International arrangements

The coverage of workers' and employers' organizations in the HCTS and the scope of collective bargaining vary by country and region. Trade unions may cover a number of sectors, which may include the HCTS, or cover particular occupational groups that are found in other sectors, e.g. workers in services in France (ILO, 2001: 103). Employers' organizations are more cohesive, and largely cover hotels and restaurants.

The International Hotel and Restaurant Association (IHRA) is the largest employers' organization representing over 750,000 establishments in 150 countries (see http://www.ih-ra.com/about/detail). The largest workers' organization, the IUF, has 326 affiliated organizations representing 10 million workers in 118 countries (see http://www.iuf.org), including the ECF (ECF-IUF).

There is only one known case of international trade union recognition between the IUF and the French Accor Group. International awareness has been facilitated through the use of websites for publicity. A dispute in a Seoul hotel came to an end in 2000 after trade unions elsewhere made representations to the Korean diplomatic mission (ILO, 2001: 116).

There are two federations of employers' organizations in Europe: The Confederation of National Associations of Hotels, Restaurants, Cafés and Similar Establishments in the European Union and European Economic Area (HOTREC) and the European Federation of Contract Catering Organizations (FERCO). For workers there is a special European Trade Union Liaison Committee on Tourism (ETLC) (ILO, 2001: 103). Social dialogue, launched by the ECF-IUF and HOTREC, takes place four times a year under the auspices of the European Commission (EC). Various joint declarations have been adopted including the 1999 Joint Declaration for the promotion of employment in hotels and restaurants, designed to reduce taxes and non-wage costs, and to improve training and certification.

The development of collective and social partnership is hampered by the reluctance among employers to promote partnership with trade unions. The challenges of global competition have caused employers to restructure and adopt new methods. Traditional occupational boundaries are breaking down, as jobs become more flexible. Hence issues on the collective bargaining agenda include the prevention of wage deterioration resulting from unclear definitions in new work patterns, and maintaining continuity of working and employment conditions where there is a change in ownership (ILO, 2001: 111). The latter is more difficult where the instigating party is an MNC based outside the host country.

Variations in global practice

The structure and scope of collective bargaining varies according to legal and national practice. Twelve African countries have collective agreements in existence since the 1970s, and almost all explicitly mention union rights (ILO, 2001: 110). While enterprise bargaining is more normative in North America, Asia and Africa, in Europe sectoral or sub-sectoral bargaining at national or regional level is more common. In France sub-sectoral bargaining is a function of the way employers are organized, and was for some time restricted to hotel and restaurant chains. More recently most independent firms adopted this procedure, even though workers are not unionized. Complete coverage is secured by extending the collective agreement to workers in all workplaces by government decree (ILO, 2001: 111).

In Australia trade unions have an almost exclusive right to represent HI employees and to make particular awards. Trade union membership is not particularly high (see Table 6.1). There is no law on trade union recognition ballots as in North America and the UK, and trade unions are not especially active. Although the Shop Distributive and Allied Employees' Union (SDA) has almost exclusive rights in fast food in all states, employers are reluctant to engage in enterprise bargaining. They will negotiate with unions where a state industrial award is perceived as too costly.

Agreements would incorporate conditions from other agreements that may offset the higher conditions under the award. Hungry Jack's (a Burger King franchise) and the SDA have reached a multi-state standard agreement, which the unions regard as easier to enforce and maintain (Allan *et al.*, 2000). Some successful enterprise agreements have addressed 'low road' practices, building in value-added features such as job rotation, training and performance management, and multi-skilling (Nankervis and Debrah, 1995).

New Zealand used to have an employment relations system similar to the Australian system. Case study 6.1 shows how in a more deregulated environment collectivism may be enduring on the surface, but is highly symbolic.

Case study 6.1 **Deregulation of employment relations in large hotels in New Zealand**

The *Employment Contracts Act 1991* replaced mandated collective bargaining and extensive trade union protection with a new regime allowing employers to engage in individualistic employment relations or innovative cooperative relations with unionized workforces. Union density within the Service Workers Union (SWU) was traditionally low in the hotel industry. The New Zealand (With Exceptions) Major Accommodation Hotel Industry Award expired in 1992.

- Collective contracts persisted but most employers abandoned traditional bargaining and moved to almost exclusively management determined 'consultation'.
- Managers espoused a more limited role for unions, including officials, although all hotels still credited union subscriptions.
- Non-union collective voice mechanisms were developed. Trade union representatives were subject to the same election procedure as their peers.
- All innovations initiated and developed by management were not consistent with high commitment strategies.

Source: Haynes and Fryer (1999, 2001).

Labour-management bargaining priorities in the US have changed post-11 September, with new considerations including job security for airline employees, and employers seeking to add provisions for 'acts of war'. There is also increased video surveillance, bio-terrorism policies, employee background checks and on-site searches of employees' belongings (Batterman and Fullerton, 2002). Current law makes virtually all changes in workplace privacy and security rules the topic of mandatory collective bargaining (Cohen, 2002).

The British experience

HI employees and, notably, employers, through bodies such as the BHA and BII, have traditionally not associated for collective bargaining purposes. The main trade unions representing HI workers are the TGWU, GMB, USDAW and NALHM. Historically membership levels have been very low, regardless of the regulatory framework in force (see Box 6.1). The LFS (2001) indicates that only 9 per cent of HI employees are covered by collective agreements, which drops to 6 per cent if public sector workplaces are excluded (Brook, 2002: 352). Trade union recognition for collective bargaining is rare, and restricted mainly to the large groups, e.g. USDAW and Compass (Moto motorway) services, the GMB and Road Chef and Jarvis Hotels (IDS, 2002, 2003).

The legal framework governing the rights, actions, duties, responsibilities and behaviours of employers and trade unions in Britain was seriously weakened in the 1980s and 1990s (for details see Chapter 7). The proportion of employees who were members of trade unions declined from 53 per cent in 1979 to 28 per cent in 1999 (Brown, 2000). Consequently similar 'hollow shell' collective agreements to those found in New Zealand have developed in Britain (Hyman, 1997). The *Employment Relations Act 1999* contained measures to facilitate trade union organization, including the statutory recognition procedures, although there has been no weakening of the constraints on industrial action.

Social partnership

Social partnership is a form of collective bargaining that places more emphasis on mutual cooperation and joint problem-solving, often extending into areas such as training, skills, flexibility, career development and quality of working life, which have not been the domain of traditional collective bargaining. It is best viewed on two levels – a relationship between the summit employer and trade union bodies, and at the workplace (Brown, 2000). Many, including the trade unions, would regard social partnership as a complementary process to collective bargaining and vehicle for union renewal (Bacon and Storey, 2000), while others see it as marginalizing trade unionism as an autonomous force, undermining workplace unionism and weakening the trade union movement (Smith and Morton, 2001).

Partnership is expected to emerge from a common response to the challenges of global competition. In the Caribbean where tourism is by far the most important economic sector, active steps to improve social partnership can be observed. One major concern of trade unions is the practices of sub-contracting and franchising, which are believed to create divisions among those working in the same workplaces (ILO, 2001: 106–7; Royle, 2000). At international level there is a social dialogue relationship between the partners in the HCTS, but it is at an early stage of development (ILO, 2001: 102).

The development of trade unions as facilitators of cooperative collective relationships, often through consultative arrangements, is a key dimension of EU social policy. In 1999 agreement between the Union of Industrial and Employers' Confederations of Europe (UNICE) and the ETUC provides a forum for social dialogue leading to agreements. These provide the framework for national governments to introduce appropriate legislation, e.g. non-discrimination for workers on fixed-term contracts in respect of hours of work and holidays. Other consultative arrangements relating to redundancies, proposed business transfers, health and safety, European Works Councils (EWCs), and the forthcoming information and consultation directive, which may involve union and non-union representatives, are discussed later in this chapter.

Reflecting the new Labour government's espousal of partnership, a Partnership at Work fund has been created to encourage employers, employees and their representatives to build trust, share information and work together to solve business problems. Since 1997 the TUC has deliberately attempted to rebuild relationships with employers by promoting a new role for trade unions based on

---

Case study 6.2 **Partnership with the GMB at Gardner Merchant**

This contract catering company, part of the French conglomerate Sodexho, recognizes the GMB in the UK. Previously each site negotiated their own interpretations of the standard ACAS recognition agreement, with emphasis on negative dispute resolution procedures. A new HR Director in 1994 spurred a reappraisal of Gardner Merchant's way of working in light of the positive collaborative experience gained from Sodexho's EWC. There was a shared desire to formulate a UK national agreement along the same lines.

The new agreement signed in 1998 recognized the legitimacy of each parties' role, a joint commitment to open discussion and improving trust, providing training opportunities and enhancing the company's reputation. It also contained a detailed disputes avoidance procedure, with strike action permissible only after all other avenues are exhausted. Joint policy statements have been issued on best practice in TUPE and the EU's Acquired Rights Directive.

Improved communication and consultation provides both sides with an early warning call about problems and potential areas of conflict. Training in consultation and planning for change was provided for local managers. There are twice-yearly Board level meetings and in early 2000 the company was seeking a national works council.

Source: IPA (2001).

Case study 6.3 Partnership in San Francisco's hotels

San Francisco's major hotels and the Hotel Employees and Restaurant Employees International Union (HERE) embarked on a new partnership-oriented approach in 1994. The 'living contract' provided a mechanism for making work-rule changes by mutual agreement during the term of the contract. Joint study teams examined issues underlying problems that would otherwise have led to a dispute. Joint solutions avoided expensive, often pointless arbitration. Rules were redesigned to make the hotels' restaurants competitive with non-union hotels. The living agreement was renewed in 1999.

Source: Korshak (2000).

---

partnership strategy, additional to collective bargaining (TUC, 1997, 1999; Brown, 2000). Nationally the trade unions believe they can play an essential role in helping to determine policy on training, jobs, investment and Europe, while at the level of the enterprise and workplace partnership agreements will help improve organizational performance and quality of working life. The joint problem-solving social partnership approach underpins the work of ACAS and the LPC, both bodies comprising equal numbers of CBI and TUC nominees plus independent members. The Information and Participation Association (IPA) shares similar ideals to the TUC on social partnership (Coupar and Stevens, 1998). Examples of social partnership are given in Case studies 6.2 and 6.3.

Trade unions

International comparisons

HCT workers across the world are less likely to be organized in trade unions than workers in other sectors, and trade union density may be as little as 10 per cent or less in industrialized countries. Even where trade unions have been afforded exclusive rights, such as in Australia and New Zealand, actual membership levels have tended to be low (Haynes and Fryer, 1999, 2001; Allan *et al.*, 2000). Figures are difficult to come by, but selected examples of density levels in the HI are given in Table 6.1.[2] In many cases they indicate density levels below a level at which the 'virtuous circle between union growth and union recognition could begin' (Bain and Price, 1983: 22).

In her survey of the HI in New Zealand, Ryan (1996) found that two-thirds of workplaces had no union members, 18 per cent had up to 50 per cent and 4 per cent had more than half. Only 10 per cent had seen any attempt at union recognition.

National figures disguise differences within sub-sectors. In large hotels, where membership is generally highest, levels of 80 per cent have been achieved in the Canadian cities of Vancouver, Toronto and Montreal (Stokes, 1997). Conversely

Table 6.1 Trade union membership in the HI by country

Country	Year	Level (%)
US	1993	<2
Canada	1998	9
Australia	1997	18/13.1
Finland	1995	65
Austria	1995	40
Italy	1995	25
Ireland	1995	20
Netherlands	1997	10
UK	1995	8
France	1995	5

Sources: Hirsch and McPherson (1993); IDS (1998b); Piso (1999); ILO (2001); Reiter (2002).

Notes: Where two figures are shown, they relate to full-time and part-time workers respectively. The most recent HI figure from the LFS shows 5% union density (Brook, 2002).

in Auckland, New Zealand membership can vary from 5 to 20 to 32 per cent (Haynes and Fryer, 1999). Although density levels were never very high (Haynes and Fryer, 2001), they dropped in the 1990s following the deregulation of employment relations, remaining higher where trade unions maintained an active role. In McDonald's in Germany trade union membership in the NGG becomes well established and rises rapidly to around 50 per cent or more after a works council has been created (Royle, 1999a). Conversely the fast food industry in Canada and the US is almost entirely non-union (Reiter, 1996). Case study 6.4 illustrates how HERE approaches organizing union membership in American hotels.

Even where union density is relatively high, as in Singapore hotels, conservative and accommodative trade unions and the institutionalization of employer–employee relations mean there is little activity or conflict (Nankervis and Debrah, 1995). As the service provided by hospitality businesses cannot be stockpiled like goods produced in a factory, industrial action is potentially more damaging and effective.

As noted in Table 6.1 trade union membership in the HI in the UK is among the lowest in Europe, and may be in decline. Arguably NALHM has been the most successful union within the HI but as Case study 6.5 indicates, membership has dropped by two-thirds. Trade unions have had a chequered history in attempting to secure recognition in larger hotels. There have been isolated cases of strike action in support of recognition, including the Savoy (1946/47), London and Torquay (1967) (see Wood, 1992: 111–19). USDAW's approach to McDonald's in the UK for 'talks about talks' was flatly rejected by the company, nor has there been any attempt by the three HI unions to make a coordinated approach to the company (Royle, 1999a). However the GMB has been actively recruiting in McDonald's and Little Chef (IDS, 2003). Recognition is pretty rare, and most likely to be found in large companies, e.g. USDAW and Compass (Moto

Case study 6.4 **Neutrality agreements and organizing tactics in new US hotels**

In the 1990s most hotels were organized on the basis of HERE approaching hotel companies several months before a new hotel was due to open seeking a neutrality agreement. Under this agreement employers give up their right to contest union organization and the right of employees to vote in a secret ballot election supervised by the National Labor Relations Board (NLRB) to determine whether they wish to be represented by HERE. By signing the employer virtually guarantees the union will be recognized as the exclusive bargaining agent. Such agreements include a card-check provision which represents a much cheaper and more effective organizing technique than the secret ballot method, which normally goes against the unions. Labour-peace and living wage ordinances coupled with the threat of sanctions from the building-trades unions to disrupt the hotel's construction, have made it easier to union organizers to obtain employers' consent to remain neutral.

Source: Stokes *et al.* (2001).

Case study 6.5 **The decline of the National Association of Licensed House Managers**

In 1997 NALHM ended 30 years of independence by joining the TGWU as an autonomous section. Membership, restricted to pubs managed by salaried managers of a brewery, as opposed to managers of free houses or tenants, peaked at 18,000 in 1982, but had declined to 6,000 by 1997. The union's demise is attributed to a combination of local conditions specific to the sector, including the major restructuring following the Mergers and Monopolies Commission Report in 1989. The subsequent Beer Orders changed the role for many pubs and the nature of their managers who became more professional and entrepreneurial.

Source: Mutch (2002).

motorway services), GMB and Roadchef and GMB and Jarvis Hotels (IDS, 2002, 2003). Since the *Employment Relations Act 1999* there have been no known recognition claims in the HI, although a number of recognition claims have been made in airlines and casinos. Summaries of these cases are posted on the CAC's website (www.cac.gov.uk/recent_decisions/).

There have been other recent examples of strike action, for reasons other than recognition. In Norway the first strike for 11 years in 1996 forced the closure of ten leading hotels, at a daily cost of £2.4 million for three of them (McIvor, 1997). A strike by bar workers in Dublin in 1994 closed 70 per cent of pubs during the World Cup (Baum, 1995). BA sustained a number of strikes among cabin crew over the 1990s. In 1997 nearly 2000 BA staff went on sick leave rather than participating in the official strike, as they feared disciplinary action. Taking turns to go sick caused considerable disruption to flights (Blyton and Turnbull, 1998: 311–12). Recent strike action in the British HI is virtually non-existent (see Chapter 7).

Recent experience in British workplaces

From WERS the state of trade membership can be ascertained in two main ways, by measuring union density and by measuring the percentage of workplaces where there are or have been trade union members in the recent past. The HI continues to sustain significantly lower trade union density in comparison with AIS and the PSS (Table 6.2). Although the picture is slightly more encouraging in larger workplaces, trade union incursion into the heart of the HI is, at best, highly marginal (Table 6.3). Recent LFS (2001) figures indicate that 5 per cent of HI employees are union members (8 per cent full-time and 3 per cent part-time), and the figure drops to 4 per cent if public sector workplaces are excluded (Brook, 2002).

In three-quarters of the small caucus of HI workplaces with union members, membership is most likely to be among managers/administrative staff. Union membership is extremely rare among other occupational groups, especially white-collar groups who are most likely to be union members in AIS and the PSS.

Table 6.2 Trade union density in context and by size of workplace (%)

	AIS	PSS	HI	<25	25–49	50–99	100+
Aggregate density	34	15	2*	2	0	0	5
Actual density							
No members	54	73	92*	92	94	94	73
1–59%	26	19	8*	7	6	6	27
60–100%	20	7	1*	1	0	0	0

Source: WERS98.

Notes: All weighted cases. Column percentages do not sum accurately due to rounding. *Significantly different at the 5% level from AIS and the PSS.

Table 6.3 Trade union density by sub-sector (%)

	Hotels	Campsites	Restaurants	Bars	Canteens
Aggregate density	0	9	1	1	15
Actual density					
No members	94	18	100	90	82
1–59%	6	82	0	10	9
60–100%	0	0	0	0	10

Source: WERS98.

Notes: All weighted cases. Column percentages do not sum accurately due to rounding.

Tables 6.4 and 6.5 indicate more details about current and past union membership issues within workplaces.

The dearth of union membership in the HI draws attention to the four issues highlighted in Table 6.4. First, there is no de-recognition or absolute decline in union membership in the HI because none of the workplaces without unions had any members five years ago. Second, unions have been slightly more active in

Table 6.4 Trade union membership in context and by size of workplace (%)

	AIS	PSS	HI	<25	25–49	50–99	100+
Any union members							
now	47	27	8*	8	6	6	27
Any union members							
5 years ago s	5	4	0*	0	0	0	0
Any recruitment							
attempts in last							
5 years r	5	5	12	13	20	2	5
Any recognition requests							
in last 5 years t	7	7	0*	0	0	0	0
Management's attitude							
towards unions w							
In favour	27	13	6*	6	7	3	4
Not in favour	17	22	22	18	28	25	28
Neutral	54	63	72**	76	65	67	69

Source: WERS98.

Notes: Yes responses to all weighted cases unless otherwise stated. *Significantly different at the 5% level from AIS and the PSS. **Significantly different at the 5% level from AIS. s Where no union members and establishment is five years or older. r Where no union members. t Where union members now or five years ago. w Excludes not an issue and non-codeable responses.

Table 6.5 Trade union membership by sub-sector (%)

	Hotels	Campsites	Restaurants	Bars	Canteens
Any union members					
now	6	82	0	10	18
Any union members					
5 years ago s	0	0	0	0	0
Any recruitment					
attempts in last					
5 years r	2	0	14	19	0
Any recognition requests					
in last 5 years t	0	0	0	0	0
Management's attitude					
towards unions w					
In favour	2	0	0	11	10
Not in favour	23	0	20	26	7
Neutral	76	100	78	64	83

Source: WERS98.

Notes: Yes responses to all weighted cases unless otherwise stated. s Where no union members and establishment is five years or older. r Where no union members. t Where union members now or five years ago. w Excludes not an issue and non-codeable responses.

Table 6.6 Non-union representatives' role in employment relations (%)

	AIS				PSS				HI			
	Negotiates	Consults	Informs	None	Negotiates	Consults	Informs	None	Negotiates	Consults	Informs	None
Pay and conditions	–	–	–	28	–	–	35	–	–	66	–	–
Recruitment and selection	–	–	–	39	–	34	–	–	56*	–	–	–
Training	–	45	–	–	–	49	–	–	–	–	66**	–
Payment systems	–	–	–	39	–	–	48	–	–	–	60	–
Grievances	–	43	–	–	–	42	–	–	60*	–	–	–
Staffing/manpower planning	–	37	–	–	–	43	–	–	–	75	–	–
Equal opportunities	–	41	–	–	–	38	–	–	–	–	–	65
Health and safety	–	58	–	–	–	62	–	–	60*	–	66*	–
Performance appraisals	–	45	–	–	–	50	–	–	60*	–	–	–

Source: WERS98.

Notes: Workplaces where there are non-union representatives or representatives of non-recognized unions (AIS N=213, PSS N=121 and the HI N=10). The table shows the most frequently used method for each employment issue. *Significantly different at the 5% level from AIS and PSS. **Significantly different at the 5% level from AIS.

attempting to recruit members in the HI, but have touched only a minority of workplaces and their attempts do not appear to have proved successful. Third, there have been no recognition requests in the last five years. Finally HI managers are significantly less likely to be in favour of trade unions. One should also caution against assuming too much from the neutral responses because Cully *et al.* (1999) suggested that managers who declare themselves neutral might actually hold negative views about trade unions. We can usefully consider the neutrality responses in Table 6.4 with an earlier observation that managers have an even higher level of preference for consulting directly with employees than with a union (Table 3.9). While a majority of AIS and PSS managers do hold negative views about unions, there is a clear indication that HI managers hold even more negative views about unions than their counterparts in AIS and the PSS.

This final observation suggests that non-union representation is unlikely to be much of a force anywhere. This is borne out by the fact that fewer than 10 per cent of workplaces have present non-union representatives or representatives of non-recognized unions, affecting one in 11 workplaces in AIS, one in 12 in PSS and one in 16 the HI. These representatives are more likely to be found in unionized workplaces, and are rarely found in non-union workplaces, suggesting that they are complementary to union representation rather than substitutes for it. Thus most HI workplaces (93 per cent) have no worker representatives of any kind compared to 70 per cent in AIS and 85 per cent in the PSS.

In the HI non-union representatives are most likely to be volunteers, whereas in AIS and the PSS the most common selection method is election by employees. In most cases these representatives sit on a consultative committee covering a wide range of issues. Non-union representatives can also deal with or play a part in employment issues such as pay, recruitment, training, pay systems, grievances, staff planning, equal opportunities, health and safety, and performance appraisal. Their involvement varies from full (negotiation), partial (consultation), token (informed) or none (see Table 6.6). Although care should be taken in drawing too much from such a small number of cases, there are still some striking differences between AIS, the PSS and the HI.

The consequences of working without unions

'Non-union representation can provide at best only a partial mechanism for employee involvement and participation in the absence of legal underpinnings' (Terry, 1999: 28), because they have no collective sanctions or any of the protections afforded to union representatives. Such representation has no real power base, as it is merely cooperative, and ultimately, at managerial discretion, often abandoned in times of crisis and change when managers should be at their most open if they are to convince employees of their commitment to participation and of its effectiveness.

Workers in non-union workplaces appear to be penalized in a number of other ways. Collective bargaining appears to facilitate access to and improvement on statutory rights (Brown *et al.*, 2000). Unionized workplaces have more alternative voice mechanisms than non-union workplaces (Benson, 2000), where workers also lose out on family leave and gender equality (Deery *et al.*, 2001). Even though trade unions have gained the right to accompany a worker in a grievance or disciplinary hearing, including where the union is not recognized, accompaniment does not imply the right to represent. Most HI employees do not actually know any trade union officials (see Chapter 8). The absence of union voice mechanisms reinforces managerial prerogative and may weaken employees' chances of resolving a dispute or grievance. In McDonald's in Australia employees raise such concerns through the Personal Action Letter (PAL), which is brought to the attention of management or head office. Few workers are aware of PAL or use it (Allan *et al.*, 2000).

The individualized nature of contractual, remuneration and bargaining arrangements provides more limited provision of procedural justice and equity (Deery *et al.*, 2001). Workers seek advice and representation outside the traditional labour movement and from voluntary organizations such as the Citizens' Advice Bureau (CAB) (Abbott, 1998). The CAB has experienced a steep rise in the number of employment problems brought to them, and is becoming increasingly active in resolving such problems, in the absence of workplace mechanisms. This may change following the introduction of new statutory minimum grievance and disciplinary procedures. On issues such as redundancy, dismissal and the unilateral variation of the terms and conditions of employment, workers also seek the help of ACAS.

Forms of workplace conflict

The absence of unions does not indicate an absence of conflict. Rather alternative forms of worker behaviour, other than strike action, are normally deployed (see Box 6.1). By worker behaviour we mean the ways and means used by workers to cope with or resist managerial control in the everyday conduct of their work, which arise from their lack of power as individuals (see Chapters 1 and 2). These can be individual and collective (Sosteric, 1996; Lucas, 1997a), including mass and individual absenteeism. More days are lost from absence than from strikes (see Chapters 4 and 7). 'As with absenteeism, pilfering is arguably more costly than strikes' (Blyton and Turnbull, 1998: 315). Rather than raise a formal grievance about low pay that is likely to be ignored, workers enhance their pay by short-changing customers. Employee theft may be responsible for one in three business failures, and is especially prevalent in food service, with employees' own estimates three times higher than their managers' (Ghiselli and Ismail, 1998). Ultimately workers may leave the organization voluntarily or involuntarily, and may seek resolution of the dispute outside the workplace, notably at employment tribunal.

Lucas (1997a) identifies how students use their tacit skills to resist managers and customers (Case study 6.6). In customer-service work flight attendants' response to work intensification is to slow down and smile less broadly. Fuller and Smith (1991) report how the use of mystery shoppers so incensed hotel workers that they also conducted a 'smile strike'.

Law (2000) notes an interesting instance of customer protest in one of the most luxurious hotels in Hong Kong, which illustrates the effectiveness of mass action in response to the perceived inequitable treatment of a customer breast-feeding in

---

Box 6.1 *Forms of workplace conflict*

Unorganized, informal and individual

Getting by
- Coping mechanisms (sharing a moan with colleagues, put up and shut up)
- Pilferage (short changing customers, occasional drink)
- 'Fiddles' and 'knock-offs' (individual to supplement low pay)
- Absence (response to work pressure, survival)

Getting back
- Pilferage (larger items/scale such as sheets, towels, bottles of spirits)
- 'Fiddles' (collective)
- Sabotage (working without enthusiasm, smile strike, misleading or limiting information given to customers, disconnecting calls from unpleasant customers)
- Absence (reassertion of control, more work for co-workers)

Getting on
- Turnover (career development, more pay)

Organized, formal and collective

---

a public area, who was asked to go somewhere more private. Eighteen women 'protested' by breast-feeding in the same area, and the hotel staff did nothing.

Why is unionization so low?

Three sets of circumstances are relevant to low levels of unionization:

- Do the structural characteristics of workplaces and workforces provide an environment in which it is possible to conceive effective levels of unionization?
- Do workers have an interest or motivation to join trade unions?
- What role do employers and trade unions play?

Structural factors

The substantial presence of small workplaces (Table 2.1) and their wide geographical dispersion pose considerable challenges to trade union recruitment and organizing strategies (Abbott, 1993; Lowe and Rastin, 2000). The ideology of a 'family culture' is a significant barrier to organizing in SMEs (Dundon *et al.*, 1999).

Case study 6.6 Resisting managers and customers in hospitality work

Getting by

One student worked four eight-hour shifts per week for a 'pittance' of £3.00 an hour managing the leisure centre of a city centre hotel. She used the extensive amount of working time spent on her own to complete all her college work. Others read books or collected data for their assignments or dissertation. None claimed they were actually skiving.

Another student stated they all stuck together with difficult customers. Where the customer gave them a £20 or £50 note, they would shout out the amount to the other person in the bar to have a witness should the customer claim the note was for a different value.

Getting back

A change in managers led to a change in management style from no procedures to enforcing the rules. Staff responded by giving customers free drinks and helping themselves.

A student serving drinks on large trays at a large arena had to step over customers and reported getting 'touched up' by men. If she reported this she knew the customer would claim it was accidental. If she had to return, she would keep the tray between her and the customer so they could not do it again. If customers were particularly horrible she would make a point of treading on their feet, of course smiling and apologizing.

Sources: Lucas (1997a); Lammont and Lucas (1997, 1999).

Workplaces under the control of one parent company may be fragmented by sub-contracting and franchising arrangements. In the US and Canada hotel restaurants are frequently leased, becoming part of the non-union restaurant sub-sector. In Las Vegas where virtually all food beverage operations are leased HERE represents 900 workers, whereas the figure would be 2,700 if they were not leased. Although trade unions are opposed to sub-contracting a priority is to negotiate protection against a deterioration of terms and conditions of employment in these circumstances (ILO, 2001: 105). Franchised units have the legal status of an independent employer, which places them outside scope of company-wide representative bodies based on a minimum headcount. Thus agreements may only apply to a minority of a company's workplaces in a particular country, as Royle (2000) demonstrates in the case of McDonald's.

Additionally work is structured and organized around highly flexible patterns to match stochastic demand, so gaining access to a critical mass of employees is very difficult for trade union organizers to achieve. The fast food production system offers protection against trade unions through a casual and youthful labour force, which is difficult to organize, and which reduces the likelihood of union pressure for higher wages and potential interruptions through strikes (Allan *et al.*, 2000).

Employees – hardly a captive bunch

Many, if not most, employees work in different departments or at different times on different contracts, which keeps communications and group identity low among workers, especially in larger workplaces. This, heightened by departmental rivalry and fuelled by high labour turnover, militates against the establishment any collective ethos. High turnover causes membership attrition, although this could be attenuated if check-off was available within large organizations with fluid internal mobility, e.g. breweries (Mutch, 2002). Individualized contracts lead to a sense of individual identity and also sharpen competition among individuals (Abbott, 1993). Individual employees doing different jobs, each with its own set of benefits, prefer to negotiate for themselves, believing strongly that they can influence their own working environment. The notion of service may instil a sense of submission, and there is little collective kudos to be gained from excellent service (ILO, 2001: 105).

A young workforce (Lowe and Rastin, 2000), and to a lesser extent part-time working, is strongly correlated to lower levels of density, especially in the UK (Brook, 2002). The GMB's strategy to recruit students on a 10p a week subscription achieved only a small level of membership (Royle, 1999a). Part-time workers are one of the least committed work groups and therefore less likely to be interested in trade unions (Hakim, 1995), although some display strong support for the ideals and protection afforded by unions (Walters, 2002). Workers with less than two years' service, temporary and zero hours workers, and sales and customer-service staff sustain substantially lower trade union density (Brook, 2002).

The issue of gender is more ambiguous, as density levels of men and women in Britain have converged towards similar levels of around 30 per cent since the early 1990s (Brook, 2002). Women with higher education qualifications have the highest density levels, and are more than twice as likely to be union members than women with no qualifications or qualifications at A-level or below (Brook, 2002). This is consistent with Lowery and Beadles' (1996) observation that industrial and craft workers are less likely to choose union representation than professional workers. Weaker affiliation to union membership among females may be attributed to their disproportionate representation in part-time (Sinclair, 1995) and casual work, and to their irregular hours. Women often feel neglected by trade unions (Gabriel, 1988; Munro, 2001) or are dissatisfied with their experience of them (Sinclair, 1995). This creates a negative perception of trade unions, as in the case of an Asian woman who found her white, male trade union official 'dismissive' and sought advice instead from the CAB (Abbott, 1998).

Employers and trade unions

The role of employers is also crucial (Case study 6.7). In the US employers cannot be compelled to grant union organizers access to their employees where other

---

Case study 6.7 **Anti-union tactics in the German fast food industry**

Anglo-Saxon-based MNCs, including McDonald's, Pizza Hut and Burger King, are more likely to adopt anti-union policies. Employment relations in most German-owned firms appear to be less antagonistic. Maredo and Churrasco enjoyed good relations with the NGG while under German ownership, but these have become more difficult since the takeover by the UK Whitbread group. A subsidiary of the UK Compass Group 'Eurest' works cooperatively with unions.

McDonald's has sought to root out or inhibit union membership by sending 'flying squads' of senior managers to trouble spots, making 'troublemakers" job duties more unpleasant, actual or threatened dismissal, or paying people to leave.

Source: Royle (1999a, 2002).

---

reasonable means are available, e.g. shopping malls and entrances to hotels (Clay and Stephens, 1995a). Where employers are unwilling to recognize trade unions, workers have less reason to join and may even fear repercussions. Positive views of trade unions are unlikely to convert into action as employees are thwarted by a sense of fatalism about the likely success of a union dealing with a hostile employer (Macaulay and Wood, 1992). Or it may well be the case that workers, instilled with a sense self-reliance and in the knowledge that work is temporary or readily available elsewhere, are simply not dissatisfied enough to seek trade union protection and representation, an issue explored in Chapter 8.

Given the difficulties HERE has had in organizing HI workers, Lowery and Beadles (1996) suggest that unions' past patterns of organizing need to be altered, as they may be targeting the 'wrong' workers (also Sinclair, 1995). In spite of the TUC's positive attempts to encourage the trade union movement to target women, ethnic minorities (Kirton and Greene, 2002) and part-time workers (Walters, 2002) sex and race inequality remains institutionalized within trade unions (Dickens, 1997; Wacjman, 2000; Munro, 2001). If unions in Britain are to stem union decline, they must overcome their traditional antipathy towards non-standard workers based on the fear that recruiting them would undercut full-time jobs (Sinclair, 1995). Such workers, including low-wage service workers, need to be the target of union recruitment and retention efforts (Waddington and Whitston, 1997; Oxenbridge, 2000; Simms *et al.*, 2000). Fundamentally 're-branding' towards non-standard workers is difficult, time-consuming and costly (Walters, 2002), even if unions change their organizing structure to facilitate their increased participation (Heery, 1998).

This is not to say that hospitality and tourism workers are 'unique' (Riley, 1985). Rather, their orientations to work (Dodrill and Riley, 1992) and their role within the capitalist relations of production (Piso, 1999) do not differentiate them from production workers. But there is a complex mix of factors that clearly contribute to an explanation of why trade unions, even where they enjoy strong institutional support, have made few incursions into large swathes of the HCTS.

A continuum of workforce participation

Participation provides employees with the opportunity to influence and take part in organizational decision-making and is, therefore, mainly pluralist. It is based on collective representation, which may be union or union-union, and is often referred to as indirect participation. Where worker representatives are elected, trade unions are generally involved. Non-elected participation tends to be ad hoc. Effective participation is dependent upon an equitable power balance. Participation normally extends to areas outside the focus of traditional collective bargaining, i.e. the effort–reward bargain. Hence social partnership dealing with issues such as training and skills can be regarded as a variant of participation. Initiatives for participation normally emanate from the state, trade unions or employees. Examples discussed below include transnational EWCs, the forth-coming national-level information and consultation directive, works councils and joint consultative committees (JCCs).

Involvement is closely associated with 'soft' and 'best practice' HRM and is management driven. As it seeks to enhance employee support and commitment to the objectives and values of the organization, it is mainly unitarist. As any increase in employee control and decision-making is limited to the job and work operation only, involvement is sometimes called task-based or direct participation (Marchington and Wilkinson, 1999). Involvement practices addressed below include briefing groups, suggestion schemes, problem-solving groups, teamworking and empowerment.

Worker representation at employers' initiative rarely addresses fundamental issues of pay and working time. Rather, it has more to do with improving manage-ment and workforce communications, and with improving day-to-day business issues and training. In one Accor hotel, while two-thirds of the staff attended meetings, only half of them participated actively. The remaining third did not bother to attend (ILO, 2001: 108). Employee support and enthusiasm for meet-ings may be patchy, particularly where management determines the 'consultation' agenda.

Since the 1980s successive WIRS/WERS have shown an increase in direct participation and a decline in indirect participation and collective bargaining in Britain (Millward *et al.*, 2000). Hence involvement 'may be desirable to enhance the status, opportunity and work satisfaction of the individual . . . it may reduce the capacity of employees to challenge and influence managerial decisions by undermining collectivism and the representational role and power of trade unions' (Salamon, 2000: 369). Involvement and participation are not discrete or mutually exclusive practices and can be depicted on a continuum (Box 6.2). Ultimately participation hinges upon the extent to which managers control workers and the degree of control afforded to workers within the organization or in their work.

Box 6.2 A continuum of employee participation

No/low involvement $\longleftrightarrow$	Receiving information $\longleftrightarrow$	Joint consultation $\longleftrightarrow$	Joint decision-making $\longleftrightarrow$	Employee control
No empowerment	Team briefing	Health and safety committee	Works council	Worker cooperative
Suggestion scheme	Workforce briefing	Consultative committee	Consultative committee	Total empowerment
Job redesign	Newsletter		Quality circles	
Share ownership	Email		Disclosure of information	
Profit-sharing	Meetings			
Problem-solving groups				
Opinion survey				

Source: Based on Blyton and Turnbull (1998: 224).

Indirect participation

European Works Councils

EWCs came into being as a result of the EWC Directive (1994), and are cross-border meetings between worker representatives and managers of companies with businesses in more than one country. Every enterprise with at least 150 employees in each of at least two countries and a total of at least 1,000 employees in the European Economic Area (EEA) is required to have an EWC. The procedure for consultation is if at least 150 employees from at least two countries require it. The meetings are for information and consultation purposes, not collective bargaining, as employee representatives have no powers to block management decisions.

A number of MNCs operating in the EU established EWCs by 'voluntary agreement' ahead of the legally required implementation date of 1996. This enabled

---

Case study 6.8 Positive outcomes from European Works Councils

- Club Méditerranée consulted and came to an agreement on closing operations and restructuring processes.
- Accor concluded an agreement with the IUF on trade union rights.
- Compass extended equal opportunities policies to all subsidiaries and promised training for all employees. Compass committed itself to becoming the 'Preferred Employer', linking customer satisfaction to employee satisfaction.

Source: ILO (2001: 115).

Case study 6.9 Pizza Express Forum

A structure for feedback and consultation for more than 250 British restaurants was established in 2000. This was developed by a working party of volunteers, with a former waiter recruited to act as full-time coordinator. Each restaurant has its own staff representative, who feeds into one of 27 Area Forums (each covers around nine restaurants). Each Area Forum elects a representative for one of three Regional Forums.

Issues raised by representatives have included a new menu and a service charge. At the National Forum representatives have brought up questions about training, payslips and recycling. Most of Pizza Express's 6,000 staff are in the UK, and the aim is to ensure that the Forum complies with rules on EWCs. Although some staff are union members, the initiative will have failed if staff see joining unions as an alternative to the Forum.

Source: Hewett (2000).

companies to appoint employee representatives instead of those determined by national law or practice. By August 2000 there were 14 EWCs, only two of which were set up after the deadline for voluntary agreements. Examples of those agreements signed jointly with trade unions are European and include Accor (French), Bass plc and Compass (UK) and Scandic Hotels (Swedish) (see Case study 6.8). By contrast agreements affecting EWCs in American MNCs, such as McDonald's, Tricon Global Restaurants and the tour operator American Express, were not signed by trade unions (ILO, 2001: 114). McDonald's was able to negotiate the kind of EWC it wanted, which applies only to one-third of their workers because franchised stores are excluded (Royle, 1999b). Britain was excluded from coverage of the Directive until the new Labour government opted into the Social Chapter in 1998. Transition arrangements meant that British-based MNCs had until 1999 to make voluntary agreements, as the UK regulations to comply with the Directive did not come into force until 2000 (Case study 6.9).

Other EU-driven consultation

Other EU directives have required the UK to legislate for consultation with representatives in circumstances of collective redundancies, transfers of undertakings and health and safety. In keeping with EWCs, representatives do not have to be union representatives, and in health and safety employers may consult directly with employees or their representatives. However a number of factors limit their practical effect in the HI (Lucas, 2001). Redundancy consultation with workers' representatives is required only when 20 or more employees at an establishment are to be made redundant within 90 days. Many workplaces will not qualify because they are too small, and the use of atypical labour, high labour turnover and dismissal to regulate headcount means the HI sustains relatively few redundancies (see Chapter 2). Because redundancies and transfers are sporadic, often situation-specific events, standing structures for such purposes are rare anywhere in Britain (Smith *et al.*, 1999). There may be little real consultation as employers may use such procedures to legitimize their decisions or to reassure workers (Sargeant, 2001).

As James (1994) has observed, the ongoing nature of health and safety may assure some continuity of management–employee dialogue. Health and safety is the one domain where there is some form of representative structure in non-union workplaces (Cully *et al.*, 1999). Workers in non-union workplaces face difficulties in gaining access to health and safety representation (James and Walters, 2002). Our WERS analysis shows, in the absence of any consultative committee or a committee that deals with health and safety matters, HI workplaces are significantly less likely to have joint committee to deal with health and safety matters (Table 6.7). Such committees are most likely to deal with health and safety matters only. HI representatives are most likely to have been volunteers, whereas slightly more democratic methods are used in AIS and the PSS.

Adding the number of workplaces with health and safety committees to the number of workplaces with a JCC that discusses health and safety conveys a more complete picture of health and safety consultation. Even on this measure only one-

Table 6.7 Health and safety arrangements in context, by size of workplace and sub-sector (%)

	AIS	PSS	HI	<25	25–49	50–99	100+
Joint committee	27	21	10*	0	13	33	61
Any representatives where no committee	37	29	14*	4	45	15	33

	Hotels	Camp sites	Restaur- ants	Bars	Canteens
Joint committee	23	24	13	0	13
Any representatives where no committee	23	0	12	11	4

Source: WERS98.

Notes: All weighted cases. *Significantly different at the 5% level from AIS and PSS.

fifth of HI workplaces consult formally on health and safety issues, significantly below AIS (48 per cent) and the PSS (37 per cent). Where there is no consultative committee that deals with health and safety issues, HI workplaces are significantly less likely to have representatives that deal with management over health and safety matters (Table 6.7).

The Directive on information and consultation adopted in 2002 is to be phased in from 2005, following consultation arising from the discussion paper *High Performance Workplaces: The Role of Employee Involvement in a Modern Economy* (www2.dti. gov/er/consultation/informconsult). It will also apply a size of firm threshold. Initially it may apply only to companies with 150 or more employees, and by 2008 it will still only affect businesses with more than 50 employees. The Directive will extend consultation beyond the issues discussed above (www2.dti.gov.uk/er/consultation/proposal). Employees have the right to be:

- informed about the business's economic situation;
- informed and consulted about employment prospects;
- informed and consulted about decisions likely to lead to substantial changes in work organization or contractual relations, including redundancies and transfers.

Information must be given in time to allow employee representatives to examine and prepare for consultation. The government is likely to encourage voluntary agreements within social partnership, imposing a statutory minimum framework where this is not possible. As with EWCs, there will be some impact among larger, but not most, HI businesses.

Works councils

Many European countries have highly formal institutional arrangements providing for works councils with written constitutions covering *inter alia* the election of representatives, frequency of meetings, and terms of reference. The German system of co-determination is often heralded as the 'best practice' model. Two-level worker participation comprises a works council (*Betriebsrat*) in the workplace, and worker representatives on the supervisory board of the enterprise (*Aufsichtsrate*). While McDonald's theoretically has a works council in every store, very few have been established because of company interference to delay and discourage any attempts to elect one (Royle, 1995, 2000). Tactics have included transferring the store into different ownership, buying out the instigators of a works council and nominating management candidates to provide a management-based agenda. Employee acquiescence and inadequate legislation have enabled McDonald's to stick to its American-style approach to participation, which is more in keeping with employee involvement, and to circumvent requirements for works councils in many other European countries (Royle, 2000: 119–49). Similar avoidance strategies are deployed by other Anglo-Saxon-based MNCs in the German fast food industry (Royle, 2002).

Joint consultative committees

Farnham and Pimlott (1995) identify three types of JCC. One covers similar terrain to works councils (integrative participation), another allows employees to influence

Table 6.8 Consultation and communication in context and by size of workplace (%)

	AIS	PSS	HI	>25	25–49	50–99	100+
System of briefings	83	82	84	79	91	96	91
Consultative committee	23	18	11***	0	25	21	53
Problem solving or							
quality groups	33	28	16*	9	17	35	48
Formal opinion survey p	39	36	43	36	46	56	58
Other dd							
Entire workforce							
meetings	42	42	47	55	40	27	36
Management chain/							
cascade	54	47	37***	28	47	54	71
Suggestion schemes	24	25	25	21	36	24	29
Newsletter	43	39	42	41	48	42	39
Disclosure of information bb							
Internal investment plans	50	46	55	52	56	64	70
Financial position of							
establishment	63	58	69	69	68	67	73
Financial position of							
organization m	66	67	78	92	67	44	57
Staffing plans	63	59	53	50	59	55	55

Source: WERS98.

Notes: Yes responses to all weighted cases unless otherwise stated. p In last five years for establishments five years or older. dd Four most frequently mentioned other ways in which management consults or communicates with employees (multi-response). bb Regularly given by management to employees or their representatives. m Where part of a larger organization or sole UK establishment. *Significantly different at the 5% level from AIS and PSS. ***Significantly different at the 5% level from AIS.

decisions before they are taken (classical consultation), while a third is largely symbolic, entailing downward communication only (pseudo participation). JCCs may be upgraded to marginalize collective bargaining and downgraded to deal with trivia.

WERS tells us that management committees for consultation, rather than negotiation, are significantly rarer in the HI, although they are only present in around one-quarter of AIS workplaces (Table 6.8). While the likelihood of such a committee increases with workplace size they are rarely present in some sub-sectors (Table 6.9). Committees are very rare in very small HI workplace and most common in large workplaces. None of the smaller HI workplaces without committees had had one during the previous five years. However, one-quarter of the large workplaces no longer had a committee (all hotels), although the reasons for its disappearance are unknown.

Where committees function in the HI, health and safety is most likely to be discussed, followed by training, working practices and welfare services and facilities. Pay and government regulations are the least frequently discussed issues. HI committees are significantly less likely to discuss employment and pay issues. There is a different emphasis on the range of issues discussed in AIS and the PSS, making for a fuller, more rounded agenda. Even so the vast majority of committees discuss

Table 6.9 Consultation and communication by sub-sector (%)

	Hotels	Campsites	Restaurants	Bars	Canteens
System of briefings	97	94	91	73	81
Consultative committee	22	28	5	9	3
Problem-solving or quality groups	25	0	17	4	49
Formal opinion survey p	36	78	50	39	62
Other dd					
Entire workforce meetings	22	6	59	61	18
Management chain/ cascade	52	100	37	30	20
Suggestion schemes	20	24	39	22	12
Newsletter	29	24	36	51	66
Disclosure of information bb					
Internal investment plans	71	100	34	55	77
Financial position of establishment	76	96	49	74	88
Financial position of organization m	64	72	76	89	71
Staffing plans	65	78	68	34	62

Source: WERS98.

Notes: Yes responses to all weighted cases unless otherwise stated. p In last five years for establishments five years or older. dd Four most frequently mentioned other ways in which management consults or communicates with employees (multi-response). bb Regularly given by management to employees or their representatives. m Where part of a larger organization or sole UK establishment.

a range of issues rather than a single topic, with the exception of restaurants where most discuss a single topic.

In the very few HI workplaces where a consultative committee deals with a range of issues (N = 13, all of which employ 50 or more workers), employee representatives are significantly more likely to be elected and not to be appointed by management than in AIS and the PSS. In AIS there are proportionately more workplaces where committees deal with a range of issues (N = 441), but representatives are less likely to be elected, and appointment by management features in one-quarter of workplaces. These committee meetings occur slightly more frequently in AIS and the PSS. HI managers were significantly more likely than their AIS and PSS counterparts to consider these committees as fairly influential or not very influential.

Direct participation

Marchington and Wilkinson (1999: 345–50) identify a fourfold schema of involvement (Box 6.3), all of which embrace empowerment to differing degrees. Whether involvement schemes benefit all or are wholly exploitative, benefiting only employers, depends on the context and the processes, and employees can simultaneously experience greater job discretion and increased satisfaction and increased work demands. Workers will always resist so it is 'unrealistic to expect these sorts of schemes to remove problems from work, given that the employment relationship in any organization is built upon both conflict and co-operation' (Marchington and Wilkinson, 1999: 359).

The use of employee involvement practices to foster an open, supportive and participatory employment relations climate will be positively linked to improving SQ (Redman and Mathews, 1998). Communication systems, based on the 'involvement' model of indirect participation are an important prerequisite to culture change (Watson and D'Annunzio-Green, 1996). Guest and Conway (2002) see a parallel between managing organizational culture and the psychological contract, as both embody people-building and high trust relationships. The process is complex and, if left to chance, will lead to poor relations with employees. Communication is most effective at entry and on-job, while communicating down the organization is the most difficult aspect. The problem for managers in attempting to communicate full and accurate information is that simple explanations may distort reality.

Most of the literature on employee involvement in the HI is concerned with empowerment and teamworking. After discussing these we focus on other involvement mechanisms drawn mainly from WERS.

Empowerment

Empowerment is a central component of SQ management and, like teamworking, is managerially led. It is wider than delegation, as power and authority are devolved, giving employees greater responsibility to solve problems, akin to Friedman's (1977) 'responsible autonomy'. Rather than providing greater autonomy or self-

---

Box 6.3 A four-fold schema of involvement

Downward communication is the most diluted, and includes written documentation, face-to-face meetings, house journals and team briefing. Its purpose is to convey information, reinforce managerial prerogative and shape employee expectations.

Upward problem solving taps into employees' knowledge and ideas, and includes suggestion schemes and ad hoc problem-solving groups or quality circles, where small groups meet voluntarily on a regular basis to identify, analyse and solve quality-related work problems. These practices are part of 'best practice' HRM (Pfeffer, 1998). Like downward communication it is essentially unitarist and 'bolted' onto the work process.

Task-based participation is integral to the job and part of everyday working life, and includes quality of working life programmes. It may entail performing more tasks at the same level or at a higher level, or some managerial/supervisory responsibility.

Teamworking and self-management (one of Pfeffer's (1998) seven key HRM practices) allows employees to take responsibility for the task, work without direct supervision, to have discretion over work methods and time, to multi-skill and to recruit team members. Managerial control is at its most subversive and effective when employees take on responsibility for peer surveillance.

Source: Derived from Marchington and Wilkinson (1999).

---

management, empowerment may lead to greater work intensification and increased stress, and may represent a form of control.

Lashley (1997) identifies four meanings of empowerment through:

- participation (autonomous work groups, job enrichment);
- involvement (quality circles, team briefings);
- commitment (share ownership, profit-sharing);
- delayering (job redesign, job enrichment).

Claims for empowerment need to take account of the way managers use these different definitions and meanings, as different forms of empowerment lead to different working arrangements and boundaries for what employees can and cannot do (Lashley, 1996). Empowerment as participation is observed in Marriott Hotels where employees have to identify and satisfy customer needs. In Harvester Restaurants where delayering requires staff to make decisions about work organization or scheduling, the culture is still largely control-oriented (Lashley, 1995b). Empowerment as involvement is practised in Hilton Hotels (team briefing), McDonald's (suggestion schemes) and Accor (quality circles).

The challenge for international companies is how to balance the consistency and certainty demanded by customers with elements of employee discretion necessary to add the nebulous quality factor to social interactions in variety of cultural contexts. Jones *et al.* (1997) report how one American hotel company encourages employees to 'share' and 'celebrate' employment stories, including access to a worldwide empowerment hotline. This helps reinforce a level of commitment perceived as necessary to go 'beyond contract'. Managers find themselves caught between the contradictory impulses of standardization and customization, and cannot abandon either. Legge (1995a) identifies a similar contradiction within quality management, which seems to argue for delegation and control simultaneously.

Marriott Corporation and Harvester Restaurants use empowerment to produce greater efficiency, improve employee commitment, and ultimately increase customer satisfaction (Lashley, 1997). At Harvester Restaurants the removal of a layer of management and the formation of employees into self-managing teams succeeded because of low turnover, the commitment of the team manager and the active support of senior managers (Ashness and Lashley, 1995). The greater autonomy and discretion afforded by teamworking may be accompanied by work intensification and increased surveillance, e.g. management, peers, customer feedback and 'mystery shoppers'. 'Quick fix' empowerment will rarely succeed.

Case study 6.10 **From empowerment to control in a Canadian nightclub**

Employees had developed an articulate and sophisticated culture with an elaborate customer-service hierarchy and system of reward and punishment, based on high-tipping customers. The main product was status not alcohol. There was low staff turnover and high flexibility, and core values were instilled in informal after-work gatherings, where employees shared stories, thereby training each other. There was high group cohesion although staff developed their own highly personalized styles of service to suit their particular customers.

The change was designed to generalize service to as wide a market as possible, with a new manager exercising control from the top. Job training was to manipulate employees' perception of their role. All intermediate supervisory posts were removed, so grievances had to be taken to the top. Employees' behaviour was monitored by 'spotters'. Superficial agreeability, a form of industrial sabotage, replaced authoritative emotional exchange. Employees were deskilled because they engaged in more limited social interaction and lost income because they had to serve different customers. After-work gatherings reduced and workers became stressed. Customers went elsewhere, sales fell, morale declined and employees lost any respect they had had for the manager.

Source: Sosteric (1996).

The key to success is communication that builds a shared understanding of what empowerment means, surrounded by commitment, ownership, skills and competencies, leadership and sustainability (D'Annunzio-Green and Macandrew, 1999).

Hales and Kildas (1998: 93) claim that 'The notion of empowerment is beset by conceptual ambiguities, contradictions and a lack of compelling supporting evidence.' Their study of five-star hotels in Amsterdam found little evidence of empowerment in spite of management rhetoric. What there was amounted to increased employee responsibility rather than greater choice over how work is done or more voice in organizational decisions. Support systems of recruitment, training and remuneration were mostly absent.

The critical issue of how to balance control and autonomy in securing both compliance and cooperation is also addressed by others. As Lashley (1995a: 28) points out, 'Employers are concerned with both employee control and commitment. Employers are merely shifting the locus of control from one imposed externally on employees, to one which generates increased self-control in each employee.' At best worker power in enhanced but in highly controlled circumstances (Rees, 1999).

Sosteric's (1996) ethnographic account of a nightclub provides a case of empowerment in reverse, as a management sought to impose direct control in a workplace where work organization was based on responsible autonomy (Case study 6.10).

Teamworking

Service industry characteristics and customer orientation are conducive to teamworking, which is one of the three key principles of SQ management (Wilkinson *et al.*, 1998). Claims that teamworking is used in two-thirds of British workplaces are rather hollow as only 5 per cent actually had autonomous work groups (Cully *et al.*, 1999).

Rees (1999) examined the nature and extent of employee involvement through teamworking in hotels, including the methods used and the levels of responsibility and autonomy afforded to teams. Two approaches were used. Task-based teams were created to make workers functionally flexible, e.g. within food and beverage operations across the bar, restaurant and room service. Problem-solving teams met to discuss improving customer service when management signalled a problem. Actual levels of discretion and responsibility were low because managers deployed various mechanisms to limit empowerment. Although the employees reported a strong sense of teamwork, they felt it should allow them to have more input into problem-solving and decision-making. Rees defines constrained responsible autonomy as 'reorganized control', as the increased level of employee involvement is within increasingly defined and measured limits.

WERS shows that HI workplaces are significantly less likely to have most of the LOG working in formally designated teams. Higher levels of teamworking occur in large HI workplaces, where three-quarters of workplaces have half or more workers so involved. The HI is also significantly more likely to have just a few or no workplaces using teamworking, especially in very small workplaces. The lack of teamworking is interesting given that it is one of Redman and Mathews' (1998) eight key HRM practices necessary to make a positive contribution to SQ (Box 3.2).

Other means of employee involvement

Workforce briefing

WERS tells us that a large majority of workplaces in AIS, the PSS and the HI operate a system of briefings for one or more sections of the workforce (Table 6.8). Nine in ten HI workplaces employing 25 or more workers operate a system of briefings. An all-inclusive approach involving the whole workforce is especially marked in very small workplaces. A more selective or tiered approach of departmental or work group/section/team briefing occurs as workplace size increases, and is most common in hotels.

Briefing occurs less frequently in the HI than in AIS and the PSS, with six in ten HI workplaces briefing on a monthly or less frequent basis compared to half in AIS. Infrequency of briefing is particularly marked in very small HI workplaces and bars, with more frequent briefing occurring in large workplaces and hotels. HI workplaces give slightly less time at meetings to questions from employees or for employees' views, and the amount of time available decreases with HI workplace size. Thus nearly two-thirds of large workplaces allocate less than a quarter of time at meetings for this purpose, while six in ten very small workplaces allow one-quarter or more of the meeting for employee feedback. This suggests that employees in very small workplaces do have more opportunity to participate in such meetings although the opportunity for them to do this is less frequent. Conversely briefing in large workplaces is less 'consultative' although it occurs more frequently.

The vast majority of HI workplaces in New Zealand communicate directly with individuals, usually on an 'as and when' basis, although more formal methods such as JCCs are found in larger workplaces (Ryan, 1996). Workplaces are less likely to seek employees' input than to supply information. Newsletters, suggestion schemes and notice boards were common only in hotels and fast food.

Problem-solving groups

The HI is significantly less likely to have problem-solving groups for specific problems or to discuss aspects of performance or quality than AIS and the PSS (Table 6.8). In the HI the probability of a group operating increases with workplace size. Where there is no group and the establishment is five or more years old, groups have been used during the last five years in only a tiny minority of workplaces.

Although such groups are more likely to be permanent in the HI than in AIS and the PSS, the HI is significantly more likely to have groups with a finite life than AIS. In the HI a group's contribution is significantly more likely to be recognized by non-financial reward and is significantly less likely to get nothing at all. Financial rewards are given in around one-third of cases.

Whether or not such groups exist, employees in most workplaces in AIS, the PSS and the HI can make suggestions for improving working methods through other channels, most commonly through their managers.

Opinion surveys

A significant minority of workplaces in AIS, the PSS and the HI has used formal surveys to elicit employees' views or opinion during the last five years (Table 6.8). In the HI this is more likely to happen in workplaces employing 50 or more workers than in workplaces employing fewer than 50 employees. The results are most likely to be made available in written form to all employees than not made fully available. However, full disclosure is more likely not to take place at all in very small HI workplaces. Chung (1997) suggests that opinion surveys enable employees to provide valuable information about guests' characteristics, appropriate people to hire and the training they need, and how best to reward employees. The results may be used to adjust HR practices in support of SQ.

Other forms of communication and consultation

The HI is most likely to communicate or consult using regular meetings with the whole workforce, while the management chain and cascading information are most likely to be used in AIS and the PSS. In addition to these two methods, regular newsletters distributed to all employees and suggestion schemes constitute the four most often used methods in AIS and the HI. Even, so one-fifth of HI workplaces (16 per cent in AIS) offers no other forms of communication and consultation. Broad-brush sub-sector patterns are shown in Table 6.9.

Disclosure of information relating to plans about organizational and establishment financial performance and internal investment and staff plans is a majority practice in AIS, PSS and HI workplaces (Table 6.8). Regular information about the financial position of the whole organization (where part of larger organization or sole UK establishment) is the issue most likely to be disclosed to employees or their representatives. Looking at all HI workplaces, financial information about the establishment is more likely to be disclosed than information about internal investment plans and staffing plans. Some sub-sector variation is evident from Table 6.9.

Discussion and review topics

Collective dialogue

How far can collective dialogue in the form of social partnership provide a more effective means than collective bargaining to regulate employment in the hospitality industry?

Trade unions

Debate the following two motions:

- There is no place for trade unions in the hospitality and tourism industries.
- Trade unions actually benefit employers and workers in the hospitality and tourism industries.

Organizing trade union members

How can trade unions organize hospitality and tourism workers more effectively?

Workplace conflict

- How many types of individual and collective workplace conflict can you identify?
- What damage does such conflict inflict on the organization?
- How can managers prevent conflict from occurring?

Consultation

What are the most effective systems and means of consultation between employers and workforce, in the following circumstances?

- A large MNC hotel company operating in America and Europe.
- A national, independent restaurant chain.
- A regional café bar company with establishments in Glasgow and Edinburgh.
- A medium-sized family-run hotel.
- A fish and chip shop.

Empowerment

Can workers really be empowered or is empowerment simply another device to maximize managerial control?

Teamworking

Can teamworking be imposed or is it only effective in certain conditions and where it evolves?

Workforce briefing

How far is workforce briefing just an exercise in management propaganda and employee 'brain-washing' or does it actually benefit both managers and workers?

7 Employment law and dispute resolution

Learning objectives

By the end of this chapter you should be able to:

- understand how the legal and institutional framework underpins the principles of justice, fairness and equity;
- appreciate the nature of individual and collective disputes and the means by which they may be resolved;
- identify the essential features of effective grievance and disciplinary procedures and the circumstances and conditions that contribute to effective individual dispute resolution within the workplace;
- evaluate the role of the employment tribunal system.

Employment law

International regulation of employment derives from ILO Conventions, e.g. the Minimum Wage Fixing Convention (1928) is one of the most widely accepted instruments of the ILO (Lucas, 1986). The way in which this had been implemented as legislation and/or collective agreements varies considerably (LPC, 2003: 251–8; also Chapter 5), reflecting the differences in national employment systems, institutional arrangements and cultures outlined in Chapter 1. Although we can discern varying extents of regulation, suggesting that the US is less regulated than Europe, this is over-simplistic as the US has substantially more employment law than Britain. Similarly a European model, if it exists, is highly diverse (Taylor, 2001a,b). Because of huge national variations, this chapter focuses mainly on UK law and practice within the context of the EU, supplemented by examples from Europe and the rest of the world.

Some 200 EU measures affect the HI, many of which are implemented into national legislation (ILO, 2001: 68). Hence it is possible to trace the roots of much UK employment protection legislation to EU Directives and other pronouncements.[1] The UK has the least employment protection legislation in the EU, while Mediterranean countries have the most. Less legislation is closely related to higher part-time, female and youth employment rates (Slinger, 2001). The principle of subsidiarity allows EU countries to implement Directives in accordance with national systems, hence more highly regulated systems are likely to manifest more legislation. Weaker coverage can arise from securing derogations for a transitional period, e.g. individual opt-outs from the 48-hour week or from failure to implement a Directive in its true spirit, which may lead to a legal challenge.[2] Many European countries contain legal regulations within collective agreements, e.g. the Spanish hospitality sectoral agreement incorporates regulations governing disciplinary procedures.

Employment law is broadly differentiated as individual rights and entitlements, that is law designed to protect individual workers, and collective rights that largely regulate the role of employers and trade unions in collective bargaining and collective disputes. The law is also designed to encourage employers to follow good practice, and to change their behaviour in the ways they deal with workers individually and collectively.

Individual rights

In many countries there are exceptions to blanket coverage of employment protection (ILO, 2001). Employers also exploit loopholes, such as using short-term casuals who do not build up any continuity of service (Head and Lucas, 2004a,b). Different legal environments in countries across the world pose operational challenges for MNCs, and may militate against maintaining a consistent sense of identity. Zuehl and Sherwyn (2001) suggest that HI companies identify policies and practices to comply with the legal requirements of all countries where they operate. Best policies will combine conformance to the most stringent legal requirements and voluntarily adopt practices that are not required. Nevertheless, there may be circumstances where a single comprehensive policy is not feasible. Case study 7.1 indicates common themes distilled from dismissal law in eleven countries (Australia, China, Egypt, France, Germany, Italy, Japan, Mexico, South Korea, the UK and the US), upon which a model termination policy has been based.

The UK experience

The 1970s saw a major expansion in individual employment protection rights to include equal pay, sex and race discrimination, and unfair dismissal. Although the 1980s and 1990s have been described as a period of deregulation, 'legal formalisation of the employment relationship increased as new regulation, both substantive and procedural was added' (Brown *et al.*, 2000: 613), increasing the importance of legal governance of the employment relationship. Most rights have been restricted to *employees* who have a contract of service or apprenticeship, and may depend on a length of service qualification. There are also some exemptions related to a worker's age[3] and size of firm.[4] The main body of this employment protection legislation is contained in the *Employment Rights Act 1996*. Disputes relating to individual rights are determined at employment tribunal (see pp. 190–4).

A major extension to the floor of statutory rights has occurred under New Labour. Some measures, e.g. the NMW and WTR, have wider application to

Case study 7.1 **Patterns in dismissal law across 11 countries**

Substantive dismissal standards

Only the US and China do not have a minimum requirement (just cause) that the employer must establish a reason for dismissal that is valid and reasonable. Just cause typically includes employee performance deficiencies and misconduct. In China, if notice is provided, an employee may be dismissed for any or no reason.

Pretermination process

A number of countries require employers to fulfil procedural requirements before an employee is dismissed, such as providing reasons for the dismissal, or giving the employee the opportunity to respond to any charges or accusations. Information in writing is required in Mexico, France and Italy. In Australia and the UK compliance with the employer's own procedure and basic principles of fairness are considered. In Egypt and South Korea, joint committees play a more substantial role in the dismissal process, while the trade unions must be informed in Germany.

Notice

In a number of countries employers are always required to give notice prior to dismissal. In some cases this is regardless of whether the dismissal satisfies applicable standards of just cause. Length of notice is often determined by length of service, e.g. in Germany and the UK. More frequently notice is required for all cases except where the employee is dismissed for just cause, e.g. in France and Australia. No notice is required in Mexico and the US.

Severance

Australia, China, Germany, the UK and the US require no severance payments other than payments that may be made in lieu of notice. In Italy and Mexico severance payments are made regardless of the reason for dismissal. Egyptian employers are required to pay compensation to a social-insurance authority based on length of employment. In Korea severance payments are made in the form of contributions towards employees' retirement allowances.

Source: Zuehl and Sherwyn (2001).

workers who work under any other contract, such as agency workers. The *Employment Relations Act 1999* allows the Secretary of State to extend any extant statutory employment rights applicable only to employees to those who are currently excluded. Failure to bring workers in scope of legal provisions such as unfair dismissal is clearly detrimental to many casual workers in the HI, where the courts continue to take a strict line (Leighton and Painter, 2001; Head and Lucas, 2004b). So-called 'casuals' with long continuous service and appreciable workloads may not be given contracts. As they do not perceive themselves to be employees, they may be disinclined to assert their rights, even though the reality may be different (Head and Lucas, 2004b). A review of the Act in 2002 has proposed that this should be effected by regulations only, which does not require primary or secondary legislation to be amended, but no indications of any actual changes in coverage have been given (www.dti.gov.uk/er/erareview).

The main changes since 1997 are summarized in Box 7.1.[5] Disputes resolution measures contained in the *Employment Relations Act 1999* and the *Employment Act 2002* are discussed in more detail later in the chapter. Appropriate websites must be consulted for up-to-date details. The DTI's website provides the most useful and comprehensive information and an extensive list of hyperlinks (www.dti.gov.uk/er/index.htm). The main body of discrimination, harassment, family-friendly, and health and safety legislation is discussed in Chapter 4, while minimum wage legislation is outlined in Chapter 5.

The main enforcement mechanism is an employment tribunal, which comprises a legally qualified chair and two lay members, one with an employer background and the other with a union or worker background. Tribunal decisions are not binding on other tribunals, but decisions reached by any of the higher courts (case law) are binding. Tribunal decisions can be appealed to the EAT, the CA or the House of Lords (HL). A case with potentially far reaching consequences may be referred to the ECJ by any of the aforementioned bodies.

Collective rights

Although collective employment law governs the rights, actions, duties, roles, responsibilities and behaviours of employers and trade unions, in practice the vast majority of legal provisions centre on trade unions. Deregulation aimed at reducing trade union power has been a key public policy theme in many English-speaking nations, including the UK, Australia and New Zealand (see Case studies 3.2 and 6.1). The role of trade unions has altered radically and been marginalized in post-Communist regimes in Central and Eastern Europe (Pollert, 1999), although some progress has been made in establishing an institutional framework. As noted in Chapter 6, a favourable legal environment rarely translates into high trade union density among hospitality and tourism workers.

The UK experience

The *Trade Disputes Act 1906* gave trade unions immunity from prosecution under the civil law, allowing them to function lawfully and conferring the right to strike

---

Box 7.1 Main recent legislation and regulations (UK)

National Minimum Wage Act 1998 (www.lowpay.gov.uk) entitles workers aged 22 and over to a minimum wage, while a lower development rate applies to young workers and adult trainees.

Human Rights Act 1998 (www.homeoffice.gov.uk/hract) allows the European Convention on Human Rights to be enforced directly in UK courts. Although the impact on employment law is likely to be limited, employment tribunals have a duty to develop common law so as to make it compatible with the Convention Rights, and to interpret and apply legislation in a way that is compatible with Convention Rights. Groups not yet covered by anti-discrimination legislation might take proceedings under the Convention.

Data Protection Act 1998 (www.hmso.gov.uk/acts/acts1998) regulates how personal data may be held, used and disclosed (based on 'data protection principles'), which now includes manual data.

Public Interest Disclosure Act 1998 (www.hmso.gov.uk/acts/acts1998) protects workers against victimization or dismissal who 'blow the whistle' on their employers' fraudulent, criminal or dangerous activities.

Working Time Regulations 1998 (www.dti.gov.uk/er/work_time_regs) applies to workers and limits the working week to an average of 48 hours a week. Restrictions are placed on nightwork. There is a right to minimum rest intervals, one day off per week, in-work rest breaks and four weeks' paid leave per annum in addition to statutory holidays.

Part-time Workers (Prevention of Less Favourable Treatment) Regulations 2000 (www.dti.gov.uk/ptime) gives part-time workers the right not to be treated less favourably than comparable full-time workers in their contractual terms and conditions, unless objectively justified.

Fixed-term Employees (Prevention of Less Favourable Treatment) Regulations 2002 gives fixed-term employees the right not to be treated less favourably than comparable full-time workers in their contractual terms and conditions, unless objectively justified.

---

and undertake peaceful picketing. The 'traditional' system of British industrial relations based on the notion of 'voluntarism' and 'free collective bargaining' was considered to be in need of reform by the 1960s (Donovan Commission). The *Industrial Relations Act 1971* sought to restrict 'too powerful' trade unions. The status quo was restored by successive *Trade Union and Labour Relations Acts* in 1974 and 1976. Short-lived statutory recognition procedures introduced under the *Employment Protection Act 1975* were repealed as unworkable in 1980.

From 1979 trade union power was seriously weakened through a process of accretion (Kessler and Bayliss, 1998), which restricted unions' capacity to function and maintain their membership base. Aggregate union membership density in Britain in workplaces employing 25 or more employees fell from 65 per cent to 36 per cent between 1980 and 1998 (Millward *et al.*, 2000). Union density (all in employment) dropped from 33.6 per cent to 26.5 per cent between 1991 and 2001 (Brook, 2002). The *Trade Union and Labour Relations Consolidation Act 1992* and the *Trade Union Reform and Employment Rights Act 1993* contain all the relevant measures, which focus on:

- More limited autonomy of trade unions and a restriction of their activities, e.g. election of officers and ballots on mergers by postal ballot.
- Measures to undermine union funds and membership, e.g. the deduction of subscriptions from pay became subject to more stringent conditions and the end of 'closed shop'.
- Restrictions on the right to strike and take industrial action, e.g. official strike subject to stringent ballot conditions, with no secondary picketing.

The *Employment Relations Act 1999* made certain improvements to the position of trade unions and worker representation:

- Trade unions have the right to claim *statutory recognition* (excluding employers with fewer than 21 employees including part-timers). If the employer refuses to recognize the trade union, the trade union may refer the claim to the CAC for a decision.
- *Dismissal for taking part in lawful industrial action is automatically unfair.*
- Workers have the *right to be accompanied* by either a fellow employee or trade union official when requested to attend a disciplinary or grievance hearing,[6] regardless of whether the employer recognizes the union. This should afford more fairness in grievance and disciplinary hearings, but accompaniment does not imply representation. There is no right to be accompanied by a lawyer, and the companion does not have the right to answer questions on the worker's behalf.

The trend has been for more voluntary recognition agreements, because employers see them as producing more favourable collective bargaining deals than statutorily determined ones. The review of the *Employment Relations Act 1999* has proposed minor changes to the recognition procedures, which favour both employers and trade unions (www.dti.gov.uk/er/erareview).

Dispute resolution

A framework of justice

As noted in Chapter 1, the rules of employment govern *inter alia* what work is done, how jobs are constituted, pay and conditions of employment and hours of work.

Standards of behaviour and performance are not set in tablets of stone. For the most part the employment relationship is a dynamic nexus that is subject to continuous adjustment and negotiation. Some matters may be subject to more formal modes of regulation, e.g. an annual pay review, than others, e.g. a short-term adjustment to working hours. Sometimes the relationship breaks down, an issue of conflict emerges and order and normality need to be restored. Disputes about the application of existing rules are usually referred to as conflicts of right. Disputes about the development of new rules through the process of collective bargaining are termed conflicts of interest.

At an individual level, formal procedures are needed to resolve any disputes that may arise from either 'unfair' managerial or 'unreasonable' worker behaviour. As Torrington *et al.* (2002: 532) note 'The organisation requires a framework of justice to surround the employment relationship so that managers and supervisors, as well as other employees, know where they stand when dissatisfaction develops'. This framework of organizational justice is a function of procedures and processes that are perceived as fair and reasonable to all parties, and an acknowledgement that power may be used unduly by either of the parties. Customers may clearly be involved in disputes, e.g. where a complaint leads to disciplinary action, but information is sparse (Case study 7.2). Informal means may also be used successfully to resolve disputes.

Particular emphasis is placed on individual dispute resolution through procedures for resolving a worker's grievance or to enable management to discipline a worker whose performance or conduct is unsatisfactory. As managers have greater power in the employment relationship, discipline is the major issue, and it is about control. Hence grievance and discipline are not necessarily complementary processes of social control (Hook *et al.*, 1996). This reflects the major shift from collective conflict in the form of strike action to individual overt conflict, manifested variously as absenteeism, labour turnover and recourse to the grievance and disciplinary process (Knight and Latreille, 2000; ACAS, 2002). Collective disputes

---

Case study 7.2 **Dispute resolution in unionized hospitality workplaces in the US**

The grievance arbitration process in collective agreements is the principal method for resolving disputes relating to interpretation of the contract and discipline and discharge. Employers are more likely to win contract claims where the burden of proof falls on the union, and to lose discipline and discharge cases where the burden of proof falls on them. They are more likely to win theft of food cases, because policies are clear and unambiguous, and less likely to win where money transactions are involved. Although offensive behaviour towards colleagues or customers in the presence of customers features prominently, an employer cannot win a case without customer testimony, and many fail to report.

Source: Murrmann and Murrmann (1997).

procedures are less likely to apply in the HI, as they are normally a function of active trade unions.

It is estimated that there are between 500,000 and 900,000 individual disputes per annum (DTI, 2001b). Hence the prominence of individual dispute resolution in recent and current employment relations policy reform (Earnshaw *et al.*, 1998, 2000; Goodman *et al.*, 1998; DTI, 2002).

The institutional framework for dispute resolution

Recent legal developments

The state has played an important role in dispute resolution since the nineteenth century. The legal framework governs the behaviour of employers and trade unions in collective bargaining, encourages employers to develop internal disputes resolution procedures, and provides employees and workers with grievance, disciplinary and dismissal rights in employment, including recourse outside the organization to an employment tribunal as a last resort.

The *Employment Rights (Dispute Resolution) Act 1998* introduced an award of two weeks' pay where an unfairly dismissed employee was prevented from using the internal appeals procedure. The *Employment Relations Act 1999* (see p. 175) and the *Employment Act 2002* both place considerable emphasis upon improving dispute resolution in the workplace, and strengthening the institutional and legal framework for resolving disputes.

The *Employment Act 2002* contains provisions aimed at improving employment relations and avoiding unnecessary employment tribunals through better communication in the workplace and improved conciliation. The tribunal system will also be streamlined. The following changes will be in place in 2004, after consultation and the drafting of Regulations, while others may follow later arising from the review of the *Employment Relations Act 1999*:

- Statutory minimum grievance and disciplinary procedures will be automatically incorporated into all contracts (i.e. employees only).
- An extension to the time limits for lodging a tribunal application will allow procedures to be completed.
- Certain categories of complaint will be prevented from being presented at tribunal.
- Tribunals can vary compensatory awards where the employer or applicant has failed to use the minimum statutory procedures. The minimum reduction/increase is 10 per cent, and can be up to 50 per cent where it is 'just and equitable' to do so.
- Wider compliance with the written statement of employment particulars will be required. Employers can rely on an offer letter or contract instead of the written statement. The exemption of employers with fewer than 20 employees from giving information on grievance and disciplinary procedures will be removed, and an employee may be awarded a minimum of two weeks' pay as compensation where the employer has failed to provide written particulars.

- The way dismissals are judged will be altered. Provided the minimum standards set out in the Act are met and the dismissal is otherwise fair, other procedural shortcomings can be disregarded. This reverses the decision in *Polkey v A. E. Dayton Services (formerly Edmund Walker (Holdings) Ltd) [1987] 503 HL and [1987] 13 CA*. This established that a dismissal will normally be unfair where a fair procedure was not followed, even if following the fair procedure would not have affected the eventual decision.

Institutional support

Institutions independent of government exist primarily to promote the voluntary settlement of individual and collective disputes, if they cannot be resolved through normal workplace procedures.

ACAS

ACAS is the most influential independent body, dealing with the prevention and resolution of individual and collective problems in the workplace by voluntary means. The ACAS mission is to improve organizations and working life through better employment relations, and its services are free to employers, trade unions and workers:

- *Advisory* activities focus on preventative measures, and include a telephone helpline, a range of publications, and projects with employers and trade unions.
- *Conciliation* is the act of reconciling or bringing together the parties with the aim of moving forward to an acceptable voluntary settlement.
- In *mediation*, a more proactive process, an ACAS officer will act as an intermediary who will make suggestions to resolve the problem.
- ACAS can also arrange for the appointment of an independent arbitrator to decide the outcome of a dispute, which may be binding in law. *Arbitration* is now available as an alternative to a tribunal hearing, currently for unfair dismissal only.

The ACAS *Annual Report 2001–02* (ACAS, 2002) shows its major workload involves providing conciliation in individual disputes (tribunal and non-tribunal). In that period 137,500 cases were completed out of 165,093 cases received. The main issues of dispute were unfair dismissal (46,363 cases), protection of wages (36,205 cases) and breach of contract (26,420 cases). Only one-quarter of cases proceeded to employment tribunal, as a conciliated settlement was reached in 42 per cent of cases and one-third of cases were withdrawn. A settlement made under the auspices of ACAS cannot proceed to tribunal. An alternative means of pre-tribunal settlement is through a compromise agreement, which is more formal and legalistic (Lucas, 1998).

Conciliation in collective disputes accounted for 1,270 completed cases, of which 92 per cent resulted in a settlement or progress towards a settlement. Pay and terms and conditions of employment and recognition were the main causes of dispute. Some 61 cases referred for arbitration and seven for mediation were concerned mainly with pay or dismissal and discipline. Only 13 cases were referred under the new arbitration scheme for unfair dismissal, suggesting that there is 'mistrust' of a single arbitrator with the power to award compensation of more than £50,000.

The ACAS helpline deals with over 750,000 calls per annum on a wide range of issues including people's rights in the workplace. Over half of 506 advisory projects were concerned with collective bargaining arrangements or communication, consultation and employee involvement. ACAS is developing its advisory work in relation to small business in conjunction with the Small Business Service.

The statutory *Code of Practice on Disciplinary and Grievance Procedures* (ACAS, 2000), discussed in more detail on pp. 181–2 and pp. 185–6, is the most influential ACAS publication, since employment tribunals and arbitrators are bound to take its provisions into account. The Code provides detailed guidance on the essential features of procedures and how they should be used in practice. Areas on which more specific guidance has been added include capability cases, confidentiality of disciplinary proceedings, grievances raised during disciplinary proceedings, use of suspension, communication of rules, stages of procedure (warnings), duration of warnings, handling of grievance and disciplinary appeals and the rights of the person accompanying the employee. This Code is under review in light of the new provisions of the *Employment Act 2002*.

CAC

The CAC's role is 'to promote fair and efficient arrangements in the workplace, by resolving collective disputes . . . either by voluntary agreement or, if necessary, through adjudication' (CAC, 2002: 12). The CAC deals with recognition and de-recognition disputes, applications for disclosure of information for collective bargaining, and disputes over the constitution of EWCs, providing they satisfy the statutory test.

The CAC's *Annual Report 2001–02* reported 118 cases of statutory recognition in the previous 12 months, bringing the total to 175 since the procedure was instituted in 2000. These procedures are based on the premise that voluntary agreement is preferable to statutory recognition, and the procedure offers a number of opportunities for the parties to step back and reach a voluntary agreement. ACAS assistance may be sought in reaching a voluntary agreement. Although there have been no recognition claims in the HI, there have been number of recognition claims have been made in airlines and casinos. Summaries of these cases are posted on the CAC's website (www.cac.gov.uk/recent_decisions/).

Grievance and disciplinary procedures

Grievances

The nature of grievances

Worker complaints and grievances are a pervasive part of workplace life and, if unresolved, can lead the negative outcomes for managers and workers.

Surprisingly the subject continues to be neglected with analysis concentrating on the nature of complaints and the procedures rather than on their causes and effects (Cully *et al.*, 1999; Lewin and Peterson, 1999; Meager *et al.*, 2002). The concept of justice is akin to that used in civil law, as grievances address an individual's claim of suffering or being wronged. Yet the outcome may be a reassertion of managerial authority where managerial behaviour leading to a grievance is attributed to a lack of clear rules (Hook *et al.*, 1996).

The three-stage approach developed by Pigors and Myers (1977) provides one way to classify individual employee disquiet:

- *Dissatisfaction* bothers the individual but is not expressed out loud. The worker might feel upset because s/he has been reprimanded for someone else's mistake, or because s/he has been given insufficient credit for dealing well with a difficult situation. The incident may be quickly forgotten, but more frequent recurrence may induce workforce resistance with negative outcomes including deterioration in performance, pilfering and sabotage or high staff turnover.
- Dissatisfaction becomes a *complaint* when the issue is articulated and brought to someone's attention. It may arise from misinformation or a misunderstanding. Provided the person dealing with the complaint has the ability to resolve the problem, it may be resolved simply by explanation.
- A *grievance* represents a more formal complaint that is presented to management and, as such, constitutes a direct challenge to managerial authority. This may explain why grievances are relatively rare. Additionally the employee may genuinely believe that nothing will happen anyway.

However, these distinctions are regarded as spurious, because most procedures preclude entering the formal stages unless formal resolution has been attempted by those immediately involved (Rollinson *et al.*, 1996).

The nature of the grievance itself also contributes to the relative rarity of grievances. 'Grievances are usually complex but are typically reformulated and misrepresented to fit acceptably simplistic classifications' (Salipante and Bouwen, 1990: 17). They are continuous, without clear beginning and endings, and may develop into an accumulation of problems. Salipante and Bouwen differentiate three main sources of conflict:

- *Environmental conflict* arises from working conditions and the nature of the work.
- *Social-substantive conflict* stems from perceived inequities in treatment or from disagreements over goals of means.
- *Social-relational conflict* derives from relationships between individuals, groups and organizations, personality conflicts, racism and sexism.

Environmental conflict may be more easy to articulate and resolve, when the problem is tangible, e.g. failure of equipment. Both types of social conflict are more problematic because they represent a challenge to management, something that many employees may feel unwilling to undertake. In these circumstances workforce resistance may be the employee's chosen means to challenge management, deployed as 'getting back', 'getting on' and 'getting by' (see Chapters 1 and 2).

Although formal procedures are necessary, it may be more effective to try and resolve grievances informally (Anon., 2002a). Variation in managers' personal frames of reference may determine whether they handle grievances in a highly prescriptive autocratic way or in a less prescriptive problem-solving manner, and may also place them at odds with organizational policy (Hook *et al.*, 1996). Managers in non-union settings may feel less inhibited about taking a prescriptive line. Alternatively newcomers may be treated more harshly than old hands, which is unfair given they have had less time to assimilate the rules of the organization, and women treated more leniently than men, raising the possibility of discrimination (Rollinson *et al.*, 1996).

Grievance procedures

The ACAS *Code of Practice on Disciplinary and Grievance Procedures* (ACAS 2000: 15–18) provides detailed managerial guidance on the principles and practice of grievance handling. Although not legally enforceable, the *Code* can be taken into account in employment tribunal proceedings. The new minimum statutory grievance procedures introduced by the *Employment Act 2002* will strengthen the position of employees in respect of procedural coverage. A modified two-step statutory procedure for former employees is also specified: statement of grievance and response. Other general requirements, which also apply in disciplinary cases, are that procedural matters must be processed without unreasonable delay, and the timing and location of meetings must be reasonable. Both sides must have the opportunity to state their cases. Appeals should be conducted by a more senior manager, so far as is reasonably practicable.

The basic principles of the ACAS guidance and new standard minimum statutory procedure are outlined in Box 7.2. Special consideration may need to be given to grievances about bullying and harassment, and in cases of whistleblowing.

Evidence from WERS shows that most non-managerial employees in HI workplaces have recourse to a formal procedure for dealing with individual grievances, although there is marginally less comprehensive coverage than in AIS and PSS. However employees in almost one-fifth of HI workplaces do not have access to grievance procedures, and they are most likely to be in smaller workplaces, hotels and bars (Tables 7.1 and 7.2). In these cases the resolution of a problem relating to working conditions would be dealt with by the responding manager or other managers. Some of these workplaces may have only one manager, making it impossible to have a staged procedure, a point that is also addressed within the ACAS Code.

Where grievance procedures exist, the vast majority of non-managerial employees in AIS, the PSS and the HI are covered. All such employees are covered in all sizes of workplace except very small workplaces (84 per cent); these are most likely to be restaurants. However as the new statutory procedures apply only to employees, other workers such as casual workers may continue to be denied access to grievance procedures.

Employees are most likely to be made aware of the procedure through the staff handbook, closely followed by the letter of appointment in AIS and the PSS. HI

Box 7.2　Grievances: ACAS guidelines and the minimum standard statutory procedure

ACAS guidelines

Stage 1 Statement of grievance, preferably in writing, to immediate superior. Where contested, the worker should be invited to attend a hearing. Where the grievance relates to the performance of a 'duty of the employer in relation to a worker', i.e. a legal duty arising from statute or common law, there is a right to be accompanied. The manager should respond in writing within five working days of the written notice or hearing.

Stage 2 If not resolved at Stage 1, the worker should be permitted to raise the matter in writing with a more senior manager. Hearing should be within five working days. Accompaniment rights as per Stage 1.The manager should respond in writing within ten working days of the hearing.

Final stage If not resolved at Stage 2, the worker should be permitted to raise the matter in writing with an even more senior manager. Time limits and accompaniment rights as per Stage 2.

Confidential records should be kept at each stage.

Minimum statutory procedure
Step 1 Statement of grievance
Step 2 Meeting
Step 3 Appeal

Source: ACAS (2000); *Employment Act 2002*.

---

workplaces are significantly less likely to inform employees of this right in the letter of appointment, especially in very small workplaces, bars and restaurants, suggesting a more informal approach to recruitment. Induction is the third most commonly used means to convey this information, in around 30 per cent of workplaces in AIS, the PSS and the HI. Use of indirect and informal means (notice board/told by manager) is most marked in restaurants.

The right to be accompanied in raising grievances is acknowledged in almost all workplaces everywhere, although almost one-fifth of restaurants have no such provision, so workers in this sub-sector would seemingly stand to benefit most from the accompaniment provisions of the *Employment Relations Act 1999*. A colleague is the most frequently mentioned source of support, followed by anyone they choose and a friend or family member. Bar employees are most likely to be able exercise choice over who accompanies them. AIS and the PSS share these general characteristics, although in AIS trade union representatives assume third-order importance before friends and family members.

Table 7.1 Formal procedural arrangements in context and by size of workplace (%)

	AIS	PSS	HI	<25	25–49	50–99	100+
Collective disputes	50	39	36**	38	28	33	50
Any dispute in last 12 months over pay/conditions	5	3	0*	0	0	3	0
Individual grievances	88	86	82	79	78	92	100
Any grievances in last 12 months	23	21	12**	9	5	24	28
Discipline and dismissals	88	86	81	75	89	90	100
Right of appeal	91	91	87	79	96	100	100
Any employees formally warned n	43	45	55	52	39	76	92
Any employee suspension (with/without pay) n	17	16	17	7	17	47	59
Any deductions from pay n	5	4	2	0	0	9	14

Source: WERS98.

Notes: All weighted cases. *Significantly different at the 5% level from AIS and PSS. **Significantly different at the 5% level from AIS. n In last 12 months.

Table 7.2 Formal procedural arrangements by sub-sector (%)

	Hotels	Campsites	Restaurants	Bars	Canteens
Collective disputes	23	100	33	36	75
Any dispute in last 12 months over pay/conditions	0	0	1	0	0
Individual grievances	73	100	93	78	86
Any grievances in last 12 months	20	6	5	11	16
Discipline and dismissals	83	100	78	80	88
Right of appeal	79	100	84	90	100
Any employees formally warned n	63	100	53	50	53
Any employee suspension (with/without pay) n	25	94	18	12	6
Any deductions from pay n	7	0	0	0	0

Source: WERS98.

Notes: All weighted cases. n In last 12 months.

Employers without procedures are much more likely to be taken to employment tribunal (DTI, 2001b). There was no prior meeting between employer and employees in two-thirds of tribunal cases. The *Employment Act 2002* implemented in 2004 will prevent particular complaints being presented at tribunal if part or all of the grievance procedure has not been completed, additional to the powers of tribunals to reduce compensation.

Use of procedures

In practice HI employees are less likely to use the grievance procedure, especially in smaller workplaces and restaurants (Tables 7.1 and 7.2). In the six out of ten workplaces where the grievance procedure had not been used in the previous 12 months, a dearth of formal grievances was deemed to reflect good management–employee relations and the practice of dealing with disputes informally. These reasons also apply in AIS and the PSS, with less emphasis on informal means. A majority of restaurants use informal methods, while a large minority claim never to have had any grievances. This tallies with other research showing that formal grievance procedures in non-union workplaces are used very rarely, as grievances are resolved informally (Earnshaw *et al.*, 1998). However, if we consider other evidence from WERS, we can infer that high dismissal and quit rates may indicate employee dissatisfaction, hence relations may not be as good as managers claim them to be. Procedural coverage does not guarantee that employees' individual problems will be resolved as grievances where workplace culture conflicts with the notion of formality.

Workers who have pursued a grievance experience a decline in performance ratings, work attendance rates and promotion rates, and are more likely to sustain higher turnover rates (Lewin and Peterson, 1999). Evidence suggests they become stigmatized and the object of employer retribution, which indicates why most employees who experience unjust treatment at work remain silent.

(Meager *et al.*, 2002) also confirm that the raising of grievances in relation to employment rights is a minority practice. Most of those reporting a 'problem' about their rights (16 per cent) do try and resolve the problem after seeking advice, with only a very small proportion staying and putting up with the situation or resigning. Where the advice suggested that the individual's treatment might have been unlawful, in two-thirds of cases the employee took the matter further. In one-fifth of cases the situation resolved itself. Irrespective of whether advice was taken, around 40 per cent decided to take action to remedy the problem, and a similar proportion left if the problem was not resolved.

As we noted above, the nature of grievances is complex and not easy to classify. Twelve types of grievance were specified in the WERS questionnaire, but in half the HI cases and around 45 per cent in AIS and the PSS, the substance of the grievance was none of these. None of the specified reasons stands out as problematic, except to the extent that in all groupings the main issue in one in four cases is pay and conditions. This issue was especially important in half of the restaurant sub-sample. Other more frequently mentioned issues, although minority responses, were relations with managers/supervisors, promotion/career development, work practices/allocation/pace and working time, and annual leave/time off. While most grievances appear to fall into Salipante and Bouwen's (1990) environmental conflict group, with the rest appearing to be social-relational, it is difficult to classify them with any degree of confidence, as we cannot know how far social-substantive issues underlie the grievance. Recent research shows that harassment and/or bullying tops the list of complaints, replacing pay and grading (Anon., 2002a).

Discipline and dismissal

The nature of discipline

Discipline is not simply about punishment and correction, but it is also about the formulation and application of rules and procedures that are fair and consistent (ACAS, 2000: 5), managerial control (Fox, 1985), strong leadership, and maintaining a performance based on teamwork and self-discipline (Torrington *et al.*, 2002: 528–9). Discipline goes beyond issues of conduct and capability and ensuring procedural adherence so that unfair dismissal cases are defended successfully. Hence discipline is more in keeping with criminal law, relying on a full investigation of the facts, the presentation of evidence, an appropriate period of time to reach a considered decision, and allowing a right of appeal (Hook *et al.*, 1996). As our discussion in Chapter 1 has shown, discipline is underpinned by rules and power relationships that are in a state of constant flux. Discipline is also implicit in HRM in the sense of both being managerial-led and requiring employee team spirit and commitment. High commitment management practices have not supplanted traditional disciplinary sanctions (Edwards, 2000). Dismissal and disciplinary sanctions are lower where unions have a significant presence (Brown *et al.*, 1998).

Acknowledging its broad and multifaceted face, discipline is defined as:

> The identifiable standards for the behaviour and performance of employees that are produced in organizations (including the formal and informal negotiation of these standards) and the sanctions that may be deployed for their breach.
>
> (Edwards, 2000: 319)

Disciplinary procedures

A large part of the ACAS *Code of Practice on Disciplinary and Grievance Procedures* (2000) addresses the issue of discipline, and other circumstances such as absence and poor performance, which may not necessarily give grounds for invoking the disciplinary process. Indeed the ACAS approach stresses improvement rather than punishment and, as for grievances, encourages informal means initially, such as coaching and counselling. Some key principles of the ACAS guidance and the new minimum statutory procedures are outlined in Box 7.3. A summary statutory procedure will apply in cases of immediate dismissal for gross misconduct. The employer must set out in writing the reason for dismissal, the basis for believing the employee is guilty of the alleged misconduct, and advise there is a right of appeal. If the employee appeals there must be a meeting, subject to the same conditions as in the main procedure.

WERS confirms that most HI workplaces have a formal procedure for dealing with discipline and dismissals (other than redundancies) for non-managerial employees, and coverage is marginally less comprehensive than in AIS and the PSS, and in very small workplaces (Table 7.1).

Box 7.3 Discipline: ACAS guidelines and the minimum standard statutory procedure

ACAS guidelines

Written rules should be clear and specific, and made available to all workers. Managers should ensure workers know and understand the rules, e.g. by explaining them during induction.

Workers should be clear of the likely consequences of breaking rules or failing to meet performance standards. A clear indication of the conduct that could lead to summary dismissal (gross misconduct) should be given, e.g. theft, physical violence.

Procedures should have regard to the requirements of natural justice, e.g. advance notice of allegations, no disciplinary action until the case has been carefully investigated and the right of appeal. Criminal charges or convictions outside employment are not automatic grounds for dismissal.

Stage 1 Oral *or* written warning, depending on the nature of the infringement, with reasons for the warning and the right of appeal. Warnings to be disregarded after appropriate period of 'good' behaviour. Written warnings should contain details of the improvement or change expected of the worker, when this is to be achieved, and that failure to improve may lead to a final warning.

Stage 2 Final written warning may follow from Stage 1 or where the infringement is sufficiently serious. This should incorporate the same principles as the first written warning.

Stage 3 Dismissal or other sanction, e.g. disciplinary transfer or suspension without pay, subject to contract. Decision to dismiss should be taken only by an appropriate designated manager and confirmed in writing. Reasons for dismissal should be stated and details of contract termination and appeal should be provided.

Confidential records should be kept at each stage.

Minimum statutory procedure
Step 1 Statement of grounds for action and invitation to meeting
Step 2 Meeting and notify decision
Step 3 Appeal and notify decision

Source: ACAS (2000); *Employment Act 2002.*

Where disciplinary procedures exist all non-managerial employees in HI are covered, which is significant although almost all are covered in AIS and the PSS. Employees in all groupings are most likely to be made aware of the procedure through the staff handbook, with the letter of appointment following a close second in AIS and the PSS. As with grievances, HI workplaces are less likely to make new recruits aware of these rights in the letter of appointment, pointing to a more informal approach, while induction is also the third most frequently mentioned means to convey this information. Use of indirect and informal means (notice board/told by manager) is also widely used in restaurants. Earnshaw *et al.* (1998) observed that documentation may be issued only to permanent staff, raising the possibility that formal procedures may not be applied to part-time and casual staff.

The presence of a disciplinary procedure does not mean that common disciplinary standards are applied to all employees, that all managers will comply on all occasions, or that the procedures will comply with employment tribunal criteria (Earnshaw *et al.*, 1998). As with grievances, an exploratory, non-threatening, non-punitive management style may be most appropriate (Fenley, 1998), but managers do not necessarily adopt the same handling styles for grievances and disciplinary issues (Hook *et al.*, 1996). Fenley (1998) suggests that managers' behaviour is likely to fit into one of four forms, noted in Case study 7.3 in relation to a highly relevant work-related issue for many HI employees. If an internal attribution (use of perceived psychological characteristics as causal behavioural explanations) is made about an employee, such as a tendency to be lazy or display the wrong attitude, severe sanctions will usually follow (Rollinson *et al.*, 1996). While Rollinson *et al.*'s (1997) study found that discipline achieves 'corrective' behaviour for about half of those formally disciplined, the other half maintained tendencies to rule-breaking. Here the way in which discipline is approached and handled is important. Taking a punitive approach is ineffective in shaping behaviour, and creates an impression in the mind of the person being disciplined that the manager is seeking retribution.

The right to be accompanied in disciplinary or dismissal proceedings is acknowledged in almost all workplaces in AIS, the PSS and the HI, although there is a marginal difference of disadvantage for employees compared to the practices adopted for grievance proceedings. A colleague or anyone they choose are the most frequently mentioned sources of support, with bar employees having the most freedom to elect anyone they choose. HI employees are significantly less likely to have the right to be accompanied by a union representative. The right of appeal against a disciplinary decision is also well established, if not universal.

Use of procedures

Use of the disciplinary procedure can be effected on a number of levels, and with differing degrees of severity. Written warnings (anything from a first to a final written warning) are more commonly used in the HI, with some differences occurring by size of workplace and sub-sector (Tables 7.1 and 7.2). Suspension with or without pay occurs on a less frequent basis in all groupings (under one-fifth), but

Case study 7.3 Four styles of discipline: drinking at work

Hard management: punitive and arbitrary

The *reconstructed punitive model* meets good employee relations practice and organizational needs. A single instance of an employee being found under the influence of alcohol at work results in dismissal. This is specified as a dismissable offence within rules that are clearly understood, and due process is observed.

The *arbitrary model* fails to meet good employee relations practice or organizational needs. An employee may be dismissed for one drinking offence where management has previously condoned or encouraged such behaviour, and due process is not observed.

Soft management: corrective vs. lax

The *reconstructed corrective model* meets good employee relations practice and organizational needs, allowing plenty of opportunity for reform, while due process is imperative. An employee who has committed a drink-related offence is given the opportunity to attend an employee assistance programme.

The *lax model* fails to meet good employee relations practice and organizational needs, entailing a failure to set standards or apply rules, and a tendency to adopt an over-indulgent attitude towards rule breakers. Managers do not mete out consistent treatment, delay interventions or overreact. Heavy drinking is condoned, without regard to health and safety or production and service standards.

Source: Fenley (1998).

---

is used more frequently in medium and large workplaces. A deduction from pay is a rarely used disciplinary sanction.

When the overall incidence of disciplinary sanctions is accounted for, more HI workplaces discipline their employees in AIS and the PSS (Table 7.3). Even though a sizeable minority of HI firms imposed no disciplinary sanctions, the use of any disciplinary sanction is more likely to occur in HI workplaces (one in 1.77) than in AIS (one in 2.24) and PSS workplaces (one in 2.17). The number of disciplinary sanctions applied is greater. HI workplaces (over half) are significantly more likely to impose ten or more disciplinary sanctions per 1,000 employees. This is even higher in very small workplaces (three-quarters) and restaurants (89 per cent). Similarly the mean number of dismissals per 1,000 employees is significantly higher in the HI.

WERS does not indicate the nature of offences that give rise to discipline or dismissal. Technically minor offences such as timekeeping are highly visible trans-

Table 7.3 Disciplinary sanctions and dismissals in last 12 months in context, by size of workplace and sub-sector

	AIS	PSS	HI	<25	25–49	50–99	100+
Any disciplinary sanctions (%)	45	47	57	52	44	85	94
Mean number per 1,000 employees	7	8	13	18	9	6	4
Number of dismissals	1	1	2	1	4	2	4
Mean number per 1,000 employees	23	26	66*	61	112	34	24

			Hotels	Camp-sites	Restaur-ants	Bars	Canteens
Any disciplinary sanctions (%)			67	100	53	53	53
Mean number per 1,000 employees			6	5	18	15	13
Number of dismissals			3	b	1	2	2
Mean number per 1,000 employees			59	1	33	94	51

Source: WERS98.

Notes: All weighted cases where sanctions used. Figures have been rounded to nearest whole number.
*Significantly different at the 5% level from AIS and PSS. b Fewer than 0.5%.

gressions, and can often be interpreted by managers as posing a direct threat to their authority. Consequently they are handled in a way out of all proportion to their seriousness (Rollinson *et al.*, 1996). Lateness, absenteeism, poor performance, unsatisfactory server/customer interface, employees not fitting with management style and poor recruitment and selection have been observed in the British HI (Earnshaw *et al.*, 1998). Tardiness and absenteeism are the two main reasons for dismissal but, in spite of a three-stage procedure, US restaurant managers find it hard to practise consistent discipline because a termination leaves the restaurant short handed. Hence less ordered techniques of discipline are used, such as shift loss, decreased hours and unpleasant duties (Dermody, 2002). Case study 7.4 illustrates how British managers may not observe the spirit of the law.

The role of law in individual dispute resolution

Legal means for resolving individual disputes vary across the world, and may include the quasi-legal mechanism of a tribunal or other body embracing a practitioner view, in addition to courts of law. Case studies 7.5 and 7.6 provide examples from the US affecting the HI. In another example an undocumented alien was not entitled to an award for missed pay in a wrongful termination case, because the individual was undocumented (Cohen, 2002). When McDonald's became established in Australia, the company challenged the award and convinced the tribunal that the job was different (lower skill) than in more conventional restaurants, thereby securing a lower rate of pay (Allan *et al.*, 2000).

Case study 7.4 Discipline and dismissal in UK hotels

Employers appeared to be trying to find ways of avoiding the effects of unfair dismissal legislation. Employers were well aware of the (then) two-year service requirement, and used it as a device to weed out unsatisfactory employees. Increases in part-time and casual workers, often with short service, meant that many workers were excluded from unfair dismissal protection. Some casual workers had long service and may actually have been employees. High dismissal rates were observed, particularly in small establishments, and employees had an above-average rate of success at tribunal. Hence the law was deficient in terms of protecting employees, and in terms of encouraging employers to adopt good practice and change their behaviour.

Source: Head and Lucas (1998, 2004a,b).

Case study 7.5 Challenging dismissal in the US

Employees can challenge dismissal by filing charges with the NLRB, claiming a violation of the protected concerted activity (PCA) provisions of the *National Labor Relations Act*. To establish a PCA the employee must be acting on behalf of other employees in complaining about wages, hours or working conditions or trying to enforce the provisions of the collective agreement. If successful reinstatement on full back pay is likely.

Source: Clay and Stephens (1994).

Employment tribunals

By the mid-1990s the UK tribunal system was becoming ill equipped to cope with the demands placed upon it by an extended system of individual rights and the expansion of tribunals' jurisdiction to include certain contract claims on termination of employment giving rise to over 70 different types of complaint. There were undue delays in cases being heard, too much legalism in tribunal proceedings and high operating costs. The *Employment Relations (Disputes Resolution) Act 1998* renamed industrial tribunals as employment tribunals. Other changes included an extension to the circumstances in which the Chair can sit alone, and giving tribunals wider powers to dispose simply and swiftly uncontested and untenable claims, without the need for a formal or full hearing. The scope of compromise agreements was widened to settle a whole range of disputes (Lucas, 1998: 11–12).

The *Employment Relations Act 1999* widened access to employment tribunals by reducing the qualifying service for unfair dismissal to one year. The maximum compensatory award was also increased from £12,000 to £50,000. This figure is

---

Case study 7.6 **Alternative dispute resolution in the US hospitality industry**

Companies that formalize an internal dispute resolution procedure may avoid huge legal costs, save time and boost employee morale. Alternative Dispute Resolution can be part of the grievance procedure, and may include mediation, arbitration, mini-trials, summary trials and peer review. Some courts now require settlement conferences to encourage settlements outside the courtroom.

Mandatory arbitration may be the most effective way to avoid the shortcomings of the American legal system (procedural inconsistencies and high monetary and time cost). Policies must normally conform to particular standards of fairness if they are to be regarded as universally enforceable, but cannot preclude employees from filing a complaint with the EEOC. There is still confusion over whether unionized employees subject to a collective agreement should be treated differently from non-union workers in respect of mandatory arbitration policies.

Sources: Goldstein (1995); Sherwyn and Tracey (1997).

---

index-linked to the retail price index and is revised annually in February with other minimum and maximum statutory awards.[7] Raising the ceiling for compensatory awards has not produced any discernible rise in applications or the value of awards. The actual loss for most, based on claimants' pay and time out of work, is relatively small. In 1999 only 148 cases reached the maximum, with the median award standing at £2,310. In 2002[8] 19 cases reached the new maximum, and the median award had risen to £3,180 (www.dti.gov.uk/er/erareview).

In the decade to 2000/1 the number of tribunal applications more than trebled to reach 130,000 per annum. A new set of Tribunal Rules of Procedure came into force in 2001 enabling all or part of a claim to be struck out at a pre-hearing review, and providing for improved disclosure and better preparation prior to the hearing. Costs can be awarded if a claim is misconceived, frivolous or vexatious, but are rarely awarded.[9] Proposals to deter unmeritorious claims by requiring a deposit of £100 were dropped on grounds on unfairness.

Registered applications fell by 14 per cent in 2001/2 to 112,227 but it is not clear how far they reflect procedural changes (Employment Tribunals Service, 2002). The number of registered appeals with the EAT also dropped. Unfair dismissal claims, which have increased (39 per cent) and *Wages Act* claims (20 per cent) are the main jurisdictions. The number of jurisdictions per application has increased from 1.4 to 1.7. Some 35 per cent of applications were settled through ACAS, 32 per cent were withdrawn, 12 per cent were successful at tribunal and the rest were either dismissed or otherwise disposed of. Costs were awarded in 169 cases (£500 at the median). Unfair dismissal compensation exceeded £15 million. The median award was £2,563 and the maximum £61,134. These levels are substantially below awards made in discrimination cases, noted in Chapter 4 (Employment Tribunals Service, 2002).

Continued reform of the tribunal system will stem from the recommendations made by the Employment Tribunal System Taskforce in 2002, addressing the administration and resourcing of the tribunal system, and placing greater emphasis on dispute resolution and earlier disclosure of information. Four sets of recommendations are made:

- Greater coherence through the establishment of a high-level body, e.g. establishing best practice.
- Greater emphasis on the prevention of disputes, e.g. via ACAS, including more extensive use of mediation.
- Earlier disclosure of information, e.g. to help employees understand if they have a case, and for each party to recognize the merits of the other's case and consider reaching a settlement.
- Right infrastructure, e.g. new information technology systems and links to ACAS.

Other recently announced proposals include the award of costs for the unreasonable conduct of representatives, e.g. unnecessary time wasting, compulsory ACAS conciliation, and improving documentation, including new forms for applicants and respondents in order to increase the amount of information to be made available to the parties. Parties who do not have legal representation will be able to recover the costs of time spent preparing their case. Changes will be incorporated into revised Rules of Procedure, which remain to be drafted.

Details of what employment tribunals do, how to apply to an employment tribunal or defend a claim, and the relevant forms can be found on www.employmenttribunals.gov.uk. Details of the role of the EAT and summaries of the EAT's appeal findings can be found on www.employmentappeals.gov.uk.

The law in practice

The Survey of Employment Tribunals 1998 established details about users of the tribunal system, some of which have yet to be addressed by the policymakers (DTI, 2001b). First, over 60 per cent of applicants are male and aged 35 or over, and the vast majority are in permanent full-time employment. One-third of applicants work in micro-firms (fewer than ten people). That said, tribunal applications do not affect most employers. Second, employees are almost three times as likely to have no representation than employers. Employees are less likely to use legal representation, with trade unions, or the CAB serving as their main sources of support. Third, only one-quarter of applications proceed to a full hearing, of which half are successful. Fourth, the success rate of applicants depends upon the jurisdiction, e.g. applicants are more successful in redundancy cases and less so in sex and race discrimination cases. Fifth, applicants face short-term stress, long-term unemployment problems and worse employment prospects. The average cost per application was £2,000.

Table 7.4 Industrial tribunal complaints in last 12 months in context, by size of workplace and sub-sector

	AIS	PSS	HI	<25	25–49	50–99	100+
Any complaint (%)	7	7	4	1	4	10	20
Mean number per 1,000 employees	24	27	42	143	31	16	11

			Hotels	Camp-sites	Restaur-ants	Bars	Canteens
Any complaint (%)			8	10	7	0	1
Mean number per 1,000 employees			13	7	73	0	34

Source: WERS98.

Notes: All weighted cases where complaint made. Figures have been rounded to nearest whole number.

Awareness of rights among working people is highly variable. High or low levels of awareness and knowledge relate to a law's visibility and length of time established, publicity and/or controversy, the existence of a visible enforcement body and relevance to particular sub-groups of the population (Meager *et al.*, 2002).

Drawing on WERS, in spite of the liberal dispensation of disciplinary sanctions and dismissal, fewer HI workplaces experienced employment tribunal complaints in the previous twelve months (Table 7.4) and also during the last five years (mainly hotels) than AIS and the PSS. Very small workplaces and restaurants sustain the highest rate of complaints. Given the significant proportion of applications made by employees working in micro-workplaces noted above, WERS, as currently constituted, is likely to understate the real level of complaints within the HI on its widest definition (Table 2.1). The needs of small business are not being served well by the tribunal system (Earnshaw *et al.*, 1998).

Differences in management style have been found between HI firms that had recently faced an unfair dismissal claim and those that had not (Goodman *et al.*, 1998). The latter emphasized the importance of creating a friendly atmosphere through good communications and building team spirit. Managers were always readily available. Managers with recent experience of a tribunal did not use 'team' measures such as pooling tips and task flexibility and showed no interest in personal problems. In fact the main reason why HI employers might lose or actually lost was procedural (Earnshaw *et al.*, 1998, 2000). Even though procedures were instituted after a case was lost for dismissing an employee who kicked a customer, the manager of a theme bar still had reservations because in a club it was difficult to distinguish between 'banter' and abuse of customers (Earnshaw *et al.*, 1998).

WERS shows that unfair dismissal is the most common ground for complaint where an employee had initiated an application to tribunal in the last 12 months, especially in AIS and the PSS and also in a large minority of HI workplaces. *Wages Act* complaints were more common in the HI, especially in hotels. There were no complaints of race discrimination in the HI.

There is no clear-cut managerial response to the experience of having received an employment tribunal application in the last five years. A majority of AIS, PSS and HI responses did not fit the six actions specified. The most common response after a tribunal application was to make sure that workplace procedures were followed. More interesting is the fact that none of the specified actions were taken in workplaces employing below 50 employees, begging the question 'Was anything done at all?'

The management response to dealing with an employment tribunal application differs between the HI and AIS and the PSS. There is more emphasis in the HI on attempting to resolve the matter without ACAS advice and a greater reluctance to reach a decision on the basis of taking independent advice on the merits of the case. Applications are also more likely to go to a hearing in the HI, although this approach is a minority response.

Collective disputes and procedures

Non-managerial employees in HI workplaces are less likely to have a collective disputes procedure than their counterparts in AIS and the PSS, and there are also some variations in coverage by size of workplace and sub-sector (Tables 7.1 and 7.2). Where such procedures exist (one in three HI workplaces), they almost always deal with health and safety and the organization of work, and in a large majority of cases the procedures also cover pay and conditions and redundancy. Provision for reference to an outside body or person where there is a failure to agree is incorporated into three-quarters of HI collective disputes procedures, slightly higher than in AIS and the PSS, but in only one-third of restaurants' procedures.

Collective disputes over pay and conditions are rare generally but are significantly less likely to affect HI workplaces than in AIS and the PSS.[10] In the previous 12 months the overall analysis indicates there were below 0.5 per cent collective disputes over pay and conditions in the HI, and that these affected only restaurants. No HI workplaces sustained industrial action, such as overtime bans, working to rule, or going slow. No strikes had occurred either in the previous 12 months or in the last five years. Such practices were also very rare in AIS and the PSS (mainly below 3 per cent). There was no secondary action in the form of picketing at the workplace during the previous 12 months in HI workplaces and this happened in only 1 per cent of AIS workplaces. Only a miniscule number of workplaces in the HI and AIS suffered significant disruption as a result of industrial action in another organization. More recent British figures for 2001 show five disputes in the HI, which accounted for 3,600 working days lost, affecting 800 workers, compared to 525,000 working days lost nationally (Davies, 2002).

Discussion and review topics

Individual rights

- Which individual employment rights have been of greatest benefit to managers, employees and workers in the HI?
- Which individual employment rights have been of least benefit to managers, employees and workers in the HI?
- Are there any obvious gaps in the scope or coverage of the law that should be filled to the benefit of managers, employees and workers?
- How effective is the law as a means to change managerial behaviour and employment practice?
- How can the law be publicized and enforced more effectively?

Grievances

How can managers create an organizational culture and climate that encourages workers to raise grievances openly without fear of retribution?

Discipline

Identify employee behaviour within hospitality and tourism workplaces that is sufficiently serious to warrant:

- summary dismissal for gross misconduct;
- a written warning;
- a verbal warning.

Employment tribunals

Arrange a visit to the Regional Office of Employment Tribunals to observe a tribunal hearing.

Analyse and evaluate the following issues, where possible:

- the role of the Chair and lay members;
- the extent to which the applicant and respondent had a fair hearing;
- whether both sides had prepared their case adequately;
- the relevance of the evidence presented;
- whether the proceedings were too legalistic;
- whether the outcome was a fair result.

8   What do the workers think?

Learning objectives

By the end of this chapter you should be able to:

- appreciate the importance of viewing the employment relationship from an employee perspective;
- identify the employee and job characteristics of the WERS employee survey respondents;
- evaluate why HI employees' views about their job, working at their workplaces and trade union representation are different from those in AIS and the PSS;
- discern more specific issues from the employee verbatim responses;
- differentiate between the merits of quantitative and qualitative research approaches in identifying themes from the employee data.

Towards a more balanced understanding

The employee survey, included in WERS for the first time, has two main consequences. First, we gain a more balanced perspective of employment relations within the workplaces reviewed in earlier chapters. Second, we can create a more detailed picture of employees' working lives – what they think about their job, about working at their workplace, and how they are represented at work (see also Cully *et al.*, 1999: 4–10, 137–91). Questionnaire evidence from 1,100 HI employees provides a large enough sample to examine all sub-sectors inclusive of canteens and campsites, and to be less circumspect in drawing conclusions than in the management survey.

WERS marks the largest, most representative, systematic attempt to explore HI employees' views about employment relations. We review the output relating to all the questions and refer briefly to some multivariate analysis in relation to the influence of employee and job characteristics on workforce representation and employee job satisfaction. Additionally we home in on a previously unpublished area – the employee verbatim responses from the last, and only open, question (D12), seeking any final comments about the workplace or the questionnaire.

Individual comments can be related to employees' identifying characteristics. For clarity of presentation these are restricted to gender, age, occupational group, contract status, weekly hours, whether part of a larger organization, workplace size and sub-sector. More details about the research questions, sample and data analysis are contained in Appendix 1. Unfortunately this survey and, particularly, the verbatim responses, provide very little useful information on the role of customers.

Learning about employees' experiences and perceptions of the employment relationship is important in developing an understanding of the psychological contract. How the workplace is managed and the organizational climate together with the individual's experience of employment help determine the three elements of the psychological contract – fairness, trust and delivery on promises made (Guest and Conway, 1998). Gallie *et al.* (1998) put it slightly differently, identifying four factors that affect people's perceptions of their job, work, workplace and well-being: the nature of the work task, social integration in the workplace, participation in decision-making and job security. We seek to uncover some facets of an implicit contract to discover whether these, in combination with the more explicit measures of employment policies and practices make for satisfied, committed employees. Different workers will demonstrate different orientations to work. What is less clear is how far these differences are influenced by the employment relationship itself rather than the differences in personal, underlying values.[1]

Recalling earlier themes

As noted in the Introduction the bulk of available literature within employment relations is drawn from management research. Earlier chapters have relied heavily on managers' side of the story, 'balanced' to varying extents by clutches of employee-based research,[2] with little evidence on customers who are crucial to developing our understanding of a triadic employment relationship.

We cannot provide answers to every question posed or offer a reciprocal view of all issues raised earlier. The employment relationship is extremely complex, hence its fascination (Cully *et al.*, 1999). Some of the economic and social concerns that impact upon a contemporary employment relationship (Ackers, 2002; Lucas and Lammont, 2003) can be revealed. We can also consider the extent to which employees may feel empowered in the context of management-driven rules and (unequal) power relationships, and shed some light on whether they identify with managers' aims (Friedman, 1977) or have multiple identities (Heery, 1993).

We can review how far some issues relating to employment, work and the work-force may influence employment relations. Do particular characteristics affect employees' orientations to work (Simons and Enz, 1995), their work experiences, perceptions of their job or their commitment to the organization? Are particular factors more likely to contribute to a negative rather than a positive turnover culture (Deery and Shaw, 1997; Rowley and Purcell, 2001)?

Some important aspects about employees' perceptions of how they are managed are revealed. The strong suggestion so far is that management style, HRM policies and practices (explicit elements of a psychological contract) are unlikely to generate a positive employee response in terms of an implicit contract embodying fairness, trust and delivery of promises.[3] The relevance of transactional and relational psychological contracts is explored (Rousseau, 1990; Guest *et al.*, 1996). How do employees see their lot? What is employees' response to high levels of recruitment activity, patchy training and far from comprehensive family-friendly policies? How do employees respond to poor pay and reward systems?

Finally we can shed more light on employees' attitudes to trade unions, representation and workplace involvement, and how this impacts upon their experiences of dispute resolution in the workplace. Reasons may emerge why trade union membership is so low, and may continue to remain so. On the AIS, PSS and HI comparison some job and employee characteristics can be expected to explain variations in responses (Cully *et al.*, 1999[4]). This does not apply to the multivariate analysis in the case of the characteristics we have controlled for in the regressions, including age and gender (see Appendix 1).

Revisiting the literature

Employee-based literature points to two important questions, as we now show. Guest and Conway's (1999) notion of 'black hole' employment emerged from a survey including questions about explicit and implicit dimensions of the psychological contract. The HI was found to be one of five 'black hole' industries marked, among other things, by the absence of trade unions and HRM, and signifying exploitation and pain. More accurately, however, most HI employees were not located in 'black holes', since only a sizeable minority (44 per cent) 'suffered' from 'black hole' employment. WERS enables us to shed light upon the extent to which a much larger number of HI employees[5] may generally have a positive employment experience, rather than a negative one.

Most 'black hole' conditions have been known about for a long time (*inter alia* Wood, 1992; Price, 1994; Lucas, 1995a, 1996a). Inference has been made from management research centring on explicit dimensions of the psychological contract, e.g. low pay, lack of trade unions and inadequate procedural arrangements, notably WIRS3 (Lucas, 1995a, 1996a). Such 'poor' employment relations practices might be expected to impact negatively on employees' job satisfaction and commitment. But other studies have begun to suggest this is not necessarily so, e.g. jobs in services have certain attributes that are traded off against factors such as low pay (Dodrill and Riley, 1992; Riley *et al.*, 1998).

To combat unwillingness among HI employers to participate in research studies, the larger chains or groups excepted, researchers have turned to less conventional methods of research inquiry. Pragmatic methodologies such as 'door stopping' employees at their workplace have been used (Macaulay and Wood, 1992). Alternatively a particular segment has been chosen, e.g. students who combine full-time study with part-time work, as a large proportion are known to work in the HI (Lucas and Ralston, 1996; Lucas, 1997a; Lammont and Lucas, 1999; Lucas and Langlois, 2001; Johnson and Lucas, 2002).

These studies of young, student employees working predominantly in non-union services provide clear and consistent evidence of employees experiencing both satisfaction and dissatisfaction within the same employment relationship. Extending the notion of transformational and transactional psychological contracts to include contingent workers (McLean Parks *et al.*, 1998) makes it possible to conceptualize students as working simultaneously under both types of contract (Curtis, 2002).

The case of students is not necessarily generalizable. However, students do share a number of common attributes with HI employees in general, as they are young, mobile, singles working part-time unsociable hours, who are not trade union members. Importantly their experiences reveal both dimensions of the psychological contract. In spite of experiencing poor pay, unpredictable hours, bad management and rude customers (inferred exploitation) these individuals can still derive satisfaction at work. Students also experience good relationships with their peers and customers, can exercise control over their work, believe strongly that they have the ability to influence their own working environment or can change it if necessary, and gain work experience in the process. That said, the HI offers work at suitable times for students who are willing and able to work. The rise in student labour participating in the HI also reflects a coincidence of needs (Lucas and Ralston, 1996; Curtis and Lucas, 2001).

This summary begs two important questions, upon which this chapter seeks to shed light:

- Is it right to infer that the existence of the conventional view of 'poor employment relations', i.e. low pay, lack of unions, etc., automatically translates into feelings of exploitation and dissatisfaction at work among workers?
- To what extent do other hospitality workers share a similar 'dual' experience to students working in the HI?

Employee and job characteristics

Significant differences in employee characteristics and job characteristics between the HI and AIS and the PSS are shown in Tables 8.1, 8.2, 8.3 and 8.4. HI employees are more likely to be female, young and, most notably, single with no dependent children. They have shorter service, work fewer hours and earn less pay, but are more likely to do jobs performed equally by men and women. Hence our three-way comparisons are likely to show a part-time, short-service and age effect in relation to employees' views about their job, what it is like to work at their workplace and their propensity to become trade union members.

Very small workplaces, restaurants and canteens employ the most females, whereas hotels are most likely to employ males. Nearly two-thirds of employees in small and medium workplaces are under the age of 30, and this is even more marked in restaurants and bars, where part-time students are likely to be employed. Employees aged 30 and above are most likely to work in large workplaces, campsites and canteens.

Although the levels of unqualified workers and those with vocational qualifications are similar across all comparisons, HI employees (11 per cent) are significantly less likely to have a first degree or above than their counterparts in AIS (21

Table 8.1 Employee characteristics in context and by size of workplace (%)

% in category	AIS	PSS	HI	<25	25–49	50–99	100+
Female	49	54	57**	64	51	55	53
Below age 30	25	33	55*	55	64	65	43
No dependent children	59	63	79*	80	82	83	72
Single	22	28	50*	49	58	58	40
Ethnic group (white)	96	96	95	96	96	96	93
No educational qualifications	26	24	28	40	20	16	30
Vocational qualifications	37	35	38	36	37	37	43
Health problem/disability	6	6	5	6	4	5	4
Total employees	28,222	12,886	1,110	341	152	288	330

Source: WERS98 employee survey.

Notes: All weighted cases. *Significantly different at the 5% level from AIS and the PSS. **Significantly different at the 5% level from AIS.

Table 8.2 Employee characteristics by sub-sector (%)

% in category	Hotels	Campsites	Restaurants	Bars	Canteens
Female	52	55	67	53	66
Below age 30	53	35	68	69	25
No dependent children	77	75	78	87	66
Single	46	30	65	60	25
Ethnic group (white)	95	98	93	96	97
No educational qualifications	23	32	21	35	42
Vocational qualifications	39	43	33	41	36
Health problem/disability	5	0	3	8	4
Total employees	460	36	213	273	123

Source: WERS98 employee survey.

Notes: All weighted cases.

per cent) and the PSS (18 per cent). Above average proportions of unqualified workers are found in very small workplaces, canteens and bars.

The employee data bear out the fact that HI employment flows fuelled by short-service workers are more rapid than in AIS. Similarly only 10 per cent of HI staff have 10 years' or more service compared to 26 per cent in AIS and 17 per cent in the PSS. Bars have a well above average percentage of short-service staff, whereas campsites and canteens have more staff with one or more year's service. HI employees are also slightly less likely to see their jobs as permanent. The use of fixed-term contracts in the HI is rare although one-fifth of campsite staff is on fixed term contracts, presumably related to seasonality.

Most HI employees work in personal and protective services (36 per cent) or other occupations (31 per cent), referred to as personal service and unskilled manual workers hereafter.[6] Employment in AIS and the PSS is more evenly spread

Table 8.3 Job characteristics in context and by size of workplace (%)

% in category	AIS	PSS	HI	<25	25–49	50–99	100+
Below 1 year's service	17	23	39*	48	45	40	26
Permanent job	92	92	83*	83	84	79	86
Personal and protective services	12	11	36*	46	42	31	27
Below 30 hours a week	26	35	50*	74	52	50	23
Earn less than £51 a week	8	12	25*	45	25	23	7
No overtime worked	48	49	63*	75	68	58	53
Work done equally by men and women	30	32	47*	50	53	46	42

Source: WERS98 employee survey.

Notes: All weighted cases. *Significantly different at the 5% level from AIS and the PSS.

Table 8.4 Job characteristics by sub-sector (%)

% in category	Hotels	Campsites	Restaurants	Bars	Canteens
Below 1 year's service	35	27	35	54	31
Permanent job	87	58	80	82	82
Personal and protective services	32	14	32	55	20
Below 30 hours a week	30	34	58	87	28
Earn less than £51 a week	49	70	78	88	61
No overtime worked	57	70	66	80	45
Work done equally by men and women	40	47	46	64	37

Source: WERS98 employee survey.

Note: All weighted cases.

across all occupational groups. In AIS the biggest group is clerical and secretarial (18 per cent). Very small and small HI workplaces and bars have the highest proportion of personal service jobs.

Half the HI sample work part-time (29 hours or less a week) compared to 26 per cent in AIS. Short hours jobs (below 10 hours) are most likely in very small and small workplaces. Three-quarters of employees in very small workplaces work part-time, whereas three-quarters of employees in large workplaces work full-time. Bars have the most short-hours staff (21 per cent) and 87 per cent work part-time. Hotels and campsites are most likely to employ full-time workers.

One-quarter of HI employees earn less than £51 per week, which is skewed towards very small workplaces. Eight in ten HI employees earn less than £181 per week compared to 37 per cent in AIS and half in the PSS. Earnings below £181 affect 90 per cent of employees in the very small workplaces and 66 per cent of employees in large workplaces.[7]

Almost two-thirds of HI employees do not usually work overtime compared to just under half in AIS and the PSS. Regular overtime is lowest in very small workplaces (75 per cent). Most employees are normally paid for overtime, with a minority taking time in lieu, particularly in large workplaces. HI employees usually work overtime because it is a job requirement, they need the money or do not want to let their work colleagues down. These latter two factors are particularly pronounced in restaurants.

The HI, particularly bars, appears to offer greater equality of opportunity for employment by gender than AIS and the PSS. The utilization of cheap student part-time labour of either sex is probably an important contributory factor. Male-only or mainly male jobs are most likely in large workplaces and female-only or mainly female jobs in very small workplaces. Restaurants have the clearest indication of women-only jobs.

What are employees' views about their job?

Table 8.5 summarizes details of employees' views about their job, indicating significant differences between HI employees and those in AIS and the PSS in all but one aspect touched by this question. On a three-way comparison most employees perceive that their jobs require very hard work. The differences lie in HI employees being more likely to have sufficient time to complete their job, being more secure in their job and worrying less about their job outside working hours. In our multivariate analysis, HI employees remained more likely than all other PSS employees to report satisfaction with the time available to complete their job and with job security after controlling for other factors. Additionally they were significantly more likely to report that work was very hard.

Within the HI, and focusing on the 'agree' responses only, there is a clear indication that work is harder and more stressful in large workplaces than in very small workplaces (Table 8.6). While it is tempting to suggest that the nature of jobs may be 'better' in these very small workplaces, we cannot rule out the possibility that employee or job characteristics may also be a contributory factor

Table 8.5 Employees' views about their job in context (%)

	AIS			PSS			HI		
	A	N	D	A	N	D	A	N	D
Requires very hard work	76	19	4	76	19	4	76	18	7*
Never enough time to get job done	40	32	28	37	32	32	26*	33	41*
Job is secure in workplace	60	21	19	63	21	17	72*	18	10*
Worry a lot about work outside working hours	24	22	54	22	22	56	17*	21	61*

Source: WERS98 employee survey.

Notes: All weighted cases. Row percentages do not sum to 100 due to rounding. Agree (A) and disagree (D) columns include strongly agree/disagree responses. N = neutral. *Significantly different at the 5% level from AIS and the PSS.

Table 8.6 Where employees agree with aspects of their job by size of workplace (%)

	<25	25–49	50–99	100+
Requires very hard work	66	75	82	80
Never enough time to get job done	22	21	25	33
Job is secure in workplace	72	78	78	63
Worry a lot about work outside working hours	13	11	18	23

Source: WERS98 employee survey.
Notes: All weighted cases. Refinement of Table 8.5. Agree includes strongly agree and agree responses.

Table 8.7 Where employees agree with aspects of their job by sub-sector (%)

	Hotels	Campsites	Restaurants	Bars	Canteens
Requires very hard work	82	77	84	59	77
Never enough time to get job done	26	24	24	18	50
Job is secure in workplace	72	41	72	76	71
Worry a lot about work outside working hours	21	17	12	10	23

Source: WERS98 employee survey.
Notes: All weighted cases. Refinement of Table 8.5. Agree includes strongly agree and agree responses.

(Tables 8.1 and 8.3). There are also differences by sub-sector (Table 8.7), but these are not as consistent as the differences by workplace size.

Two further questions sought employees' views about the amount of influence they have in performing their work, and how satisfied they are with four particular aspects of their job. Gallie *et al.* (1998) assert the degree of discretion and influence over work is important. In relation to the first, a large majority of employees in AIS, the PSS and the HI concur that they do have influence over the range of tasks undertaken, the pace of work and how to do the work. The extent of influence is more likely to be 'some' than 'a lot'. HI employees in large workplaces and campsites are most 'empowered', and employees in very small workplaces and bars are the least 'empowered' in terms of having a lot of influence over their work.

Tables 8.8 and 8.9 summarize responses to the second question. A clear majority is satisfied with the amount of influence they have over their job, the sense of achievement they get from their work and the amount of respect they get from supervisors/line managers. In the case of the latter HI employees are significantly more likely to report satisfaction than their counterparts in AIS and the PSS. Pay is the exception where a significant minority of employees across all comparisons is dissatisfied. Satisfaction with all four job aspects is greatest in very small workplaces, and decreases as workplace size increases. While bar staff are most satisfied

Table 8.8 Employees' job satisfaction in context and by size of workplace (%)

Satisfied with	AIS	PSS	HI	<25	25–49	50–99	100+
Amount of influence							
over job	58	60	64**	70	60	60	63
Amount of pay	36	37	32***	37	36	30	26
Sense of achievement							
from work	64	63	67	68	67	66	65
Respect from supervisors/							
line managers	58	60	68*	76	68	66	60

Source: WERS98 employee survey.

Notes: All weighted cases. Satisfied with includes very satisfied and satisfied responses. *Significantly different at the 5% level from AIS and PSS. **Significantly different at the 5% level from AIS. ***Significantly different at the 5% level from PSS.

Table 8.9 Employees' job satisfaction by sub-sector (%)

Satisfied with	Hotels	Campsites	Restaurants	Bars	Canteens
Amount of influence					
over job	64	65	55	69	66
Amount of pay	26	22	31	42	35
Sense of achievement from					
work	67	59	60	67	78
Respect from supervisors/					
line managers	62	59	54	82	68

Source: WERS98 employee survey.

Notes: All weighted cases. Satisfied with includes very satisfied and satisfied responses.

with their pay and managers, the differences by sub-sector are more varied than by workplace size.

What is it like to work here?

Employment practices and the organization

During the 12 months prior to the survey there were similar levels of discussion between employees and supervisors in the HI, the PSS and AIS concerning job-related matters of job progress, promotion opportunities, training needs and pay (Tables 8.10 and 8.11). However, it is only in relation to job progress where a majority reports that discussion has occurred. HI employees in very small workplaces are less likely to experience such discussion than their counterparts in large workplaces. A significant minority of employees in very small and small workplaces and bars are seemingly denied the opportunity for discussion on any of these matters.

In the previous year broadly similar levels of training were organized or paid for by the employer in the HI, the PSS and AIS, affecting around six in ten employees, although more HI employees received less than two days' training.

Table 8.10 Job-related matters discussed with supervisor in context and by size of workplace (%)

	AIS	PSS	HI	<25	25–49	50–99	100+
Job progress	58	60	53	42	45	60	62
Promotion chances	20	21	22	19	18	22	25
Training needs	47	47	44	45	27	47	49
Pay	28	35	36**	32	35	39	39
None of these	27	26	30	37	37	24	23

Source: WERS98 employee survey.

Notes: All weighted cases. Yes responses. **Significantly different at the 5% level from AIS.

Table 8.11 Job-related matters discussed with supervisor by sub-sector (%)

	Hotels	Campsites	Restaurants	Bars	Canteens
Job progress	58	55	52	38	69
Promotion chances	21	27	23	18	29
Training needs	44	49	51	35	54
Pay	38	31	36	32	42
None of these	26	37	21	44	25

Notes: All weighted cases. Yes responses.

Source: WERS98 employee survey.

Canteen staff fare best, with three-quarters receiving some training. However four in ten employees across all comparisons received no training.

Nearly half of employees in AIS, the PSS and the HI have no access to family-friendly arrangements. Where these apply flexible working hours is the most common practice, although accessible to fewer than one in four employees. Parental leave is significantly less likely to be available in the HI than in AIS and the PSS. Campsites have an above average level (20 per cent) of workplace nursery/help with cost of childcare (HI 2 per cent).

Where an employee needs a day off at short notice, employees in AIS (45 per cent) and the PSS (37 per cent) are most likely to use paid leave. By contrast HI workplaces (17 per cent) are significantly less likely to use paid leave and significantly more likely to take unpaid leave (41 per cent). This increases to around half of all employees in very small workplaces, bars and restaurants.

Tables 8.12, 8.13 and 8.14 summarize employees' views about the organization. Table 8.12 reveals two aspects where HI employees express a significantly different view from their counterparts in AIS and the PSS. Perhaps surprisingly, given the lack of family-friendly measures in place, two-thirds of HI employees believe that managers understand their need to meet family responsibilities and six in ten affirm that people are encouraged to develop their skills. Being loyal and proud to tell people who they work for are the views of a clear majority across all comparisons, while half the employees share the values of the organization. A relatively small minority of employees across all comparisons appear not to be committed to the organization. Our multivariate analysis sharpens the difference

Table 8.12 Employees' views about the organization in context (%)

	AIS			PSS			HI		
	A	N	D	A	N	D	A	N	D
Share many of the values of the organization	52	33	14	52	34	13	54	35	10
Managers understand about employees having to meet family responsibilities	54	25	21	56	25	18	65*	21*	13*
People are encouraged to develop their skills	51	25	23	52	26	22	59*	25	16*
Feel loyal to the organization	66	23	10	68	23	10	70	22	7
Proud to tell people who you work for	57	31	12	58	32	11	61	29	9

Source: WERS98 employee survey.

Notes: All weighted cases. Row percentages do not sum to 100 due to rounding. Agree (A) and disagree (D) columns include strongly agree/disagree responses. N = neutral. *Significantly different at the 5% level from AIS and the PSS.

between HI employees and those in the rest of the PSS, showing that HI employees are more likely to state that they share the values of the organization and feel loyal to it. They continue to report that managers also understand about employees having to meet family responsibilities and encourage employees to develop their skills after controlling for other factors.

Employees in very small HI workplaces manifest greater general commitment than those in large workplaces (Table 8.13) and bar staff appear the most committed by sub-sector (Table 8.14). These findings may be explained by the fact that workers in smaller workplaces can more easily identify with an organization that they can actually see and relate to. Commitment is more likely to be a function of employees' relationship with their managers and peers and the extent to which they feel involved, an issue to which we now turn.

Workplace involvement and commitment

Three questions sought to ascertain employees' views on how helpful particular methods of communication were, how often they were asked for their views on five key business issues and how good managers were at maintaining two-way dialogue, dealing with problems and treating employees fairly. Tables 8.15 and 8.16 summarize responses to the first question. A good majority of HI employees find notice boards and meetings with managers most helpful, and in both cases the difference is significant. There is strong endorsement that meetings are helpful in very small workplaces, as one-fifth of employees do not have access to a notice board, a situation also observed in bars. There are no management–employee meetings in nearly one-quarter of restaurants. Email is not used widely to com-

Table 8.13 Where employees demonstrate commitment to the organization by size of workplace (%)

	<25	*25–49*	*50–99*	*100+*
Share many of the values of the organization	62	55	49	50
Managers understand about employees having to meet family responsibilities	78	65	64	51
People are encouraged to develop their skills	61	57	60	58
Feel loyal to the organization	74	78	70	65
Proud to tell people who you work for	63	66	59	60

Source: WERS98 employee survey.

Notes: All weighted cases. Refinement of Table 8.12. Agree responses only (strongly agree/agree). Neutral and disagree responses are not included.

Table 8.14 Where employees demonstrate commitment to the organization by sub-sector (%)

	Hotels	*Campsites*	*Restaurants*	*Bars*	*Canteens*
Share many of the values of the organization	53	52	41	63	64
Managers understand about employees having to meet family responsibilities	55	51	64	79	75
People are encouraged to develop their skills	57	59	61	67	52
Feel loyal to the organization	70	51	65	81	65
Proud to tell people who you work for	67	40	47	67	59

Source: WERS98 employee survey.

Notes: All weighted cases. Refinement of Table 8.12. Agree responses only (strongly agree/agree). Neutral and disagree responses are not included.

municate information, hence HI employees are significantly less likely to find it helpful than their counterparts in AIS and the PSS. Fewer HI employees receive a newsletter or magazines, but those who do generally find it helpful. The more limited importance of newsletters and email in the HI is likely to reflect workplace and job characteristics.

In relation to the second question, HI employees are significantly more likely to be consulted (frequently and sometimes) on health and safety (73 per cent) than employees in AIS (63 per cent) and the PSS (60 per cent). This is also true of staff matters, including redundancy (35 per cent) compared to AIS (30 per cent) and the PSS (28 per cent). Health and safety is the issue where there is most likely to be consultation, providing some evidence to justify the suggestion it may be a catalyst for developing management–employee dialogue (James, 1994). However, as

Table 8.15 Employees' views of helpful methods for keeping up to date in context and by size of workplace (%)

	AIS	PSS	HI	<25	25–49	50–99	100+
Notice boards	65	65	73*	69	74	77	75
Email	29	30	17*	20	15	11	21
Newsletter or magazines	55	48	45**	51	33	37	51
Meetings with managers	59	60	69*	77	67	67	64

Source: WERS98 employee survey.

Notes: All weighted cases. Helpful includes very helpful and helpful responses. *Significantly different at the 5% level from AIS and the PSS. **Significantly different at the 5% level from AIS.

Table 8.16 Employees' views of helpful methods for keeping up to date by sub-sector (%)

	Hotels	Campsites	Restaurants	Bars	Canteens
Notice boards	75	76	81	67	68
Email	16	24	9	17	35
Newsletter or magazines	42	59	39	46	62
Meetings with managers	64	59	63	82	73

Source: WERS98 employee survey.

Notes: All weighted cases. Helpful includes very helpful and helpful responses.

the management survey demonstrates, this is not being achieved through any system of employee representation. A similar proportion of employees across all comparisons is consulted about changes to work practices (around 60 per cent) and future plans (around half) for the workplace, but only one in three is asked for their views about pay. Yet a sizeable core of employees in AIS, the PSS and the HI are never or hardly ever asked for their views on all these issues. Nearly half of all employees are never consulted about staffing issues and pay, one-third are never consulted about future plans for the workplace, and one-quarter are never consulted about changes to work practices. Employees in very small workplaces are more likely to be consulted over these issues than their counterparts in large workplaces, particularly in relation to future plans. Sub-sectoral variations are slight, with canteen staff having the most involvement and restaurant staff the least.

The third question drew employees into making a more considered evaluation of how good their managers were in the six areas shown in Table 8.17. Here we can see some striking differences between HI employees and their counterparts in AIS and the PSS, with HI employees giving their managers a significantly higher level of endorsement for all these dimensions of management style. Even so it is notable, and consistent with the preceding discussion, that managers are least good at involving employees and responding to their suggestions. Most striking is the high level of support for good management–employee relations in the HI, even though this is not quite as rosy as their managers' view of very good or good employment relations (97 per cent HI, 90 per cent AIS and PSS). In our multivariate analysis HI employees remained more likely than employees in the rest of

Table 8.17 How good are managers in context? (%)

	AIS			PSS			HI		
	Good	Neither	Poor	Good	Neither	Poor	Good	Neither	Poor
Keeping everyone up to date about proposed changes	44	26	29	47	26	27	61*	21*	18*
Providing everyone with a chance to comment on proposed changes	32	30	39	33	30	36	43*	30	26*
Responding to suggestions from employees	33	33	34	37	33	30	49*	28*	22*
Dealing with employees' work problems	49	27	24	53	25	21	66*	19*	15*
Treating employees fairly	52	26	22	56	24	19	67*	19*	14*
Management/ employee relations	55	27	18	61	24	15	73*	18*	9*

Source: WERS98 employee survey.

Notes: All weighted cases. Row percentages do not sum to 100 due to rounding. Good columns include very good responses and poor columns include very poor responses. *Significantly different at the 5% level from AIS and the PSS.

the PSS to report that their managers were good in all six areas after controlling for other factors. HI managers may have better interpersonal skills than managers elsewhere. A close physical working relationship with employees builds close bonds and engenders trust. Unequivocally there is a high level of mutual satisfaction about the state of employment relations in the HI in the absence of systems of employee representation. This begins to suggest that the necessary level of dissatisfaction to prompt joining a trade union is not present among HI employees (Barling *et al.*, 1992).

Tables 8.18 and 8.19 reveal clear distinctions by workplace size, with employees in very small workplaces demonstrating a much higher level of positive endorsement for their managers' style, which more or less reduces as workplace size increases. Perhaps then, the notion that 'small is beautiful' has some resonance? Bar staff show the highest level of support for management style, with those working in campsites manifesting the least.

Representation at work

The employee data allow us to probe some of the issues explored in Chapter 6, and to form a more considered view about why HI employees are not highly unionized. Again we find striking, significant differences between HI employees and those in AIS and the PSS. The extent of non-unionization among HI employees is shown in Table 8.20, both in terms of actual membership and past

Table 8.18 Where employees rate their managers as good by size of workplace (%)

	<25	25–49	50–99	100+
Keeping everyone up to date about proposed changes	74	57	61	50
Providing everyone with a chance to comment on proposed changes	64	38	38	31
Responding to suggestions from employees	62	53	46	39
Dealing with employees' work problems	72	72	68	54
Treating employees fairly	80	68	66	54
Management/employee relations	83	81	75	58

Source: WERS98 employee survey.

Notes: All weighted cases. Refinement of Table 8.17. Good includes very good and good responses.

Table 8.19 Where employees rate their managers as good by sub-sector (%)

	Hotels	Campsites	Restaurants	Bars	Canteens
Keeping everyone up to date about proposed changes	55	48	65	73	54
Providing everyone with a chance to comment on proposed changes	34	26	42	63	48
Responding to suggestions from employees	42	47	47	70	43
Dealing with employees' work problems	57	47	69	82	57
Treating employees fairly	59	52	67	85	60
Management/employee relations	66	61	71	90	66

Source: WERS98 employee survey.

Notes: All weighted cases. Refinement of Table 8.17. Good includes very good and good responses.

membership, with the multivariate analysis confirming that HI employees are different from employees in the rest of the PSS after controlling for other factors. Tables 8.20 and 8.21 indicate small concentrations membership in large workplaces, campsites and canteens, demonstrating the extent of employees' lack of union affiliation in the three sub-sectors that dominate the HI.

Tables 8.22 and 8.23 show the lack of contact or knowledge about trade unions or more general workplace representation among HI employees, especially in smaller workplaces, restaurants and bars which are numerically so important. This may be a determinant as well as an outcome of low unionization. Not knowing any representatives is also confirmed in the multivariate analysis after controlling for other factors, making it clearly an important contributory factor affecting HI employees' perceptions of trade unions. Large numbers of widely dispersed workplaces pose huge organizational difficulties for trade unions. Workplaces are too

Table 8.20 Employees' trade union membership in context and by size of workplace (%)

% in category	AIS	PSS	HI	<25	25–49	50–99	100+
Trade union member	39	20	6*	4	0	3	14
Have never been a member	43	60	76*	80	86	81	65

Source: WERS98 employee survey.
Notes: All weighted cases. *Significantly different at the 5% level from AIS and the PSS.

Table 8.21 Employees' trade union membership by sub-sector (%)

% in category	Hotels	Campsites	Restaurants	Bars	Canteens
Trade union member	4	12	5	3	22
Have never been a member	75	64	82	83	62

Source: WERS98 employee survey.
Note: All weighted cases.

small to make realistic representation viable, which reinforces a perception of self-reliance among employees.

Equally, less than supportive managers (Tables 8.24 and 8.25), including a sizeable core of hostile ones, are not conducive to trade union representation. Interestingly, the employee data highlight managers as being more opposed to trade unions than is claimed by the managers themselves (see Table 4.4). Although we cannot know how far the perceived neutrality of most managers belies levels of hostility that managers do not make explicit,[8] very few employees consider their managers to be favourably disposed towards trade unions. Employees in very small workplaces and bars[9] suggest there is more hope for trade unions compared to those in large workplaces and hotels where organization efforts have been targeted in the past. In the HI, membership seems to be lower where management is more supportive of trade unions.

It is, then, not surprising to find that most HI employees believe they are the best person to represent themselves in dealing with key employment issues with managers whom they know well personally (Table 8.26). Employees appear most confident to represent themselves in challenging managers about their work, followed by disciplinary proceedings and seeking a pay increase. This is confirmed in the multivariate analysis showing that HI employees are different from those in the rest of the PSS, after controlling for other factors. Hence while HI employees see themselves as more empowered and self-reliant, one might argue that a limited range of alternatives forces them to behave in this way.

The self-help option is most marked in very small workplaces and more or less declines as workplace size increases. Hence it is least favoured in those workplaces most likely to have employees who are union members (large workplaces, campsites and canteens), particularly in pay and disciplinary matters (Tables 8.27 and 8.28).

Table 8.22 Contact with trade unions or other worker representatives in context and by size of workplace (%)

% in category	AIS	PSS	HI	<25	25–49	50–99	100+
Frequent	9	6	5*	6	1	6	6
Occasional	27	16	9*	6	4	8	16
Never	24	23	16*	11	17	17	20
I am a representative	2	1	3*	5	1	2	2
Do not know any representatives	37	53	66*	71	76	66	56

Source: WERS98 employee survey.

Notes: All weighted cases. Excludes other/multi-coded responses. *Significantly different at the 5% level from AIS and the PSS.

Table 8.23 Contact with trade unions or other worker representatives in context by sub-sector

% in category	Hotels	Campsites	Restaurants	Bars	Canteens
Frequent	5	4	3	7	5
Occasional	10	21	6	4	21
Never	18	26	18	10	15
I am a representative	3	0	0	7	0
Do not know any representatives	63	49	73	71	57

Source: WERS98 employee survey.
Note: All weighted cases. Excludes other/multi-coded responses.

Table 8.24 Employees' perception of management attitude towards trade unions in context and by size of workplace

% in category	AIS	PSS	HI	<25	25–49	50–99	100+
In favour	18	10	8*	19	2	3	4
Neutral	54	55	59*	64	68	63	47
Not in favour	28	34	33*	17	30	34	49

Source: WERS98 employee survey.

Notes: All weighted cases. Excludes other/multi-coded responses. *Significantly different at the 5% level from AIS and the PSS.

Table 8.25 Employees' perception of management attitude towards trade unions by sub-sector

% in category	Hotels	Campsites	Restaurants	Bars	Canteens
In favour	3	12	3	23	4
Neutral	51	57	62	68	65
Not in favour	46	31	35	9	31

Source: WERS98 employee survey.
Note: All weighted cases. Excludes other/multi-coded responses.

Table 8.26 Preferred representation in dealing with employment issues in context (%)

	AIS			PSS			HI		
	Myself	Trade union	Other	Myself	Trade union	Other	Myself	Trade union	Other
Increase in pay	43	42	14	56	27	16	65*	17*	17
Complaint about working here	66	23	10	73	16	11	79*	9*	11
Facing disciplinary action	49	36	13	61	23	16	73*	10*	16

Source: WERS98 employee survey.

Notes: All weighted cases. Row percentages do not sum to 100 due to rounding. Excludes other/multi-coded responses. *Significantly different at the 5% level from AIS and the PSS.

Table 8.27 Prefer to represent themselves in dealing with employment issues by size of workplace

% in category	<25	25–49	50–99	100+
Increase in pay	69	71	69	55
Complaint about working here	81	87	79	75
Facing disciplinary action	81	78	74	62

Source: WERS98 employee survey.

Note: All weighted cases.

Table 8.28 Prefer to represent themselves in dealing with employment issues by sub-sector

% in category	Hotels	Campsites	Restaurants	Bars	Canteens
Increase in pay	69	51	54	72	58
Complaint about working here	76	68	79	85	80
Facing disciplinary action	70	56	71	86	62

Source: WERS98 employee survey.

Note: All weighted cases.

In the small number of workplaces where there is a union or staff association present, HI employees report that unions do indeed make a difference. They are significantly more likely to report than their counterparts in AIS and the PSS that unions are taken seriously by management (64 per cent) and make a difference to what it is like to work here (53 per cent). Most also agree that unions take notice of their members' problems, a view that is also shared by AIS and PSS employees. We cannot infer anything useful from the workplace size and sub-sector analysis because the numbers of cases are too small.

Responding to an open question

Almost one-third of employees (338) offered some additional comments, over three-quarters (261) of which relate specifically to job satisfaction or dissatisfaction. A small number offered a more balanced view, combining both satisfaction and dissatisfaction (Table 8.29) (see Appendix 1). We should note that a minority of those providing written comments (22 per cent) made no reference to job satisfaction, and have been excluded from the analysis presented in Table 8.29. Many of these offered comments about the questionnaire itself and its utility, or simply did not feel many of the questions were applicable to their circumstances. Interestingly, a few of these were the bulk of the small number readily identifiable as students, who indicated that the job was part of their course or no more than casual employment unrelated to a career. Hence the value of these comments in broadening our understanding of issues surrounding job satisfaction beyond the student population that we have necessarily relied upon in earlier studies (Lucas, 1997a,b; Lammont and Lucas, 1999; Lucas and Langlois, 2001; Johnson and Lucas, 2002).

Interestingly the qualitative responses appear to convey a different perception of employees' job satisfaction than the survey and point to a higher level of dissatisfaction. One possible explanation for this apparent mismatch might be that the verbatim responses are coming from the least satisfied workers. The verbatim responses are, of course, only one variable of job satisfaction, among many others provided by WERS, and need to be interpreted with caution. On the one hand, they may serve as a synopsis of the extent of employee satisfaction. On the other hand, they may be unrepresentative because aggrieved or frustrated employees with no effective means of seeking redress for their grievances at work are more likely to take the opportunity to 'make a protest' to an anonymous entity. Equally the silent majority (over 700 employees) who chose not to add supplementary comments may include many who believe that expressing a view will serve no useful purpose. These suggest other circumstances which, if considered in combination with other factors, may explain why workers do not also reach the threshold of joining trade unions.

The job satisfaction responses are readily classifiable into five main categories: hours/pay/conditions of employment; management/colleagues; the respondent's own job; other workplace issues; and employee representation. Similar classification is not possible for the 'balanced view' responses, because they contain a more complex mix of factors. Only two employee characteristics demonstrate

Table 8.29 HI employees' unsolicited comments about work

	Overall (% in brackets)	Hours/pay/ conditions	Managers/ colleagues	Own job	Workplace general	Repre- sentation
Dissatisfied	155 (59)	64	27	19	46	9
Satisfied	70 (27)	3	28	15	25	1
Balanced view	36 (14)					
Total	261					

Source: WERS98 employee survey.

Notes: Overall figures in column 1 exclude comments classified as not applicable or incomplete (N = 261). The row numbers exceed the overall total in column 1 because a few respondents clearly identified more than one factor in the overall classification.

a significant relationship (at the 5 per cent level) with job dissatisfaction. Respondents working in multi-site workplaces and in the age group 20–49 years are more likely to express dissatisfactions compared to respondents working in single-site workplaces and those aged below 20 years and aged 50 and above. There are no significant differences for factors such as gender, part-time and occupational group. It is important to note that the overwhelming majority of comments cannot be attributed to part-time students, because they are most likely to derive from full-time females working in chain hotels and restaurants employing 50 or more workers (Tables A.25 and A.26).

It is also the case that workers in the same workplace can have widely differing views of their experience. In terms of clusters of responses (11 workplaces with seven or more), most belong to large chains. For example in one large chain hotel only one of fourteen respondents indicated satisfaction, while in eight other workplaces a majority, usually a large one, expressed dissatisfaction. Only two workplaces had a majority of satisfied employees – a small hotel and a medium-sized independent hotel.

Employee dissatisfactions

Hours of work, pay and conditions of employment

These issues, often mentioned together, prompted the most adverse comments. The particular circumstances varied, including issues like: 'I'm seasonal, so I don't get holidays and sick pay'; 'Not paid for all hours worked'; 'Premium rates should apply at weekends or for unsocial hours'; 'Pay is poor relative to colleagues in the same job'; 'No breaks'; 'Insufficient time between shifts'.

The unfairness of the effort–reward exchange and the difficulty of challenging this are indicated as follows:

> I am increasingly concerned about the number of hours I am having to put in to get the job done. Additional responsibilities which do not warrant an increase in pay . . . the company expects staff to share a job out between them if another member of staff leaves and be happy to do it. If you question this

you are being branded as disloyal (permanent female clerical worker aged 40–49 working 55 hours in a large chain restaurant).

Why can't I go when I have finished? I'm supposed to leave at 4.00 p.m. and it is not before 4.30–5.00, and I am not paid for this (permanent female unskilled manual worker aged 40–49 working 50 hours in a large chain hotel).

As a wife and mother working part-time I have no rights. If I take time from work, I will not get paid. My employers think that a minimum wage would be a terrible thing, and if I didn't like getting paid £3.00 an hour, then I could leave. My employer can cut and increase my hours at any time. I have no contract over my job (temporary female unskilled manual worker aged 30–39 working in a small independent hotel).

I had 15 very happy years working in X. I now work for contractors with less pay, no sick pay, no pension, less holidays, more work. These have been the worst five years since we were all made redundant by X and taken over by Y (permanent male unskilled manual worker aged 30–39 working 38 hours in a large chain canteen).

Recently I have been doing the food orders, the job of a kitchen senior. Our kitchen senior has left and no one replaced her, thus I am doing the job with no extra pay or recognition (fixed-term female unskilled manual worker working 45 hours in a very small chain campsite).

Workplace issues

Just over half the dissatisfactions were directed at general problems within the workplace, such as frequent change, high turnover, poor communications, low morale, lack of consultation, threat of violence, poor food handling procedures, unfair sacking of staff with less than two years' service and not enough staff:

Most of the answers to this questionnaire would have been different 12 months ago. The company is changing and facing 50 per cent redundancies in permanent staff. The management is holding all the cards too closely to their chest, systems and working practices are archaic (permanent male manager aged 40–49 working in a large chain campsite).

Would like more responsibilities in setting and maintaining higher standards and decision-making (permanent male skilled worker aged 30–39 working 44 hours in a large chain hotel).

The company is just interested in making profit for itself than in helping the staff. IiP just looks good to the shareholders (permanent male personal service worker aged 25–29 working 21 hours in a very small chain bar).

It would be more hygienic if there were cleaners rather than us handling food and then doing some cleaning. We then continue to serve food, which can allow germs to get into the food (temporary female sales worker below 20 years working 16 hours in a very small chain restaurant).

I have recently joined a good company but I cannot understand why good staff can be sacked for no reason if they have worked full-time for under two years. Something must be done to protect staff from bad employees and poor companies who are able to mess up people's lives (permanent male personal service worker aged 30–39 working 60 hours in a small independent hotel).

This comment reflects an overwhelming degree of dissatisfaction expressed by six of eight workers in this workplace:

I am appalled at this particular company's approach to team members in regard to pay, consultation, conditions and policies. They are almost pre-historic (permanent female clerical worker aged 25–29 working 40 hours in a large chain campsite).

Managers and colleagues

Problems with managers (poor, patronizing, autocratic, inconsistent, lazy, do not allow complaints, bullying) were far more common than problems with colleagues (lazy, poor teamwork):

The assistant manager is a patronizing ponce. His attitude towards the staff and in front of guests is disgusting and undermining. It is only a matter of time before somebody will lose their job by answering him back (permanent female unskilled manual worker aged 30–39 working 27 hours in a large independent hotel).

I feel that management at X are far too laid back and young, e.g. bar and restaurant manager is only 22 and regularly disappears off the premises while on duty. Also we are expected to work 2 p.m.–4 a.m. and return to work at 10 a.m. the next day on some occasions (temporary male personal service worker below 20 years working 46 hours in a medium-sized chain hotel).

The trouble being a club steward is that you are never considered as part of the whole working. You are always kept in the dark. It's like the secret service, club business is only for committee men (permanent male personal service worker aged 60 or more working 65 hours in a very small independent bar).

Our workplace would run more smoothly if other staff pulled their weight (permanent female personal service worker aged 40–49 working 39 hours in a very small chain restaurant).

I find this workplace the most stressful I've worked in due to the bullying tactics of the manager, which seem to be ignored by the people she's accountable to . . . stress becomes difficult to keep from private life and general health (permanent female clerical worker aged 20–24 working 42 hours in a medium-sized chain hotel).

Lack of representation

Complaints about the lack of representation were extremely rare, although there was some indication of highly negative managerial attitudes to trade unions in a handful of cases:

I would like to see trade unions more easily accessible, also a list of workers' rights for part-time staff (permanent female sales worker aged 20–24 working 19 hours in a small independent hotel).

We have no worker representation for any given circumstances for any grievances or pay conditions. Any problems have to go through our supervisors. Also our managers have a company pension, we cannot have one (permanent male skilled worker aged 40–49 working 42 hours in a large independent hotel).

I would like to see a catering union formed for this type of workplace . . . people I work with including myself are working 10+ hours without a break (permanent female personal service worker aged 40–49 working in a medium sized chain restaurant).

This managerial respondent's comment might be inferred as espousing unitarism:

I don't think unions are suited to this type of environment. Nor, given the culture here, I would think that unions could resolve or communicate better – this is already happening (permanent female manager aged 25–29 working 50 hours in a small chain canteen).

Employee satisfactions

Social relationships

Employees derived most job satisfaction from social relationships, particularly with colleagues (friendly, staff help each other, staff friendly and understanding, good team):

My workplace is a really great place to work. I have made lots of friends and the work is really enjoyable (temporary female personal service worker below 20 years working 8 hours in a small chain bar).

Very friendly people that I work beside makes my job more enjoyable (permanent female personal service worker aged 25–29 working 20 hours in a medium-sized independent hotel).

Although the comments offered by most of the small number of respondents identifiable as students were treated as non-applicable, this one echoes the sentiments of many students in our earlier research (Lucas, 1997a,b; Lammont and Lucas, 1999; Lucas and Langlois, 2001; Johnson and Lucas, 2002):

I enjoy work mainly because the majority of part-time staff are my age and we are all at the same college. My job is fun . . . but I would like more say in events and changes but as I am only 16 and part-time I don't get any. Managers are always understanding and helpful if anyone has a problem (permanent female personal service worker below 20 years working 20 hours in a medium-sized chain hotel).

A smaller number reported good relationships with their managers (good or helpful management, non-ageist, non-sexist employer).

Although a younger worker cited above was critical of management in this workplace, his older colleague had a different story to tell:

Where I work the staff are all very friendly and help with any problems that I have. I am new to this type of work, my previous work was in coal-mines but the management have been very good in helping me adapt to the massive change (permanent male unskilled manual worker aged 50–59 working 38 hours in a medium-sized chain hotel).

The workplace

A similar number considered the workplace a good place to work (good safety, well-structured training, nice environment). As the first respondent indicates long hours are not necessarily a source of complaint:

In general, a very good working relationship between client and workforce. Good health and safety attitude and kept up to date on all aspects of the job contract and future work with reference to the future of the unit (permanent male skilled worker aged 40–49 working 68 hours in a large chain canteen).

I am due to retire . . . I have worked for the hotel for nearly 17 years and have enjoyed the challenge immensely, very rewarding job and thoroughly enjoyable (permanent female personal service worker aged 60 or more working 40 hours in a medium-sized chain canteen).

Since our new manager started we have been through some major changes to the country club. These should be beneficial to everyone as we are being trained to a higher standard including courses, which are very important to our career (permanent male personal service worker aged 20–24 working 40 hours in a large independent hotel).

Balanced views of employees

A number of the respondents gave a more balanced view, reporting both good and bad features about their work situation. While employees enjoyed their job and valued the support of colleagues, the criticisms were generally levelled at the way they were managed:

> Too much responsibility without empowerment. Physically stretched without sufficient resources. Lack of training and development, lack of capital investment. Very proud of my team and the job they do in the circumstances (permanent manager working 60 hours in a medium-sized chain canteen).

> There are no incentives . . . nothing to be aiming for. Not enough appreciation for what I do. A large amount of false management giving false hopes. I enjoy my job and the people I work with but the whole management body is pretty bad (permanent female clerical worker aged 20–24 working 42 hours a week in a large chain hotel).

> All the staff in my workplace seem very friendly to work with. My job itself is not too pleasant . . . I get messy and it is quite a dangerous area . . . lots of pots and pans and slippery floors which can cause accidents (permanent female unskilled manual worker aged 50–59 working 28 hours in a medium-sized independent hotel).

Themes from the employee survey

A number of themes can be identified in relation to employees' views about their job and workplace and how they are represented at work. They centre upon explicit and implicit dimensions and relational and transactional dimensions of a psychological contract. We can expect a part-time, short-service age effect, except where we have controlled for these factors in the multivariate analysis.

Views about the job

For most hospitality employees work is hard, but jobs are secure and not stressful. This may be a function of a significant youthful, part-time contingent working little overtime. Employees also have some job discretion, and are happy with the extent to which they are 'empowered'. They feel a sense of achievement and believe they command the respect of their managers. Pay is the only aspect where there is any real dissatisfaction, suggesting that most do not get a fair day's pay for a fair day's work. This is borne out by the relatively low pay of HI employees. When we take HI employees as a discrete group, they display greater satisfaction (adequate time to undertake work that is more secure) than employees in the rest of the PSS, in spite of work being harder. This suggests that a significant amount of customer interface[10] may offer the potential to provide more satisfaction for those who may also be suited to this type of work.

Views about the workplace

Employment practices

Most employees do not have the opportunity to discuss all job-related matters with their superior, except job progress. Four in ten employees received no training in the previous 12 months. Around half have no access to family-friendly policies, but this is not a major consideration to a group where dependent children are relatively rare. Most have to take unpaid time if they want to take a day off at short notice, but it may well be the case that they are able to make up lost time. Hence there is evidence that 'poor' employment practices are in place for many, reaffirming what was observed from the management survey in earlier chapters.

The organization

Managers understand employees' family needs, although one might expect this would not be a major consideration for young singles without dependants. People are encouraged to develop their skills. Although we cannot say how far this group matches the majority that had received training in the previous 12 months, it is conceivable that skills development may occur outside a formal training. HI employees as a discrete group do have different expectations of their managers and organization than employees in the rest of the PSS. Managers are seen to be supportive and encouraging, while a higher level of commitment (loyalty to an organization whose values are espoused) is noteworthy.

Involvement and commitment

HI employees are generally kept up to date by a combination of meetings with managers and information posted on notice boards, rather than by more contemporary means of newsletters and email. Hence they enjoy a closer personal interface with their superiors, who may also be relatively young. This is likely to reflect a small workplace effect, which also militates against any effective form of representation developing. Most employees are consulted on health and safety, which is likely to be an ongoing consideration where there is food handling with risks to employees and customers alike. Views on core substantive issues in the employment relationship, notably pay, are less frequently sought.

HI employees are generally very happy with their managers, particularly believing that employment relations are good. However managers are least good at involving employees and responding to suggestions, suggesting their style tends more towards the autocratic or paternalistic than the participative. HI employees as a discrete group are more positive about their managers than employees in the rest of the PSS, suggesting empathy and a shared ethos that may be lacking elsewhere.

Representation at work

HI employees are less likely to be trade union members, and membership is lowest in the largest sub-sectors – hotels, restaurants and bars. Most employees do not know any trade union or non-union representatives. HI employees' level of know-ledge and awareness about 'workplace democracy' is significantly lower than for employees in the rest of the PSS. Employees do not see managers as openly favouring unions, yet membership is lower where management is more supportive. Employees prefer to represent themselves, and are notably more self-reliant in matters of pay and discipline than employees in the rest of the PSS. Even if they have little choice and may actually be happy with this state of affairs, one might question the wisdom of this, given they are dissatisfied with their low pay. Nevertheless, where unions are present they are seen to make a difference. The part-time, short-service and age effect may be a factor that contributes to extremely low levels of union membership, yet controlling for these factors still finds HI employees to be different. If representation does not actually matter to HI employees, they will not seek to change the situation, so the HI remains an infertile ground for either union or non-union representation.

Do 'poor' employment relations lead to feelings of exploitation and dissatisfaction?

Findings from the management survey contained in the previous chapters in most respects are not wholly different from those established from WIRS3 (Lucas, 1995a, 1996a). They show that employment policies and practices in HI work-places compare less favourably to those observed in workplaces in AIS and the PSS (see Appendix 2). Prima facie these explicit dimensions of the psychological contract do not suggest that implicit dimensions of fairness, trust and delivery of promises will be met. But of course this is highly dependent upon the substance of employees' expectations, which can vary considerably.

In reality many HI employees working in gender-neutral workplaces are more or less satisfied with their job, workplace, managers and organization, and are perceptibly more upbeat than their counterparts in AIS and the PSS. The main negative issue is pay. HI employees are well informed enough, more or less indiffer-ent to the lack of involvement or representation, and consider they are well able to look after their own interests in the workplace. Ultimately managers and employees working in close proximity develop close personal bonds, and share a highly positive view of the state of employment relations in their workplaces. There is a high trust relational psychological contract for many of them. 'Poor' employ-ment relations in conventional academic terms do not necessarily lead to feelings of alienation, exploitation and dissatisfaction for many HI employees, where certain attributes of the job are valued and traded off against low pay.

Do hospitality employees have a simultaneous transactional and relational psychological contract?

The preceding section has highlighted a number of aspects around loyalty and commitment that point to facets of a relational psychological contract. There are also transactional facets present. We can infer that the presence of a sizeable minority of short-service employees involves a transaction of regular job change for those unable to secure career development because there is little training or no job hierarchy, especially in smaller workplaces. Some employees may not invest so much of themselves in their jobs, as moving on is relatively easy. The expectation of necessarily leaving to 'get on' reinforces a sense of self-reliance and lowers employees' expectations in terms of involvement and representation.

The notion of a transactional contract is different from Rousseau's (1990, 1995), where good financial reward is a trade-off for low security. Employees accept HI jobs in the knowledge that pay is not particularly good, even by 'getting on'. Their expectations are being met elsewhere. For many of these employees the direct customer relationship is in their hands, even though they may not be in direct customer contact, e.g. chefs. Employees know their managers want them to provide good service, so there is a unity of understanding, if not a unity of economic interest. They know what their managers are trying to achieve, so there is no need to question it or no grounds for resisting it.

Employees in WERS do not necessarily reflect the perspective of many students, who have no orientation to HI work on a longer-term basis. For these young people part-time working is an economic necessity and means to an end in a specific set of circumstances. But they do share a transactional contract that embodies a relative acceptance of low pay in exchange for other compensations that have a strong social connotation. Hence we can point to a psychological contract that embraces both dimensions, which may be more relational to managers and customers than transactional to the employee.

Finally, one might argue that employees' questions were focused too closely on their own job or work, and need to be broadened to include other issues in the employment relationship. WERS does not provide answers to explain why so many HI employees quit the workplace or why their work expectations may differ from those held by employees working elsewhere. Further research is needed to develop more fully an explanation of why an academic view of 'good' employment relations may not be shared by the parties themselves. How far does the nature of a triadic employment relationship, rather than the personal values of the employees, affect the state of the psychological contract?

Discussion and review topics

Psychological contract

How useful are the notions of relational and transactional contracts?

Explicit and implicit dimensions of a psychological contract

Why do employment policies and practices that are regarded as 'poor' not produce feelings of alienation or dissatisfaction among HI employees?

Are hospitality employees unique?

Can you explain why HI employees may be different from employees in the rest of the PSS?

Quantitative or qualitative method?

What particular insights are gained from the verbatim responses that are not forthcoming from the survey evidence?

Knowing more about employees at work

If you were designing the employee survey for the next WERS:

- What issues would you want to know about?
- What type of questions would you ask?

9 Conclusions and future issues

Comparative international themes

Hospitality and tourism employment is important to very many countries across the globe. Although the influence of large MNCs is spreading, most employment is in small, independent enterprises. Much work is unpaid or low-paid. There is heavy reliance on females and young labour and, in some countries, on migrants. Most work is regarded as semi-skilled or unskilled, and there has been some deskilling. Training is often basic, with firms tending to buy in skills from the labour market. The HCTS also manifests different occupational categories compared to other private services. Many workers engage directly with customers, while others whose work is still geared towards providing good customer service have a more indirect customer relationship, necessitating us to acknowledge that the employment relationship is triadic. Part-time and atypical employment is common, and may be increasing amid countries' desire to create more flexible labour markets. The labour force is highly mobile, often with a short-term orientation to the HCTS, generating high labour turnover and leaver rates. Recruitment and retention is particularly problematic, particularly for managers where a lack of professionalism may impede business success in developing and transitional economies.

These characteristics, in combination with the fact that most workers are not trade union members, constitute what might be termed 'vulnerable' employment. Hence it is not surprising to find regulation of the employment relationship is of global concern in areas such as minimum wages, equal pay and working time. However, wide recognition is given to lower minimum rates for young workers, and unequal pay persists, reinforcing the importance of women and young people as cheap labour.

Different economic, social, legal and political factors create particular cultures and a variety of employment systems, even within the same region. Hence considerable variation of regulatory regimes remains within EU countries that are ostensibly subject to the same broad employment standards. Some countries have well-developed and relatively comprehensive systems of VET and collective bargaining arrangements. Where union membership is low, more complete coverage may be secured by extending collective agreements to all workers by government decree. The drive for flexibility and the deregulation of labour markets stands at odds with increased regulation of employment. Cultural barriers may prevent the wider application of measures to combat discrimination. New work organization may be especially challenging in transitional countries in Central and Eastern Europe.

Global changes have contributed to economic uncertainty and a more turbulent market, creating new sets of challenges for managers. Management style is influenced by constraints and choices related to product and labour markets, organizational status and structure, size of workplace and culture. While managers' personal frame of reference influences choice, managers are most likely to place high priority on seeking to control labour costs, and have little incentive to take the 'high road' to employment.

Although we have been able to use data from 50 countries, a limitation is that most research is western-centric and drawn from 'Anglo' countries. This provides a clearer, if only partial, view of key employment relations issues in the US, Australia and New Zealand, which may have parallels in the UK. We have some information about the positive and negative influence of MNCs on employment practices in hotels, restaurants, fast food and contract catering in host countries, while hotels in the transitional Slovakian economy offer a corollary as they are still immune from international influence. More examples from Africa and Latin America would have been interesting and useful.

The state of employment relations in Britain

Managerial evidence

WERS reaffirms that employment relations in the British HI are unequivocally different from AIS and the PSS across a wide range of employment practices, one explicit dimension of a psychological contract. Many features of global application also characterize the British HI as 'vulnerable' employment. More specific workplace practices of disadvantage include pay, how it is determined and conditions of employment. HI employees have less access to family-friendly measures, comprehensive induction and training, performance appraisal and a healthy and safe environment. Disciplinary sanctions are more commonplace. On the positive side there is also less use of grievance procedures, although this could signify fear rather than contentment and more IiP accreditation. The balance of evidence overwhelmingly points to the 'bleak house' (Sisson, 1993) and 'black hole' (Guest and Conway, 1999) scenarios.

Employment relations are an important part of managerial work, where decisions are most likely to be concentrated in the hands of one or two managers in the absence of specialist internal and external advice. The extent of unionization is marginal, and not compensated by other means of consultation. Managers probably hold negative views about unions. Even though managers would rather consult with employees than with unions, they do neither. The 'unbridled individualism' thesis developed from WIRS3 seems to be reaffirmed by the WERS management evidence. Managers transact the employment relationship from a unitary perspective.

In assessing the management evidence on its own, we must remind ourselves that three-quarters of HI workplaces are multi-site, and include some very large employers. Strong strategic integration is suggested. HI workplaces are much more cost-conscious and work on a lower wage cost:sales ratio. While a strong proprietorial and family effect is also evident, in most cases this is about control of a large organization, not a stereotypical single site family business. Most of the very small workplaces employing 10 to 24 employees included for the first time in WERS are chain pubs. WERS is most likely to convey a big organization picture of employment relations and is less helpful in providing particular insights into the practices of small, independent operators. This form of employment relations is most likely to be discernible in small workplaces employing between 25 and 49 employees.

The clear implication is that big firms are not necessarily good firms, where employment policies and practices in HI workplaces within a cost-control framework continue to contradict the conventional notion 'good' employment relations. This is supported by the findings of most other UK studies, although some clearly provide evidence of 'better' practice that is more relational.

While WERS provides considerable support for a cost-control 'low road' and transactional approach to employment relations throughout the HI, it does not detail or explain managerial rationale or motive. It is argued that outcomes such as the lack of representation, consultation and grievances are likely to be a function of managers working in close proximity with employees with whom close personal bonds develop where customers are ever present. This leads to a relationship of affiliation based on shared understanding of the importance of providing good customer service and 'mucking in' together. The suggestion of affiliation (similar to Scase's (1995) fraternalism) is well established within the management literature (Chapter 3 and Lucas, 1995a: 30–4), but does not necessarily imply unitarism because 'liberal' managers may still recognize difference among employees as a whole.

Employee evidence

The employee survey appears to throw up some contradictions. In spite of demonstrably 'poor' employment policies and practices, HI employees are remarkably positive about their work, workplace, organization and their relationship to them, more so than their counterparts in AIS and the PSS. They are more satisfied with the way they are treated by their managers. Pay is the only area of notable dissent. Employees are largely isolated from any trade union presence, contact or activity. They feel informed enough, considering themselves well able to look after themselves in transactions with their managers about employment issues.

Undoubtedly a number of these observations can be linked to employee and job characteristics, including age, part-time hours and short service. They must also link to the highly interpersonal nature of customer-service employment relationships, providing further support for affiliation. This creates a unity of understanding towards customer service if not a unity of economic interest. Employees who believe their future is in their own destiny and concur with their managers that employment relations are good cannot be said to be masochistic or powerless. There is neither a need to question their situation nor a need to resist it. These employees can be said to espouse 'enfranchised realism' built upon a trade-off between low pay and other factors. 'Resigned realism' might be more appropriate for those who are relatively powerless, while others may suffer real exploitation.

Even more striking is the finding that in a number of respects HI employees are indeed different from employees in the rest of the PSS, when characteristics including age, length of service, pay, size of workplace and type of organization are controlled for. This suggestion in a customer-service context is not new, but now more convincingly demonstrated across a larger sample of employees working in all sub-sectors of the HI. Importantly there is now more compelling evidence to suggest that trade unions face an even more daunting task in attempting to recruit members and organize HI workplaces.

Customers and gender

Customers are an important influence on employment relations in the HI, and often interrelate with gender where the issue is women's rather than men's disadvantage. Managing and experiencing the service encounter are important facets of an employment relationship that hinges upon a socio-economic exchange, not simply an economic nexus around the price of labour. The social composition of service work is part of the product, which managers see as a legitimate area for intervention. The locus of managerial control extends beyond workers' behaviour to include emotions, speech and appearance. Labour may be manufactured to appeal to customers, particularly males, and internalize customer prejudices. Female labour may be sexualized, requiring workers to flirt or suffer harassment to earn tips. These are barriers to women's equality, and may reflect that social attitudes have moved more slowly than legal requirements. Workers respond by developing coping strategies. Alternatively customer-service work may also be highly rewarding and contribute to high levels of job satisfaction among some workers. To some job flirt may simply be an individual response of using one's skills to best effect and be a highly empowering experience, which stands at odds with notions of desexualized labour and equality.

Customers are also unpredictable and their unsatisfactory behaviour may impact on managers and workers. Where customers are drawn into managerial control strategies, e.g. high reliance on tips, employees will suffer stress if tips are non-existent or derisory or they have to draw upon behaviours that do not come naturally. Customer/guest information used to guide hiring, performance assessment for pay or other purposes, including training needs, promotion, discipline and dismissal, may be unreliable, including an unwillingness by customers to testify in formal proceedings, e.g. employment tribunals.

While there is evidence that HI employees are more likely to work in more gender-equal workplaces, some management practices are clearly not gender-neutral. Women's work may be defined as unskilled to keep costs low. The use of proxy measures in appraisal, e.g. 'being there', may penalize women working part-time. There is also some evidence that trade unions have not always served women's interests well. Assumptions of women's lower commitment may shape the core–periphery and determine which jobs are full-time or part-time, with the latter receiving less favourable terms and conditions. Cost-cutting underpins job segregation. The same assumptions can also be applied to young workers, affecting men and women alike. Labour markets perpetuate gender segregation where collective bargaining is more likely to benefit men, decentralized pay increases the probability of low pay and minimum wage systems treat young workers less favourably. It remains to be seen how far new legislation will enable these gaps to be closed. More studies are needed that take a perspective that embeds customers, gender and youth within the analysis of employment relations in the HI.

Continuity and change

Continuity is provided by the bulk of managerial evidence but, importantly, change is heralded by employee evidence enabling us to reassess the state of employment relations in the HI. To do so inevitably runs the risk of oversimplification, as there are undoubtedly many types of employment relationship in many different contexts. WERS does not probe issues that have particular relevance to a triadic employment relationship based on close individual bonds between managers and workers within a customer-service ethos.

Overall management's approach is highly cost-control-driven, which inevitably results in particular outcomes, including low pay, flexible employment and hire and fire. Whether these outcomes are necessarily 'good' or 'bad' is a moot point. Not all managers deliberately set out to exploit their workers. Many are not unreasonable people, although some are bullies and exploit power unreasonably. Rather, most are faced with making difficult choices within the constraints of their own spheres of influence. One might argue that the choices of an owner-manager of a small firm operating in a tight market are more constrained than the choices of the HR director of large, profitable chain. This might excuse relatively 'poor' policies and practices in a boarding house. The broad picture of British employment relations portrays a larger-firm view, where, arguably, more profitable employers could and should do better.

Yet most hospitality employees do not see themselves as a bunch of losers in the face of overbearing, unfair or unreasonable managers. Their work and employment expectations are not unrealistic, and are largely met where low pay is traded off against other factors in a customer-service employment relationship that can be high trust and positive. Most believe they have control of their own destinies, and have little incentive to seek trade union protection. Others are more powerless and even though they can move on, some may become locked in a cycle of low trust exploitative employment relationships. For some customer-service work is highly rewarding. For others it is undoubtedly less so, threatening the unity of purpose where they are unable to provide good service to awkward customers.

We can now state with greater certainty that the metaphors of 'bleak house' (management evidence) and 'black hole' (employee evidence) are wanting. Both are based on only one side of a story that is much more complex. We see an

---

Box 9.1 *Dimensions of a socio-economic customer-service employment relationship*

Management
Affiliated, liberal individualism ⟷ Unbridled individualism ⟷ Determined opportunism

Fair cost-control employment policies and practices ⟷ Exploitative cost-control employment policies and practices

Workers
Enfranchised realism ⟷ Resigned realism ⟷ Exploitation

Relational psychological contract ⟷ Transactional psychological contract

Customers
Direct interface ⟷ Indirect effect

Rewarding, predictable and satisfied ⟷ Awkward, unpredictable and dissatisfied

Work
Gender neutral ⟷ Gendered

Satisfying and empowering ⟷ Dissatisfying and exploitative

High trust ⟷ Low trust

---

employment relationship that is rather different from Edwards' (2003a) employer–employee relationship mediated by trade unions or employee representatives and the state. The locus is a function of dimensions related to three sets of actors within particular types of work, and also embodies explicit gender and implied youth perspectives (Box 9.1). This allows for a variety of employment relationships in the HI, which are an outcome of the dimensions mediated by the state. The omission of any reference to collectivism and representation is made somewhat reluctantly, but as its possibility is so very marginal its inclusion across some dimensions would arguably detract from the reality of employment relations in the HI.

Future prospects

Relative consensus between managers and employees does not imply employment relations are not in need of reform. There are no easy solutions, particularly if we extend reform to include customers, and this requires further consideration, so we stick to conventional prescriptions for the time being. If we assume that trade unions and systems of employee representation are never to become a force in the

HI, then we have to look to the state. The first possibility is alternative collective measures that will serve the interests of small firms. One obvious route would be to reappraise the notion of legally enforceable state-sponsored collective bargaining on an industry basis. This would take account of particular industries' needs, in effect a more sophisticated and comprehensive version of the wages councils. Similar arrangements already operate outside Britain, but do not necessarily place hospitality workers at a much higher point in the earnings distribution. Such collective agreements would provide a bigger safety net than the NMW, which should be retained for its simplicity, and could create a sense of collective responsibility and awareness. The second possibility is that an extension of employment rights to workers would also provide greater protection for 'vulnerable' hospitality workers currently excluded from rights, such as unfair dismissal. In the current climate the latter option looks the most realistic, but may be slow in coming.

Appendix 1

Background characteristics of the WERS98 sample

Methodology

About the survey

WERS is a nationally representative sample survey of workplaces in Britain with ten or more employees. WERS has a slightly modified title from its predecessor surveys (WIRS1, 2 and 3 in 1980, 1994, 1990), largely to reflect contemporary employment relationships. Indeed the nature and scope of the survey was altered significantly to reflect the declining influence of trade unions and the rise of more individual employment relationships. WERS covers all industry sectors, except agriculture and coal-mining, and includes both private and publicly owned establishments. WERS is sponsored by the DTI, the ESRC, ACAS and the PSI, the latter supported in part by funds from the Leverhulme Trust. Its main findings are contained in Cully *et al.* (1999).

The main aims of WERS were to:

- examine the state of the contemporary employment contract;
- explore how employee relations practices at the workplace impact upon its performance and competitiveness;
- assess whether there has been a transformation in workplace employment relations in Britain.

WERS also provides a benchmark against which New Labour's legislative changes can be assessed, and evidence of continuity and change in employment relations (Millward *et al.*, 2000).

Interview data were gathered from managers and worker representatives, and a panel survey was undertaken to explore issues of continuity and change within workplaces that had participated in WIRS3. Two major innovations in WERS were the inclusion of very small workplaces employing 10–24 employees and an employee survey. The sample was weighted to compensate for the higher probability of large workplaces being selected.

A new approach

The data presented and discussed in this book offer a distinct and different perspective from the main primary analysis of WERS. Cully *et al.* (1999) discuss very small workplaces (10–24 employees) in a separate chapter, and do not integrate them within their overall analysis. Here the full data set inclusive of these workplaces is used (DTI, 1999). This gives a more comprehensive account of employment relations in AIS,[1] the PSS[2] and, especially, the HI,[3] as these small workplaces comprise 61 per cent of the HI sample within WERS.[4]

The inclusion in WERS of an employee survey for the first time is important because we gain a more balanced perspective of employment relations within the same workplaces, and can create a more detailed picture of employees' working lives. The main issues explored are what employees think about their job, about working at their workplace, and how they are represented at work (see also Cully *et al.*, 1999: 4–10).

Three main sources of data have been used in preparing this book:

- specified output from the management questionnaire;
- all output from the employee questionnaire;
- verbatim responses from the employee questionnaire.

No use could be made of the worker representative questionnaire due to the low incidence of unionization in the HI or the panel survey because of the small number of cases.

Appropriate questions in the *management questionnaire* were identified, where possible with a view to achieving consistency with WIRS3 data (Lucas, 1995a). The main areas omitted were in relation to aspects of representation at work and collective bargaining, because of the marginal influence of trade unions within the HI. On the basis of the author's requirements, NIESR staff created the necessary variables and produced the statistical output (see Acknowledgements).

Selected frequency output is presented in this book to serve two main purposes:

- to compare and contrast the HI (N = 121) with AIS (N = 2,191) and the PSS (N = 1,218);
- to enable closer inspection of differences within the HI by size of workplace and sub-sector.

No question selection was necessary for the *employee questionnaires*, where all of the data collected in the survey proved relevant. The responses for the HI (N = 1,077), AIS (N = 28,215) and the PSS (N = 14,412) are presented in the same format as the management survey results. It should be noted that the AIS and PSS samples both include the HI.

Subsequently permission was obtained via the WERS User Sub-committee to access restricted data in the form of *employee verbatim responses* from the employee questionnaire. Question D12 asked 'Do you have any final comments you would like to make about your workplace, or about this questionnaire?'. Comments were provided voluntarily by a sub-set of respondents. We present these qualitative responses for HI employees only (N = 338), which represent 30 per cent of all HI employees who responded to the survey. We can identify each response by work-place size, industry sub-sector, gender, age group, occupational group, contract status, weekly hours (including overtime), whether part of a larger organization, and the percentage of the workforce that are female and part-time (identifying characteristics).

Data analysis

The relatively small sample size of the HI *management questionnaire* responses effec-tively rules out the use of statistical refinements beyond simple frequencies. Tests of significance (at the 5 per cent level) are restricted to a comparison of the HI with AIS and the PSS in all tables for purposes of simplicity and clarity. These tests are calculated using the unweighted bases (Table A.1).

Simple frequencies are also presented for the *employee questionnaire*. Tests of signif-icance (at the 5 per cent level) are made on the same basis as the management questionnaire, using the unweighted bases (Table A.2).

Additionally some multivariate analysis has been used to determine whether HI employees are more or less likely than employees in the rest of the PSS to demon-strate particular views or characteristics. The particular outcomes that have been tested in this way are contained in Tables 8.5 (employees' views about their job), 8.12 (employees' views about the organization), 8.17 (how good are managers), and 8.20, 8.22 and 8.26 (trade union membership and representation). The multi-variate analysis takes on a different form from all the other analysis because hospitality employees have been removed from private services, so that each of the samples tested is discrete. Regressions automatically test at all levels of statistical significance (1, 5 and 10 per cent), but we do not report the full details here.[5] Results that are significant at the 5 per cent level are noted briefly in the text.

The multivariate analysis takes the form of a series of probit regression models in which dichotomous variables representing particular outcomes are regressed upon a number of control variables. These control variables comprise:

- each of the eight variables relating to employee characteristics contained in Tables 8.1 and 8.2;
- six of the variables relating to job characteristics contained in Tables 8.3 and 8.4 excluding the occupational group (personal and protective services);
- a dummy variable indicating employees working in single, independent estab-lishments;
- five dummy variables to control for establishment-size effects;
- a dummy variable identifying employees in the HI.

The interest is focused on the hospitality dummy, which indicates whether the specified outcome is any more or less likely among HI employees than among other PSS employees after controlling for the other characteristics included in the model.

Table A.1 The management sample in context, by size of workplace and sub-sector (number of cases)

	AIS	PSS	HI	<25 employees	25–49 employees	50–99 employees	100+ employees	Hotels	Camp-sites	Restaur-ants	Bars	Canteens
Weighted base	2,191	1,363	160	98	32	22	8	39	2	41	65	12
Unweighted base	2,191	1,218	121	29	27	33	32	51	4	30	23	12

Source: WERS98.

Table A.2 The employee sample in context, by size of workplace and sub-sector (number of cases)

	AIS	PSS	HI	<25 employees	25–4 employees	50–99 employees	100+ employees	Hotels	Camp-sites	Restaur-ants	Bars	Canteens
Weighted base	28,222	12,886	1,110	341	152	288	330	460	36	213	273	123
Unweighted base	28,215	14,412	1,077	165	178	318	416	524	68	215	134	127

Source: WERS98 employee survey.

The original probit coefficients have been transformed into changes in proba-
bilities. This is achieved by evaluating the change in the probit index that arises
from a unit change in each independent variable when all other variables are
held at their mean value. The transformed coefficient on the hospitality dummy
can then be interpreted as the change in the probability of the outcome (e.g. union
membership) that is associated with working in the HI rather than the remainder
of the PSS for the average employee, after the influences of the specified characteristics have been removed. If each regression model were to include only
the hospitality dummy and no other control variables, the transformed coefficient on the hospitality dummy would correspond to the raw difference in proba-
bilities obtained from the initial tabular analysis presented in particular tables in
Chapter 8.

The main identifying characteristics of each of the *employee verbatim responses* have
also been subjected to simple frequency analysis to identify the parameters of the
sub-sample. Then responses have been subjected to content analysis along three
constructs of job satisfaction – only satisfied, only dissatisfied, and both satisfied
and dissatisfied. These constructs and the identifying characteristics were subsequently analysed using the Statistical Package for the Social Sciences (SPSS).
The responses of the large majority (77 per cent) who gave comments on job satisfaction (N = 261) were not distributed normally. Hence non-parametric statistical
tests were conducted: the Mann-Whitney test to compare two unrelated groups,
the Median test to compare two or more unrelated groups and the Kruskal-
Wallace test to compare three or more unrelated groups. These tests determine if
any of the employee characteristics have a significant relationship with job
(dis)satisfaction (at the 5 per cent level). The results must be treated with some
caution because they are not representative of all employees surveyed. Only
two employee characteristics demonstrated a significant relationship with job
dissatisfaction (see Chapter 8).

How WERS is presented

This Appendix (general background), the main body of the text (specific employment relations observations) and Appendix 2 (summary employment relations
practices and outcomes) contain tables that present key frequencies to illustrate
some of the general differences between HI and AIS and PSS workplaces, a
number of which are statistically significant. Tables are based on all weighted cases
(Tables A.1 and A.2) unless otherwise specified. Notes are given with each table
to indicate these differences.

Tables are also the most effective way to show broad-brush patterns within the
HI by size of workplace and sub-sector. However, statistically testing the intra-HI
figures from the *management questionnaire* serves little purpose, because the
unweighted bases are so low. Some caution needs to be exercised in drawing
conclusions from the small samples, especially in the case of campsites and
canteens because of the very small number of cases (both sum to fewer than 20).
Hence these two sub-sectors are shown only in tables, and not included in the
discussion. Although there is scope for applying statistical tests to the intra-HI

figures in the *employee questionnaire* because the unweighted bases are larger numerically, we prefer to maintain consistency with the approach used elsewhere in the book. Nevertheless we can be less cautious about the sub-sectoral results, and include campsites and canteens in the discussion. The main general features from the management and employee questionnaires are presented separately in two subsequent sections.

Some responses referred to in the discussion and tables relate to a sub-sample of all weighted cases, e.g. following a filter question. In these cases size of the sub-sample will normally be noted. Gratuitous use of figures and percentages is avoided within the discussion, particularly in the management questionnaire because of the small sample sizes. Thus the discussion focuses on general tendencies (vast majority, large minority) or more general measures such a half, two-thirds or one in ten.

Using statistical data of this kind can only establish patterns and broad trends, but it does provide a reliable and valid basis from which more focused empirical work can be undertaken. Even so, one the limitation of WERS remains the exclusion of workplaces employing fewer than ten employees (see Chapter 2), so we still have an incomplete picture of employment relations in their total context. Further, these data shed no light on the role played by customers in determining employees' experience of work, which we contend is integral to understanding customer-service work employment relationships.

Terminology

The following terms are used to describe workplace size:

* very small workplaces (10–24 employees);
* small workplaces (25–49 employees);
* medium workplaces (50–99 employees);
* large workplaces (100+ employees).

The term smaller workplaces is used to denote workplaces employing fewer than 50 employees. Where comparisons are drawn between AIS, the PSS and the HI, while these are normally referred to by their acronyms, they may also be referred to as 'all groupings' or 'on all comparisons'.

Management questionnaire

Workplace profile

This section presents key workplace features of WERS. The HI contains more very small workplaces (10–24 employees) than AIS, although the only statistically significant difference is in the mean number of employees per workplace (Table A.3). From Table A.4, we can see that a majority of these very small workplaces are bars, while most very large workplaces are hotels.

Table A.3 Workplace size in context (percentage of workplaces by numbers employed)

Number of employees	AIS	PSS	HI
10–24	50	56	61
25–49	26	25	20
50–99	13	11	13
100+	11	8	5
Total (%)	100	100	100
Mean number of employees	62	47	34**
Weighted base	2,191	1,363	160
Unweighted base	2,191	1,218	121

Source: WERS98.

Notes: Column percentages do not sum to 100 due to rounding. ** Significantly different at the 5% level from AIS.

It is important to note that the characteristics of the HI sample have altered markedly between WIRS3 in 1990 and WERS in 1998, with the inclusion of very small workplaces (Table A.5). Even if we remove very small workplaces from the WERS sample (Table A.6), it is notable that bars constitute a much larger proportion of small workplaces in 1998. However, this still does not represent the full industry picture (see Chapter 2), so other characteristics of the WERS sample, e.g. gender and age composition of the workforce, may differ from those established from sources like the LFS.

Employee characteristics

The main characteristics of employees within HI workplaces (by gender and working hours) are shown in Tables A.7, A.8 and A.9. Full-time denotes working hours of 30 or more per week, while part-time denotes working hours below 30 per week.

Gender and working hours

Similar proportions of females work in HI and AIS, but their distribution differs significantly. Although half or more of the workforce is female in three-quarters of HI workplaces, there are very high concentrations of females (71 per cent+) in more AIS workplaces than in HI workplaces (Table A.10). Smaller HI workplaces are most likely to have a high proportion of females. Table A.11 illustrates how the distribution of female employees differs by sub-sector.

However, significantly more females in the HI work part-time than in AIS and the PSS, so there is a more substantive part-time female contingent in many workplaces. The growth of part-time employment among males means that HI workplaces are twice as likely to have part-time employees. There is a more substantive part-time female contingent in smaller workplaces, bars and restaurants.

Table A.4 Hospitality workplaces by sub-sector and number of employees (1998) (% in brackets)

	10–24 employees	25–49 employees	50–99 employees	100+ employees	All sub-sectors	Range of employees	Mean number of employees
Hotels	12 (12)	9 (28)	13 (60)	6 (66)	39 (24)	10–340	57
Campsites and short stay accommodation	1 (1)	0	0	0 (6)	2 (1)	16–283	58
Restaurants	26 (26)	8 (26)	6 (30)	1 (10)	41 (26)	10–252	32
Bars	50 (52)	13 (41)	1 (6)	0	65 (41)	10–64	20
Canteens and catering	9 (9)	2 (5)	1 (5)	1 (14)	12 (8)	16–406	40
All hospitality	98 (100)	32 (100)	22 (100)	8 (100)	160 (100)	10–406	34
Range of employees	10–24	25–48	52–95	100–406	10–406		
Mean number of employees	16	34	67	160	34		

Source: WERS98.

Notes: All weighted cases. Row and column numbers and column percentages do not sum accurately due to rounding.

Table A.5 Hospitality workplaces by sub-sector and number of employees (1990) (% in brackets)

	25–49 employees		50–99 employees		100+ employees		All sub-sectors		Mean number of employees
Hotels	22	(37)	14	(54)	5	(33)	41	(41)	64
Campsites and short-stay accommodation	0		b	(2)	2	(13)	2	(2)	140
Restaurants	20	(34)	9	(35)	2	(13)	31	(31)	49
Bars	7	(12)	1	(4)	2	(13)	10	(10)	59
Clubs	3	(5)	b	(2)	0		3	(3)	35
Canteens and catering	7	(12)	1	(4)	4	(27)	12	(12)	90
All hospitality	59	(100)	26	(100)	15	(100)	99	(100)	62

Source: WIRS3.

Notes: All weighted cases. Row and column numbers and column percentages do not sum accurately due to rounding. b Fewer than 0.5.

Table A.6 Hospitality workplaces by sub-sector and number of employees (excluding 10–24 employees) (1998) (% in brackets)

	25–49 employees		50–99 employees		100+ employees		All sub-sectors		Range of employees	Mean number of employees
Hotels	9	(28)	13	(60)	6	(66)	27	(44)	250–340	75
Campsites and short-stay accommodation	0		0		c		c		148–283	166
Restaurants	8	(26)	6	(30)	1	(10)	16	(26)	25–252	56
Bars	13	(41)	1	(6)	0		15	(24)	26–64	35
Canteens and catering	2	(5)	1	(5)	1	(14)	4	(7)	30–406	86
All hospitality	32	(100)	22	(100)	8	(100)	62	(100)	25–406	62
Range of employees	25–48		52–95		100–406		25–406			
Mean number of employees	34		67		160		62			

Source: WERS98.

Notes: All weighted cases. Row and column numbers and column percentages do not sum accurately due to rounding. c Fewer than 1%.

Table A.7 Hospitality workforce composition by gender (%)

	Male	Female	All employees
By gender	43	57	100
Full-time	58	40	48
Part-time	42	60	52
Total	100	100	100

Source: WERS98.

Note: All weighted cases.

Table A.8 Hospitality workforce composition by working hours (%)

	Full-time	Part-time	All employees
By working hours	48	52	100
Male	52	35	
Female	48	65	
Total	100	100	

Source: WERS98.

Note: All weighted cases.

Table A.9 Hospitality workforce composition by gender and working hours (%)

	Full-time	Part-time	All employees
Males	25	18	43
Females	23	34	57
Total	48	52	100

Source: WERS98.

Note: All weighted cases.

Table A.10 Workforce composition in context and by size of workplace (%)

	AIS	PSS	HI	<25	25–49	50–99	100+
Females (all) a	58	66	57	62	59	53	55
71%+	37	32	22**	23	28	10	12
50%+	60	60	77*	86	64	60	79
Part-time (all) a	26	33	51*	61	61	51	34
71%+	16	21	40*	46	43	23	4
50%+	32	35	72*	81	71	49	25
Male (full-time) a	45	40	25*	20	20	27	35
71%+	25	23	4*	6	0	0	2
50%+	36	35	10*	9	7	15	17
Female (part-time) a	21	25	34**	43	39	30	24
71%+	6	7	7	6	19	0	4
50%+	23	23	39*	50	30	13	4

Source: WERS98.

Notes: All weighted cases. a Aggregate percentage. *Significantly different at the 5% level from AIS and PSS. ** Significantly different at the 5% level from AIS.

Table A.11 Workforce composition by sub-sector (%)

	Hotels	Campsites	Restaurants	Bars	Canteens
Females (all) a	56	53	57	58	64
71%+	5	0	33	16	69
50%+	77	90	73	76	97
Part-time (all) a	37	22	59	78	38
71%+	0	0	47	65	17
50%+	44	0	77	96	26
Male (full-time) a	33	43	24	11	28
71%+	0	0	13	0	1
50%+	15	10	19	2	3
Female (part-time) a	26	18	40	47	30
71%+	0	0	6	12	12
50%+	9	0	47	55	26

Source: WERS98.

Notes: All weighted cases. a Aggregate percentage.

Table A.12 Other workforce characteristics in context and by size of workplace (%)

	AIS	PSS	HI	<25	25–49	50–99	100+
Employees <21 years							
20%+	14	23	55*	54	52	64	45
None	44	35	12*	16	5	6	2
Mean (%)	8	12	24*	20	32	31	22
Employees 51+ years							
20%+	32	36	16*	22	11	0	10
None	14	17	39*	44	51	15	0
Mean (%)	15	14	8	9	7	6	10
Mean (%) of disabled employees	1	1	1	1	1	1	1
Mean (%) of ethnic minority employees	4	4	3	2	3	7	6

Source: WERS98.

Notes: All weighted cases. *Significantly different at the 5% level from AIS and PSS. Means are rounded.

Table A.13 Other workforce characteristics by sub-sector (%)

	Hotels	Campsites	Restaurants	Bars	Canteens
Employees <21 years					
20%+	53	0	69	56	16
None	5	82	19	9	20
Mean (%)	22	2	29	25	15
Employees 51+ years					
20%+	11	6	19	9	59
None	8	0	46	62	0
Mean (%)	10	19	8	5	17
Mean (%) of disabled employees	1	5	b	2	b
Mean (%) of ethnic minority employees	4	b	6	2	1

Source: WERS98.

Notes: All weighted cases. b Fewer than 0.5%. Means are rounded.

The HI has a significantly lower concentration of full-time males than AIS and the PSS. Bars and very small workplaces have very low concentrations of full-time males.

Other characteristics

The HI has significantly greater reliance on young workers aged 20 or less than AIS and the PSS (Table A.12). Conversely significantly more HI workplaces employ no workers aged 51 and over compared to AIS and the PSS. Differences in the age profile of employees by size of workplace and sub-sector are shown in Tables A.12 and A.13. These tables also indicate that disabled and ethnic minority employees are marginal to most workplaces.

Occupational groups

The HI workforce comprises a large proportion of manual workers. Above average proportions of manual workers are found in medium and large workplaces, and in hotels and restaurants. Relatively few bar staff are manual workers. Almost all HI workplaces have manual workers and managers. There are significant differences in some occupational groupings in the HI compared to AIS and the PSS (Tables A.14 and A.15).

Workplace status

Two-thirds of all HI workplaces are public limited companies (PLCs), which is significantly higher than in AIS and the PSS. The vast majority of HI workplaces are wholly or predominantly UK owned and controlled. Very few workplaces are Head Offices. Differences in workplace status are shown in Table A.16 and A.17.

HI organizations include some very large employers. Just over one-fifth of multi-site workplaces are part of a very large organization employing 100,000+ workers; these are almost always restaurants or bars. Over one-third of very small workplaces in the HI belong to these very large employers. Eighty-five per cent of HI multi-site workplaces are part of an organization employing 1,000+ workers. Hotels are most likely to be part of an organization employing fewer than 1,000 workers.

Very small workplaces are most likely to be bars that are brewery owned. Indeed within the very largest HI organizations (500+ sites), half of the workplaces are very small workplaces. Similarly, at the other end of the spectrum (2–10 sites) nearly 60 per cent of HI workplaces are very small. In other words, where very small HI workplaces are part of a larger organization, they are most likely to be part of an organization with very few or very many sites.

In the one-third of HI workplaces that are not PLCs, individual or family interest over the company is high, especially in small workplaces and restaurants. A majority of controlling owners are actively involved in the day-to-day management of these workplaces on a full-time basis, particularly in bars and large workplaces, although the likelihood of such involvement is below that in AIS and the PSS. The HI has relatively few franchises. The level of franchises is not as high as might have been expected in restaurants.

Table A.14 Workplaces with employees in the specified occupational group in context and by size of workplace (%)

	AIS	PSS	HI	<25	25–49	50–99	100+
Managers and senior administrators	90	91	95	94	93	100	100
Professional	44	36	16*	13	16	21	41
Technical	31	25	7*	2	6	21	33
Clerical and secretarial	77	70	38*	28	27	80	92
Sales	36	45	49	48	43	54	57
Non-management/ non-manual	92	91	67*	60	70	85	100
Craft and skilled services	39	36	42	29	60	59	83
Personal and protective services	26	20	36***	31	28	61	63
Operative and assembly	20	16	12***	11	7	13	34
Routine unskilled	54	51	65*	60	75	69	86
Any manual workers	78	73	95	95	95	93	100
Aggregate (%)	44	40	65*	50	61	73	78
71%+	30	28	49*	41	59	61	79
50%+	44	38	62*	53	63	90	95

Source: WERS98.

Notes: All weighted cases. *Significantly different at the 5% level from AIS and the PSS. ***Significantly different at the 5% level from the PSS.

Table A.15 Workplaces with employees in the specified occupational group by sub-sector (%)

	Hotels	Campsites	Restaurants	Bars	Canteens
Managers and senior administrators	100	100	94	91	100
Professional	22	4	14	12	19
Technical	19	81	0	2	10
Clerical and secretarial	68	100	31	14	81
Sales	42	23	18	70	63
Non-management/ non-manual	73	100	41	76	90
Craft and skilled services	66	100	27	39	24
Personal and protective services	60	23	34	19	57
Operative and assembly	9	4	20	9	3
Routine unskilled	82	100	45	67	71
Any manual workers	95	100	96	97	80
Aggregate (%)	73	67	72	39	73
71%+	65	19	74	28	33
50%+	91	100	78	30	80

Source: WERS98.

Note: All weighted cases.

Table A.16 Workplace status in context and by size of workplace (%)

	AIS	PSS	HI	<25	25–49	50–99	100+
Multi-site	68	61	77***	79	67	89	64
Mean number of employees	69	54	33*	16	34	66	162
Single site h	30	38	23***	21	33	11	34
Mean number of employees	45	35	36	18	34	75	150
Franchise j	4	5	9	11	4	10	4
Head Office g	11	15	4***	2	0	17	8
Proprietorial/family controlled i	51	49	72*	66	95	61	66
Age of workplace							
<5 years	16	19	21	27	11	15	13
5–20 years	44	49	26*	12	42	47	53
20+years	40	31	53***	60	47	39	34

Source: WERS98.

Notes: All weighted cases unless otherwise specified. *Significantly different at the 5% level from AIS and the PSS. ***Significantly different at the 5% level from the PSS. h Excludes cases of sole UK workplaces of a foreign organization. j Excludes public sector in AIS. g Where part of a larger organization. i Excludes PLCs. Means are rounded.

Table A.17 Workplace status by sub-sector (%)

	Hotels	Campsites	Restaurants	Bars	Canteens
Multi-site	69	100	75	81	86
Mean number of employees	54	58	31	21	40
Single site h	30	0	25	19	14
Mean number of employees	60	0	33	16	41
Franchise	1	0	6	9	49
Head Office g	15	0	4	0	2
Proprietorial/family controlled i	77	0	87	56	73
Age of workplace					
<5 years	11	0	35	22	9
5–20 years	35	0	27	18	30
20+years	53	100	38	60	62

Source: WERS98.

Notes: All weighted cases unless otherwise specified. h Excludes cases of sole UK workplaces of a foreign organization. g Where part of a larger organization. i Excludes PLCs. Means are rounded.

New HI workplaces (less than five years old) are most likely to be restaurants or very small workplaces. Older workplaces (more than 20 years old) are most likely to be pubs employing fewer than 25 employees. Over one-fifth of HI workplaces have seen changes in ownership over the past five years. Such change is most likely to have affected very small and large workplaces, with small workplaces largely unaffected.

Workplace employment change

In terms of the general economic conditions within which workplaces function, in the five-year period before WERS more HI workplaces suffered job losses than in AIS or the PSS and fewer HI workplaces experienced employment growth. Just over half of HI workplaces remained stable or expanded employment, suggesting that labour cost control was an important consideration for a sizeable minority, notably in very small workplaces and bars. However in the 12 months before WERS job losses were slightly higher in AIS and the PSS, and HI workplaces were significantly more likely to have experienced stable employment than AIS. The increased proportion of HI workplaces reporting no change, together with work-places reporting employment growth (three-quarters) suggest that economic conditions had become more favourable to the HI, with hotels being most likely to sustain job growth. However, job loss, and hence labour cost control, continued to affect more very small workplaces. Employment flows in the 12-month period before WERS, which detail a significantly greater degree of movement among permanent staff in and out of HI workplaces than in AIS and the PSS, are discussed in detail below.

Workplace performance

The nature of HI workplaces is significantly different from AIS and the PSS, with most describing themselves as producers of goods and services for consumers. AIS and PSS workplaces (one-quarter) are significantly more likely to be suppliers of goods and services to other companies.

The vast majority of HI workplaces regard themselves as having many competitors, especially bars, indicating that the HI operates in significantly more competitive domestic conditions than workplaces in AIS and the PSS. This is also related to workplace size, with almost all very small workplaces regarding themselves as being in this position. The proportions in this category fall as workplace size increases, such that just over half of large workplaces regard themselves as having many competitors.

A majority of HI workplaces believe their market is growing, but significantly fewer operate in mature markets compared to AIS and the PSS. Just over one-third of firms in all cases operate in a declining or turbulent market, with bars most likely to report their market as declining or turbulent.

Significantly more HI workplaces work on a low wage cost:sales ratio, with over half having a ratio of less than 25 per cent, and this particularly affects very small and small workplaces. In general the proportion of wage costs increases with workplace size, although significantly fewer HI workplaces have a ratio of 50 per cent or more. Bars are most likely to have the lowest ratios, while hotels are most likely to have wage cost:sales ratios of 25 per cent or more.

As noted in Chapter 3 (Tables 3.5 and 3.6), HI workplaces are significantly less likely to have attained BS5750 or ISO9000 than in AIS and the PSS. This is not to say that quality is unimportant. Monitoring quality is significantly more likely to be a management task in the HI. Customer surveys are of secondary importance for quality purposes and, as in AIS and the PSS, are used in around half the workplaces. Other methods, including inspection by a specialist section and individual employee monitoring of quality, are used less frequently in the HI. Medium and large workplaces and hotels deploy the widest combination of quality monitoring measures to the greatest extent, whereas very small workplaces and bars rely heavily on managerial monitoring.

HI workplaces are significantly more cost-control conscious in terms of keeping records of sales/fees/budget, costs, profits and labour costs than in AIS and the PSS. These records are kept in almost all workplaces, by size and sub-sector. However, HI workplaces are significantly less likely to keep absenteeism records. The majority of bars do not record labour turnover and absence. Other types of records (quality, labour turnover and training) are kept by a majority of workplaces. Productivity is least likely to be recorded on all comparisons, in around half of all workplaces.

Slightly more HI workplaces (over half) than in AIS and the PSS have used benchmarking over the past five years, but it is used least in hotels and restaurants.

Table A.18 does not indicate any significant differences between the HI and AIS and the PSS in terms of how they assess business performance. Very small workplaces are more circumspect about their financial performance, with a core reporting average performance (Tables A.19 and A.20). Small and medium workplaces report above-average productivity levels. There is a clear pride in the quality of product or service.

Table A.18 Assessment of business performance in context (%)

	AIS			PSS			HI		
	Above average	Average	Below average	Above average	Average	Below average	Above average	Average	Below average
Financial performance	49	32	7	51	32	6	57	24	14
Labour productivity	43	36	3	44	38	4	39	47	9
Quality of product or service	70	20	2	76	16	1	74	24	0

Source: WERS98.

Notes: All weighted cases. Row percentages do not sum to 100 because responses where no comparison is possible or relevant data are not available have been excluded. Above average combines a lot better and better responses. Below average combines below and a lot below responses.

Table A.19 Assessment of business performance by size of workplace (%)

	<25			25–49			50–99			100+		
	Above average	Average	Below average	Above average	Average	Below average	Above average	Average	Below average	Above average	Average	Below average
Financial performance	51	28	14	70	7	23	62	29	8	65	32	0
Labour productivity	32	50	0	52	47	2	54	31	12	30	63	0
Quality of product or service	76	23	0	70	30	0	72	25	3	82	12	1

Source: WERS98.

Notes: All weighted cases. Row percentages do not sum to 100 because responses where no comparison is possible or relevant data are not available have been excluded. Above average combines a lot better and better responses. Below average combines below and a lot below responses.

Table A.20 Assessment of business performance by sub-sector (%)

	Hotels			Campsites			Restaurants			Bars			Canteens		
	Above average	Average	Below average	Above average	Average	Below average	Above average	Average	Below average	Above average	Average	Below average	Above average	Average	Below average
Financial performance	54	32	11	18	10	72	62	24	15	52	23	17	85	15	0
Labour productivity	38	51	7	90	10	0	55	31	1	32	50	0	19	82	0
Quality of product or service	81	13	2	90	4	6	80	19	0	62	38	0	96	4	0

Source: WERS98.

Notes: All weighted cases. Row percentages do not sum to 100 because responses where no comparison is possible or relevant data are not available have been excluded. Above average combines a lot better and better responses. Below average combines below and a lot below responses.

Three-quarters of AIS and PSS workplaces reported an increase in labour productivity in the previous five years compared to under two-thirds in the HI. Very small workplaces and bars were least likely to report increased productivity over this period. A good majority of workplaces across all groups reported an increase in labour costs relative to all other costs in the last five years, and this had affected proportionately more HI workplaces, especially small workplaces.

Workplace change

Almost all workplaces in all groups reported some workplace change in the last five years, with a majority stating there had been a lot of change. Details of specific changes presented in Table A.21 show a remarkable degree of consistency with one small exception. This indicates that HI workplaces have been more innovative in introducing performance-related pay to non-managerial employees. Tables A.22 and A.23 report how specific aspects of change have affected workplaces by size and sector. As a rule very small workplaces and bars have been less innovative, although there were differences in the types of changes made.

The most important cause of HI workplace change has been employee-related matters (e.g. changes to payments systems or working time) (43 per cent), and this was significantly greater than in AIS and the PSS. Three-quarters of bars reported this as the most important reason. Market and competitive change was the most important factor in AIS and the PSS (around 40 per cent). The next three most important factors in the HI were other market conditions (34 per cent), managerial changes (32 per cent) and customer pressure (19 per cent). The HI was especially immune to change caused by legislation/government policy, with no very small workplaces mentioning this as a cause of change. Quality issues and increases in communications and consultation were also of minor importance to the vast majority of HI workplaces.

The HI has been as active as AIS and the PSS in introducing workplaces changes in the last five years, although there are slight differences in the types of changes made. In the HI there is less use of technology and work techniques, and greater use of changes to pay, working time, the organization of work and, particularly, the introduction of a new product or service. Where more than one change has been introduced by management (six in ten HI workplaces) new technology is the change that has had most impact on employees. The introduction of initiatives to involve employees (one-quarter of these HI workplaces) has had a significantly more important impact on employees than in AIS and the PSS. The most important change that HI management was not able to introduce was to payment systems, and this was significant, although it affected a very small number of cases, all of which were very small restaurants.

Employee questionnaire

Closed questions

Thirty-six questions focused on information about employees' jobs, working at the workplace, representation at work and details about their personal and job

Table A.21 Workplace change in the last five years in context (%)

	AIS			PSS			HI		
	Up	Same	Down	Up	Same	Down	Up	Same	Down
Supervisors' employee relations responsibilities	56	43	1	53	46	1	62	38	0
Importance of employee relations matters in setting organizational goals/objectives	77	32	1	66	33	1	65	35	1
How hard people work	77	21	2	73	24	3	78	19	3
Flexibility to move employees from one task to another	58	40	3	55	42	3	63	31	5
Employees' influence over their job	59	37	4	58	40	2	56	43	1
Amount of information provided about the workplace	75	24	0	74	24	1	79	20	2
Proportion of non-managerial pay related to performance	32	67	2	41	56	2	52**	47	1
Employee influence over managerial decision-making	52	47	2	51	47	1	50	48	2
Proportion of women in managerial posts	34	62	5	35	59	5	42	50	8

Source: WERS98.

Notes: All weighted cases where establishment has been operating for at least five years (AIS, N = 1,945, PSS, N = 1,171, HI, N = 116). Row percentages do not sum to 100 due to rounding. ** Significantly different at the 5% level from AIS. Up and down combine a lot and a little responses.

Table A.22 Workplace change in the last five years by size of workplace (%)

	<25			25–49			50–99			100+		
	Up	Same	Down	Up	Same	Down	Up	Same	Down	Up	Same	Down
Supervisors' employee relations responsibilities	55	45	0	69	30	0	75	25	0	63	37	0
Importance of employee relations matters in setting organizational goals/objectives	62	38	0	71	29	0	62	35	3	63	37	0
How hard people work	80	20	0	78	17	4	75	18	6	65	23	12
Flexibility to move employees from one task to another	57	34	9	69	31	0	69	28	3	80	18	2
Employees' influence over their job	53	45	2	61	39	0	56	42	2	58	43	0
Amount of information provided about the workplace	78	20	2	75	25	0	82	15	3	87	14	0
Proportion of non-managerial pay related to performance	60	40	0	43	57	0	44	53	3	36	59	4
Employee influence over decision-making	60	38	2	30	69	0	46	49	5	51	49	0
Proportion of women in managerial posts	29	63	9	56	40	4	66	23	10	49	46	4

Source: WERS98.

Notes: All weighted cases where establishment has been operating for at least five years. Row percentages do not sum to 100 due to rounding. Up and down combine a lot and a little responses.

Table A.23 Workplace change in the last five years by sub-sector (%)

	Hotels			Campsites			Restaurants			Bars			Canteens		
	Up	Same	Down	Up	Same	Down	Up	Same	Down	Up	Same	Down	Up	Same	Down
Supervisors' employee relations responsibilities	66	34	0	18	82	0	79	20	0	48	52	0	81	19	0
Importance of employee relations matters in setting organizational goals/objectives	58	39	2	100	0	0	54	46	0	69	31	0	76	24	0
How hard people work	80	11	9	94	6	0	73	24	3	76	25	0	97	3	0
Flexibility to move employees from one task to another	82	18	0	28	72	0	61	37	2	48	41	11	99	0	1
Employees' influence over their job	55	40	5	90	10	0	63	36	1	43	57	0	91	9	0
Amount of information provided about the workplace	77	16	7	100	0	0	89	11	0	73	27	0	79	21	0
Proportion of non-managerial pay related to performance	44	53	2	76	24	0	38	62	0	59	41	0	69	31	0
Employee influence over decision-making	46	47	7	6	94	0	68	31	1	40	60	0	70	30	0
Proportion of women in managerial posts	57	37	6	100	0	0	54	41	4	31	58	12	25	75	0

Source: WERS98.

Notes: All weighted cases where establishment has been operating for at least five years. Row percentages do not sum to 100 due to rounding. Up and down combine a lot and a little responses.

Table A.24 Hospitality employees by workplace size and sub-sector (% in brackets)

	10–24 employees	*25–49 employees*	*50–99 employees*	*100+ employees*	*All sub-sectors*
Hotels	2 (b)	65 (14)	172 (37)	221 (48)	460
Campsites and short- stay accommodation	8 (22)	0	0	28 (78)	36
Restaurants	64 (30)	28 (13)	90 (42)	31 (15)	213
Bars	208 (76)	50 (18)	15 (6)	0	273
Canteens and catering	60 (49)	8 (7)	11 (9)	44 (36)	123
Total employees	341	152	288	330	1,100

Source: WERS98 employee survey.

Notes: All weighted cases. Row and column numbers and percentages do not sum accurately due to rounding. b Fewer than 0.5%.

Table A.25 Main organizational characteristics of the employees providing verbatim responses

Characteristic	*%*
Workplace size	
10–24 employees	12
25–49 employees	16
50–99 employees	29
100+ employees	43
Range 10–406	
Sub-sector	
Hotels	54
Campsites	7
Restaurants	20
Bars	8
Canteens	11
Multi-site	73
Single site	27
Females	
71%+	17
50%+	65
Part-time	
71%+	13
50%+	33

Source: WERS98 employee survey.

Notes: Percentages have been rounded. Column sub-totals do not sum to 100 due to rounding.

characteristics. Table A.24 shows that the employee responses come mainly from bar employees in very small workplaces and hotel employees in medium and large workplaces, which is consistent with the workplace profile shown in Table A.4.

Open question (D12)

As noted above in the Methodology, the employee verbatim responses do not follow a normal distribution. Tables A.25 and A.26 show key organizational and personal identifying characteristics.

Table A.26 Main personal characteristics of the employees providing verbatim responses

Characteristic	%
Male	46
Female	54
Age	
Under 30	53
30+	47
Main occupational groups	
Personal and protective services	33
Other occupations	28
Clerical and secretarial	16
Hours of work (including overtime)	
Under 16	12
16–29	19
30–48	55
49+	13
Range 4–89	
Contract	
Temporary	12
Fixed-term	5
Permanent	82

Source: WERS98 employee survey.

Notes: Percentages have been rounded. Column sub-totals do not sum to 100 due to rounding.

Appendix 2
Employment relations practices and outcomes

These tables are designed to enable:

- tutors to set questions that require students to analyse and evaluate statistical data for an assignment or extended essay;
- students to develop their analytical and research skills, by learning how to interpret and synthesize statistical data.

Table A.27 Key characteristics of workplaces in context and by size of workplace (% of workplaces)

Characteristic	AIS	PSS	HI	<25	25–49	50–99	100+
Multi-site	68	61	77***	79	67	89	64
Single site h	30	38	23***	21	33	11	34
Franchise j	4	5	9	11	4	10	4
Head Office g	11	15	4***	2	0	17	8
Proprietorial/family controlled i	51	49	72*	66	95	61	66
Females (all) a	58	66	57	62	69	53	55
Part-time a	26	33	51*	61	61	51	34
Female part-time a	21	25	34*	43	39	30	24
Male full-time a	45	40	25*	20	20	27	35
Manual workers a	44	40	65*	50	61	73	78
Temporary agency workers	20	16	8*	8	4	13	21
Full-time contracts 1 year+	16	13	9	11	4	6	7
Trade union density a	34	15	2*	2	0	0	5
	No.	No.	No.	No.	No.	No.	No.
Mean employees <21 years	8	12	24*	20	32	31	22
Mean employees 51+ years	15	14	8	9	7	6	10
Mean disabled employees	1	1	1	1	1	1	1
Mean ethnic minority employees	4	4	3	2	3	7	6
Mean employees per workplace	62	47	34**	16	34	67	160

Source: WERS98

Notes: All weighted cases unless otherwise stated. h Excludes cases of sole UK workplaces of a foreign organization. g Where part of larger organization. i Excludes PLCs. j Excludes public sector in AIS. a Aggregate percentage. *Significant at the 5% level with AIS and the PSS. **Significant at the 5% level with AIS. ***Significant at the 5% level with the PSS.

Table A.28 Key characteristics of workplaces by sub-sector (% of workplaces)

Characteristic	Hotels	Campsites	Restaurants	Bars	Canteens
Multi-site	69	100	75	81	86
Single site h	30	0	25	19	14
Franchise	1	0	6	9	49
Head Office g	15	0	4	0	2
Proprietorial/family controlled i	77	0	87	56	73
Females (all) a	56	53	57	58	64
Part-time a	37	22	59	78	38
Female part-time a	26	18	40	47	30
Male full-time a	33	43	24	11	28
Manual workers a	73	67	72	39	73
Temporary agency workers	14	0	3	0	52
Full-time contracts 1 year+	4	6	16	9	0
Trade union density a	0	9	1	1	15
	No.	No.	No.	No.	No.
Mean employees <21 years	22	2	29	25	15
Mean employees 51+ years	10	19	8	5	17
Mean disabled employees	1	5	b	2	b
Mean ethnic minority employees	4	b	6	2	1
Mean employees per workplace	0	9	1	1	15

Source: WERS98.

Notes: All weighted cases unless otherwise stated. h Excludes cases of sole UK workplaces of a foreign organization. g Where part of larger organization. i Excludes PLCs. j Excludes public sector in AIS. a Aggregate percentage. b Fewer than 0.5%.

Table A.29 Management organization and structure for employment relations in context and by size of workplace (% of workplaces)

	AIS	PSS	HI	<25	25–49	50–99	100+
Organization g							
HR Director l	60	63	71	78	64	53	86
Higher-level manager spending most time on ER k	76	76	71	69	75	66	85
Workplace							
Formal strategic plan	74	69	75	75	67	78	93
HR specialist	20	17	10**	2	24	8	59
Manager with primary responsibility for ER	88	87	89	89	95	80	80
Mean time spent on ER	32	31	35	31	42	38	47
'Specialist' job responsibility for ER ff	61	61	61	58	61	72	74
Total years' experience in HR ff	14	14	16	16	18	12	11
Formal HR qualification ff	35	30	39	40	51	21	39
Few non-management staff supervising others d	63	69	74	78	71	67	53
Most supervisors trained in HR skills f	25	23	38***	34	48	39	44
No external help with ER	52	51	75*	90	54	57	25
Investors in People	34	31	50*	62	30	31	50
BS5750/ISO9000	24	21	11*	16	0	9	15

Source: WERS98.

Notes: All weighted cases unless otherwise stated. d Below 20%. g Where part of larger organization. ff Excludes cases where managers are more concerned with other responsibilities. f 60% and above where non-managerial employees supervise other workers. l Excludes Head Offices. k Private sector including Head Offices. *Significant at the 5% level with AIS and the PSS. **Significant at the 5% level with AIS. ***Significant at the 5% level with the PSS.

Table A.30 Management organization and structure for employment relations by sub-sector (% of workplaces)

	Hotels	Campsites	Restaurants	Bars	Canteens
Organization g					
HR Director l	57	100	61	82	100
Higher-level manager spending most time on ER k	37	93	55	94	82
Workplace					
Formal strategic plan	69	100	83	70	86
HR specialist	14	10	4	9	26
Manager with primary responsibility for ER	89	72	88	100	35
Mean time spent on ER	31	36	29	40	36
'Specialist' job responsibility for ER ff	63	94	69	48	90
Total years' experience in HR ff	17	15	15	15	14
Formal HR qualification ff	41	100	30	24	88
Few non-management staff supervising others d	72	90	82	79	28
Most supervisors trained in HR skills f	38	100	45	29	63
No external help with ER	63	90	84	77	67
Investors in People	32	10	68	48	66
BS5750/ISO9000	5	0	2	11	60

Source: WERS98.

Notes: All weighted cases unless otherwise stated. d Below 20%. g Where part of larger organization. ff Excludes cases where managers are more concerned with other responsibilities. f 60% and above where non-managerial employees supervise other workers. l Excludes Head Offices. k Private sector including Head Offices.

Table A.31 Employment practices and outcomes in context and by size of workplace (% of workplaces unless otherwise specified)

Practice	AIS	PSS	HI	<25	25–49	50–99	100+
Internal/external applicants given equal treatment	75	73	86*	91	87	71	67
Personality/attitude tests	19	21	15	6	39	18	27
Performance/competency tests	48	43	25*	19	35	29	42
Standard induction ee	73	73	77	69	84	100	97
Induction 1 day or less	33	36	44	42	35	55	56
Few or none receive off-job training d ee	45	48	57	64	48	49	30
Functionally flexible training ee	54	55	51	61	30	35	23
Equal opportunities and diversity policy	67	62	70	75	67	48	78
Equality policy effects measured v	16	9	9	8	6	23	7
Full-time to part-time working gg	46	43	54	47	62	76	55
Increased use of part-time staff o	33	35	34	28	40	48	31
Standard employment contracts ee	83	80	77	68	93	86	89
Outcomes							
New recruits x	27	34	63*	62	72	64	33
Few or no vacancies filled internally d	68	70	73	83	60	44	44
Achieve experienced worker standard after 1 month ee	27	33	53*	57	41	53	49
Labour turnover x	19	23	42**	43	37	49	31
Leavers x	32	33	78*	70	115	68	45

Mean aa	No.	No.	No.	No.	No.	No.	No.
Resignations	175	220	515	527	542	491	341
Dismissals	23	26	66*	61	112	34	24
Redundancies	26	35	13*	4	47	5	2
Retirements	26	26	10*	7	25	3	7
Absence	5	4	5	6	3	6	5
Work-related illness	73	66	57	97	28	26	13
Injuries	98	127	198	284	117	96	47
Disciplinary sanctions	7	8	13	18	9	6	4
Industrial tribunal complaints	24	27	42	143	31	16	11

Source: WERS98.

Notes: gg Most common family-friendly practice. x Mean percentage of total employees employed one year ago. ee LOG. d Below 20%. o Last five years. v Where policy exists. aa Mean number per 1,000 employees. *Significant at the 5% level with AIS and the PSS. ** Significant at the 5% level with AIS.

Table A.32 Employment practices and outcomes by sub-sector (% of workplaces unless otherwise specified)

	Hotels	Campsites	Restaurants	Bars	Canteens
Practice					
Internal/external applicants given equal treatment	73	100	94	89	83
Personality/attitude tests	16	82	10	15	19
Performance/competency tests	38	72	27	6	68
Standard induction ee	72	94	79	80	72
Induction 1 day or less	39	19	48	42	81
Few or none receive off-job training d ee	53	4	79	61	17
Functionally flexible training ee	18	0	35	25	55
Equal opportunities and diversity policy	45	100	69	78	86
Equality policy effects measured v	10	0	3	2	56
Full-time to part-time working gg	43	18	62	53	71
Increased use of part-time staff o	40	0	38	25	51
Standard employment contracts ee	93	100	65	72	85
Outcomes					
New recruits x	59	5	66	71	24
Few or no vacancies filled internally d	63	22	67	83	73
Achieve experienced worker standard after 1 month ee	64	82	42	56	35
Labour turnover x	39	20	61	33	23
Leavers x	72	19	93	85	24
Mean aa	*No.*	*No.*	*No.*	*No.*	*No.*
Resignations	28	4	16	13	10
Dismissals	3	b	1	2	2
Redundancies	b	1	b	1	0
Retirements	1	1	b	17	11
Absence	4	1	10	4	4
Work-related illness	22	71	96	78	27
Injuries	64	42	409	112	335
Disciplinary sanctions	6	5	18	15	13
Industrial tribunal complaints	13	7	73	0	34

Source: WERS98.

Notes: gg Most common family-friendly practice. x Mean percentage of total employees employed one year ago. ee LOG. d Below 20%. o Last five years. v Where policy exists. aa Mean number per 1,000 employees. b Fewer than 0.5.

Table A.33 Pay practices and outcomes in context and by size of workplace (% of workplaces unless otherwise specified)

	AIS	PSS	HI	<25	25–49	50–99	100+
Practice							
Parties involved in decision-making y ee							
Board-level	44	51	44	41	53	39	49
Higher-level	33	32	46	46	46	50	33
Workplace-level	40	48	37	25	43	65	47
Annual pay review ee	89	88	66*	58	83	71	92
Regular paid/unpaid overtime ee	42	44	73*	83	57	44	9
Any variable pay y	53	63	62	62	61	60	78
Profit-related pay	32	40	40	39	41	38	60
Employee share ownership	15	20	28**	27	39	21	24
Most non-managerial employees subject to performance appraisal e	80	86	75	72	70	86	86
Sales revenue: wages/labour costs <25%	29	34	52*	60	49	28	14
Outcomes							
Half or more of workforce earning below £3.50 per hour	8	12	33*	34	49	15	8
No non-pay terms and conditions ee	11	14	30*	29	43	18	26
Labour costs increased relative to other costs o	69	74	76	75	88	73	57
Mean hourly earnings	£6.21	£5.47	£3.62**	£3.14	£3.52	£3.57	£4.12

Source: WERS98.

Notes: y Multi-response question. ee LOG. o Last five years. e 60% and above. *Significant at the 5% level with AIS and the PSS. **Significant at the 5% level with AIS. *Significant at the 5% level with AIS.

Table A.34 Pay practices and outcomes by sub-sector (% of workplaces unless otherwise specified)

	Hotels	Campsites	Restaurants	Bars	Canteens
Practice					
Parties involved in decision-making y ee					
Board-level	44	0	73	40	5
Higher-level	29	100	46	43	88
Workplace-level	66	0	23	35	24
Annual pay review ee	85	24	37	68	100
Regular paid/unpaid overtime ee	55	22	80	76	80
Any variable pay y					
Profit-related pay	59	100	58	64	69
Employee share ownership	15	24	27	40	19
Most non-managerial employees subject to performance appraisal e	76	94	79	63	96
Sales revenue: wages/labour costs <25%	4	8	50	80	62
Outcomes					
Half or more of workforce earning below £3.50 per hour	18	0	31	48	12
No non-pay terms and conditions ee	12	22	27	48	7
Labour costs increased relative to other costs o	72	82	65	82	95
Mean hourly earnings	£3.97	£3.13	£3.26	£3.04	£4.07

Source: WERS98.

Notes: y Multi-response question. ee LOG. o Last five years. e 60% and above.

Table A.35 Collective and individualized employment relations practices and outcomes in context and by size of workplace (% of workplaces unless otherwise specified)

	AIS	PSS	HI	<25	25–49	50–99	100+
Practice							
Aggregate trade union density	34	15	2*	2	0	0	5
Neutral management attitude to unions	54	63	72**	76	65	67	69
Higher trade union density o u	9	18	0*	0	0	0	0
Any union recruitment o r	5	5	12	13	20	2	5
Request for recognition o	7	7	0*	0	0	0	0
Non-union representatives q	1 in 11	1 in 12	1 in 16	1 in 14	0	1 in 22	1 in 4
Health and safety committee	27	21	10*	0	13	33	61
Any safety representatives where no committee	37	29	14*	4	45	15	33
Collective disputes procedure z	50	39	36**	38	28	33	50
Grievance procedure z	88	86	82	79	78	92	100
Right to be accompanied in grievance hearing	98	97	95	93	95	100	100
Disciplinary/dismissal procedure z	88	86	81	75	89	90	100
Right to be accompanied in disciplinary hearing	95	93	93	89	100	100	94
Right of appeal against discipline	91	91	87	79	96	100	100
Outcomes							
Collective disputes over pay/ conditions	5	3	0*	0	0	0	0
Strike o	3	1	0*	0	0	0	0
Picketing	1	1	0*	0	0	0	0
Disruption from industrial action elsewhere	3	4	1	0	0	5	0
Use of grievance procedure	23	21	12**	9	5	24	28
Use of any disciplinary sanctions	45	47	57	52	44	85	94
Use of warnings	43	45	55	52	39	76	92
Use of suspension with/ without pay	17	16	17	7	17	47	59
Use of deduction from pay	5	4	2	0	0	9	14
Any industrial tribunal claim	7	7	4	1	4	10	20
Any industrial tribunal claim o	14	12	8	0	14	23	41
Mean aa	*No.*	*No.*	*No.*	*No.*	*No.*	*No.*	*No.*
Disciplinary sanctions	7	8	13	18	9	6	4
Dismissals	23	26	66*	61	112	34	24
Industrial tribunal complaints	24	27	42	143	31	16	11

Source: WERS98.

Notes: All instances relate to last 12 months except o which indicate last five years. z Non-managerial employees. q Where non-union reps or reps of non-recognized unions present. r Where no union members. u Where number or percentage of trade union members known and establishment five years or older. aa Mean number per 1,000 employees. *Significant at the 5% level with AIS and the PSS. **Significant at the 5% level with AIS.

Table A.36 Collective and individualized employment relations practices and outcomes by sub-sector (% of workplaces unless otherwise specified)

	Hotels	Camp-sites	Restaur-ants	Bars	Canteens
Practice					
Aggregate trade union density	0	9	1	1	15
Neutral management attitude to unions	76	100	78	64	83
Higher trade union density o u	0	0	0	0	0
Any union recruitment o r	2	0	14	19	0
Request for recognition o	0	0	0	0	0
Non-union representatives q	1 in 20	1 in 2	1 in 41	1 in 16	0
Health and safety committee	23	24	13	0	13
Any safety representatives where no committee	23	0	12	11	4
Collective disputes procedure z	23	100	33	36	75
Grievance procedure z	73	100	93	78	86
Right to be accompanied in grievance hearing	100	100	82	100	100
Disciplinary/dismissal procedure z	83	100	78	80	88
Right to be accompanied in disciplinary hearing	99	100	87	91	99
Right of appeal against discipline	79	100	84	90	100
Outcomes					
Collective disputes over pay/ conditions	0	0	1	0	0
Strike o	0	0	0	0	0
Picketing	0	0	0	0	0
Disruption from industrial action elsewhere	0	0	2	0	2
Use of grievance procedure	20	6	5	11	16
Use of any disciplinary sanctions	67	100	53	53	53
Use of warnings	63	100	53	50	53
Use of suspension with/without pay	25	94	18	12	6
Use of deduction from pay	7	0	0	0	0
Any industrial tribunal claim	8	10	7	0	1
Any industrial tribunal claim o	24	0	8	1	0
Mean aa	*No.*	*No.*	*No.*	*No.*	*No.*
Disciplinary sanctions	6	5	18	15	13
Dismissals	59	1	33	94	51
Industrial tribunal complaints	13	7	73	0	34

Source: WERS98.

Notes: All instances relate to last 12 months except o which indicate last five years. z Non-managerial employees. q Where non-union reps or reps of non-recognized unions present. r Where no union members. u Where number or percentage of trade union members known and establishment five years or older. aa Mean number per 1,000 employees.

Table A.37 Participation and involvement practices and outcomes in context and by size of workplace (% of workplaces)

	AIS	PSS	HI	<25	25–49	50–99	100+
Practice							
Little or no formal team-working d ee	29	31	50*	60	45	33	18
System of briefings	83	82	84	79	91	96	91
Briefing monthly or less often	47	50	60	76	51	41	15
Less than 25% time allowed for employees' questions or views	43	44	50	43	61	58	64
Consultative committee	23	18	11**	0	25	21	53
Performance/quality groups	33	28	16*	9	17	35	48
Formal opinion surveys p	39	36	43	36	46	56	58
Regular information on internal investment	50	46	55	52	56	64	70
Regular information on financial position of establishment	63	58	69	69	68	67	73
Regular information on financial position of organization m	66	67	78	92	67	44	57
Regular information on staffing plans	63	59	53	50	59	55	55
Benchmarking against other workplaces	46	46	56	55	59	51	53
Outcomes							
Above-average financial performance	49	51	57	51	70	62	65
Above-average labour productivity	43	44	39	32	52	54	30
Above-average product/ service quality	70	76	74	76	70	72	82
Very good/good management/employee relations	90	90	98*	100	94	99	93

Source: WERS98.

Notes: ee LOG. m Where part of larger organization or sole UK establishment. d Below 20%. p In last five years for establishments five years or older. *Significant at the 5% level with AIS and the PSS. **Significant at the 5% level with AIS.

Table A.38 Participation and involvement practices by sub-sector (% of workplaces)

	Hotels	Campsites	Restaurants	Bars	Canteens
Practice					
Little or no formal team-working d ee	37	0	62	57	14
System of briefings	97	94	91	73	81
Briefing monthly or less often	98	100	76	85	100
Less than 25% time allowed for employees' questions or views	66	96	23	60	39
Consultative committee	22	28	5	9	3
Performance/quality groups	25	0	17	4	49
Formal opinion surveys p	36	78	50	39	62
Regular information on internal investment	71	100	34	55	77
Regular information on financial position of establishment	76	96	49	74	88
Regular information on financial position of organization m	64	72	76	89	71
Regular information on staffing plans	65	78	68	34	62
Benchmarking against other workplaces	45	78	48	64	67
Outcomes					
Above-average financial performance	54	18	62	52	85
Above-average labour productivity	38	90	55	32	19
Above-average product/service quality	81	90	80	62	96
Very good/good management/employee relations	100	100	94	100	98

Source: WERS98.

Notes: ee LOG. m Where part of larger organization or sole UK establishment. d Below 20%. p In last five years for establishments five years or older.

Notes

1 Whither employment relations and hospitality?

1 Rose (2001: 20–7) gives a more detailed overview, while Kessler and Bayliss (1998: 1–109) provide a comprehensive account of developments from the mid-1940s to the mid-1990s. Edwards (2003b) provides the most contemporary account.

2 One of the earlier attempts to regulate employment internationally through the ILO was Convention No. 26, The Minimum Wage Fixing Convention, which Britain ratified in 1929 (Lucas, 1986: 15–16).

3 The application of the Transfer of Undertakings (Protection of Employment) Regulations 1981 has been beset with difficulty and uncertainty. New Regulations are due in 2004.

4 Even so industrial relations is retained in Edwards (2003b).

5 The approach used in this book is to focus on three key actors in the employment relationship – the employer, worker and customer. More conventional approaches have taken a different focus, using the state, employers and trade unions as the three key actors (Edwards, 1995, 2003a; Dickens, 1997). Korczynski (2002) provides the first HRM analysis to take the customer seriously.

6 The first triplet supports United and, such is her fanaticism, that she doesn't give a damn about fair play as long as United beat City. The second triplet is equally fanatical about his team. Their sister is more objective, not on account of any inherent difference in their personalities, but because she is a neutral observer who supports Villa.

7 Nicholls (1999: 11–54) provides a comprehensive and detailed account of the theoretical approaches to employee relations adding systems theory, feminist theory, comparative theory and postmodernism to the approaches discussed here. See also Salamon (2000: 1–39) and Rose (2001: 27–47).

8 Taylor (2001a) argues that the lack of attention being focused on the nature of power relationships in the workplace in contemporary Britain is a strategic mistake.

9 Collective action among different employers is rare.

10 Acknowledged by Dunlop (1958: 49), but only in passing.

11 The amount of revenue generated in the international market by McDonald's is 49 per cent and 53 per cent by KFC (Lee and Chon, 2000). Leat and Woolley (1999) provide a detailed account of MNCs and their implications for employee relations. Royle (2000) discusses the case of McDonald's in Europe.

12 Although dated, Ferner and Hyman (1998) address changing industrial relations in Europe, while Leat (1999) provides useful accounts of the EU and its implications for employment relations. More recent data can be found in journals such as the European Journal of Industrial Relations.

13 Two recent edited collections offer accounts of international issues within hospitality and tourism that are complementary to those discussed here. D'Annunzio-Green *et al.* (2002) explore international perspectives on HRM, including employee relations. Royle

and Towers' (2002) examination of labour relations in the global fast food industry, with particular focus on how MNCs operate within national systems, is more relevant in terms of employment relations. To avoid unnecessary duplication and repetition, very little of their material has been incorporated into this book.

14 Salamon (1999: 179–208, 2000: 282–309) discusses the role of the state and government respectively.

15 Salamon (2000: 456–88) provides a detailed account of the processes of conciliation and arbitration.

16 Loretto *et al.* (2000) provides a useful review of the efficacy of codes of practice.

17 A new network of Sector Skills Councils (SSC) replaced the NTOs in 2002.

2   Employment and work

1 Doherty and Manfredi (2001) state that the line between the public and private division of labour is hard to draw, and is obscured by illegal practices. They cite a married couple running a 19-bedroom hotel with a 300-cover restaurant with the help of two cooks and one occasional part-time worker as 'very suspicious'.

2 Locating consistent statistical measures of HI employment and establishments in the UK over time is problematic, because the ways in which the data have been collected and reported have changed in the last few years (H*t*F, 1999, 2001, 2002). For example in 1998 the AES, which estimates the number of establishments shown in Tables 2.1 and 2.2, was replaced by the Annual Business Inquiry (ABI) using a different methodology. Figures based on the ABI (2000) show a vastly reduced number of HI establishments – 150,692 employing an average of seven employees (H*t*F, 2002). Tables 1.1, 2.1, 2.2, 2.3, 2.4, 2.5, 2.6, 2.12 present available data (ONS, 1996; H*t*F, 1999, 2000, 2002; National Statistics (NS), 2001) primarily to *indicate key differences* between the HI and the UK/Britain that are most appropriate to this analysis. To achieve this, it has been necessary to use figures for different years.

3 Occupational segregation is both horizontal (women are concentrated in particular occupations) and vertical (women are concentrated in lower-status jobs in particular occupations). In practice these are not necessarily discrete forms of segregation, as Maxwell (1997) and Woods and Viehland (2000) show in their studies of female hotel managers. Rubery and Fagan's (1993) suggestion that occupational segregation is weak in the UK compared to France, Italy and Spain is challenged by Burrell *et al.* (1997) in their study of women in hotels in these countries. Jordan (1997) argues that tourism organizations reproduce and rationalize job segregation in relation to the culture of tourism, where informal recruitment systems serve to reproduce existing organization structures.

4 In Britain around one million students in full-time education under the age of 25 are in employment (NS, 2002). The proportion of full-time students in this age group in employment rose from 23 to 37 per cent between 1984 and 1996 (Lucas and Lammont, 1998).

5 Choi *et al.* (2000) foresee an increase in the migration of hospitality labour in an increasingly globalized economy. With the aid of increasingly advanced technologies, this could be used to solve labour shortages in particular countries.

6 For a recent and more detailed review of the skills debate and its implications for education and training, see Nickson *et al.* (2002, 34–48)

7 Korczynski (2002) provides a more detailed and highly coherent analysis in relation to service work more generally.

8 Korczynski (2002) rejects Ritzer's analysis, arguing that only 4 per cent of jobs in the US are McDonaldized.

9 The problem of high turnover is a recurrent theme within international hospitality literature, but space does not allow us to develop this issue in detail. Key recent sources are noted in the text. Other recent sources include the following: Mok and Luk (1995), Simons and Enz (1995), Simons (1995), Berger and Ghei (1995), Young and Lundberg

(1996), La Lopa (1997), Kaak *et al.* (1998), Pizam and Thornburg (2000), Hinkin and Tracey (2000), Simons and Hinkin (2001), Stalcup and Pearson (2001), Lam *et al.* (2001a,b, 2002), Birdir (2002), Gustfason (2002) and Warech (2002).

10 Iverson and Deery (1997) found that union loyalty exerted a positive influence on reducing turnover.

11 Downsizing has been a prevalent activity in US lodging and foodservice organizations during the 1990s, particularly among major international hotel groups and fast food operators (Hutchinson *et al.*, 1997). The authors propose a set of managerial recommendations to minimize stress and negative reactions from employees.

12 'Rolling up' holiday pay may be unlawful and defeat the Directive's purpose to provide workers with rest periods, according to a Scottish Court of Session decision in 2003 in *MBS Structures v Munro* [2003] IRLR 350. The EAT in *Marshalls Clay Products v Caulfield and Other Cases* [2003] IRLR 552 has since taken a different line. 'Rolling up' is lawful if the wage is clear in the contract and topped up by a percentage sum identified as holiday pay, or the contract provides for pay before or during leave.

13 In early 2003 the Employment Appeal Tribunal (EAT) in *Ashby v Addison and Addison* ruled that the WTR do not apply to children below the maximum compulsory school age. Hence they are excluded from the definition of 'worker' and not entitled to paid holidays. The *Children and Young Person's Act 1933* gives children the right to two weeks' holiday, but not paid holiday. The EAT also upheld the finding that the employee, a paper deliverer, had been both wrongly and unfairly dismissed.

14 Cultural differences account for national differences in practice in the EU (Raghuram *et al.*, 2001). Increased part-time employment is reported elsewhere in the world, for example in the US (McLean Parks *et al.*, 1998, Stamper and Van Dyne, 2001) and Australia (Junor, 1998).

15 Unfair dismissal waivers were abolished in 1999.

16 McLean Parks *et al.* (1998) argue that a better understanding of employees' attitudes and behaviours can be achieved by extending the notion of the psychological contract, which has been viewed mainly in relation to full-time workers, to contingent workers. This could be achieved by measuring the dimensions rather than the content of contracts across different work arrangements, different types of job and across national boundaries. Stamper and Van Dyne (2001) suggest the short-term cost benefits of part-time workers may be offset by a lack of organizational citizenship, which may undermine the quality of customer service.

17 Service work embraces five traditional attributes – intangibility, perishability, variability, simultaneous production and consumption, and inseparability – although not all service work has all of these attributes (Korczynski, 2002: 4–7).

3 The role of management in employment relations

1 We are not able to develop any significant gender analysis of management style, although differences in the management style of men and women have been observed (Rutherford, 2001).

2 Frenkel (2000) cites labour costs in services as 60 per cent, but this is clearly too high for the HI.

3 Davidson *et al.* (2001: 445) provide the first attempt to describe organizational climate as 'the here-and-now interactions between members of an organization', which has its roots in a psychological approach aimed to identify common dimensions across organizations. They differentiate it from culture, which describes the uniqueness of each organization in terms of its history, represented in descriptions from myths, symbols, rites and stories.

4 For an overview of national industrial relations systems, the EU and ILO, see Section 2, Hollinshead and Leat (1995). Chapters within Royle and Towers (2002) also provide details about national systems in selected countries in America, Europe and Asia-Pacific.

5 This is based on Fox's (1974) elaboration of his unitary and pluralist dichotomy. Purcell has since elaborated upon these five styles, often in conjunction with others (e.g. Kessler and Purcell, 1995), as have others, including Marchington and Parker (1990). The small firms literature also has the potential to provide a way forward, although much conceptual work has been located outside the HI or in unionized establishments, e.g. Rainnie (1989) and Scase (1995).

6 This approach may not be relevant in other countries, where managers in the HI manage within more highly regulated institutional frameworks. This issue remains an interesting topic for future development.

7 For more details about the general nature of HRM and personnel management, the reader can consult texts such as Legge (1995a), Bach and Sisson (1999), Sisson and Storey (2000), Torrington *et al.* (2002) and Boxall and Purcell (2003). Korczynski (2002) offers a dedicated text on HRM in service work.

8 Dickens (1998) argues that this shift away from specialists will weaken equal opportunities policies, as line managers as less likely to be as aware of these issues.

9 For further comment, see Nickson and Wood (2000) and Hoque (2000).

10 There are no HI organizations listed as employers' associations at the Certification Office for Trade Unions and Employers' Assocations. Only the Brewers and Licensed Retailers Association of Scotland is shown as unlisted (www.certoffice.org/annual report). Hence none is formally constituted for employment relations purposes.

4 Resourcing, development and fair treatment

1 Liability for negligent hiring in the US reinforces the importance of making appropriate background checks. Even where employees are off duty the employer may be liable for their behaviour if the employer knew or should have known that the employee was likely to behave in a certain manner, e.g. if there was a history of violent behaviour (Clay and Stephens, 1995b).

2 This is the occupation that accounts for the greatest proportion of non-managerial employees. Adoption of this approach was 'a heuristic device to prevent the interview becoming unduly long and unwieldy by having to repeat questions for each occupational group present at the workplace. Conversely, it necessarily constrained our view of diversity across groups within the workplace' (Cully *et. al.*, 1999).

3 A more detailed account of tourism education and training across the world is given in ILO (2001: 90–101). Issues addressed include training needs, new skill requirements, continuous training, competencies, certification, training providers and social dialogue.

4 H*t*F (2002) reports the recent uptake and stock of a range of qualifications and awards, but does not report how far national targets have been met.

5 Orientation and socialization are used elsewhere to describe this process.

6 The number of job grades for the LOG is slightly higher in the HI than in AIS and the PSS. In the HI in 45 per cent of workplaces there are four or more grades in the LOG compared to 37 per cent in the PSS and 39 per cent in AIS. In the HI the number of grades increases with workplace size. Hotels are most likely to have such jobs.

7 Dickens (1997) asserts that Britain has some of the most sophisticated race discrimination legislation in Europe. Monaghan (2000) provides a useful review of the practical effects of race discrimination.

8 In the UK the *Criminal Justice and Public Order Act 1994* also covers harassment on a variety of grounds, including sex and race, in the street, at work or at home. Offenders may be imprisoned or fined.

9 In the past only Northern Ireland had religious discrimination, where employers have a statutory requirement to monitor and take action.

10 There is a fine line between harassment and bullying, and not all harassment is of a sexual nature. McMahon (2000) sees harassment as oriented at some personal characteristic of the victim, whereas bullying is the abuse of power manifested as a repeated pattern of aggressive behaviour. Her Irish study found that harassment in Northern Ireland was sectarian, whereas harassment in the Republic was sexual.

11 In the US no consensus has emerged on this issue. Three areas of concern have emerged – how the accommodation request is made, how to handle reassignments and whether to permit telecommuting as a substitute to working on the premises (Kreismann and Palmer, 2001).
12 Proposals for a new statutory body to enforce the law in these all areas and encompass the work of the EOC, CRE and DRC are being considered.
13 Busby and Middlemiss (2001) identify sources for the development of specific anti-discrimination legislation for gays and lesbians.
14 See also note 3 to Chapter 7.
15 This excludes full-time union officers, in contrast to the accompaniment rights in grievance and disciplinary hearings.
16 Whether this is deliberate or due to space constraints, as in this book, is not clear. James and Walters (1999) and Walters (2001) provide useful more detailed reviews of health and safety issues. See also the HSE website.
17 Passive smoking is an emerging issue. While Young (1997) advises employers to ban smoking to avoid litigation, Cuthbert and Nickson (1999) find that employers who ban smoking voluntarily oppose legislation banning it altogether, as it would remove their competitive advantage.
18 Smith's (2001) work is the first real attempt to quantify the extent of stress in Britain, but not the causes. Surprisingly his sample of 103 catering workers showed them to be among the least stressed group (twenty-fourth of 27 occupations).

5 Pay, reward and performance

1 Effects in terms of race and disability are also acknowledged. Proportionally both groups are smaller than the gender division, and are less visible.
2 Rose (2001: 216–20) provides a useful summary of international minimum wage systems. More recent examples are contained in Appendix 5 of LPC (2003).
3 Questionnaires already apply in discrimination cases.
4 In the US Sturman (2001) addresses this issue by comparing the pay levels of jobs according to knowledge, skills and abilities to determine whether the low-pay problem suggested by pay averages can be substantiated. Pay levels for low human capital jobs were relatively close (due to a minimum wage floor) while the differences were greater for high human capital jobs. The HI paid 85 per cent less for moderate complexity jobs and 78 per cent less for high complexity jobs. This is likely to exacerbate skill shortages among the most skilled.
5 '–' Data have been suppressed due to confidentiality or, where the sample size is small or the relative standard error is greater than 5 per cent, because the data are not considered to be of sufficient statistical reliability. The NES release criteria currently require that any estimate:
   a of a mean is based on a sample size of at least 30 and that the associated standard error does not exceed 5 per cent.
   b of a quantile such as a percentile, quartile or median, or of a percentage, is based on a sample size of at least 10 and that the sample size is either at least 225 or that the relative standard error is less than 20 per cent.
   The standard error provides a measure of the quality of the estimates provided in the table. These are expressed as percentages of the estimated values. The population value of the variable being estimated in the table will be within two standard errors of the estimated value in 95 per cent of samples. Another way to think of this is that two standard errors provides a '95 per cent confidence interval' for the estimate.

6 Representation, participation and involvement

1 The principles of negotiation are discussed in Torrington *et al.* (2002: 628–44).
2 The EU figures for 1995 from ILO (2001) are something of a mystery, because the source cited, Visser (1998), does not show any data for the hotel and restaurant sector.

7   Employment law and dispute resolution

1 The early development and influence of EU social policy is reviewed in Lucas (1996b).
2 The EC has already warned that the UK is not complying fully with the Working Time Directive, because there is no obligation on employers actively to prevent working in excess of 48 hours. There is some doubt that the facility for opt-outs will continue beyond 2003, because no other member states have taken advantage of this facility.
3 Two tribunals hearing cases of 'forced retirement' of two male workers over 65 ruled indirect sex discrimination and a right to claim unfair dismissal and redundancy payments. The EAT subsequently upheld an appeal by the government. Age discrimination will have to be outlawed by 2006 (Anon., 2002b).
4 In 2004 the small firms exemption under the *Disability Discrimination Act 1995* (see Chapter 4) and in regard to the issuing details of disciplinary procedures (this Chapter) will be removed. The only remaining size exemption will be for employers with fewer than five employees, who are not required to issue a formal health and safety policy.
5 At the time of writing the proposals arising from the review of the *Employment Relations Act 1999* were subject to consultation. Major changes to individual rights are not expected.
6 The right to accompaniment extends only to grievance hearings that concern the performance of a 'duty by an employer in relation to a worker', which could include contractual commitments. Thus a grievance about equal pay would qualify, as it relates to a statutory duty, whereas a grievance about a pay rise would not.
7 Most awards comprise an element based on a week's pay. From 1 February 2003 the following maxima apply: a week's pay is £260, while the unfair dismissal compensation comprises a basic award (£7,800), compensatory award (£53,500) and additional award (£6,760–£13,520: 26–52 weeks' pay).
8 For the period February to August, after the compensatory award had increased to £52,600. Over 12 months to March 2002, when the compensatory award stood mainly at £51,700, 37 claimants were awarded above £50,000, but this includes the basic award (Employment Tribunals Service, 2002).
9 In *Gee v Shell UK Ltd*, the CA warned that tribunals should not be too hasty in awarding costs, finding no grounds in this case because the claim was not frivolous, vexatious, abusive, disruptive or otherwise unreasonable. The tribunal had erred in warning that she faced substantial costs because her claim had little chance of success (Anon., 2003a).
10 The separate but related issue of worker behaviour is considered in individual and collective forms in Chapters 1, 2 and 6.

8   What do the workers think?

1 Upchurch *et al.* (2000) review the managerial challenges of trying to motivate Russian hotel workers in an economy only recently exposed to capitalism. Russian workers are not used to being recognized for achievements, having worked under a 'work-production' mentality where individual efforts were often punished. Financial rewards are the most effective tool, with recognition and advancement beginning to be seen as effective.
2 This is most evident within Chapter 2, with Chapter 3 also containing recent HRM research drawn from employee research.
3 WERS finds a positive relationship between 'good' HRM based on high commitment practices and employee job satisfaction and commitment (Cully *et al.*, 1999).
4 The main variations offered by Cully *et al.* (1999) are gender, hours of work and occupation, with managers reporting the most job influence. Part-timers are positive about their treatment, although they are treated less favourably than full-timers in terms of pay and training. Young part-timers have substantially lower levels of commitment and job satisfaction than older part-timers, with part-time mothers falling in the middle.

5 Guest and Conway (1999) surveyed 1,000 employees in total across AIS, so we can assume that the HI responses were small numerically.

6 Personal service occupations include chefs/cooks, waiting and bar staff (three of the largest occupational groups) and housekeepers (see Table 2.6). Almost all protective service occupations are found outside the HI, e.g. police, fire service. Other occupations (in services) include kitchen porters/hands, counterhands/catering assistants (these two groups comprise the largest occupation in Table 2.6), hotel porters and cleaners/domestics. It is not clear how receptionists are classified, but other sales or other service occupations seem the most likely occupational categories.

7 Although precise comparisons are not possible, we can note that NES data for 1998 show that full-time employees on adult rates in AIS received average gross annual earnings of £385.15 compared to £255.30 in the HI. Part-time male manual workers in AIS received gross weekly earnings of £123.20 compared to £67.40 in the HI. Part-time female manual workers in AIS received gross weekly earnings of £88.50 compared to £65.30 in the HI (ONS, 1998b).

8 See Chapter 6, 'Recent experience in British workplaces' (pp. 146–9).

9 While brewery employers have been perceived as sympathetic to trade unions, many no longer own breweries where union organization is traditionally strong. There is no direct evidence that unions have experienced much organizing success with breweries' newer ventures within hotels, restaurants and themed bars and pubs.

10 This characteristic is difficult to identify with any precision from occupational groupings and is not included in the multivariate analysis. Tables 8.3 and 8.4 show personal service workers, but they are not the only occupation with a customer interface. Occupational group is to be included in a re-run of the multivariate analysis, for a paper based on Lucas (2001).

Appendix 1: Background characteristics of the WERS98 sample

1 AIS denotes the whole economy (except agriculture and coal-mining), covering SIC 1992 Codes D–Q.

2 PSS denotes all SIC Codes G–Q, not owned by the state or a public body.

3 HI denotes SIC Code H. This comprises hotels, camping sites and other short-stay accommodation, restaurants, bars, canteens and catering.

4 Within the full population, including micro-workplaces with fewer than ten employees, workplaces employing 25 or more employees account for 11 per cent of all workplaces in AIS and almost 70 per cent of employment. In the HI there are only 4 per cent of workplaces of this size, which employ 41 per cent of all employees. The HI is dominated by micro-workplaces (85 per cent), which account for 36 per cent of employment (H*t*F, 1999).

5 These are discussed in a separate, more detailed paper based on Lucas (2001). The multivariate analysis unit contains a further eight dummy variables in addition to those detailed here.

References

Aalberts, R. J. and Seidman, L. H. (1996) 'Sexual-harassment policies for the workplace: a tale of two companies', *Cornell Hotel and Restaurant Administration Quarterly*, 37, 5, 78–85.

Abbott, B. (1993) 'Small firms and trade unions in services in the 1990s', *Industrial Relations Journal*, 24, 2, 308–17.

Abbott, B. (1998) 'The emergence of a new industrial relations actor: the role of the citizens' advice bureaux?', *Industrial Relations Journal*, 29, 4, 257–69.

ACAS (2000) *Code of Practice on Disciplinary and Grievance Procedures*, London: ACAS.

ACAS (2002) *Working Together Annual Report 2001–02*, London: ACAS.

Ackers, P. (2002) 'Reframing employment relations: the case for neo-pluralism', *Industrial Relations Journal*, 33, 1, 2–19.

Adib, A. and Guerrier, Y. (2001) 'The experience of tour reps in maintaining and losing control of holidaymakers', *International Journal of Hospitality Management*, 20, 4, 339–52.

Adkins, L. (1995) *Gendered Work: Sexuality, Family and the Labour Market*, Buckingham: Open University Press.

Allan, C., Bamber, G. and Timo, N. (2000) ' "McDonaldization" and employment relations: a study of MNE fast food operators in Australia', *International Human Resource Issues*, 1, 1, 28–45.

Almond, P. and Rubery, J. (1998) 'The gender impact of recent European trends in wage determination', *Work, Employment and Society*, 12, 4, 675–93.

Anastassova, L. and Purcell, K. (1995) 'Human resource management in the Bulgarian hotel industry: from command to empowerment?', *International Journal of Hospitality Management*, 14, 2, 171–85.

Anon. (2002a) 'Don't nurse a grievance: resolving disputes at work', *IRS Employment Review*, 759: 7–13.

Anon. (2002b) 'Tribunal ends age barrier to unfair dismissal and redundancy claims', *IRS Employment Review*, 760: 45.

Anon. (2003a) 'Costs warning put "undue pressure" on unfair dismissal claimant', *IRS Employment Review*, 768: 45.

Anon. (2003b) 'Time to talk: how and why employers conduct appraisals', *IRS Employment Review*, 769: 8–14.

Argyris, C. (1960) *Understanding Organizational Behaviour*, Homewood, IL: Dorsey Press.

Armstrong, M. (2000) 'The name has changed but has the game remained the same?', *Employee Relations*, 22, 6, 576–93.

Arrowsmith, J. and Sisson, K. (1999) 'Pay and working time: towards organization-based systems?', *British Journal of Industrial Relations*, 37, 1, 51–75.

Arrowsmith, J. and Sisson, K. (2001) 'International competition and pay, working time and employment: exploring the processes of adjustment', *Industrial Relations Journal*, 32, 2, 136–53.

Ashness, D. and Lashley, C. (1995) 'Empowering service workers in Harvester Restaurants', *Personnel Review*, 24, 8, 17–32.

Atkinson, J. (1984) 'Manpower strategies for flexible organisations', *Personnel Management*, 16, 28–31.

Bach, S. and Sisson, K. (eds) (1999) *Personnel Management: A Comprehensive Guide to Theory and Practice*, 3rd edn, Oxford: Blackwell.

Bacon, N. and Storey, J. (2000) 'New employee relations strategies in Britain: towards individualism or partnership?', *British Journal of Industrial Relations*, 38, 3, 407–27.

Bagguley, P. (1987) *Flexibility, Restructuring and Gender: Changing Employment in Britain's Hotels*, Lancaster: Lancaster Regionalism Group, University of Lancaster.

Bagguley, P. (1990) Gender and labour flexibility in hotel and catering', *The Service Industries Journal*, 10, 4, 737–47.

Bain, G. S. and Price, R. (1983) 'Union growth: dimensions, determinants and density', in G. S. Bain (ed.) *Industrial Relations in Britain*, Oxford: Blackwell.

Balchin, A. (1994) 'Part-time workers in the multiple retail sector: small change from employment protection legislation?', *Employee Relations*, 16, 7, 43–57.

Barber, N. and Pittaway, L. (2000) 'Expatriate recruitment in South East Asia: dilemma or opportunity?', *International Journal of Contemporary Hospitality Management*, 12, 6, 352–9.

Barclay, J. M. (2001) 'Improving selection interviews with structure: organisations' use of "behavioural" interviews', *Personnel Review*, 30, 1, 81–101.

Barham, C. and Leonard, J. (2002) 'Trends and sources of data on sickness absence', *Labour Market Trends*, April, 177–85.

Barling, J., Fullagar, C. and Kelloway, E. K. (1992) *The Union and its Members: A Psychological Approach*, New York: Oxford University Press.

Barron, P. (1997) 'An analysis of Australian students' images of the hospitality industry: a focus on new recruits', *Australian Journal of Hospitality Management*, 4, 2, 13–20.

Barron, P. and Maxwell, G. (1998) 'Employee job perceptions: a comparison of Scottish and Australian fast food units', *Australian Journal of Hospitality Management*, 5, 1, 33–9.

Barrows, C. W., Gallo, M. and Mulleady, T. (1996) 'AIDS in the US hospitality industry: recommendations for education and policy formulations', *International Journal of Contemporary Hospitality Management*, 8, 1, 5–9.

Batterman, L. R. and Fullerton, J. F. III (2002) 'Collective bargaining after September 11: what about job security and workplace security?', *Cornell Hotel and Restaurant Administration Quarterly*, 43, 5, 93–108.

Baum, T. (1995) *Managing Human Resources in the European Tourism and Hospitality Industry*, London: Chapman Hall.

Baum, T. (1996) 'Unskilled work and the hospitality industry: myth or reality', *International Journal of Hospitality Management*, 15, 3, 207–9.

Baum, T. and Nickson, D. (1998) 'Teaching human resource management in hospitality and tourism: a critique', *International Journal of Contemporary Hospitality Management*, 10, 2, 75–9.

Baum, T., Amoah, V. and Spivack, S. (1997) 'Policy dimensions of human resource management in the tourism and hospitality industries', *International Journal of Contemporary Hospitality Management*, 9, 5/6, 221–9.

Beardwell, I. J. (1996) 'How do we know how it really is?', in I. J. Beardwell (ed.) *Contemporary Industrial Relations: A Critical Analysis*, Oxford: Oxford University Press.

Benson, J. (2000) 'Employee voice in union and non-union Australian workplaces', *British Journal of Industrial Relations*, 38, 3, 453–9.

Berger, F. and Ghei, A. (1995) 'Employment tests: a facet of hospitality hiring', *Cornell Hotel and Restaurant Administration Quarterly*, 36, 6, 28–35.

Beynon, H., Grimshaw, D., Rubery, J. and Ward, K. (2002) *Managing Employment Change*, Oxford: Oxford University Press.

Bird, C., Lynch, P. A. and Ingram, A. (2002) 'Gender and employment flexibility within hotel front offices', *The Service Industries Journal*, 22, 3, 99–116.

Birdir, K. (2002) 'General manager turnover and root causes', *International Journal of Contemporary Hospitality Management*, 14, 1, 43–7.

Blyton, P. and Turnbull, P. (1998) *The Dynamics of Employee Relations*, 2nd edn, Basingstoke: Macmillan.

Bodvarsson, O. B. and Gibson, W. A. (2002) 'Tipping and service quality: a reply to Lynn', *The Social Science Journal*, 39, 3, 471–6.

Bonamy, J. and May, N. (1997) 'Service and employment relationships', *The Service Industries Journal*, 17, 4, 544–63.

Boxall, P. and Purcell, J. (2003) *Strategy and Human Resource Management*, Basingstoke: Palgrave.

Boyd, C. (2001) 'HRM in the airline industry: strategies and outcomes', *Personnel Review*, 30, 4, 438–53.

Braverman, H. (1974) *Labor and Monopoly Capital*, New York: Monthly Review Press.

Breiter, D. and Woods, R. H. (1997) 'An analysis of training budgets and training needs assessment in mid-sized hotels in the United States', *Journal of Hospitality and Tourism Research*, 21, 2, 86–97.

Broadbridge, A. (1997) 'Why earnings differentials are different for men and women in retailing', *The Service Industries Journal*, 17, 2, 221–36.

Brook, K. (2002) 'Trade union membership: an analysis of data from the autumn 2001 LFS', *Labour Market Trends*, July, 343–55.

Brown, D. and Crossman, A. (2000) 'Employer strategies in the face of a national minimum wage: an analysis of the hotel sector', *Industrial Relations Journal*, 31, 3, 206–19.

Brown, W. (2000) 'Putting partnership into practice in Britain', *British Journal of Industrial Relations*, 38, 2, 299–316.

Brown, W., Deakin, S., Hudson, M., Pratten, C. and Ryan, P. (1998) *The Individualisation of Employment Contracts in Great Britain*, Research paper for the DTI, Cambridge: Centre for Business Research, Department of Applied Economics, University of Cambridge, June.

Brown, W., Deakin, S., Nash, D. and Oxenbridge, S. (2000) 'The employment contract: from collective procedures to individual rights', *British Journal of Industrial Relations*, 38, 4, 611–29.

Buick, I. and Thomas, M. (2001) 'Why do middle managers in hotels burn out?', *International Journal of Contemporary Hospitality Management*, 13, 6, 304–9.

Burns, P. M. (1997) 'Hard-skills, soft-skills: undervaluing hospitality's service smile', *Progress in Tourism and Hospitality Research*, 3, 3, 239–48.

Burrell, J., Manfredi, S., Rollin, H., Price, L. and Stead, L. (1997) 'Equal opportunities for women employees in the hospitality industry: a comparison between France, Italy, Spain and the UK', *International Journal of Hospitality Management*, 16, 2, 161–79.

Busby, N. and Middlemiss, S. (2001) 'The equality deficit: protection against discrimination on the grounds of sexual orientation in employment', *Gender, Work and Organisation*, 8, 4, 387–410.

Cameron, D., Gore, J., Desombre, T. and Riley, M. (1999) 'An examination of the reciprocal effects of occupation culture and organisation culture: the case of chefs in hotels', *International Journal of Hospitality Management*, 18, 3, 225–34.

Cappelli, P. and Crocker-Hefter, A. (1996) 'Distinctive human resources are firms' core competencies', *Organisational Dynamics*, 25, 1, 7–22.

Casey, B. (2001) 'Tipping in New Zealand restaurants', *International Journal of Hospitality Management*, 20, 2, 219–25.

Casey, B., Metcalf, H. and Millward, N. (1997) *Employers' Use of Flexible Labour*, London: PSI.

Cassell, C. (1996) 'A fatal attraction?: strategic HRM and the business case for women's progression at work', *Personnel Review*, 25, 5, 51–66.

Central Arbitration Committee (CAC) (2002) *Annual Report 2001–02*, London: CAC.

Charles, R. O. and McCleary, K. W. (1997) 'Recruitment and retention of African-American managers', *Cornell Hotel and Restaurant Administration Quarterly*, 38, 1, 24–9.

Cheng, A. and Brown, A. (1998) 'HRM strategies and labour turnover in the hotel industry: a comparative study of Australia and Singapore', *International Journal of Human Resource Management*, 9, 1, 136–54.

Choi, J., Woods, R. H. and Murrmann, S. K. (2000) 'International labor markets and the migration of labor forces as an alternative solution for labor shortages in the hospitality industry', *International Journal of Contemporary Hospitality Management*, 12, 1, 61–7.

Chung, B. G. (1997) 'Collecting and using employee feedback: an effective way to understand customers' needs', *Cornell Hotel and Restaurant Administration Quarterly*, 38, 5, 50–7.

Clark, T., Gospel, H. and Montgomery, J. (1999) 'Running on the spot? A review of 20 years of research on the management of human resources in comparative and international perspective', *International Journal of Human Resource Management*, 10, 3, 520–44.

Clay, J. M. and Stephens, E. C. (1994) 'Protected employee concerted activity: hospitality-industry implications', *Cornell Hotel and Restaurant Administration Quarterly*, 35, 5, 12–15.

Clay, J. M. and Stephens, E. C. (1995a) 'Union organizers access to hotels' private property', *Cornell Hotel and Restaurant Administration Quarterly*, 36, 1, 20–8.

Clay, J. M. and Stephens, E. C. (1995b) 'Liability for negligent hiring: the importance of background checks', *Cornell Hotel and Restaurant Administration Quarterly*, 36, 5, 74–81.

Clay, J. M. and Stephens, E. C. (1996) 'Child-labor laws and the hospitality industry', *Cornell Hotel and Restaurant Administration Quarterly*, 37, 6, 20–5.

Claytor, A. (2002) 'Review of research and evaluation on investors in people', *Labour Market Trends*, January, 47–8.

Clegg, H. A. (1979) *The Changing System of Industrial Relations in Great Britain*, Oxford: Blackwell.

Clifford, N., Morley, M. and Gunnigle, P. (1997) 'Part-time work in Europe', *Employee Relations*, 19, 6, 555–67.

Coffey, B. S. and Anderson, S. E. (1998) 'Career issues for women association executives: mentors, pay, equity and boards of directors', *Cornell Hotel and Restaurant Administration Quarterly*, 39, 1, 34–9.

Cohen, E. A. (2002) 'Collective bargaining regarding safety and security issues', *Cornell Hotel and Restaurant Administration Quarterly*, 43, 5, 109–18.

Cooke, F. L. (2001) 'Human resources strategy to improve organisational performance: a route for firms in Britain', *International Journal of Management Reviews*, 3, 4, 321–39.

Coupar, W. and Stevens, B. (1998) 'Towards a new model of industrial partnership', in P. Sparrow and M. Marchington (eds) *Human Resource Management: The New Agenda*, London: Financial Times/Pitman.

Cully, M., Woodland, S., O'Reilly, A. and Dix, G. (1999) *Britain at Work*, London: Routledge.

Curtis, S. (2002) 'The nature of the psychological contract for undergraduates working part-time during term-time'. Paper presented to the Manchester Metropolitan University Business School Doctoral Symposium, March.

Curtis, S. and Lucas, R. E. (2001) 'A coincidence of needs? Employers and full-time students', *Employee Relations*, 23, 1, 38–54.

Cuthbert, L. and Nickson, D. (1999) 'Smoking in the restaurant industry: time for a ban?', *International Journal of Contemporary Hospitality Management*, 11, 1, 31–6.

D'Annunzio-Green, N. (2002) 'An examination of the organizational and cross-cultural challenges facing international hotel managers in Russia', *International Journal of Contemporary Hospitality Management*, 14, 6, 266–73.

D'Annunzio-Green, N. and Macandrew, J. (1999) 'Re-empowering the empowered: the ultimate challenge?', *Personnel Review*, 28, 3, 258–78.

D'Annunzio-Green, N., Maxwell, G. A. and Watson, S. (eds) (2002) *Human Resource Management: International Perspectives in Hospitality and Tourism*, London: Continuum.

Davidson, M., Manning, M., Timo, N. and Ryder, P. (2001) 'The dimensions of organizational climate in four- and five-star Australian hotels', *Journal of Hospitality and Tourism Research*, 25, 4, 444–61.

Davies, J. (2002) 'Labour disputes in Britain 2001', *Labour Market Trends*, November, 589–603.

Deery, M. and Jago, L. K. (2002) 'The core and periphery: an examination of the flexible workforce model in the hotel industry', *International Journal of Hospitality Management*, 21, 4, 325–38.

Deery, M. and Shaw, R. (1997) 'An exploratory analysis of turnover culture in the hotel industry in Australia', *International Journal of Hospitality Management*, 16, 4, 375–92.

Deery, M. and Shaw, R. (1999) 'An investigation of the relationship between employee turnover and organizational culture', *Journal of Hospitality and Tourism Research*, 23, 4, 387–400.

Deery, M., Walsh, J. and Knox, A. (2001) 'The non-union workplace in Australia: bleak house or human resource innovator?', *International Journal of Human Resource Management*, 12, 4, 669–83.

Department of Trade and Industry (DTI) (1998) *Fairness at Work*, Cmnd 3968, London: HMSO.

Department of Trade and Industry (DTI) (1999) *Workplace Employee Relations Survey: Cross-section, 1998* [computer file], 4th edn, Colchester: UK Data Archive [distributor], 22 December, SN: 3955.

Department of Trade and Industry (DTI) (2001a) *Dispute Resolution in Britain: A Background Paper*. Available on-line at: http://www.dti.gov.uk/er/individual/et.

Department of Trade and Industry (DTI) (2001b) *Creating a Work-Life Balance: A Good Practice Guide for the Hospitality Industry*, London: DTI.

Department of Trade and Industry (DTI) (2002) *Employment Tribunal System Taskforce Report*. Available on-line at: http://www.employmenttribunalsystemtaskforce.gov.uk.

Dermody, M. B. (2002) 'Recruitment and retention practices in independent chain restaurants', *International Journal of Hospitality and Tourism Administration*, 3, 1, 107–17.

Dickens, L. (1994) 'The business case for women's equality: is the carrot better than the stick?', *Employee Relations*, 16, 8, 5–18.

Dickens, L. (1997) 'Gender, race and employment equality in Britain: inadequate strategies and the role of industrial relations actors', *Industrial Relations Journal*, 28, 4, 282–91.

Dickens, L. (1998) 'What HRM means for gender equality', *Human Resource Management Journal*, 8, 1, 23–40.

Dodrill, K. and Riley, M. (1992) 'Hotel workers' orientations to work', *International Journal of Contemporary Hospitality Management*, 4, 1, 25–35.

Doherty, L. (2002) Human resource management in hospitality: time to come in from the cold? Paper presented to the 20th Annual International Labour Process, University of Strathclyde, April.

Doherty, L. and Manfredi, S. (2001) 'Women's employment in Italian and UK hotels', *International Journal of Hospitality Management*, 20, 1, 61–76.

Doherty, L. and Stead, L. (1998) 'The gap between male and female pay: what does the case of hotel and catering tell us?', *The Service Industries Journal*, 18, 4, 126–44.

Donovan Commission (1968) *Royal Commission on Trade Unions and Employer's Associations Report*, London: HMSO.

Doyle, B. (1995) *Disability, Discrimination and Equal Opportunities*, London: Mansell.

Dundon, T., Grugulis, I. and Wilkinson, A. (1999) ' "Looking out of the black-hole": non-union relations in an SME', *Employee Relations*, 21, 3, 251–66.

Dunlop, J. (1958) *Industrial Relations Systems*, New York: Henry Holt.

Earnshaw, J. and Morrison, L. (2001) 'Workplace stress claims following the John Walker decision', *Personnel Review*, 30, 4, 468–87.

Earnshaw, J., Goodman, J., Harrison, R. and Marchington, M. (1998) *Industrial Tribunals, Workplace Disciplinary Procedures and Employment Practice*, Department of Trade and Industry Employment Relations Research Series, No. 2, London: DTI.

Earnshaw, J., Marchington, M. and Goodman, J. (2000) 'Unfair to whom? Discipline and dismissal in small establishments', *Industrial Relations Journal*, 31, 1, 62–73.

Edwards, P. (1995) 'The employment relationship' in P. Edwards (ed.) *Industrial Relations Theory and Practice in Britain*, Oxford: Blackwell.

Edwards, P. (2000) 'Discipline: towards trust and self-discipline?', in S. Bach and K. Sisson (eds) *Personnel Management*, 3rd edn, Oxford: Blackwell.

Edwards, P. (2003a) 'The employment relationship and the field of industrial relations', in P. Edwards (ed.) *Industrial Relations Theory and Practice in Britain*, 2nd edn, Oxford: Blackwell.

Edwards, P. (ed.) (2003b) *Industrial Relations Theory and Practice in Britain*, 2nd edn, Oxford: Blackwell.

Edwards, P. and Gilman, M. (1999) 'Pay equity and the National Minimum Wage: what can theories tell us?', *Human Resource Management Journal*, 9, 1, 20–38.

Employment Tribunals Service (2002) *Annual Report and Accounts 2001–2002*, London: Employment Tribunals Service. Available on-line at: http://www.ets.gov.uk.

Equal Opportunities Commission (2002) *Towards the Goal of Equality: Annual Report 2001/2*, Manchester: EOC.

Erickson, R. J. and Wharton, A. S. (1997) 'Inauthenticity and depression: assessing the consequences of interactive service work', *Work and Occupations*, 24, 2, 188–213.

Esichaikul, R. and Baum, T. (1998) 'The case for government involvement in human resource development: a study of the Thai hotel industry', *Tourism Management*, 19, 4, 359–70.

Fagan, C. (2001) 'Time, money and the gender order: work orientations and working-time preferences in Britain', *Gender, Work and Organization*, 8, 3, 239–66.

Farnham, D. and Pimlott, J. (1995) *Understanding Industrial Relations*, 5th edn, London: Cassell.

Faulkner, B. and Patiar, A. (1997) 'Workplace induced stress among operational staff in the hotel industry', *International Journal of Hospitality Management*, 16, 1, 99–117.

Feldman, D. C., Doerpinghaus, H. I. and Turnley, W. H. (1995) 'Employee reactions to temporary jobs', *Journal of Managerial Issues*, 7, 2, 127–41.

Fenley, A. (1998) 'Models, styles and metaphors: understanding the management of discipline', *Employee Relations*, 20, 4, 349–64.

Ferner, A. and Hyman, R. (eds) (1998) *Changing Industrial Relations in Europe*, 2nd edn, Oxford: Blackwell.

Finegold, D., Wagner, K. and Mason, G. (2000) 'National skill-creation systems and career paths for service workers: hotels in the United States, Germany and the United Kingdom', *International Journal of Human Resource Management*, 11, 3, 497–516.

Flanders, A. (1974) 'The tradition of voluntarism', *British Journal of Industrial Relations*, 12, 3, 352–70.

Fombrun, C., Tichy, N. M. and Devanna, M. A. (1984) *Strategic Human Resource Management*, New York: Wiley.

Forrest, A. (1993) 'Women and industrial relations theory', *Relations Industrielles*, 48, 409–40.

Foucault, M. (1979) *The Will to Knowledge: The History of Sexuality 1*, London: Allen Lane Penguin Press.

Fox, A. (1966) *Industrial Sociology and Industrial Relations*, London: HMSO.

Fox, A. (1974) *Beyond Contract*, London: Faber and Faber.

Fox, A. (1985) *Man Mismanagement*, 2nd edn, London: Faber and Faber.

Frenkel, S. J. (2000) 'Introduction: service work and its implications for HRM', *International Journal of Human Resource Management*, 11, 3, 469–76.

Friedman, A. L. (1977) *Industry and Labour*, London: Macmillan.

Fulford, M. D. and Enz, C. A. (1995) 'Human resources as a strategic partner in multi-unit restaurants', *Cornell Hotel and Restaurant Administration Quarterly*, 36, 3, 24–9.

Fuller, L. and Smith, V. (1991) 'Management by customers in a changing economy', *Work, Employment and Society*, 5, 1, 1–16.

Gabriel, Y. (1988) *Working Lives in Catering*, London: Routledge.

Gallie, D., White, M., Cheng, Y. and Tomlinson, M. (1998) *Restructuring the Employment Relationship*, Oxford: Oxford University Press.

Gennard, J. and Kelly, J. (1995) 'Human resource management: the views of personnel directors', *Human Resource Management Journal*, 5, 1, 15–32.

Gennard, J. and Kelly, J. (1997) 'The unimportance of labels: the diffusion of the personnel/HRM function', *Industrial Relations Journal*, 28, 1, 27–42.

Ghiselli, R. and Ismail, J. A. (1998) 'Employee theft and efficacy of certain control procedures in commercial food service operations', *Journal of Hospitality and Tourism Research*, 22, 2, 174–87.

Gibb, S. (2001) 'The state of human resource management: evidence from employees' views of HRM systems and staff', *Employee Relations*, 23, 4, 318–36.

Gilbert, D. and Guerrier, Y. (1997) 'UK hospitality managers past and present', *The Service Industries Journal*, 17, 1, 115–32.

Gilbert, D., Guerrier, Y. and Guy, J. (1998) 'Sexual harassment issues in the hospitality industry', *International Journal of Contemporary Hospitality Management*, 10, 2, 48–53.

Gilman, M., Edwards, P., Ram, M. and Arrowsmith, J. (2002) 'Pay determination in small firms in the UK: the case of the response to the National Minimum Wage', *Industrial Relations Journal*, 33, 1, 52–67.

Ginn, J., Arber, S., Brannen, J., Dale, A., Dex, S., Elias, P., Moss, P., Pahl, J., Roberts, C. and Rubery, J. (1996) 'Feminist fallacies: a reply to Hakim on women's employment', *British Journal of Sociology*, 47, 1, 167–73.

Goldstein, J. I. (1995) 'Alternatives to high-cost litigation', *Cornell Hotel and Restaurant Administration Quarterly*, 36, 1, 28–33.

Goodman, J., Earnshaw, J., Marchington, M. and Harrison, R. (1998) 'Unfair dismissal cases, disciplinary procedures, recruitment methods and management style: case study evidence from three industrial sectors', *Employee Relations*, 20, 6, 536–50.

Gore, J., Kelliher, C. and Riley, M. (2002) 'Re-framing functional flexibility'. Paper presented to the 20th Annual International Labour Process, University of Strathclyde, April.

Gospel, H. (1992) *Markets, Firms and the Management of Labour in Modern Britain*, Cambridge: Cambridge Polity Press.

Gospel, H. and Palmer, G. (1993) *British Industrial Relations*, 2nd edn, London: Routledge.

Goss, D. and Adam-Smith, D. (2001) 'Pragmatism and compliance: employer responses to the working time regulations', *Industrial Relations Journal*, 32, 3, 195–208.

Goss, D., Goss, F. and Adam-Smith, D. (2000) 'Disability and employment: a comparative critique of UK legislation', *International Journal of Human Resource Management*, 11, 4, 807–21.

Goss-Turner, S. (1999) 'The role of the multi-unit manager in branded hospitality operations', *Human Resource Management Journal*, 9, 4, 39–57.

Grant, D. (1999) 'HRM, rhetoric and the psychological contract: a case of "easier said than done" ', *International Journal of Human Resource Management*, 10, 2, 327–50.

Grant, D. and Oswick, C. (1998) 'Of believers, atheists and agnostics: practitioner views of HRM', *Industrial Relations Journal*, 28, 3, 178–93.

Green, F. (2001) 'It's been a hard day's night: the concentration and intensification of work in late twentieth-century Britain', *British Journal of Industrial Relations*, 39, 1, 53–80.

Grimshaw, D., Ward, K. G., Rubery, J. and Beynon, H. (2001) 'Organisations and the transformations of the internal labour market', *Work, Employment and Society*, 15, 1, 25–54.

Groeschl, S. and Doherty, L. (1999) 'Diversity management in practice', *International Journal of Contemporary Hospitality Management*, 11, 6, 262–8.

Guerrier, Y. and Adib, A. S. (2000) ' "No, we don't provide that service": the harassment of hotel employees by customers', *Work, Employment and Society*, 14, 4, 689–705.

Guerrier, Y. and Adib, A. S. (2002) 'Tour reps at work: an exploration of emotional labour processes'. Paper presented to the 20th Annual International Labour Process, University of Strathclyde, April.

Guerrier, Y. and Lockwood, A. (1989) 'Core and peripheral employees in hotel operations', *Personnel Review*, 18, 1, 9–15.

Guest, D. (1987) 'Human resource management and industrial relations', *Journal of Management Studies*, 24, 5, 503–21.

Guest, D. (1989) 'Human resource management: its implications for industrial relations and trade unions', in J. Storey (ed.) *New Perspectives on Human Resource Management*, London: Routledge.

Guest, D. (1999) 'Human resource management: the workers' verdict', *Human Resource Management Journal*, 9, 2, 5–25.

Guest, D. (2001) 'Human resource management: when research confronts theory', *International Journal of Human Resource Management*, 12, 7, 1092–106.

Guest, D. and Conway, N. (1998) '*Fairness at Work* and the psychological contract', *Issues in People Management*, London: IPD.

Guest, D. and Conway, N. (1999) 'Peering into the black hole: the downside of new employment relations in the UK', *British Journal of Industrial Relations*, 37, 3, 367–89.

Guest, D. and Conway, N. (2002) 'Communicating the psychological contract: an employer perspective', *Human Resource Management Journal*, 12, 2, 22–38.

Guest, D. and Hoque, K. (1996) 'Human resource management and the new industrial relations', in I. J. Beardwell (ed.) *Contemporary Industrial Relations: A Critical Analysis*, Oxford: Oxford University Press.

Guest, D., Conway, N., Briner, R. and Dickman, M. (1996) *The State of the Psychological Contract in Employment*, London: IPD.

Gummesson, E. (1991) 'Marketing orientation revisited: the crucial role of the part-time marketer', *European Journal of Marketing*, 25, 2, 60–75.

Gustafson, C. M. (2002) 'Employee turnover: a study of private clubs in the US', *International Journal of Hospitality Management*, 14, 3, 106–13.

Hakim, C. (1995) 'Five feminist myths about women's employment', *British Journal of Sociology*, 46, 3, 429–55.

Hakim, C. (1997) 'A sociological perspective on part-time work', in H.-P. Blossfeld and C. Hakim (eds) *Between Equalisation and Marginalisation: Women Working Part-time in Europe and the USA*, Oxford: Oxford University Press.

Hales, C. and Kildas, A. (1998) 'Empowerment in five-star hotels: choice, voice or rhetoric?', *International Journal of Contemporary Hospitality Management*, 10, 3, 88–95.

Hales, C., Tamangani, Z., Walker, A. and Murophy, N. (1996) 'Factors influencing adoption of NVQs in small hospitality businesses', *International Journal of Contemporary Hospitality Management*, 8, 5, 5–9.

Halim, H. T. (2001) 'Human resource practices within the service quality philosophy', Ph.D. thesis, Manchester Metropolitan University.

Hall, E. (1993) 'Smiling, deferring and flirting: doing gender by giving "good service"', *Work, Employment and Society*, 20, 4, 452–71.

Hall, L. and Torrington, D. (1998) 'Letting go or holding on: the devolution of operational personnel activities', *Human Resource Management Journal*, 8, 1, 41–55.

Hardy, S. and Adnett, N. (2002) 'The parental leave directive: towards a family-friendly social Europe', *European Journal of Industrial Relations*, 8, 2, 157–72.

Haynes, P. and Fryer, G. (1999) 'Changing patterns of HRM and employment relations in New Zealand: the large hotel industry', *Asia Pacific Journal of Human Resources*, 37, 2, 33–43.

Haynes, P. and Fryer, G. (2000) 'Human resources, service quality and performance: a case study', *International Journal of Contemporary Hospitality Management*, 12, 4, 240–8.

Haynes, P. and Fryer, G. (2001) 'More form than substance? Collective bargaining and employee voice in the Auckland luxury hotel industry', *International Journal of Employment Studies*, 9, 2, 109–29.

Head, J. (1998) 'The impact of individual employment legislation on the employment relationship in the hospitality industry', Ph.D. thesis, Manchester Metropolitan University.

Head, J. and Lucas, R. E. (1998) 'The impact of unfair dismissal rights on the employment relationship in the hospitality industry', *International Journal of Hospitality Management*, 17, 3, 243–51.

Head, J. and Lucas, R. E. (2004a, forthcoming) 'Does individual employment legislation constrain the ability of hospitality employers to "hire and fire"', *International Journal of Hospitality Management*, 23, 2.

Head, J. and Lucas, R. E. (2004b, forthcoming) 'Employee relations in the non-union hotel industry: a case of "determined individualism"?', *Personnel Review*, 33, 6.

Health and Safety Commission (HSC) (2001) *HSC Annual Report and HSC/E Accounts 2000/1*, Sudbury: HSE.

Heery, E. (1993) 'Industrial relations and the customer', *Industrial Relations Journal*, 24, 4, 284–95.

Heery, E. (1997) 'Annual review article 1996', *British Journal of Industrial Relations*, 35, 1, 87–109.

Heery, E. (1998) 'Campaigning for part-time workers', *Work, Employment and Society*, 12, 2, 351–66.

Hendry, C. and Pettigrew, A. (1986), 'The practice of strategic human resource management', *Personnel Review*, 15, 5, 3–8.

Herzberg, F. (1966) *Work and the Nature of Man*, London: Staples Press.

Hewett, J. (2000) 'Staff have their say at Pizza Express', *IPA Bulletin No. 1*, November, 1.

Hinkin, T. R. and Tracey, R. B. (2000) 'The cost of turnover: putting a price on the learning curve', *Cornell Hotel and Restaurant Administration Quarterly*, 41, 3, 14–21.

Hirsch, B. T. and MacPherson, D. A. (1993) 'Union membership and coverage files from the Current Population Survey: note', *Industrial and Labour Relations Review*, 46, 574–8.

Hjalager, A. and Andersen, S. (2000) 'Tourism employment: contingent work or professional career?', *Employee Relations*, 23, 2, 115–29.

Hochschild, A. R. (1983) *The Managed Heart: Commercialisation of Human Feeling*, Berkeley: University of California Press.

Hofstede, G. (1980) *Culture's Consequences: International Differences in Work-related Values*, Beverly Hills, CA: Sage.

Hofstede, G. (1991) *Cultures and Organizations: Software of the Mind*, London: McGraw-Hill.

Hollinshead, G. (1999) 'Management', in G. Hollinshead, P. Nicholls and S. Tailby (eds) *Employee Relations*, London: Financial Times Prentice Hall.

Hollinshead, G. and Leat, M. (1995) *Human Resource Management: An International and Comparative Perspective*, London: Pitman.

Hollinshead, G., Nicholls, P. and Tailby, S. (1999) *Employee Relations*, London: Financial Times Prentice Hall.

Holloway, J. (1985) 'Between gratitude and gratuity: commentary on Shamir', *Annals of Tourism Research*, 12, 2, 239–58.

Hook, C., Rollinson, D. J., Foot, M. and Handley, J. (1996) 'Supervisor and manager styles in handling discipline and grievance, part 1: comparing styles in handling discipline and grievance', *Personnel Review*, 25, 3, 20–34.

Hoque, K. (1999a) 'New approaches to HRM in the UK hotel industry', *Human Resource Management Journal*, 9, 2, 64–76.

Hoque, K. (1999b) 'Human resource management and performance in the UK hotel industry', *British Journal of Industrial Relations*, 37, 3, 419–43.

Hoque, K. (1999c) *Human Resource Management in the Hotel Industry*, London: Routledge.

Hoque, K. (2000) 'HRM in the UK hotel industry: a response', *Human Resource Management Journal*, 10, 4, 91–3.

Hoque, K. and Noon, M. (2001) 'Counting angels: a comparison of personnel and HR specialists', *Human Resource Management Journal*, 11, 3, 5–22.

Hospitality Training Foundation (H*t*F) (1997) *Target the Top*, London: Hospitality Training Foundation.

Hospitality Training Foundation (H*t*F) (1999) *Key Facts and Figures for the Hospitality Industry*, London: Hospitality Training Foundation.

Hospitality Training Foundation (H*t*F) (2000) *Labour Market Review for the Hospitality Industry*, London: Hospitality Training Foundation.

Hospitality Training Foundation (H*t*F) (2001) *Labour Market Review 2001*, London: Hospitality Training Foundation.

Hospitality Training Foundation (H*t*F) (2002) *Labour Market Review 2002*, London: Hospitality Training Foundation.

Hunter, L., McGregor, A., MacInnes, J. and Sproull, A. (1993) 'The "flexible firm": strategy and segmentation', *British Journal of Industrial Relations*, 31, 3, 383–407.

Huselid, M. (1995) 'The impact of human resource management practices on turnover, productivity, and corporate financial performance', *Academy of Management Journal*, 38, 3, 653–72.

Hutchinson, J. C., Murrmann, S. K. and Murrmann, K. F. (1997) 'Planning and implementing an effective downsizing program', *International Journal of Hospitality Management*, 16, 1, 23–38.

Hyams, P. and Fryer, G. (2000) 'Human resources, service quality and performance: a case study', *International Journal of Contemporary Hospitality Management*, 12, 4, 240–8.

Hyman, R. (1989) *The Political Economy of Industrial Relations*, Basingstoke: Macmillan.

Hyman, R. (1997) 'The future of employee representation', *British Journal of Industrial Relations*, 35, 3, 25–56.

Iles, P. (1995) 'Learning to work with difference', *Personnel Review*, 24, 6, 44–60.

Incomes Data Services (IDS) (1998a) 'Sweden: Employment in the hotel and catering sector', *IDS Employment Europe*, 439, July, 21–2.

Incomes Data Services (IDS) (1998b) ' "Atypical" jobs sustain growth in Dutch hotels', *IDS Employment Europe*, 442, October, 18–20.

Incomes Data Services (IDS) (1998c) 'Pay and conditions in the Spanish hospitality sector', *IDS Employment Europe*, 443, November, 18–19.

Incomes Data Services (IDS) (1999) 'New agreements set minima in Italy's hospitality sector', *IDS Employment Europe*, 449, May, 20–1.

Incomes Data Services (IDS) (2001) 'Pay in hotels', *IDS Report* 825, January, 10–15.

Incomes Data Services (IDS) (2002) 'Pay in hotels', *IDS Report* 858, June, 16–21.

Incomes Data Services (IDS) (2003) 'Pay in pubs and restaurants', *IDS Report* 876, March, 16–21.

Ineson, E. M. (1996) 'Selection for vocational courses: a consideration of the viewpoint of graduate employers', *International Journal of Contemporary Hospitality Management*, 8, 6, 10–17.

Ineson, E. M. and Kempa, R. F. (1997) 'Selecting students: is there an education–industry mismatch?', *International Journal of Contemporary Hospitality Management*, 9, 3, 128–41.

International Labour Organization (ILO) (2001) *Human Resources Development, Employment and Globalization in the Hotel, Catering and Tourism Sector*, Report for discussion at the Tripartite Meeting on the Human Resources Development, Employment and Globalization in the Hotel, Catering and Tourism Sector, Geneva: International Labour Organization.

IPA (2001) 'Partnership – mini case studies for Gardner Merchant'. Available on-line at: www.partnership-at-work.co.uk.

Iverson, K. (2000a) 'The paradox of the contented female manager: an empirical investigation of gender differences in pay expectation in the hospitality industry', *International Journal of Hospitality Management*, 19, 1, 33–51.

Iverson, K. (2000b) 'Managing for effective workforce diversity: identifying issues that are of concern for employees', *Cornell Hotel and Restaurant Administration Quarterly*, 41, 2, 31–8.

Iverson, R. D. and Deery, M. (1997) 'Turnover culture in the hospitality industry', *Human Resource Management Journal*, 7, 4, 71–82.

James, P. (1994) 'Worker representation and consultation: the impact of European requirements', *Employee Relations*, 16, 7, 1, 33–42.

James, P. and Walters, D. (1999) *Regulating Health and Safety at Work: the Way Forward*, London: Institute of Employment Rights.

James, P. and Walters, D. (2002) 'Worker representation in health and safety: options for regulatory reform', *Industrial Relations Journal*, 33, 2, 141–56.

James, P., Cunningham, I. and Dibben, P. (2002) 'Absence management and the issues of job retention and return to work', *Human Resource Management Journal*, 12, 2, 82–94.

Jameson, S. (2000) 'Recruitment and training in small firms', *Journal of European Industrial Training*, 24, 1, 43–9.

Johnson, K. and Lucas, R. E. (2002) 'Student employment in services: a UK, Central and Eastern European perspective', *Research and Practice in Human Resource Management Journal*, 10, 1, 53–67.

Jones, C., Nickson, D. and Taylor, G. (1997) 'Whatever it takes? Managing empowered workers and the service encounter in an international hotel chain', *Work, Employment & Society*, 11, 3, 541–54.

Jones, C., Thompson, P. and Nickson, D. (1998) 'Not part of the family? The limits to managing the corporate way in international hotel chains', *International Journal of Human Resource Management*, 9, 6, 1048–63.

Jordan, F. (1997) 'An occupational hazard? Sex segregation in tourism employment', *Tourism Management*, 18, 8, 525–34.

Junor, A. (1998) 'Permanent part-time work: new family-friendly standard or high intensity cheap skills (Precarious Employment)?' *Labor and Industry*, 8, 3, 1–16.

Kaak, S. R., Field, H. S., Giles, W. F. and Norris, D. R. (1998) 'The weighted application blank: a cost-effective tool that can reduce labour turnover', *Cornell Hotel and Restaurant Administration Quarterly*, 39, 2, 18–24.

Kalleberg, A. L. (2001) 'Organising flexibility: the flexible firm in a new century', *British Journal of Industrial Relations*, 39, 4, 479–504.

Kandola, R. and Fullerton, J. (1994) *Managing the Mosaic*, London: IPD.

Keenoy, T. (1997) 'HRMism and the languages of representation', *Journal of Management Studies*, 34, 5, 825–41.

Keenoy, T. (1999) 'HRM as hologram: a polemic', *Journal of Management Studies*, 36, 1, 1–23.

Keep, E. and Mayhew, K. (1999) 'The assessment: knowledge, skills and competitiveness', *Oxford Review of Economic Policy*, 15, 1–15.

Kelliher, C. and Johnson, K. (1997) 'Personnel management in hotels – an update: a move to human resource management?', *Progress in Tourism and Hospitality Research*, 3, 4, 321–31.

Kelliher, C. and Perrett, G. (2001) 'Business strategy and approaches to HRM: a case study of new developments in the United Kingdom restaurant industry', *Personnel Review*, 30, 4, 421–37.

Kelliher, K., Riley, M. and Jones, P. A. (2000) 'Implementing functional flexibility: training for a multi-skilled workforce', Proceedings of the 9th Annual CHME Hospitality Research Conference, 80–92, University of Huddersfield.

Kelly, J. (1997) 'Industrial relations: looking to the future', *British Journal of Industrial Relations*, 35, 3, 393–8.

Kessler, I. and Purcell, J. (1995) 'Individualism and collectivism in theory and practice', in P. Edwards (ed.) *Industrial Relations Theory and Practice in Britain*, Oxford: Blackwell.

Kessler, S. and Bayliss, F. (1998) *Contemporary British Industrial Relations*, 3rd edn, London: Macmillan.

Kirton, G. and Greene, A. (2002) 'The dynamics of positive action in UK trade unions: the case of women and black members', *Industrial Relations Journal*, 33, 2, 157–72.

Kivelä, J. J. and Chu, C. Y. H. (2001) 'Delivering quality service: diagnosing favorable and unfavorable service encounters in restaurants', *Journal of Hospitality and Tourism Research*, 25, 3, 251–71.

Knight, K. G. and Latreille, P. L. (2000) 'Discipline, dismissals and complaints to employment tribunals', *British Journal of Industrial Relations*, 38, 4, 533–55.

Knutson, B. J. and Schmidgall, R. S. (1999) 'Dimensions of the glass ceiling in the hospitality industry', *Cornell Hotel and Restaurant Administration Quarterly*, 40, 6, 64–75.

Kochan, T. and Barocci, T. (1985) *Human Resource Management and Industrial Relations: Text, Readings and Cases*, Boston, MA: Little Brown.

Korczynski, M. (2002) *Human Resource Management in Service Work*, Basingstoke: Macmillan.

Korshak, S. R. (2000) 'The labor–management partnership: San Francisco's hotels and the employees' union try a new approach', *Cornell Hotel and Restaurant Administration Quarterly*, 41, 2, 14–29.

Krakover, S. (2000) 'Partitioning seasonal employment in the hospitality industry', *Tourism Management*, 21, 5, 461–71.

Kreismann, R. and Palmer, R. (2001) 'Reasonable accommodation under the ADA: what's an employer to do?', *Cornell Hotel and Restaurant Administration Quarterly*, 42, 5, 24–33.

La Lopa, J. M. (1997) 'Commitment and turnover in resort jobs', *Journal of Hospitality and Tourism Research*, 21, 2, 11–26.

Lam, T., Zhang, H. and Baum, T. (2001a) 'An investigation of employees' job satisfaction: the case of hotels in Hong Kong', *Tourism Management*, 22, 2, 157–65.

Lam, T., Baum, T. and Pine, R. (2001b) 'Study of managerial job satisfaction in Hong Kong's Chinese restaurants', *International Journal of Contemporary Hospitality Management*, 13, 1, 35–42.

Lam, T., Lo, A. and Chan, J. (2002) 'New employees' turnover intentions and organizational commitment in the Hong Kong hotel industry', *Journal of Hospitality and Tourism Research*, 26, 3, 217–34.

Lammont, N. and Lucas, R. E. (1997) 'Context-dependent skills in service work: deployment of tacit skills by young people in the hospitality, leisure and retail industries'. Paper presented at the British Sociological Association Annual Conference, York, April.

Lammont, N. and Lucas, R. E. (1999) ' "Getting by" and "getting on" in service work: lessons for the future of accounting?', *Critical Perspectives on Accounting*, 10, 4, 809–30.

Lashley, C. (1995a) 'Towards an understanding of employee empowerment in hospitality services', *International Journal of Contemporary Hospitality Management*, 7, 1, 27–32.

Lashley, C. (1995b) 'Empowerment through delayering: a pilot study at McDonald's restaurants', *International Journal of Contemporary Hospitality Management*, 7, 2, 29–35.

Lashley, C. (1996) 'Research issues for employee empowerment in hospitality organisations', *International Journal of Hospitality Management*, 15, 4, 333–46.

Lashley, C. (1997) *Empowering Service Excellence: Beyond the Quick Fix*, London: Cassell.

Lashley, C. (1998) 'Matching the management of human resources to service operations', *International Journal of Contemporary Hospitality Management*, 10, 1, 24–33.

Lashley, C. (1999) 'Employee empowerment in services: a framework for analysis', *Personnel Review*, 28, 3, 169–91.

Lashley, C. and Best, W. (2002) 'Employee induction in licensed retail organisations', *International Journal of Contemporary Hospitality Management*, 14, 1, 6–13.

Lashley, C. and Taylor, S. (1998) 'Hospitality retail operations types and styles in the management of human resources', *Journal of Retailing and Consumer Services*, 5, 3, 153–65.

Lashley, C. and Watson, S. (1999) 'Researching human resource management in the hospitality industry', *International Journal of Tourism and Hospitality Research*, 1, 1, 19–40.

Law, J., Pearce, P. L. and Woods, B. A. (1995) 'Stress and coping in tourist attraction employees', *Tourism Management*, 16, 4, 277–84.

Law, R. (2000) 'Breast-feeding in public: should this be allowed in hotels?', *International Journal of Hospitality Management*, 19, 1, 89–92.

Leat, M. (1999) 'The European Union', in G. Hollinshead, P. Nicholls and S. Tailby (eds) *Employee Relations*, London: Financial Times Prentice Hall.

Leat, M. (2001) *Exploring Employee Relations*, London: Butterworth-Heinemann.

Leat, M. and Woolley, J. (1999) 'Multinationals and employee relations', in G. Hollinshead, P. Nicholls and S. Tailby (eds) *Employee Relations*, London: Financial Times Prentice Hall.

Lee, C. and Chon, K. (2000) 'An investigation of multicultural training practices in the restaurant industry: the training cycle approach', *International Journal of Contemporary Hospitality Management*, 12, 2, 126–34.

Lee, C. and Kang, S. (1998) 'Measuring earnings inequality and median earnings in the tourism industry', *Tourism Management*, 19, 4, 341–48.

Lee-Ross, D. (1999) 'Seasonal hotel jobs: an occupational and a way of life', *International Journal of Tourism Research*, 1, 4, 239–53.

Legge, K. (1995a) *Human Resource Management: The Rhetorics, The Realities*, Basingstoke: Macmillan.

Legge, K. (1995b) 'HRM: rhetoric, reality and hidden agendas', in J. Storey (ed.) *Human Resource Management: A Critical Text*, London: Routledge.

Leidner, R. (1993) *Fast Food Fast Talk: Service Work and the Routinization of Everyday Life*, Berkeley: University of California Press.

Leighton, P. and Painter, R. W. (2001) 'Casual workers: still marginal after all these years?', *Employee Relations*, 23, 1, 75–93.

Levitt, T. (1972) 'Production-line approach to service', *Harvard Business Review*, Sept/October, 50, 5, 41–50.

Lewin, D. and Peterson, R. B. (1999) 'Behavioural outcomes of grievance activity', *Industrial Relations*, 38, 4, 554–76.

Lewis, P. (2000) 'Pregnancy and maternity leave: employment law as a family friend?', *Industrial Relations Journal*, 31, 2, 130–43.

Liff, S. and Wajcman, J. (1996) ' "Sameness" and "difference" revisited: which way forward for equal opportunity initiatives?', *Journal of Management Studies*, 33, 1, 79–94.

Loretto, W., Duncan, C. and White, P. J. (2000) 'Industrial relations codes of practice: the 1999 Age Discrimination Code in context', *Employee Relations*, 22, 2, 146–63.

Low Pay Commission (LPC) (1998) *The National Minimum Wage: First Report of the Low Pay Commission*, Cm 3976, London: The Stationery Office.

Low Pay Commission (LPC) (2000) *The Story So Far: Second Report of the Low Pay Commission*, Cm 4571, London: The Stationery Office.

Low Pay Commission (LPC) (2001a) *Making a Difference: Third Report (Volume One) of the Low Pay Commission*, Cm 5075, London: The Stationery Office.

Low Pay Commission (LPC) (2001b) *Making a Difference: The Next Steps. Third Report (Volume Two) of the Low Pay Commission*, Cm 5175, London: The Stationery Office.

Low Pay Commission (LPC) (2002) *The National Minimum Wage Annual Report 2001/2002*. Available on-line at: http://www.dti.gov.uk/er/nmw.

Low Pay Commission (LPC) (2003) *The National Minimum Wage: Fourth Report of the Low Pay Commission, Building on Success*, London: The Stationery Office. Available on-line at: http://www.dti.gov.uk/er/nmw.

Lowe, G. and Rastin, S. (2000) 'Organizing the next generation: influences on young workers' willingness to join unions in Canada', *British Journal of Industrial Relations*, 38, 2, 203–22.

Lowery, C. M. and Beadles, N. A. II (1996) 'Predictors of union election outcomes and union support in the hospitality industry', *International Journal of Hospitality Management*, 15, 3, 255–67.

Lucas, R. E. (1986) 'British wages councils: a critique of developments 1959–1983', unpublished thesis, 2 volumes, University of Manchester, 1–960.

Lucas, R. E. (1989) 'Minimum wages: strait-jacket or framework for the hospitality industry into the 1990s?', *International Journal of Hospitality Management*, 8, 3, 197–214.

Lucas, R. E. (1995a) *Managing Employee Relations in the Hotel and Catering Industry*, London: Cassell.

Lucas, R. E. (1995b) 'Some age-related issues in hotel and catering employment', *The Service Industries Journal*, 15, 2, 234–50.

Lucas, R. E (1996a) 'Industrial relations in hotels and catering: neglect and paradox', *British Journal of Industrial Relations*, 34, 2, 267–86.

Lucas, R. E. (1996b) 'Social policy', in R. Thomas (ed.) *The Hospitality Industry, Tourism and Europe: Perspectives on Policies*, London: Cassell, 135–52.

Lucas, R. E. (1997a) 'Youth, gender and part-time work: students in the labour process', *Work, Employment and Society*, 11, 4, 595–614.

Lucas, R. E. (1997b) 'Maximising labour flexibility through the employment of part-time student labour', in M. Foley, J. Lennon and G. Maxwell (eds) *Strategy and Culture: Current Themes in Hospitality, Tourism and Leisure*, London: Cassell, 99–113.

Lucas, R. E (1998) 'Developments in resolving individual disputes', *Employee Relations Review*, 7, 9–15.

Lucas, R. E. (2001) 'Small voice or no voice: workers in a non-union sector and the state of industrial relations'. Paper presented to the BUIRA Annual Conference, Manchester Metropolitan University, July.

Lucas, R. E. (2002a) 'Fragments of HRM in hospitality? Evidence from the 1998 Workplace Employee Relations Survey', *International Journal of Contemporary Hospitality Management*, 14, 5, 207–12.

Lucas, R. E. (2002b) 'Illuminating the darker side of employment relations in the service sector', *Employee Relations Review*, 20, 18–25.

Lucas, R. E. and Johnson, K. (2003) 'Managing students as a flexible labour resource in hospitality and tourism in Central and Eastern Europe and the UK', in S. Kusluvan (ed.) *Managing Employee Attitudes and Behaviours in the Tourism Industry*, New York: Nova Science.

Lucas, R. E. and Lammont, N. (1998) 'Combining work and study: an empirical study of full-time students in school, college and university', *Journal of Education and Work*, 11, 1, 41–56.

Lucas, R. E. and Lammont, N. (2003) 'A triadic employment relationship: service work and the influence of customers', *Review of Employment Topics*, 6, 1, 55–89.

Lucas, R. E. and Langlois, S. M. (2000a) *Planning for the National Minimum Wage: Case Study Evidence from Firms in the Hospitality and Clothing Industries*. Report for the Low Pay Commission, Manchester: CHER, Manchester Metropolitan University, June.

Lucas, R. E. and Langlois, S. M. (2000b) *The National Minimum Wage and the Employment of Young People, Parts 1 and 2*. Report for the Low Pay Commission, Manchester: CHER, Manchester Metropolitan University, December.

Lucas, R. E. and Langlois, S. M. (2001) *The National Minimum Wage: What Can Young Workers Tell Us?* Report for the Low Pay Commission, Manchester: CHER, Manchester Metropolitan University, August.

Lucas, R. E. and Langlois, S. M. (2003) 'Anticipating and adjusting to the National Minimum Wage in the hospitality and clothing industries', *Policy Studies*, 24, 1, 33–50.

Lucas, R. E. and Laycock, J. (1991) 'An interactive personnel function for managing budget hotels', *International Journal of Contemporary Hospitality Management*, 3, 3, 33–6.

Lucas, R. E. and Radiven, N. A. (1998) 'After wages councils: minimum pay and practice', *Human Resource Management Journal*, 8, 4, 5–19.

Lucas, R. E. and Ralston, L. M. (1996) 'Part-time student labour in the hospitality industry: strategic choice or pragmatic response?', *International Journal of Contemporary Hospitality Management*, 8, 2, 21–4.

Lucas, R. E. and Ralston, L. M. (1997) 'Youth, gender and part-time employment: a preliminary appraisal of student employment', *Employee Relations*, 19, 1, 51–66.

Lucas, R. E. and Rowson, B. (2002) 'The Minimum Wage low road', *Hospitality Review*, 4, 3, 31–6.

Lucas, R. E., Johnson, K. and Marinova, M. (2003) *Student Employment in Central and Eastern Europe: Some Lessons in the Hospitality and Tourism Industries in Bulgaria, Hungary and Slovakia*, Manchester: International Centre for Research and Consultancy, Manchester Metropolitan University.

Lucas, R. E., Marinova, M., Kucerova, J. and Vetrokova, M. (forthcoming) 'HRM practice in emerging economies: a long way to go in the Slovak hotel industry?', *International Journal of Human Resource Management*.

Lynn, M. (1997) 'Tipping customs and status seeking: a cross-country study', *International Journal of Hospitality Management*, 16, 2, 221–4.

Lynn, M. (2000) 'National character and tipping customs: the needs for achievement, affiliation and power as predictors of the prevalence of tipping', *International Journal of Hospitality Management*, 19, 2, 205–10.

Lynn, M. (2001) 'Restaurant tipping and service quality: a tenuous relationship', *Cornell Hotel and Restaurant Administration Quarterly*, 42, 1, 14–20.

Lynn, M. and Gregor, R. (2001) 'Tipping and service: the case of hotel bellmen', *International Journal of Hospitality Management*, 20, 3, 299–303.

Mabey, C., Skinner, D. and Clark, T. (1998) *Experiencing Human Resource Management*, London: Sage.

Macaulay, I. R. and Wood, R. C. (1992) 'Hotel and catering employees' attitudes towards trade unions', *Employee Relations*, 14, 3, 20–8.

McCarty, J., Shrum, L., Conrad-Katz, T. and Kanne, T. (1990) 'Tipping as consumer behaviour: a qualitative investigation', in M. Goldberg (ed.) *Advances in Consumer Research*, Vol. 17, Association for Consumer Research, 723–8.

McGregor, D. (1960) *The Human Side of Enterprise*, New York: McGraw-Hill.

McGunnigle, P. and Jameson, S. (2000) 'HRM in UK hotels: a focus on commitment', *Employee Relations*, 22, 4, 403–22.

MacHatton, M. T., Van Dyke, T. and Steiner, R. (1997) 'Selection and retention of managers in the US restaurant sector', *International Journal of Contemporary Hospitality Management*, 9, 4, 155–60.

McIvor, G. (1997) 'Strikes force out guests at Norway hotels', *Financial Times*, 18 April.

McLean Parks, J., Kidder, D. L. and Gallagher, D. G. (1998) 'Fitting square pegs into round holes: mapping the domain of contingent work arrangements onto the psychological contract', *Journal of Organisational Behaviour*, 19, 697–730.

McMahon, L. (2000) 'Bullying and harassment in the workplace', *International Journal of Contemporary Hospitality Management*, 12, 6, 384–7.

McNabb, R. and Whitfield, K. (2000) ' "Worth so appallingly little": a workplace-level analysis of low pay', *British Journal of Industrial Relations*, 38, 4, 585–609.

Mallinson, H. and Weiler, B. (2000) 'Cross-cultural awareness of hospitality staff: an evaluation of a pilot training program', *Australian Journal of Hospitality Management*, 7, 1, 35–44.

Marchington, M. (1992) 'Managing labour relations in a competitive environment', in A. Sturdy, D. Knights and H. Willmott (eds) *Skill and Consent: Contemporary Studies in the Labour Process*, London: Routledge.

Marchington, M. and Grugulis, I. (2000) ' "Best practice" human resource management: perfect opportunity or dangerous illusion?', *International Journal of Human Resource Management*, 11, 4, 905–20.

Marchington, M. and Parker, P. (1990) *Changing Patterns of Employee Relations*, Hemel Hempstead: Harvester Wheatsheaf.

Marchington, M. and Wilkinson, A. (1999) 'Direct participation', in S. Bach and K. Sisson (eds) *Personnel Management: A Comprehensive Guide to Theory and Practice*, 3rd edn, Oxford: Blackwell.

Marginson, P., Armstrong, P., Edwards, P. and Purcell, J. with Hubbard, N. (1993) *The Control of Industrial Relations in Large Companies: An Initial Analysis of the Second Company Level Industrial Relations Survey*, Warwick Papers on Industrial Relations No. 45, Coventry: IRRU.

Mars, G. and Mitchell, P. (1976) *Room for Reform?*, Milton Keynes: Open University Press.

Mars, G. and Nicod, M. (1984) *The World of Waiters*, London: Allen and Unwin.

Mars, M., Bryant, D. and Mitchell, P. (1979) *Manpower Problems in the Hotel and Catering Industry*, Farnborough, Gower.

Marshall, G. (1986) 'The workplace culture of a restaurant', *Theory, Culture and Society*, 3, 1, 33–47.

Mattson, J. and den Haring, M. J. (1998) 'Communication dynamics in the service encounter: a linguistic study in a hotel conference department', *International Journal of Service Industry Management*, 9, 5, 416–35.

Maxwell, G. A. (1997) 'Hotel general management: views from above the glass ceiling', *International Journal of Contemporary Hospitality Management*, 9, 5/6, 230–5.

Maxwell, G. A., Blair, S. and McDougall, M. (2001) 'Edging towards managing diversity in practice', *Employee Relations*, 23, 5, 468–82.

Mayer, K. J. (2002) 'Human resource practices and service quality in theme parks', *International Journal of Contemporary Hospitality Management*, 14, 4, 169–75.

Meager, N., Tyers, C., Perryman, S., Rick, J. and Willison, R. (2002) *Awareness, Knowledge and Exercise of Individual Employment Rights*, Employment Relations Research Series 15, Brighton: Institute for Employment Studies.

Milkman, R. (1998) 'The new American workplace: high road or low road?', in P. Thompson and C. Warhurst (eds) *Workplaces of the Future*, Basingstoke: Macmillan.

Millett, B. (2002) 'Performance management in international hospitality and tourism', in N. D'Annunzio-Green, G. A. Maxwell and S. Watson (eds) *Human Resource Management: International Perspectives in Hospitality and Tourism*, London: Continuum.

Millward, N., Stevens, M., Smart, D. and Hawes, W. R. (1992) *Workplace Industrial Relations in Transition*, Aldershot: Dartmouth.

Millward, N., Bryson, A. and Forth, J. (2000) *All Change at Work?*, London: Routledge.

Mok, C. and Luk, Y. (1995) 'Exit interviews in hotels: making them a more powerful management tool', *International Journal of Hospitality Management*, 14, 2, 187–94.

Monaghan, K. (2000) *Challenging Race Discrimination at Work*, London: Institute of Employment Rights.

Morris, J. A. and Feldman, D. C. (1996) 'The dimensions, antecedents and consequences of emotional labour', *Academy of Management Review*, 21, 4, 986–1010.

Mumford, E. (1995) 'Contracts, complexity and contradictions: the changing employment relationship', *Personnel Review*, 24, 8, 54–70.

Munro, A. (2001) 'A feminist trade union agenda? The continued significance of class, gender and race', *Gender, Work and Organisation*, 8, 4, 454–71.

Murrmann, S. K. and Murrmann, K. F. (1997) 'Characteristics and outcomes of grievance arbitration decisions in hospitality firms', *International Journal of Hospitality Management*, 16, 4, 361–74.

Mutch, A. (2002) 'A managerial trade union and changes in the hospitality industry: the National Association of Licensed House Managers, 1970–1997'. Paper presented to the 20th Annual International Labour Process, University of Strathclyde, April.

Nankervis, A. R. and Debrah, Y. (1995) 'Human resource management in hotels', *Tourism Management*, 16, 7, 507–13.

National Statistics (2001) *Labour Force Survey Quarterly Supplement, No. 15, Summer*, London: the Stationery Office.

National Statistics (2002) *Labour Force Survey Quarterly Supplement, No. 18, Spring*, London: the Stationery Office.

Nicholls, P. (1999) 'The context and theory in employee relations', in G. Hollinshead, P. Nicholls and S. Tailby (eds) *Employee Relations*, London: Financial Times Prentice Hall.

Nickson, D. (1997) 'Continuity or change in the international hotel industry', in M. Foley, J. Lennon and G. Maxwell (eds) *Hospitality, Tourism and Leisure Management Issues in Strategy and Culture*, London: Cassell.

Nickson, D. and Wood, R. C. (2000) 'HRM in the UK hotel industry: a comment', *Human Resource Management Journal*, 10, 4, 88–90.

Nickson, D., Baum, T., Losekoot, E., Morrison, A. and Frochot, I. (2002) *Skills, Organizational Performance and Economic Activity in the Hospitality Industry: A Literature Review*, Warwick: University of Warwick, SKOPE.

Offe, C. (1985) *Disorganised Capitalism: Later Transformations of Work and Politics*, Cambridge: Polity Press.

Office for National Statistics (ONS) (1996) *The Annual Employment Survey*, London: Stationery Office.

Office for National Statistics (ONS) (1998a) *Labour Force Survey Quarterly Supplement No. 3, Summer*, London: Stationery Office.

Office for National Statistics (ONS) (1998b) *New Earnings Survey, Parts A and F*, London: Stationery Office.

Office for National Statistics (ONS) (2002) *New Earnings Survey, Parts A and F*, London: Stationery Office.

Osterman, P. (1999) *Securing Prosperity*, Princeton: Princeton University Press.

Oxenbridge, S. (2000) 'Trade union organising among low-wage service workers: lessons from America and New Zealand', Research Working Paper No. 160, University of Cambridge, ESRC Centre for Business.

Paraskevas, A. J. (2000) 'Management selection practices in Greece: are hospitality recruiters any different?', *International Journal of Hospitality Management*, 19, 3, 241–59.

Paraskevas, A. (2001) 'Internal service encounters in hotels: an empirical study', *International Journal of Contemporary Hospitality Management*, 13, 6, 285–92.

Partlow, C. G. (1996) 'Human-resources practices in TQM hotels', *Cornell Hotel and Restaurant Administration Quarterly*, 37, 5, 67–77.

Patterson, M. G., West, M. A., Lawthom, R. and Nickell, S. (1998) *Impact of People Management Practices on Business Performance*, Issues in People Management No. 22, London: IPD.

Paxson, M. C. (1995) 'State parental leave law compliance in the United States: an industry comparison', *International Journal of Hospitality Management*, 14, 2, 157–69.

Peccei, R. and Rosenthal, P. (1997) 'The antecedents of employee commitment to customer service: evidence from a UK service context', *International Journal of Human Resource Management*, 8, 1, 66–86.

Pfeffer, J. (1994) *Competitive Advantage Through People*, Boston: Harvard Business School Press.

Pfeffer, J. (1998) *The Human Equation: Building Profits By Putting People First*, Boston: Harvard Business School Press.

Phillips, A. and Taylor, B. (1980) 'Sex and Skill', *Feminist Review*, 6, 7, 13–21.

Pigors, P. and Myers, C. S. (1977) *Personnel Administration*, 8th edn, Maidenhead: McGraw-Hill.

Piso, A. (1999) 'Hotel and catering workers: class and unionisation', *Employee Relations*, 21, 2, 176–88.

Pizam, A. and Thornburg, S. W. (2000) 'Absenteeism and voluntary turnover in Central Florida hotels: a pilot study', *International Journal of Hospitality Management*, 19, 2, 211–17.

Pizam, A., Uriely, N. and Reichel, A. (2000) 'The intensity of the tourist–host social relationship and its effects on satisfaction and change of attitudes: the case of working tourists in Israel', *Tourism Management*, 21, 4, 395–406.

Polanyi, M. (1967) *The Tacit Dimension*, New York: Doubleday.

Pollack, J. D. (2001) 'Exemption under the Fair Labor Standards Act: the cost of mis-classifying employees', *Cornell Hotel and Restaurant Administration Quarterly*, 42, 5, 16–23.

Pollert, A. (1991) *Farewell to Flexibility?*, Oxford: Blackwell.

Pollert, A. (1999) Trade unionism in transition in Central and Eastern Europe', *European Journal of Industrial Relations*, 5, 2, 209–34.

Powell, S. and Wood, D. (1999) 'Is recruitment the millennium time bomb for the industry worldwide?', *International Journal of Contemporary Hospitality Management*, 11, 4, 138–41.

Pratten, J. D. and Curtis, S. (2002) 'Attitudes towards training in UK licensed retail', *International Journal of Hospitality Management*, 21, 4, 393–403.

Price, L. (1994) 'Poor personnel practice in the hotel and catering industry: does it matter?', *Human Resource Management Journal*, 4, 4, 44–62.

Pugh, D. and Hickson, D. (1996) *Writers on Organizations*, 5th edn, Penguin: Harmondsworth.

Purcell, J. (1999) 'Best practice and best fit: chimera or cul-de-sac?', *Human Resource Management Journal*, 9, 3, 26–41.

Purcell, J. and Ahlstrand, B. (1989) 'Corporate strategy and the management of employee relations in the multi-divisional company', *British Journal of Industrial Relations*, 27, 3, 396–417.

Purcell, J. and Sisson, K. (1983) 'Strategies and practice in the management of industrial relations', in G. Bain (ed.) *Industrial Relations in Britain*, Oxford: Blackwell.

Purcell, K. (1996) 'The relationship between career and job opportunities: women's employment in the hospitality industry as a microcosm of women's employment', *Women in Management Review*, 11, 5, 17–24.

Purcell, K. and Purcell, J. (1998) 'In-sourcing, outsourcing and the growth of contingent labour as evidence of flexible employment strategies', *European Journal of Work and Organizational Psychology*, 7, 1, 39–60.

Purcell, K. and Quinn, J. (1996) 'Exploring the education–employment equation in hospitality management: a comparison of graduates and HNDs', *International Journal of Hospitality Management*, 15, 1, 51–68.

Purcell, K., McKnight, A. and Simm, C. (1999) *The Lower Earnings Limit in Practice: Part-time Employment in Hotels and Catering*, Manchester: EOC.

Qu, H. and Yee Cheng, S. (1996) 'Attitudes towards utilizing older workers in the Hong Kong hotel industry', *International Journal of Hospitality Management*, 15, 3, 245–54.

Radiven, N. A. and Lucas, R. E. (1996) 'Wages council abolition and small hotels', *International Journal of Contemporary Hospitality Management*, 8, 5, 10–14.

Radiven, N. A. and Lucas, R. E. (1997a) 'Minimum wages and pay policy in the British hospitality industry: past impact and future implications', *Progress in Tourism and Hospitality Research*, 3, 2, 149–63.

Radiven, N. A. and Lucas, R. E. (1997b) 'Minimum wages: past, present and future issues with particular reference to British hotels', *International Journal of Hospitality Management*, 16, 4, 345–59.

Radiven, N. A. and Lucas, R. E. (2001) 'Abolition of wages councils: pay policy in hospitality', in A. Roper and Y. Guerrier (eds) *A Decade of Hospitality Management Research*, Newbury: Threshold Press.

Raghuram, S., London, M. and Larsen, H. H. (2001) 'Flexible employment practices in Europe: country versus culture', *International Journal of Human Resource Management*, 12, 5, 738–53.

Rainnie, A. (1989) *Industrial Relations in Small Firms*, London: Routledge.

Redman, T. and Mathews, B. P. (1998) 'Service quality and human resource management', *Personnel Review*, 27, 3, 57–77.

Rees, C. (1995) 'Quality management and HRM in the service industry: some case study evidence', *Employee Relations*, 17, 3, 99–109.

Rees, C. (1999) 'Teamworking and service quality: the limits of employee involvement', *Personnel Review*, 28, 5/6, 455–73.

Reiter, E. (1996) *Making Fast Food*, 2nd edn, Montreal and Kingston: McGill-Queen's University Press.

Reiter, E. (2002) 'Fast-food in Canada: working conditions, labour law and unionization', in T. Royle and B. Towers (eds) *Labour Relations in the Global Fast-food Industry*, London: Routledge.

Riley, M. (1985) 'Some social and historical perspectives on unionisation in the UK hotel industry', *International Journal of Hospitality Management*, 4, 3, 99–104.

Riley, M. (1992) 'Functional flexibility in hotels: is it feasible?', *Tourism Management*, 13, 4, 363–7.

Riley, M. and Lockwood, A. (1997) 'Strategies and measurement for workforce flexibility: an application of functional flexibility in a service setting', *International Journal of Operations and Production Management*, 17, 4, 413–19.

Riley, M., Lockwood, A., Powell-Perry, J. and Baker, M. (1998) 'Job satisfaction, organisation commitment and occupational culture: a case from the UK pub industry', *Progress in Tourism and Hospitality Research*, 4, 2, 159–68.

Riley, M., Gore, J. and Kelliher, C. (2000) 'Economic determinism and human resource management practice in the hospitality and tourism industry', *Tourism and Hospitality Research*, 2, 2, 118–28.

Ritzer, G. (1996) *The McDonaldization of Society: An Investigation into the Changing Characteristics of Contemporary Social Life*, Newbury Park, CA: Pine Forge Press.

Ritzer, G. (1998) *The McDonaldization Thesis: Exploration and Extensions*, London: Pine Forge Press.

Robson, P., Dex, S., Wilkinson, F. and Cortes, O. S. (1999) 'Low pay, labour market institutions, gender and part-time work: cross-national comparisons', *European Journal of Industrial Relations*, 5, 2, 187–208.

Rollinson, D., Hook, C., Foot, M. and Handley, J. (1996) 'Supervisor and manager styles in handling discipline and grievance, part 2: approaches to handling discipline and grievance', *Personnel Review*, 25, 4, 38–55.

Rollinson, D., Handley, J., Hook, C. and Foot, M. (1997) 'The disciplinary experience and its effect on behaviour', *Work, Employment and Society*, 11, 2, 283–312.

Rose, E. (2001) *Employment Relations*, London: Financial Times Prentice Hall.

Ross, G. F. (1995) 'Work stress and personality measures among hospitality industry employees', *International Journal of Contemporary Hospitality Management*, 7, 6, 9–13.

Ross, G. F. (1997) 'Travel agency employment perceptions', *Tourism Management*, 18, 1, 9–18.

Rousseau, D. M. (1990) 'New hire perceptions of their own and their employer's obligations: a study of psychological contracts', *Journal of Organizational Behaviour*, 11, 389–400.

Rousseau, D. M. (1995) *Psychological Contracts in Organizations: Understanding Written and Unwritten Agreements*, London: Sage.

Rowley, G. and Purcell, K. (2001) ' "As cooks go, she went": is labour churn inevitable?', *International Journal of Hospitality Management*, 20, 2, 163–85.

Rowson, B. (2002) 'Minimum wage, minimal effect: the impact of the NMW on small regional hotels', *Journal of Hospitality and Tourism Management*, 9, 2, 198–202.

Royle, T. (1995) 'Corporate versus societal culture: a comparative study of McDonald's in Europe', *International Journal of Contemporary Hospitality Management*, 7, 2, 52–6.

Royle, T. (1999a) 'The reluctant bargainers? McDonald's, unions and pay determination in Germany and the UK', *Industrial Relations Journal*, 30, 2, 135–50.

Royle, T. (1999b) 'Where's the beef? McDonald's and its European works council', *European Journal of Industrial Relations*, 5, 3, 327–47.

Royle, T. (1999c) 'Recruiting the acquiescent workforce: a comparative analysis of McDonald's in Germany and the UK', *Employee Relations*, 21, 6, 540–55.

Royle, T. (2000) *Working for McDonald's in Europe: The Unequal Struggle?*, London: Routledge.

Royle, T. (2002) 'Multinational corporations, employers' associations and trade union exclusion strategies in the German fast-food industry', *Employee Relations*, 24, 4, 437–60.

Royle, T. and Towers, B. (eds) (2002) *Labour Relations in the Global Fast-food Industry'*, London: Routledge.

Rubery, J. (1989) 'Precarious forms of work in the United Kingdom', in G. Rodgers and J. Rodgers (eds) *Precarious Jobs in Labour Market Regulation: The Growth of Atypical Employment in Western Europe*, Brussels: International Institute for Labour Studies, Free University of Brussels.

Rubery, J. (1995) 'Performance-related pay and the prospects for gender pay equity', *Journal of Management Studies*, 32, 5, 637–54.

Rubery, J. and Fagan, C. (1993) 'Occupational segregation of women and men in the European community', supplement to *Social Europe*, 3/93, 95–105.

Rutherford, S. (2001) 'Any difference? An analysis of gender and divisional management styles in a large airline', *Gender, Work and Organization*, 8, 3, 326–45.

Ryan, R. (1996) *Employment Relations in Hotels, Cafés and Restaurants: Summary Survey Results*, Wellington, NZ: Industrial Relations Centre.

Salamon, M. (1999) 'The state in employee relations', in G. Hollinshead, P. Nicholls and S. Tailby (eds) *Employee Relations*, London: Financial Times Prentice Hall.

Salamon, M. (2000) *Industrial Relations Theory and Practice*, 4th edn, London: Financial Times Prentice Hall.

Salipante, P. F. and Bouwen, R. (1990) 'Behavioural analysis of grievances: conflict, sources, complexity and transformation', *Employee Relations*, 12, 3, 17–22.

Sandiford, P. J. and Seymour, D. (2002) 'Emotional labor in public houses: reflections on a pilot study', *Journal of Hospitality and Tourism Research*, 26, 1, 54–70.

Sargeant, M. (1999) *Age Discrimination in Employment*, London: Institute for Employment Rights.

Sargeant, M. (2001) 'Employee consultation', *Employee Relations*, 23, 5, 483–97.

Scase, R. (1995) 'Employment relations in small firms', in P. Edwards (ed.) *Industrial Relations Theory and Practice in Britain*, Oxford: Blackwell.

Schein, E. H. (1978) *Career Dynamics: Matching Individual and Organisational Needs*, Reading, MA: Addison-Wesley.

Schuler, R. S. and Jackson, S. E. (1987) 'Linking competitive strategies with human resource management practices', *Academy of Management Executive*, 1, 3, 207–19.

Sehkaran, S. N. and Lucas, R. E. (2001) *The National Minimum Wage and Young Workers: A Comparison Between Urban and Rural Areas*, Report for the Low Pay Commission, Manchester, CHER, Manchester Metropolitan University, August.

Sehkaran, S. N. and Lucas, R. E. (2002) 'Hospitality to hostility: dealing with a low response rate in postal surveys'. Paper presented at 11th Annual CHME Research Conference, Leeds Metropolitan University, April.

Sehkaran, S. N. and Lucas, R. E. (2003) 'Equality of wages between young and older workers?' Paper presented at the Performance and Review Conference, Manchester Metropolitan University, April.

Seymour, D. (2000) 'Emotional labour: a comparison between fast food and traditional service work', *International Journal of Hospitality Management*, 19, 2, 159–71.

Shamir, B. (1984) 'Between gratitude and gratuity: an analysis of tipping', *Annals of Tourism Research*, 11, 1, 59–78.

Shaw, M. and Patterson, J. (1995) 'Management-development programs: a Canadian perspective', *Cornell Hotel and Restaurant Administration Quarterly*, 36, 1, 34–9.

Sherry, J. E. H. (1995) 'Employers' liability for GM's sexual harassment: a recurring work-place problem', *Cornell Hotel and Restaurant Administration Quarterly*, 36, 4, 16–17.

Sherwyn, D. (2003) 'Arbitration of employment discrimination law suits: actions that make a difference', *Cornell Hotel and Restaurant Administration Quarterly*, 43, 6, 62–72.

Sherwyn, D. S. and Sturman, M. C. (1997) 'Job sharing: a potential tool for hotel managers', *Cornell Hotel and Restaurant Administration Quarterly*, 43, 5, 84–91.

Sherwyn, D. S. and Sturman, M. C. (2002) 'Job sharing: a potential tool for managers', *Cornell Hotel and Restaurant Administration Quarterly*, 43, 5, 84–91.

Sherwyn, D. S. and Tracey, J. B. (1997) 'Mandatory arbitration of employment disputes: implications for policy and practice', *Cornell Hotel and Restaurant Administration Quarterly*, 38, 5, 58–66.

Sherwyn, D. S. and Tracey, J. B. (1998) 'Sexual-harassment liability in 1998: good news or bad news for employers and employees?', *Cornell Hotel and Restaurant Administration Quarterly*, 39, 5, 14–21.

Sherwyn, D. S., Lankau, M. J. and Eigen, Z. (1999) 'The good, the bad and the ugly: the peculiar discrimination case of Joe's Stone Crabs', *Cornell Hotel and Restaurant Administration Quarterly*, 40, 5, 10–17.

Simms, M., Heery, E., Delbridge, R., Salmon, J. and Simpson, D. (2000) 'Organising women'. Paper presented to the 50th BUIRA Annual Conference, Warwick, 7–9 July.

Simons, T. (1995) 'Interviewing job applicants: how to get beyond first impressions', *Cornell Hotel and Restaurant Administration Quarterly*, 36, 6, 21–7.

Simons, T. and Enz, C. A. (1995) 'Motivating hotel employees: beyond the carrot and stick', *Cornell Hotel and Restaurant Administration Quarterly*, 36, 1, 20–7.

Simons, T. and Hinkin, T. (2001) 'The effect of employee turnover on hotel profits: a test of multiple hotels', *Cornell Hotel and Restaurant Administration Quarterly*, 42, 4, 65–9.

Sinclair, D. (1995) 'The importance of sex for the propensity to unionize', *British Journal of Industrial Relations*, 33, 2, 173–90.

Sinclair, M. T. (1997) *Gender, Work and Tourism*, London: Routledge.

Singh, S. (1997) 'Developing human resources for the tourism industry with reference to India', *Tourism Management*, 18, 5, 299–306.

Sisson, K. (1993) 'In search of HRM', *British Journal of Industrial Relations*, 31, 2, 201–10.

Sisson, K. and Storey, J. (2000) *The Realities of Human Resource Management: Managing the Employment Relationship*, Buckingham: Open University Press.

Slinger, T. (2001) 'Some labour market implications of employment legislation', *Labour Market Trends*, 109, 9, 445–54.

Smith, A. (2001) 'Perceptions of stress at work', *Human Resource Management Journal*, 11, 4, 74–86.

Smith, J., Edwards, P. and Hall, M. (1999) *Redundancy Consultation: A Study of Current Practice and the Effects of the 1995 Regulations*, DTI Employment Relations Research Series, London: DTI, 5. Available on-line at: http://www.dti.gov.uk/emar.

Smith, M. (2000) 'Employers to discuss rights for temporary agency staff', *Financial Times*, 5 May.

Smith, M. A. (1985a) 'A participant observer study of a "rough" working-class pub', *Leisure Studies*, 4, 3, 293–306.

Smith, M. A. (1985b) 'The publican: role conflict and aspects of social control', *The Service Industries Journal*, 5, 1, 23–36.

Smith, P. and Morton, G. (2001) 'New Labour's reform of Britain's employment law: the devil is not only in the detail but in the values and policy too', *British Journal of Industrial Relations*, 39, 1, 119–38.

Soeder, J. (1998) 'Vital signs: who are these people?', *Restaurant Hospitality*, April.

Sosteric, M. (1996) 'Subjectivity in the labour process: a case study in the restaurant industry', *Work, Employment and Society*, 10, 2, 319–29.

Sparrowe, R. T. and Iverson, K. M. (1999) 'Crack in the glass ceiling? An empirical study of gender differences in income in the hospitality industry', *Journal of Hospitality and Tourism Research*, 23, 1, 4–20.

Spradley, J. P. and Mann, B. J. (1975) *Cocktail Waitress: Women's Work in a Man's World*, New York: Alfred A. Knopf.

Stacey, M. and Short, A. (2000) *Challenging Disability Discrimination at Work*, London: Institute for Employment Studies.

Stalcup, L. D. and Pearson, T. A. (2001) 'A model of the causes of management turnover in hotels', *Journal of Hospitality and Tourism Research*, 25, 1, 17–30.

Stamper, C. L. and Van Dyne, L. (2001) 'Work status and organisational citizenship behaviour: a field study of restaurant employees', *Journal of Organizational Behaviour*, 22, 5, 517–36.

Stokes, A., Murphy, R. L., Wagner, P. E. and Sherwyn, D. S. (2001) 'Neutrality agreement: how unions organize new hotels without an employee ballot', *Cornell Hotel and Restaurant Administration Quarterly*, 42, 5, 86–96.

Stokes, D. (1997) 'Bargaining power', *Hotelier*, Toronto, March–April, 27–30.

Storey, J. (1989) *New Perspectives on Human Resource Management*, London: Routledge.

Storey, J. (1992) *Developments in the Management of Human Resources*, Oxford: Blackwell.

Storey, J. (1995) 'Human resource management: still marching on, or marching out?', in J. Storey (ed.) *Human Resource Management: A Critical Text*, London: Routledge.

Storey, J. (2001) *Human Resource Management: A Critical Text*, 2nd edn, London: Thomson Learning.

Streeck, W. (1987) 'The uncertainties of management in the management of uncertainty: employers, labor relations and industrial adjustment in the 1980s', *Work, Employment and Society*, 1, 3, 281–308.

Sturman, M. C. (2001) 'The compensation conundrum: does the hospitality industry short-change itself and its employees?', *Cornell Hotel and Restaurant Administration Quarterly*, 42, 2, 70–6.

Taylor, M. S. and Berger, L. (2000) 'Hotel managers' executive education: challenges and opportunities', *Cornell Hotel and Restaurant Administration Quarterly*, 41, 4, 84–93.

Taylor, R. (2001a) *The Future of Employment Relations*, Swindon: ESRC.

Taylor, R. (2001b) *The Future of Work–Life Balance*, Swindon: ESRC.

Taylor, R. (2002a) *Britain's World of Work: Myths and Realities*, Swindon: ESRC.

Taylor, R. (2002b) *Diversity in Britain's Labour Market*, Swindon: ESRC.

Taylor, R. (2002c) *Managing Workplace Change*, Swindon: ESRC.

Taylor, S. and Lyon, P. (1995) 'Paradigm lost: the rise and fall of McDonaldization', *International Journal of Contemporary Hospitality Management*, 7, 2, 64–8.

Taylor, S. and Tyler, M. (2000) 'Emotional labour and sexual difference in the airline industry', *Work, Employment and Society*, 14, 1, 77–95.

Terry, M. (1999) 'Systems of collective employee representation in non-union firms in the UK', *Industrial Relations Journal*, 30, 1, 16–30.

Tilly, C. (1992) 'Dualism in part-time employment', *Industrial Relations*, 31, 2, 330–47.

Timo, N. (2001 ' "Lean or just mean?": the flexibilisation of labour in the Australian hotel industry', *Research in the Sociology of Work*, 10, 287–309.

Torrington, D., Hall, L. and Taylor, S. (2002) *Human Resource Management*, 5th edn, Harlow: Pearson Education.

Townley, B. (1994) *Reframing Human Resource Management*, London: Sage.

Tracey, J. B. and Nathan, A. E. (2002) 'The strategic and operational roles of human resources: an emerging model', *Cornell Hotel and Restaurant Administration Quarterly*, 43, 4, 17–26.

Trades Union Congress (1997) *Partners for Progress: Next Steps for New Unionism*, London: TUC.

Trades Union Congress (1999) *Partners for Progress: New Unionism at the Workplace*, London: TUC.

Tregaskis, O. (1997) 'The "non-permanent" reality!', *Employee Relations*, 19, 6, 535–54.

Truss, C., Gratton, L., Hope-Hailey, V., McGovern, P. and Stiles, P. (1997) 'Soft and hard models of human resource management: a reappraisal', *Journal of Management Studies*, 34, 1, 53–73.

Truss, C., Gratton, L., Hope-Hailey, V., Stiles, P. and Zaleska, J. (2002) 'Paying the piper: choice or constraint in changing HR functional roles', *Human Resource Management Journal*, 12, 2, 39–63.

Tyler, M. and Abbott, P. (1998) 'Chocs away: weight watching in the contemporary airline industry', *Sociology*, 32, 3, 433–50.

Upchurch, R. S., Davies, R. and Sverdlin, O. (2000) 'Motivation of the Russian worker: an evolutionary process', *Tourism Management*, 21, 5, 509–14.

Urry, J. (1990) *The Tourist Gaze: Leisure and Travel in Contemporary Society*, London: Sage.

Visser, J. (1998) 'European trade unions in the mid-1990s', in B. Towers and M. Terry (eds) *Industrial Relations Journal Annual Review 1997*, Oxford: Blackwell.

Waddington, J. and Whitston, C. (1997) 'Why do people join trade unions in a period of membership decline?', *British Journal of Industrial Relations*, 35, 4, 515–46.

Waddoups, C. J. (1999) 'Union wage effect in Nevada's hotel and casino industry', *Industrial Relations*, 38, 4, 577–83.

Wajcman, J. (2000) 'Feminism facing industrial relations in Britain', *British Journal of Industrial Relations*, 38, 2, 183–201.

Walby, S. (1987) *Flexibility and the Changing Sexual Division of Labour*, Working Paper No. 36, Lancaster Regionalism Group.

Walsh, J. (1999) 'Myths and counter-myths: an analysis of part-time female employees and their orientations to work and working hours', *Work, Employment and Society*, 13, 2, 179–203.

Walsh, J. (2001) 'Human resource management in foreign-owned workplaces: evidence from Australia', *International Journal of Human Resource Management*, 12, 3, 425–44.

Walsh, J. and Deery, S. (1999) 'Understanding the peripheral workforce: evidence from the service sector', *Human Resource Management Journal*, 9, 2, 50–63.

Walters, D. R. (2001) *Health and Safety in Small Enterprises*, Brussels: Peter Lang.

Walters, S. (2002) 'Female part-time workers' attitudes to trade unions in Britain', *British Journal of Industrial Relations*, 40, 1, 49–68.

Walton, R. E. (1985) 'From control to commitment in the workplace', *Harvard Business Review*, March/April, 77–84.

Ward, K., Grimshaw, D., Rubery, J. and Beynon, H. (2001) 'Dilemmas in the management of temporary work agency staff', *Human Resource Management Journal*, 11, 4, 3–21.

Warech, M. A. (2002) 'Competency-based structured interviewing at the Buckhead Beef Company', *Cornell Hotel and Restaurant Administration Quarterly*, 43, 1, 70–7.

Warhurst, C. and Thompson, P. (1998) 'Hands, hearts and minds: changing work and workers at the end of the century', in P. Thompson and C. Warhurst (eds) *Workplaces of the Future*, London: Macmillan.

Warhurst, C., Nickson, D., Witz, A. and Cullen, A. M. (2000) 'Aesthetic labour in interactive service work: some case study evidence from the "New" Glasgow', *The Service Industries Journal*, 20, 3, 1–18.

Watson, S. and D'Annunzio-Green, N. (1996) 'Implementing cultural change through human resources: the elusive organization alchemy?', *International Journal of Contemporary Hospitality Management*, 8, 2, 25–30.

Weber, K. (1998) 'Women's career progression in the Las Vegas casino industry: facilitators and constraints', *Journal of Hospitality and Tourism Research*, 22, 4, 431–49.

Weiermair, K. (1996) 'Human resources in the alpine tourist industry: workers and entrepreneurs'. Paper presented at the International Congress on Alpine Tourism, Innsbruck, May.

Welch, R. and Leighton, P. (1996) 'Individualizing employee relations: the myth of the personal contract', *Personnel Review*, 25, 5, 37–50.

Wharton, A. S. (1993) 'The affective consequences of service work: managing emotions on the job', *Work and Occupations*, 20, 2, 205–32.

Whitehouse, G., Lafferty, G. and Boreham, P. (1997) 'From casual to permanent part-time? Non-standard employment in retail and hospitality', *International Journal of Employment Studies*, 8, 2, 33–48.

Whitehouse, G., Zetlin, D. and Earnshaw, J. (2001) 'Prosecuting pay equity: evolving strategies in Britain and Australia', *Gender, Work and Organisation*, 8, 4, 365–86.

Wilkinson, A., Redman, T., Snape, E. and Marchington, M. (1998) *Managing with Total Quality Management: Theory and Practice*, Basingstoke: Macmillan.

Wilson, E. (2002) 'Waiting in vain', *The Guardian, G2*, 26 October, 16–17.

Wood, R. C. (1992) *Working in Hotels and Catering*, London: Routledge.

Wood, R. C. (1997) *Working in Hotels and Catering*, 2nd edn, London: ITB Press.

Wood, S. (1995) 'The four pillars of HRM: are they connected?', *Human Resource Management Journal*, 5, 5, 49–59.

Woods, R. H. (1999) 'Predicting is difficult, especially about the future: human resources in the new millennium', *International Journal of Hospitality Management*, 18, 4, 443–56.

Woods, R. H. and Kavanaugh, R. R. (1994) 'Gender discrimination and sexual harassment as experienced by hospitality-industry managers', *Cornell Hotel and Restaurant Administration Quarterly*, 35, 1, 16–21.

Woods, R. H. and Sciarini, M. P. (1995) 'Diversity programs in chain restaurants', *Cornell Hotel and Restaurant Administration Quarterly*, 36, 3, 18–23.

Woods, R. H. and Viehland, D. (2000) 'Women in hotel management: gradual progress, uncertain prospects', *Cornell Hotel and Restaurant Administration Quarterly*, 41, 5, 51–4.

Woods, R. H., Sciarini, M. P. and Breiter, D. (1998) 'Performance appraisals in hotels: widespread and valuable', *Cornell Hotel and Restaurant Administration Quarterly*, 39, 2, 25–9.

World Travel and Tourism Council (WTTC) (2000) *Tourism Satellite Accounting Research, Estimates and Forecasts for Government and Industry, Year 2000*, London: WTTC (CD-ROM).

Worsfold, P. (1999) 'HRM, performance, commitment and service quality in the hotel industry', *International Journal of Contemporary Hospitality Management*, 11, 7, 340–8.

Worsfold, P. and McCann, C. (2000) 'Supervised work experience and sexual harassment', *International Journal of Contemporary Hospitality Management*, 12, 4, 249–55.

Wyld, D. C. (1995) 'The Family and Medical Leave Act: what hospitality managers need to know', *Cornell Hotel and Restaurant Administration Quarterly*, 36, 4, 54–63.

Young, C. A. and Lundberg, C. C. (1996) 'Creating a good first day on the job: allaying newcomers' anxiety with positive messages', *Cornell Hotel and Restaurant Administration Quarterly*, 37, 6, 26–33.

Young, K. A. (1997) 'Environmental tobacco smoke and employees', *Cornell Hotel and Restaurant Administration Quarterly*, 38, 1, 36–42.

Zapf, D. (2002) 'Emotion work and psychological well-being: a review of the literature and some conceptual considerations', *Human Resource Management Review*, 12, 2, 237–68.

Zuehl, J. J. and Sherwyn, D. S. (2001) 'Identifying uniform employment termination practices for multinational employers', *Cornell Hotel and Restaurant Administration Quarterly*, 42, 5, 72–85.

Index